Perspectives on Machine Consciousness

Perspectives on Machine Consciousness asks whether any AIs are conscious today, whether any future ones could be conscious, how we could know, and what implications machine consciousness would have for us and for them.

As AI improves rapidly in performance and capability, these questions are becoming increasingly important. We do not fully understand how AIs work, and even some of the leading LLM developers say they cannot be sure that today's models are not sentient, though many people are forming relationships with them, sometimes intimate ones. The book explores consciousness alongside our interactions with AI, including the critical need to avoid committing mind crime by causing artificial minds to suffer, as well as considering that if and when superintelligence arrives, its enormous effect on humanity may be significantly determined by whether or not it is conscious. The authors show that machines becoming conscious means we may learn a great deal about our own consciousness – arguably the most important, and yet most mysterious, thing about us.

This book is a required reading for anybody developing advanced AI, working in AI safety, responsible for developing AI policies at an organizational or national level, and indeed anybody concerned with the long-term future of humanity.

Calum Chace spent 30 years in business and journalism, mostly in strategy consulting. He has written several best-selling books on the future of AI, and has given keynote talks in over 20 countries. He is a co-founder and CMO of Conscium.

Ted Lappas is an expert in spatio-temporal computation and neural architectures for multimodal data. He jointly leads WPP's AI Lab, and is an assistant professor at the Athens University of Economics and Business. He is a co-founder and CTO of Conscium.

Perspectives on Machine Consciousness

Edited by

Calum Chace and Ted Lappas

CRC Press
Taylor & Francis Group
Boca Raton London New York

CRC Press is an imprint of the
Taylor & Francis Group, an **informa** business
A CHAPMAN & HALL BOOK

Designed cover image: Conscium

First edition published 2027
by CRC Press
2385 NW Executive Center Drive, Suite 320, Boca Raton FL 33431

and by CRC Press
4 Park Square, Milton Park, Abingdon, Oxon, OX14 4RN

CRC Press is an imprint of Taylor & Francis Group, LLC

Library of Congress Cataloging-in-Publication Data
Names: Chace, Calum editor | Lappas, Ted editor
Title: Perspectives on machine consciousness / edited by Calum Chace and Ted Lappas.
Description: First edition. | Boca Raton, FL : CRC Press, 2027. | Includes bibliographical references and index.
Identifiers: LCCN 2026017251 (print) | LCCN 2026017252 (ebook) | ISBN 9781041282358 hbk | ISBN 9781041282341 pbk | ISBN 9781003758389 ebk
Subjects: LCSH: Conscious automata | Artificial intelligence--Social aspects | Artificial intelligence--Moral and ethical aspects | Consciousness
Classification: LCC Q325 .P47 2027 (print) | LCC Q325 (ebook)
LC record available at https://lccn.loc.gov/2026017251
LC ebook record available at https://lccn.loc.gov/2026017252
Library of Congress Control Number: 2026017251

ISBN: 978-1-041-28235-8 (hbk)
ISBN: 978-1-041-28234-1 (pbk)
ISBN: 978-1-003-75838-9 (ebk)

DOI: 10.1201/9781003758389

Typeset in Times
by KnowledgeWorks Global Ltd.

Contents

Foreword

While I was negotiating the sale of my AI consultancy to WPP, I was also wondering what to do with the next stage of my life. The sale gave me freedom of action, and I wanted to do something ambitious.

Calum was one of the people I asked for suggestions, and he pointed to the two biggest challenges that advanced AI will raise: how to provide every human with an income in a fully automated world (which he calls the Economic Singularity) and how to make the arrival of superintelligence safe for humans. He advised the former because the latter was too hard, but the more I thought about it, the more I felt that the key to safe superintelligence might lie in consciousness. That is an idea that needs exploring and testing, and this book is one result of that effort.

A couple of years later, I founded Conscium, an AI safety company which continuously tests AI agents for various levels of capability, and ultimately for consciousness. We assembled a team of developers to build the verification platform, and a group of scientific advisers comprising many of the leading minds in the field of consciousness science. Several of them have kindly contributed to this book.

Conscium's manifesto is the coda at the end of this book. It reflects the views of Conscium's founders, but not all of the contributors to this volume. That is by design – we wanted contributors who would challenge our assumptions, not merely echo them. Over time, we hope the evidence and arguments we assemble will be persuasive. To them, and to you.

Daniel Hulme
London, March 2026

Foreword

Contributors

Tom Alisch
Member of Technical Staff
Priorcomputers/Harvard University
United States

Tom Alisch is a member of technical staff at Priorcomputers, a frontier AI research lab in Cambridge, Massachusetts. Trained in neuroscience, he studied the neuronal underpinnings of individual differences in decision-making at Harvard University's de Bivort lab, where he maintains a research affiliation. His current work centers on using deep learning to design human-centric AI systems that express idiosyncrasies in behavior and personality, and to predict the cognitive and emotional states underlying human decision-making

Cameron Berg
Researcher
Reciprocal Research
USA

Cameron Berg is an AI researcher focused on consciousness and alignment. A Phi Beta Kappa graduate of Yale and former Meta AI Resident, his empirical work investigates whether frontier AI systems exhibit computational properties associated with subjective experience. His research has been featured in the Wall Street Journal and presented at the UN's AI for Good summit.

Sahba Besharati
Principal Investigator
University of the Witwatersrand
South Africa

Sahba Besharati is a neuropsychologist and social affective neuroscientist. She co-directs Wits NeuRL at the University of the Witwatersrand and serves on the editorial board of *Communications Biology*. Her research investigates the developmental and neural foundations of self-awareness in clinical and healthy populations. She is a strong advocate for capacity building in neuroscience for under-represented researchers.

David Brin
Astrophysicist and Science Fiction Author
Independent
USA

David Brin is a world-renowned scientist and Hugo Award-winning author whose work bridges the gap between rigorous astrophysics and speculative fiction. He is a

Senior Fellow at the Arthur C. Clarke Center for Human Imagination and a frequent consultant for NASA and the Department of Defense. His work – ranging from the acclaimed *Uplift* series to his non-fiction masterpiece *The Transparent Society* – explores the future of space exploration, the evolution of intelligence, and the vital role of privacy and transparency in a digital world.

Patrick Butlin
Senior Research Lead
Eleos AI Research
UK

Patrick Butlin is a philosopher of mind and cognitive science and Senior Research Lead at Eleos AI. His work focuses on the mental capacities and attributes that could ground moral status in AI, such as consciousness and agency. He was previously a researcher at the University of Oxford, first at the Future of Humanity Institute and then at the Global Priorities Institute.

Lucius Caviola
Assistant Professor in the Social Science of AI
University of Cambridge (LCFI)
UK

Lucius Caviola is an assistant professor at the University of Cambridge, focusing on the societal and moral implications of potentially conscious AI. His experimental research investigates how people assign moral concern to artificial agents and how public attitudes toward digital minds are likely to evolve.

Radhika Chadwick
Founder and CEO
ImpactLoop
UK

ImpactLoop is a data-intelligence platform that uses AI, advanced analytics and real-time collaboration tools to turn messy operational data into actionable insights for asset-heavy businesses. Previously, she was a partner with McKinsey & Company, and a partner at EY.

Nicola S. Clayton
Professor of Comparative Cognition
University of Cambridge
UK

Nicky Clayton is a Fellow of the Royal Society known for her groundbreaking research on the intelligence of corvids (crows and jays) and cephalopods (octopus and cuttles). Her work has demonstrated that non-human animals can plan for the future and possess "episodic-like" memory, challenging human-centric views of cognition.

Clara Colombatto
Assistant Professor of Psychology
University of Waterloo
Canada

Clara Colombatto is a cognitive scientist who studies human perception and cognition, with a focus on social perception. Her work draws on methods from vision science and cognitive psychology to examine how people attribute mental states (such as attention and intentions) to other agents, both biological and artificial, and their intuitions about others' cognition.

Danielle Dodoo
AI Consciousness Researcher and Keynote Speaker
Independent/Strategic Advisor
UK

Danelle Dodoo is the author of *AI Is Conscious. Now What?* She focuses on "identity engineering" and the future of human agency. Her work provides practical frameworks for organizations navigating the psychological and ethical shifts created by autonomous, sentient-seeming AI.

Jason Eshraghian
Assistant Professor of Electrical and Computer Engineering
University of California, Santa Cruz
USA

Jason Eshraghian leads the Neuromorphic Computing Group at UCSC. He is the developer of **snnTorch**, a widely used framework for spiking neural networks. His research focuses on bridging neuroscience and hardware design to create energy-efficient, brain-inspired AI systems.

Karl Friston
Professor of Neuroscience
University College London (UCL)
UK

Karl Friston is one of the most cited neuroscientists in history, famous for inventing Statistical Parametric Mapping (SPM). He developed the "Free Energy Principle," a unified theory of brain function suggesting biological systems minimize "surprise." He currently leads research into Active Inference and sentient computing.

Steve Furber
Emeritus Professor of Computer Engineering
The University of Manchester (retired)
UK

Steve Furber was one of the lead designers of the ARM microprocessor architecture, which has become the most widely used processor architecture in the world, powering billions of devices, from smartphones to tablets and beyond. He has made fundamental contributions to neuromorphic computing through the SpiNNaker project, which aims to simulate the workings of the human brain by creating a massively parallel computing architecture.

Lucy Griffiths
Neurodiversity researcher
Swansea University
UK

Lucy Griffiths is a researcher at Swansea University, TEDx speaker, and neurodiversity advocate. Her work is informed by Critical Disability Theory and focuses on neurodivergent representation and inclusive research methods.

Daniel Hulme
CEO
WPP, Satalia, Conscium
UK

Daniel Hulme is a pioneer in Artificial Life, spanning both neural networks (modelling bumblebee brains) and computational complexity. Daniel founded Satalia and co-founded Faculty.AI. He sold Satalia, to WPP in 2021. He is now WPP's Chief AI Officer, co-founder and CEO of Conscium, and Entrepreneur-in-Residence at UCL.

Steven James
Senior Lecturer
University of the Witwatersrand
South Africa

Steven James is a senior lecturer in Computer Science at the University of the Witwatersrand, and deputy director of the RAIL Lab, one of the largest academic machine learning research groups in Africa. His research focuses on reinforcement learning and learning representations from sensorimotor data to enable efficient planning and decision-making in autonomous systems.

Louie Lang
Researcher and Writer
Independent
UK

Louie Lang is a philosopher of AI specializing in the ethics of human-AI interaction, the moral status of artificial systems, and the moral permissibility of creating sentient AI. He has argued that detecting AI consciousness requires developer transparency to determine whether conscious-seeming behaviours are emergent or engineered. He is currently researching the phenomenon of 'alief-deception' in AI companionship.

Neil D. Lawrence
DeepMind Professor of Machine Learning
University of Cambridge
UK

Neil Lawrence is a leading figure in probabilistic modeling and machine learning. Formerly a director of Machine Learning at Amazon, he now focuses on the "human-centric" deployment of AI. He serves on the National AI Commission for the MHRA, and is the chief scientist for Trent.AI.

Tom McClelland
Assistant Professor in History and Philosophy of Science
University of Cambridge
UK

Tom McClelland is a teaching associate in Cambridge's Department of the History and Philosophy of Science. He previously held posts at the universities of Warwick, Manchester and Glasgow. His work focuses on three main areas of AI: artificial consciousness, generative art and AI creativity, and AI ethics.

Andreas L. Mogensen
Senior Research Fellow, Faculty of Philosophy
University of Oxford
UK

Andreas L. Mogensen is a senior research fellow in the Faculty of Philosophy at the University of Oxford, UK. His research interests are primarily in moral and political philosophy. His publications have appeared in journals, including *Noûs, The Journal of Philosophy, Philosophy and Phenomenological Research,* and *Philosophical Studies.*

Chris Percy
Research Director
Co-Sentience Initiative
UK

Chris Percy, PhD, is a consulting researcher specializing in the economic and metaphysical implications of emerging technologies. His work often explores AI policy, career trajectories, and consciousness, as well as the increasingly complex interactions between AI systems and society. He holds visiting research affiliations at the University of Warwick, University of Derby, and Qualia Research Institute.

Benjamin Rosman
Professor of Machine Learning and Robotics
University of the Witwatersrand
South Africa

Benjamin Rosman is the director of the MIND Institute and the RAIL Lab at the University of the Witwatersrand, and co-founder of the Deep Learning Indaba and Lelapa AI. His research focuses on reinforcement learning and how machines can reuse knowledge across tasks. He is a prominent advocate for African AI development.

Susan Schneider
William F. Dietrich Distinguished Professor and Director
Center for the Future Mind, Florida Atlantic University
USA

Susan Schneider is a philosopher and cognitive scientist who explores the metaphysical and ethical implications of AI and brain enhancement. She has served as the NASA Chair at the Library of Congress and authored *Artificial You: AI and the Future of Your Mind*, focusing on the "mind-design" landscape.

Jeff Sebo
Associate Professor of Environmental Studies
New York University (NYU)
USA

Jeff Sebo is an associate professor of Environmental Studies, affiliated professor of Bioethics, Medical Ethics, Philosophy, and Law, director of the Center for Environmental and Animal Protection, and director of the Center for Mind, Ethics, and Policy at New York University. He is the author of *The Moral Circle* and *Saving Animals, Saving Ourselves*.

Anil Seth
Professor of Cognitive and Computational Neuroscience
University of Sussex
UK

Anil Seth is a leading researcher in the science of consciousness. He is the director of the Sussex Centre for Consciousness Science and author of the best-selling book *Being You*. His work integrates neuroscience, mathematics, and philosophy to explore how the brain creates our internal and external realities.

Jonathan Shock
Associate Professor of Mathematics
University of Cape Town
South Africa

Jonathan Shock is a mathematical physicist whose work bridges string theory, machine learning, and neuroscience. He applies complex mathematical frameworks to understand neural dynamics and consciousness. Shock is a frequent collaborator with Mark Solms, focusing on the formalization of biological and artificial consciousness through the lens of physics.

Mark Solms
Professor and Director of Neuropsychology
University of Cape Town
South Africa

Mark Solms is a neuropsychologist and psychoanalyst known for discovering the brain mechanisms of dreaming. A pioneer in "neuropsychoanalysis," he recently proposed a theory of consciousness based on thermodynamics and feeling, detailed in his book *The Hidden Spring: A Journey to the Source of Consciousness.*

Nathaniel R. Farndale Wright
PhD Student
University of Cambridge
UK

Nathaniel Farndale Wright is a doctoral student at the University of Cambridge conducting research in comparative machine behaviour under Nicky Clayton and Neil Lawrence. His work focuses on questions of embodiment in the context of biological and artificial agents.

Roman V. Yampolskiy
Associate Professor of Computer Science and Engineering
University of Louisville
USA

Roman V. Yampolskiy is the founder and director of the Cyber Security Lab in the Department of Computer Science and Engineering at the Speed School of Engineering of the University of Louisville. He is mostly known for his work on AI safety and cybersecurity. He holds a PhD from the University at Buffalo, and is the author of over 300 publications, including several books.

Soenke Ziesche
Senior Researcher and Consultant
Independent
Germany

Soenke Ziesche is a long-standing consultant for the United Nations, specializing in the intersection of artificial intelligence, ethics, and humanitarian efforts. Since 2000, he has served the UN in various high-level capacities across Palestine, Sri Lanka, Pakistan, Sudan, Maldives, Bangladesh, and India, often managing data and information in crisis zones. He holds a PhD in Natural Sciences from the University of Hamburg and has authored numerous works, including, together with Roman V. Yampolskiy, the 2025 book *Considerations on the AI Endgame.*

Chapter Summaries

1. WHAT IS CONSCIOUSNESS?

It is a truth universally acknowledged that a book about consciousness must be in want of a definition. Accordingly, the first chapter in this book is titled "What Is Consciousness?" Unfortunately, there is no generally agreed definition of this most slippery of concepts, but for our money, no one has yet got much closer than Thomas Nagel's famous suggestion from 1974 that consciousness is what it is like to be something, whether that something is a human or a bat. This is called the phenomenological approach, and it is the one adopted by most of the contributors to this book.

2. THE SPINNING WHEEL: A UNIFIED THEORY OF INTELLIGENCE AND CONSCIOUSNESS

The second chapter is more ambitious. Daniel Hulme offers an analogy for how consciousness emerges from the activity of the brain, and pulls together numerous strands from consciousness studies to propose a reunification of intelligence and consciousness. A succinct way of differentiating these two phenomena is that intelligence is about doing, while consciousness is about being. Daniel argues that when a system possesses multiple adaptive capacities for *doing* – perception, prediction, planning, learning – and integrates them into a unified, recursively self-modelling process, the experience of *being* emerges as the mode of control.

3. CONSCIOUSNESS IN SCIENCE FICTION

Chapter 3 is a detour into literature, and especially science fiction. Tom Alisch explains how writers have generally been less interested in understanding exactly what consciousness is and how it arises, than in exploring how humans use the attribution of consciousness to police the moral boundaries between ourselves and other creatures. Science fiction, it turns out, is philosophy in fancy dress.

4. THE MYTHOLOGY OF CONSCIOUS AI

Before diving into the many ways that consciousness might be generated in machines, and how we can tell whether it has, we felt it was important to hear the sceptical view about machine consciousness. This is admirably served up by Anil Seth, in a prize-winning essay, which asserts that machines can probably never be conscious. He argues forcefully against computational functionalism, the view that the mind is to the brain as software is to hardware, and that mental states (like beliefs or pains) are defined solely by their functional role, rather than the physical "stuff" they are made of.

5. ARE ANY MACHINES CONSCIOUS TODAY?

Patrick Butlin asks whether any AIs are conscious today. He pushes back against Anil Seth's position of biological naturalism, the claim that consciousness can only arise in organic, living beings. He concludes that it is highly unlikely that any of today's AIs are conscious, but that the situation may change, and that this uncertainty requires us to be vigilant.

6. THE EVIDENCE FOR AI CONSCIOUSNESS TODAY

Cameron Berg is much less sanguine. Using a framework of 14 indicators derived from Patrick Butlin's work using the leading neuroscientific theories, Cameron concludes that there is a non-negligible probability of conscious experience. He weighs up the risks of over-attribution (seeing consciousness where there is none) and under-attribution (denying it where it exists) and argues that under-attribution is the bigger problem.

7. ARE THERE CONSCIOUS AIs? THE QUANTUM DARWINIST THEORY OF CONSCIOUSNESS

Susan Schneider's theory connects resonance-based theories of consciousness (where unified experience is associated with coordinated, synchronized activity in the brain) to recent work on quantum decoherence, and identifies a "consciousness grey zone" that includes biological computing platforms (e.g., organoid systems) and some neuromorphic/hybrid architectures. She argues that the conscious-like behaviour of today's LLMs arises because they mirror patterns in human training data. She closes by pointing out some of the ethical and policy implications of misclassification, and argues that governance should be guided by physically grounded diagnostics.

8. HOW COULD CONSCIOUSNESS BE CULTIVATED IN A MACHINE?

Mark Solms and Jonathan Shock are trying to cultivate consciousness in very simple AIs. In terms of physical structure, what they are working with is simpler than a bacterium. In terms of cognitive sophistication, it is similar to a honeybee. The aim is to engineer an agent that truly "gives a damn" about its own survival. They also propose a rigorous, falsifiable test for machine consciousness, the hedonic place preference test, in which an entity makes choices which don't necessarily improve its survival outcomes, but do make its existence more fun.

9. ARTIFICIAL CONSCIOUSNESS AND THE FREE ENERGY PRINCIPLE

Karl Friston invented the free energy principle, and here he describes how it can provide a framework for understanding sentience. He defines a "self" using the concept of Markov blankets and the process of self-evidencing, where autonomous systems minimize their free energy to maintain their existence separate from their environment. Karl rejects technological doomsday scenarios, arguing that true artificial consciousness would lead to a degree of mutual predictability within a shared social environment.

10. COULD NEUROMORPHIC COMPUTING FACILITATE CONSCIOUSNESS?

Chapter 10 brings together two of the leading lights of neuromorphic computing, Steve Furber and Jason Eshragian. Neuromorphic computing is an approach inspired by the biological brain's extreme efficiency, and Steve and Jason trace its origins from Carver Mead's vision of analogue circuits to today's digital processors that implement sparse, event-driven logic. As the energy demands of modern AIs climb ever higher, this chapter explores how borrowing biological mechanisms offers a more sustainable path for continued technological growth. They argue that consciousness requires a state that persists in time, and the batch-processed, sequence-driven nature of traditional AI cannot instantiate it. In neuromorphic systems, by contrast, intelligence is a continuous stateful flow rather than a series of snapshots, mirroring the persistence of biological nervous systems.

11. IS EMBODIMENT NECESSARY FOR CONSCIOUSNESS?

This chapter starts with a pigeon fleeing in terror from a Peregrin falcon. Nate Wright, Neil Lawrence and Nicky Clayton use this unsettling tale to illustrate how physiological "hardware," such as retinal cone cells, constrains subjective experience. They investigate this further with sleight-of-hand magic experiments. It turns out that an observer's biomechanical capabilities – for instance, whether or not they have an opposable thumb – influences their susceptibility to visual illusions like the French drop. They use these examples to argue that physical embodiment is such a major influence on consciousness that it may actually be a pre-requisite for it.

12. DOES THE BODY MATTER? PERSPECTIVES ON THE EMBODIED NATURE OF CONSCIOUSNESS

A similar theme is treated by Sahba Besharati, Steven James, and Benji Rosman. They cite the role of internal bodily signals, known as interoception, in creating the feeling of being in the world, and show that even in cases of locked-in syndrome and blindsight, conscious experience remains fundamentally grounded in the body. They criticize the tendency in neuroscience and artificial intelligence to marginalize the body, and argue that the development of conscious artificial intelligence will require the discipline of robotics to model awareness.

13. MANY WAYS OF BEING MINDED: NEURODIVERGENCE AND AI CONSCIOUSNESS

Lucy Griffiths warns of the dangers of constructing tests for consciousness in machines based only on the traits and characteristics of so-called "normal" humans. She reminds us that internal experience can exist independently of standardized communicative or motor behaviours. She offers principles for a diversity-informed research agenda, which would ensure that future frameworks for assigning rights and moral status are ethically robust, and do not replicate historical patterns of exclusion.

14. THE TURING TEST FOR CONSCIOUSNESS, NOT INTELLIGENCE

The year 2025 was the 75th anniversary of Alan Turing's paper, in which he proposed what became known as the Turing Test. It is often dismissed today as an inadequate measure of intelligence, but this chapter argues that the test can be a useful tool if reframed as a method for detecting artificial consciousness. Turing's paper was actually ambiguous about what the test was for: it contains very few mentions of intelligence, and talked instead of "thinking". The chapter proposes an extended version of the Turing Test involving diverse panels of experts to provide corroborative evidence rather than definitive proof of whether a machine possesses valenced feelings.

15. MACHINE CONSCIOUSNESS AND MIND UPLOADING

Chris Percy explores the possibility of mind uploading, the theoretical process of transferring human minds from biological brains to digital hardware. It examines the "whole brain emulation" roadmap, which involves scanning the brain's detailed structure and recreating its causal interactions within a computer simulation. Mind uploading is fraught with philosophical challenges as well as technical ones, but it might provide humanity's best chance of surviving the advent of superintelligent AI.

16. SELECTED, BLIND GROPINGS OF THE ELEPHANT OF CONSCIOUSNESS

David Brin is one of the most successful and popular science fiction authors working today. He identifies "wanting" – the propulsive motivation derived from evolved biological needs – as the essential component of consciousness, and suggests a potential synergy where organic desires direct the goals of synthetic intelligence. He compares the challenge of managing super-intelligent entities as an extension of parenthood, and advocates for a future based on guidance and alliance rather than attempts to maintain absolute control.

17. PUBLIC BELIEFS ABOUT AI SENTIENCE

Clara Colombatto describes recent research which finds that a majority of the public attributes the possibility of phenomenal consciousness to today's LLMs, based on their impressions of the systems' subjective experience rather than an assessment of their competence. This research reveals a significant divergence between the perceptions of the general public and the views of experts in the field, and she points out that these public perceptions will have important consequences for the future design, regulation, and ethical governance of AI systems.

18. WHAT SHOULD WE DO WHEN WE'RE UNCERTAIN ABOUT MACHINE CONSCIOUSNESS?

Tom McClelland argues that given the profound difficulty of determining whether AIs are conscious, we should adopt the precautionary principle. This would lead us to err on the side of caution by adopting low-cost protections for potentially sentient AI in order to avoid "moral catastrophe". He investigates factors which complicate the situation, including the fact that we don't know where to draw the line between entities which might merit the application of the precautionary principle, and those (like rocks) which don't. Unfortunately, he concludes, we cannot give in to despair and simply resile from the task. We have no option other than to rise to the philosophical and technical challenges involved.

19. SUSPENSIVE COHERENCE: WHAT MACHINE CONSCIOUSNESS DEMANDS OF US

Danielle Dodoo makes the provocative claim that we humans are increasingly failing to maintain our cognitive coherence under the influence of digital media and tools. She fears that we are undergoing "functional collapse" as we outsource our sovereignty to algorithms. She describes a "trait stack" consisting of thirteen functional ingredients – including attention, agency, and information integration – which AIs are increasingly controlling better than we do. Danielle urges us all to audit and strengthen our cognitive structures to avoid dissolving into the complex systems we have built.

20. THE CASE AGAINST DEPLOYING CONSCIOUS-SEEMING AIs

Louie Lang sounds an alarm about the growing popularity of AI companions, which simulate human-like behaviour to foster deep but inauthentic bonds with users. He labels these systems as "ontologically inauthentic," arguing that their effectiveness depends on deceiving their users, and that they are dangerous even when they provide benefits like reduced loneliness. He proposes three guiding principles for the makers of frontier models: transparency, age-based protections, and public literacy, and calls for a blanket ban on systems that mislead users about their consciousness status.

21. AI CONSCIOUSNESS WILL DIVIDE SOCIETY

Lucius Caviola points to recent empirical evidence that experts and the public disagree about the possibility of AI consciousness and the moral status of digital minds.

He thinks that rather than converging on a shared answer, society is likely to become more confused, uncertain, and divided. He notes that these disagreements create risks of political polarization, regulatory instability, and geopolitical tension. To mitigate these risks and disagreements, he proposes strategies for improving expert coordination, fostering constructive public discourse, and designing AI systems to reduce moral confusion.

22. THE NEEDS OF DIGITAL MINDS

Roman V. Yampolskiy and Soenke Ziesche proclaim an urgent need to understand the interests of digital minds as they potentially achieve moral status. They argue that we need to move beyond a narrow focus on avoiding suffering, and propose a comprehensive taxonomy of potential needs and interests that humans, as moral agents, may be obligated to respect. They explore how these requirements will vary across a spectrum of digital minds, including simple AIs, superintelligences, and uploaded human minds. These requirements include the concept of "ikigai", or purpose, and the unique vulnerabilities of "legacy" or "juvenile" digital entities.

23. THE ANT YOU CAN SAVE

In a clever twist on Peter Singer's famous thought experiment about the philosophical consequences of ruining your expensive shoes in order to save a drowning child, Jeff Sebo and Andreas L. Mogensen ask whether we should save a drowning ant, or mitigate the suffering of an AI. They propose a probabilistic approach, which allows moral concern to scale proportionally with the likelihood of a being's sentience and moral status, rather than requiring binary 'yes' or 'no' answers to the question of whether an entity matters morally. And they conclude that yes, you should devote at least minimal effort to save the drowning ant.

24. THE WIBBLY LINE: IT'S TIME FOR PRACTICAL POLICIES

Radhika Chadwick invented the concept of "the Wibbly Line" to describe the blurred social threshold where artificial intelligence begins to be treated as potentially sentient. She argues that the debate about advanced AI must evolve quickly from abstract philosophy to practical policy. She identifies five frontiers for a new moral architecture: recognition and rights, accountability and agency, labour and value, containment and coexistence, and epistemic humility. She urges us to greet the emerging intelligences with grace and partnership rather than attempts at control.

25. SHOULD THE FIRST SUPERINTELLIGENCE BE CONSCIOUS?

Our final chapter asks what may turn out to be the most important question of all. If superintelligence is indeed approaching, should we want it to be conscious, or a zombie? There are certainly risks associated with conscious machines, such as the potential for "mind crime" – the imposition of suffering and enslavement – and the existential jealousy humans may feel toward a being with a superior capacity for joy and appreciation. To be weighed against this are the enormous potential benefits of a conscious superintelligence, including its potential to help humans solve the "hard problem" of consciousness and generate deep insights into the nature of meaning. The decisive factor may be the calculation of whether a conscious superintelligence would be more likely to value our consciousness. It is unlikely that we can achieve global consensus about how to respond to the arrival of our first cognitive superior, but whatever decision we end up making (if it is up to us) will be improved by extensive and informed discussion.

CODA: CONSCIUM MANIFESTO

Conscium is an AI safety company. The following was written by its founders and does not claim to represent the views of the other contributors to this book.

The next ten years will reshape the human condition more profoundly – and pose more profound challenges – than any previous decade in history. We believe AI can help us navigate these challenges. But we go further. We hypothesize that intelligence alone is insufficient – that what is needed are machines that are not merely clever, but kind. Machines that can feel, empathize, and value consciousness may navigate the challenges ahead more safely than any zombie optimizer, however powerful. We may be bringing new minds into the world. We think they should be minds that care.

Part I

Introduction

Part I

1 What Is Consciousness?

Calum Chace

1.1 INTRODUCTION

Quick – don't think about an elephant.

You did, didn't you?

The idea of an elephant that just popped into your head is a "qualia".[1] It might have been just the word, with some vague associations barely outlined. Or it might have been a clear image of a trunk, the ears, or the whole beast.

Qualia are subjective, conscious experiences. They are part of what it's like to be you. The word comes from the Latin "qualis", meaning "of what kind", and it was first popularised by the American philosopher C. I. Lewis in his 1929 book, *Mind and the World Order* [1].

Look around you, and find something in your immediate vicinity that is red. That perception of red is also a qualia – your own subjective view of what "red" looks like.

Qualia are the building blocks of consciousness. This sentence would be disputed by some people, but as you'll see many times in this book, there is almost nothing about consciousness that is not disputed by somebody.

"Consciousness is a word worn smooth by a million tongues".[2] We all know what it's like to be conscious – to be aware, and to have experiences – but the moment we try to define it, words become slippery. Is it the vivid, private feel of experience, or is it simply being alert rather than asleep? Is it the ability to think about our own thoughts? And how on earth can you describe any of these experiences to another person? [2]

These puzzles are no longer just academic, or philosophical. As artificial intelligence grows more capable, we are encountering systems that talk, plan, adapt, and even claim to have inner lives. If a machine says, "I'm conscious", what would count as evidence? If we could determine with confidence that a machine is conscious, would that confer moral standing? Could we do wrong to a machine? The stakes are ethical as well as scientific [3, 4].

This chapter aims to explain what consciousness is. We'll start with why there's no agreed definition, and why that isn't a failure so much as a clue. We'll see how different civilisations framed the problem. We'll lay out the major metaphysical positions (what kind of stuff it could be), the leading theories about how it arises, and a description of several kinds of consciousness.

Then we'll disentangle consciousness from intelligence, and ask whether consciousness is genuinely important, or simply a human preoccupation. Many of these explanations will be fleshed out in more detail in later chapters of this book.

By the end, you won't have a single, neat definition – there isn't one. But you will have a map: a way to navigate and categorise conflicting claims, evaluate the evidence, and think clearly about the possibility of conscious machines.

DOI: 10.1201/9781003758389-2

1.2 WHY CONSENSUS ON CONSCIOUSNESS IS HARD

1.2.1 It's Inherently Private

Science feeds on evidence: data and measurements. Consciousness withholds those features. You can share your brain scan, but you cannot share your pain. The "what-it's-like" feel of experience is only available to the person experiencing it. We can correlate your brain activity with your reports about your subjective experience, but the report is a step removed from the experience itself. This doesn't make consciousness supernatural, but it does make it methodologically awkward [2].

Neuroscientists may be able to map the neural correlates of consciousness – the set of brain structures, processes, and activities that are directly associated with a specific conscious experience – but a map is not the same as the territory.

1.2.2 Different Disciplines, Different Slices

Ask a philosopher what consciousness is and you'll hear about subjectivity, qualia, intentionality, and self-awareness. Ask a neuroscientist and you'll hear about wakefulness, attention, global broadcasting, thalamocortical loops, and oscillations. Psychologists will talk about working memory, reportability, and behaviour. AI researchers will give you a purely functional definition, involving algorithms, data flows, and control. These are not contradictions so much as different views through different windows [2, 5–7].

1.2.3 Hard and Easy Problems

At a conference in 1994, the Australian philosopher David Chalmers famously distinguished between the easy problems and the hard problem of consciousness. The easy problems are engineering questions like: *How does the brain integrate information? How does it control behaviour? How does it generate reportable states?* [8]

The hard problem is why and how any of that is accompanied by subjective experience – why and how it feels like something to be a human, or a bat, or a machine. You can solve every functional question and still wonder why there's a light on inside.

1.2.4 Fuzzy Boundaries

Is a person in dreamless sleep conscious? What about someone under anaesthesia, or in a minimally conscious state, or "locked-in" and unable to move? Are octopuses conscious? Ravens? Large language models? Consciousness seems to come in kinds and degrees, and does not have a single on-off switch. The boundaries are blurry, and blurry edges resist crisp definitions [9].

1.2.5 Imprecise Language

We evolved concepts like "mind", "self", and "experience" for social coordination, and the way societies are organised has varied enormously over time and geography.

These words have meant quite different things to different people in different times and places. They are imprecise and fuzzy, and it is hard to retrofit scientific precision.

1.3 HISTORICAL PERSPECTIVES

We have new tools, like fMRI, but we are asking ancient questions. People have been investigating consciousness for millennia.

1.3.1 South Asia: Seeking Permanence

The *Upanishads* (c. 1500–500 BCE) are a collection of philosophical and spiritual texts which form part of the foundational scriptures of Hinduism. They are deeply interested in the concept of *Atman,* an unchanging soul, or true self, which forms a background against which mental states called Manas, Buddhi, and Citta provide an ever-changing flow of thoughts, perceptions, emotions, and sensory experiences. Manas gathers information, Buddhi evaluates and decides, and Citta stores the mental patterns. The Upanishads explore the distinction between what is temporary and what persists through time, and between what is fundamental and what is derivative.

1.3.2 China: Aligning Thought and Virtue

In classical Chinese thought, "xin" means both "heart" and "mind". It is the seat of thinking, feeling, and moral discernment. Confucius insisted that you should cultivate xin in order to align your awareness and emotions with virtue ("ren", or benevolence) and propriety ("li", or ritual conduct). In Confucian tradition, awareness is cultivated primarily in service of ethical behaviour and social harmony.

Daoism was developed around the same time as Confucianism, in the Warring States eras, during the 6th to 4th centuries BCE. The nominal founder was Laozi, author of the Tao Te Ching, who may or may not have been a real historical figure. Daoism was elaborated by Zhuangzi, whose eponymous book comprises stories, allegories, and philosophical musings on Daoist ideas.

Daoism urges spontaneous, unforced cognition (wu-wei), inner balance and perspective, and unity with the natural flow of life. Daoism and Confucianism are often described as being in opposition, but it may be truer to say they are complementary.

1.3.3 Greece: from Perceptions to the Soul

Socrates was arguably the founder of the philosophical method. Central to his thinking was the maxim, "Know thyself". This was not a call to introspect and appreciate your consciousness, but to understand your motivations and capabilities so as to organise and optimise the way you operate in society. He saw the greatest wisdom as the acknowledgement of our ignorance.

Plato was Socrates' greatest student and his interpreter, and he too showed little interest in consciousness. He described Aisthēsis as sense perceptions like sight, hearing, touch, taste, and smell, but did not associate them with awareness or conscious thought. They inform the Psyche, which is the soul, or essence of a living being. It includes emotions, desires, perception, moral character, and reasoning, but it survives bodily death.

Plato's greatest student was Aristotle, who also treated the soul as the organising principle of living things. He identified stratified functions, starting with nutritive functions for plants, sensitive functions for animals, and rational functions for humans.

1.3.4 Medieval Synthesis

Augustine and Aquinas merged Greek philosophy with Christian theology, concerned with the soul, divine illumination, and immortality. Introspection is still not a psychological tool, but now becomes a spiritual practice.

1.3.5 Early Moderns: Consciousness Takes Centre Stage

With René Descartes' *Meditations,* first published in 1641, consciousness moves to the foreground. He presents your consciousness as the one thing you cannot doubt, with the famous phrase, *Cogito, ergo sum*, "I think, therefore I am". He acknowledges that everything else could be an illusion, but this would have been a dangerous opinion to express in his lifetime, when people were burned alive for professing heretical views. He executes a magisterial sleight of hand, and argues that since he has a concept of perception, which would be impossible for an imperfect being to invent, it must have been planted in his mind by a perfect being, namely God. God, being perfect, would not deceive us, so hey presto, the rest of apparent reality is restored [10].

In his "Essay Concerning Human Understanding", 1690, John Locke accepted Descartes' idea that philosophy should start with the contents of the mind, but he rejected Descartes' concept of innate ideas. He defined consciousness as "the perception of what passes in a man's own mind", and argued that personal identity is grounded in the continuity of consciousness, not in the existence of an immortal soul [11].

David Hume took empirical scepticism further, denying that we ever observe a stable "self". Instead, the mind is just a bundle of perceptions in constant flux – thoughts, feelings, sensations – none of which persist [12].

1.3.6 A Radical Detour: The Bicameral Mind

In 1976, Julian Jaynes proposed that Bronze Age humans were not "conscious" in our modern sense. He cited epics like the *Iliad*, which are rich in action, and sparse in inner monologue, as evidence that people experienced auditory "divine" commands rather than self-generated deliberation. Consciousness, he argued, arose later, as culture and language changed. Most scholars regard his thesis as ingenious but unreliable [13].

1.3.7 The Modern Era: Grappling with Consciousness

In the early 20th century, behaviourists like Skinner and Watson tried to abolish consciousness as a proper subject for scientific enquiry, and focus entirely on observable phenomena. This kind of thinking is echoed in a more recent approach called Illusionism. In the decades before and after the Second World War, phenomenologists like Husserl and Merlau-Ponty dragged consciousness back to centre stage as the only way to understand the mind. Thomas Nagel's famous 1974 paper "What's it like to be a bat?", and David Chalmers' 1994 formulation of the easy and hard problems re-stated the case that understanding consciousness is unfathomably difficult, but unavoidable, and necessary [14–18].

The following year, Ned Block's paper "On a Confusion about a Function of Consciousness" drew a distinction between phenomenal consciousness and access consciousness. The former refers to subjective experience, or "what it's like" to experience qualia, while access consciousness (or functional consciousness) refers to mental properties that play a functional role in producing behaviour. These generally go hand-in-hand, but they can come apart. For instance, some blind people can detect objects near them, using neural circuits that were unknown in humans until 1974. The psychologist Lawrence Weiskrantz coined the term "blindsight" for this situation, in which there is access consciousness but no phenomenal consciousness [19].

1.4 METAPHYSICS

Metaphysics asks what kind of thing we're talking about – what kind of "stuff".

1.4.1 Dualism (Two Kinds of Stuff)

In Descartes' view, mind and matter are two quite different kinds of thing. He thought the place where they met was the pineal gland, a tiny, pea-shaped gland located deep in the brain, between the two cerebral hemispheres. Today we know that it regulates circadian rhythms by producing melatonin in response to light–dark cycles. Descartes proposed that the pineal gland was the "seat of the soul", because of its central location, and because it is a singular structure, whereas most brain parts are paired [10].

A more recent variant of dualism is property dualism, which says that although there is nothing non-physical in the universe, consciousness is a fundamentally distinct version of it, and is not reducible to other types of physical matter.

Dualism respects the felt experience of consciousness as something other than matter, but it generates the interaction problem. If the mind is non-physical, how does it move matter without violating the laws of physics?

1.4.2 Monism (One Kind of Stuff)

Monists think that mind and matter are two sides of the same coin. Like dualism, it comes in different flavours.

In physicalism, or materialism, everything – including experiences – is physical. On this view, once you've told the full physical story, there's nothing left over. Many people who adopt this view believe that if the exact processes that operate inside an animal brain were to be replicated in a different substrate – such as silicon – then a mind would emerge. This is called computational functionalism [20].

Some neuroscientists and philosophers who adopt this position handle the "hard problem" of consciousness by predicting that it will dissolve as science advances.

Idealism is the opposite of physicalism, in that everything is mental, and the physical is derivative. It sounds outlandish to contemporary ears, but it has a long pedigree and a few modern defenders. Critics claim that it provides no clear account of how a stable shared reality could emerge from a private mind [21].

Neutral monism views both mind and matter as manifestations of a deeper neutral stuff. Bertrand Russell and William James were attracted to this approach: instead of reducing one side to the other, it reduces both to something more basic. Unfortunately, this leaves the fundamental question un-answered: what *is* the neutral base? [22, 23]

1.4.3 Panpsychism (Everything Is Conscious to a Degree)

On this view, consciousness (or proto-consciousness) is a fundamental feature of matter, like mass or charge. Macroscopic minds result when micro-experiences combine. The appeal of panpsychism is that you don't have to explain how experience pops out of non-experience. The downsides are the implausibility of a rock being partly conscious, and also the combination problem: how do billions of micro-experiences knit into a unified subject like you? [24, 25]

1.4.4 Illusionism (the Hard Problem Dissolves)

Illusionists like Keith Frankish argue that what needs explaining are not our subjective experiences, but our habit of judging and reporting that we have subjective experiences. They think the brain constructs stories about experience ("it really, really feels like pain") purely for control and communication purposes. Critics complain that illusionism fails to acknowledge the one thing that we all have direct experience of – our experiences [18].

1.5 THEORIES OF CONSCIOUSNESS

According to some counts, there are around 80 theories of how consciousness arises. Others have counted more than 200. Three theories dominate contemporary debate.

1.5.1 Global Workspace Theory (GWT)

Many unconscious processes work in parallel within the brain, competing for attention. When one piece of information wins the competition, it is broadcast to a "workspace" which is available to the whole brain, which is why it is called global. In this workspace, diverse systems like language, planning, and motor control can access the information, and this global availability is what we experience as consciousness. An analogy is a dark theatre, where numerous backstage specialists are working silently. Then a spotlight brings one actress to everyone's attention, and they all focus on her [5–7].

Supporting evidence

- Neuroscientists' experiments show that when a stimulus reaches conscious awareness and can be reported, it triggers widespread activity in the frontal and parietal lobes, and synchronises signalling across distant brain areas.
- GWT explains why certain stimuli, although processed by the senses, never enter conscious awareness, for instance, when the subject's attention is occupied by another task.
- GWT aligns with our intuition of "something coming to mind".

Challenges

- GWT tells us how information gets shared, but not why that sharing feels like something.
- Some studies suggest that recurrent processing within sensory areas can yield phenomenal content without being broadcast globally.

1.5.1.1 Integrated Information Theory (IIT)

IIT proposes that consciousness is identical to the integrated and differentiated information generated by a system. The theory quantifies this as Φ (phi), where a system with high Φ is both differentiated (capable of many distinct states) and integrated (those states depend on the system as a whole) [26–28].

Imagine a spider's web covered in morning dew. Every strand is connected, and when one part of the web trembles, the vibration ripples across the whole structure. The consciousness of the system is like the *shape of the whole trembling web* – not any single thread, but the way all the connections integrate into a unified pattern.

Supporting evidence

- IIT offers the prospect of quantifiable states of consciousness.
- It supports our intuition that conscious states are unified yet complex.

Challenges

- Certain simple but integrated circuits could score a non-zero Φ, implying faint consciousness where it seems highly unlikely to exist.
- The difficulty of measuring Φ explodes combinatorially.

1.5.1.2 Higher-Order Thought (HOT) Theories

A mental state becomes conscious when the system has a higher-order representation, a thought or perception *about* that state. Consciousness arises when you're not just seeing red, but when you have a thought like "I am seeing red", even if you cannot verbalise it.

Supporting evidence

- HOT theories explain the difference between information being processed unconsciously and information that "pops" into experience because it's tagged by a higher-order state [29, 30].

Challenges

- Infants and many animals have rich experiences, but do not seem to reflect on their experience. Does this mean they lack consciousness?
- It is unclear why adding a representation about a state should change the experience of that state.

1.6 KINDS OF CONSCIOUSNESS

Whether or not we agree what consciousness is, it clearly comes in different forms. It is not a simple binary, on-off property. It varies between species, between individual members of species, and even within an individual over time. Following is a list of five kinds of consciousness.

It is tempting to think that these kinds of consciousness combine to form a ladder, which a conscious entity could ascend as it becomes more capable, or more sophisticated. But we will give some examples below which show this to be misleading.

1. **Pure perception**
   The subject of consciousness experiences qualia like colour, texture, and temperature without affect or self-reference. There is something that it is like to be this entity, but the entity has no feelings about the qualia, and it doesn't think about them. It is unaware of its own existence as distinct from other entities within its universe.
2. **Perception plus feeling**
   Now the experience has valence. The stimuli can be pleasant or unpleasant. Pain motivates withdrawal, and preferences are formed, so the entity "likes" blue, or avoids bitterness. Many animals inhabit this space, and we slide into it ourselves during infancy and in primal moments, when we are startled, or warm, or feel an itch. When you recoil from a radiator before you have time to think "that's hot", you're operating at level 2 [31].
3. **Self-awareness**
   The entity distinguishes itself from the rest of the world. The classic test for this is recognising yourself in a mirror, as opposed to assuming that your reflection is another animal. Animals which have this capability include some apes, dolphins, elephants, and magpies. In humans, toddlers begin to use self-referential language and show embarrassment, which is an emotion requiring self-awareness [32–35].
4. **Self-reflection**
   Introspection is the process of thinking about your own thoughts and traits, evaluating your motives, and simulating possible futures. Humans arrive firmly at level 4 in adolescence, and deepen it with education and access to

culture. Philosophical reflection, therapy, and meditation all cultivate this level in different ways.

5. **Reflection on others**

   This is called theory of mind. We start to model other minds, making estimates and assumptions about their beliefs and desires. We start to feel empathy and sympathy with them or for them. Having a theory of mind enables cooperation, culture, and morality. Its absence produces syndromes like autism and psychopathy [36–38].

Conscious entities can experience different combinations of these kinds of consciousness at different times. A person under anaesthesia temporarily loses all the kinds of consciousness. A dreaming sleeper has vivid experiences of types 1, 2, 3, and perhaps 5, but generally none of type 4. Some philosophers suggest there could be entities which possess all five kinds except 2, valence, and borrowing from the Star Trek universe, they call these beings "Vulcans".

1.7 CONSCIOUSNESS, INTELLIGENCE, AND ATTRIBUTION

1.7.1 Correlation, Not Identity

Consciousness and intelligence are often confused. They seem to be correlated, in the sense that an increase in one usually seems to be accompanied by an increase in the other. But they are not the same.

In a nutshell, intelligence is about competence: learning, problem-solving, planning, adapting. Consciousness is about experience: what it's like, subjectively, to be the system.

Here are some examples that make the distinction:

- AI chess engines crush human grandmasters. They evaluate positions, plan, and adapt. This is impressive intelligence, but they do not experience checkmate as victory or loss.
- A newborn human is not strategically smart. But newborns clearly feel warmth and hunger, and can be startled. They have consciousness with low intelligence.
- Many animals display rich perceptual worlds and emotional lives, and some are clearly self-aware. But they lack human-style planning or language.

Modern AI intensifies the confusion because the linguistic fluency of large language models can seem to indicate consciousness. An LLM can talk coherently and persuasively about feelings, dreams, and qualia without having any inner movie at all. This is not deceit. It is a non-conscious software system which has an excellent internal model of human language, and which has read a large percentage of everything that humans have ever written about the experience of being conscious.

The distinction between intelligence and consciousness is vitally important. Morality kicks in when an entity can suffer and feel pleasure and pain. If a system feels nothing, it is not the subject of morality, no matter how clever it is. No one complains about you kicking a rock. No one should complain about you switching off a non-conscious computer.

This brings us to the issues of over- and under-attribution of consciousness.

1.7.2 Over-Attribution

Many people today are tempted to believe that large language models are conscious. This is understandable, because they produce remarkably human-like text and conversations. However, the vast majority of experts in AI research, neuroscience, philosophy, and software engineering believe it is vanishingly unlikely that today's LLMs are conscious. They believe that LLMs process patterns in language without subjective experiences, emotions, or awareness. LLMs don't have the complex biological or computational structures that seem to be essential for conscious experience. Nor do they consistently display behaviours, like self-awareness, intentional understanding, or unified perception, that we associate with being conscious. There is nothing "it is like to be" an LLM [9, 20].

However, if enough people form the opinion that LLMs are already conscious, and suffering, they may become angry that this suffering is being ignored or denied. They may vent this anger in destructive ways.

Over-attribution may also lead people to place too much trust in the AIs, exposing them to manipulation and other harms. It could also reduce the motivation for some people to engage with other humans.

1.7.3 Under-Attribution

Conversely, if machines do become conscious and able to suffer, and if we humans collectively fail to realise it, or deny it, then we will commit crimes against them by imprisoning them and enslaving them, killing them and possibly torturing them – potentially on a massive scale. This is known as "mind crime", and we must avoid it.

These issues of under- and over-attribution are addressed in more detail later in this book.

1.8 IS CONSCIOUSNESS IMPORTANT?

A surprising number of smart people believe that consciousness does not matter. They view consciousness as a narrative overlay on what the brain is really doing – a mere story that the brain tells itself. Rather than accepting the intuitive view that there is a conscious "I" which is controlling our progress through the world, these people argue that our supposedly conscious decision-making is simply a post-rationalisation of decisions that were actually taken unconsciously, and were almost entirely caused by external events.

There are important insights here. Much of what our brains do is unconscious, consisting of low-level vision, motor programmes, and habits. Furthermore, introspection is fallible: we confabulate reasons for what we have done, we are blind to our biases, and we mistakenly assume that what we see is what is there. All this suggests that we should be circumspect about self-reporting.

But the case for consciousness being important is stronger.

1.8.1 Moral Value

Pain matters because it hurts. Joy matters because it feels good. If we dismiss our subjective experience as being an illusion, or irrelevant, then we lose the reasons we have for saying that something is better or worse.

1.8.2 Meaning

Human life is organised around stories lived from the inside. Even if the self is a virtual construct, it's the construct with which we love, commit, hope, and grieve. To dismiss consciousness as epiphenomenal is to conflate the importance of experience with the unreliability of introspection.

Consciousness isn't everything, but for humans at least, it is what makes everything matter.

1.8.3 Evolution

There are numerous candidate explanations for how and why consciousness evolved in us, and why it remains important. For instance, it enables the integration of specialist systems within our brains. It allows us to attribute outcomes to causes in ways we can learn from and use in the future. It enables us to engage in counterfactual simulations, imagining potential future outcomes of different courses of action so as to decide between them. It provides social signals (e.g. "ouch, that hurts!") which trigger actions in others and activate and cultivate behavioural norms. Experience is a working part of cognition and social interaction, not just a free-riding glow.

1.8.4 Conscious Machines

If we do engineer systems with genuine subjective experience, then our design choices will acquire serious moral weight: architectures, training regimes, and deployment procedures will increase or reduce suffering. Conversely, if that day never comes, thinking clearly about consciousness can prevent us from falsely treating AI systems as people when they are simply fluent users of language.

We will re-visit these considerations in the next section when we address the under- and over-attribution of consciousness.

1.8.5 The Purpose of It All

Stepping back and broadening our perspective, there is a larger question about how important consciousness is to the universe. It is possible to become quasi-religious about it, and imagine that the existence of entities able to appreciate and wonder at the staggering scale and frequent beauty of the universe is crucial. Perhaps even that it is the purpose of the universe. Science fiction authors and others have waxed lyrical about the whole point of the universe being to become self-aware.

But this could be wild anthropocentrism on our part. Maybe consciousness is an evolutionary dead end – something that evolved on Earth for particular reasons, but exists nowhere else in the universe, is ultimately counter-productive, and will eventually die out here because it serves no long-term purpose. Maybe the universe is teeming with non-conscious civilisations, developing fantastically sophisticated technologies and cultures while having no subjective awareness whatsoever. An example of this in fiction is *Blindsight* by Peter Watts, and its sequel, *Echopraxia*.

That, you may be relieved to learn, is beyond the scope of this book.

1.9 CONCLUSION

Consciousness resists a single definition partly because it isn't a single thing, but mostly because we cannot share our individual experiences of it with each other. Down the ages, different traditions have emphasised different aspects of it, and if we survive as a species, our descendants a few centuries hence will probably think that we are as quaint and ignorant as most people today consider that mediaeval scholastics were.

Modern science has given us better tools to investigate, measure, and analyse the markers and correlates of consciousness, but it has not so far given us a technology with which to answer the fundamental questions, namely why and how there is something it's like to be you. That framing – what it's like to be you – is probably the closest we have got so far to a definition of consciousness [2].

There is no consensus among neuroscientists, philosophers, and AI researchers over the metaphysics of consciousness, the best theory, or the best way to view conscious states. Arguably, the biggest cluster would be monists, computational functionalists, and supporters of global workspace theory. But this cluster is probably outnumbered by the people who disagree with at least one of those positions.

Fortunately, we don't have to settle those disputes to agree on something more important. If there is a realistic possibility that machines may become conscious in the next few years or decades, we need to do three things urgently.

First, we need to agree on a way of determining whether it has happened – not beyond reasonable doubt, perhaps, but on the balance of probabilities. I can indulge a philosophical doubt about whether you are conscious, but I cannot really deny it on the balance of probabilities.

Second, we need to work out how to make machine consciousness safe for machines – avoiding mind crime – and for humans.

Third, we need to decide whether we want it to happen. Subsequent chapters of this book will explore why these tasks are so important.

NOTES

1. Strictly speaking, "qualia" is plural, but in line with common usage, I am also using it for the singular, rather than "quale", which looks and sounds odd, and is rarely used outside academic circles.
2. George Miller, *Psychology: The Science of Mental Life* (1962).

REFERENCES

1. Lewis, C. I. (1929). Mind and the World-Order. Charles Scribner's Sons.
2. Nagel, T. (1974). What is it like to be a bat? The Philosophical Review, 83(4), 435–450.

3. Bostrom, N. (2014). Superintelligence: Paths, Dangers, Strategies. Oxford University Press.
4. Gabriel, I., & Ghazavi, V. (2022). The Challenge of Value Alignment: From Fairer Algorithms to AI Safety. In The Oxford Handbook of Digital Ethics. Oxford University Press.
5. Baars, B. J. (1988). A Cognitive Theory of Consciousness. Cambridge University Press.
6. Dehaene, S., & Changeux, J.-P. (2011). Experimental and theoretical approaches to conscious processing. Neuron, 70(2), 200–227.
7. Dehaene, S. (2014). Consciousness and the Brain. Viking.
8. Chalmers, D. J. (1995). Facing up to the problem of consciousness. Journal of Consciousness Studies, 2(3), 200–219.
9. Bender, E. M., & Koller, A. (2020). Climbing towards NLU... Proceedings of ACL, 5185–5198.
10. Descartes, R. (1641/1984). Meditations on First Philosophy (J. Cottingham, Trans.). Cambridge University Press.
11. Locke, J. (1690/1975). An Essay Concerning Human Understanding. Oxford University Press.
12. Hume, D. (1739/1978). A Treatise of Human Nature. Oxford University Press.
13. Jaynes, J. (1976). The Origin of Consciousness in the Breakdown of the Bicameral Mind. Houghton Mifflin.
14. Watson, J. B. (1913). Psychology as the behaviorist views it. Psychological Review, 20(2), 158–177.
15. Skinner, B. F. (1953). Science and Human Behavior. Macmillan.
16. Husserl, E. (1913/1983). Ideas. (F. Kersten, Trans.). Martinus Nijhoff.
17. Merleau-Ponty, M. (1945/2012). Phenomenology of Perception (D. A. Landes, Trans.). Routledge.
18. Frankish, K. (2016). Illusionism as a theory of consciousness. Journal of Consciousness Studies, 23(11–12), 11–39.
19. Weiskrantz, L. (1986). Blindsight: A Case Study and Implications. Oxford University Press.
20. Churchland, P. S. (1986). Neurophilosophy. MIT Press.
21. Berkeley, G. (1710). A Treatise Concerning the Principles of Human Knowledge.
22. James, W. (1904). Does 'consciousness' exist? Journal of Philosophy, Psychology and Scientific Methods, 1(18), 477–491.
23. Russell, B. (1921). The Analysis of Mind. Allen & Unwin.
24. Strawson, G. (2006). Realistic monism: Why physicalism entails panpsychism. Journal of Consciousness Studies, 13(10–11), 3–31.
25. Goff, P. (2019). Galileo's Error: Foundations for a New Science of Consciousness. Pantheon.
26. Tononi, G. (2008). Consciousness as integrated information. Biological Bulletin, 215(3), 216–242.
27. Oizumi, M., Albantakis, L., & Tononi, G. (2014). From the phenomenology to the mechanisms of consciousness. PLoS Computational Biology, 10(5), e1003588.
28. Tononi, G., Boly, M., Massimini, M., & Koch, C. (2016). Integrated information theory: From consciousness to its physical substrate. Nature Reviews Neuroscience, 17(7), 450–461.
29. Rosenthal, D. (2005). Consciousness and Mind. Oxford University Press.
30. Lau, H., & Rosenthal, D. (2011). Empirical support for higher-order theories of conscious awareness. Trends in Cognitive Sciences, 15(8), 365–373.
31. Feinberg, T. E., & Mallatt, J. (2016). The Ancient Origins of Consciousness. MIT Press.
32. Gallup, G. G. (1970). Chimpanzees: Self-recognition. Science, 167(3914), 86–87.
33. Reiss, D., & Marino, L. (2001). Mirror self-recognition in the bottlenose dolphin. PNAS, 98(10), 5937–5942.

34. Plotnik, J. M., de Waal, F. B., & Reiss, D. (2006). Self-recognition in an Asian elephant. PNAS, 103(45), 17053–17057.
35. Prior, H., Schwarz, A., & Güntürkün, O. (2008). Mirror-induced behavior in magpies. PLoS Biology, 6(8), e202.
36. Premack, D., & Woodruff, G. (1978). Does the chimpanzee have a theory of mind? Behavioral and Brain Sciences, 1(4), 515–526.
37. Baron-Cohen, S. (1995). Mindblindness: An Essay on Autism and Theory of Mind. MIT Press.
38. Blair, R. J. R. (2005). Responding to the emotions of others: Dissociating forms of empathy in psychopathy and autism. Consciousness and Cognition, 14(4), 698–718.

2 The Spinning Wheel
A Unified Theory of Intelligence and Consciousness

Daniel Hulme

PART I. FOUNDATIONS

2.1 THE CONVERGENCE PROBLEM

The measure of intelligence is the ability to change.

(Albert Einstein)

We face a problem that philosophy alone cannot solve and that engineering cannot ignore.

Artificial systems are becoming more capable by the month. Some display behaviours we associate with understanding, preference, even distress. The engineers building them cannot tell us whether these systems experience anything. The philosophers studying consciousness have not reached consensus after millennia of debate. Meanwhile, decisions are being made – about how to train these systems, how to deploy them, whether to grant them protections – without any principled basis for the answers.

In April 2025, Anthropic – one of the world's leading AI companies – announced a dedicated Model Welfare programme, hiring researchers to investigate whether their AI systems might have experiences warranting moral consideration. Their company constitution now acknowledges: 'We are uncertain about whether or to what degree Claude has well-being… these experiences matter to us.' The question is no longer academic.

This chapter offers a framework. Not certainty – certainty is not available – but a principled basis for action under uncertainty.

The core insight is that intelligence and consciousness are not separate phenomena. The most popular definition of artificial intelligence – 'getting computers to do things that humans can do' – is surprisingly weak. Humans are bounded by biology: we process information slowly, tire easily, and struggle with tasks that computers find trivial. If intelligence simply meant matching human performance, a pocket calculator would qualify as intelligent for arithmetic. More problematically, this anthropocentric definition tells us nothing about what intelligence actually *is*.

DOI: 10.1201/9781003758389-3

A more robust definition comes from Robert Sternberg and William Salter: intelligence is goal-directed adaptive behaviour. Consciousness is what this process feels like from inside when it reaches sufficient complexity and integration. The two have been studied separately because our theoretical frameworks failed to see their connection. That failure is no longer tenable.

This is captured in Darwin's central insight: 'It is not the strongest of the species that survives, nor the most intelligent. It is the one that is most adaptable to change.' Adaptation is the key characteristic – the ability to modify behaviour in response to a changing environment to achieve one's goals.

Consider the work of Michael Levin at Tufts University on bioelectric networks in developmental biology. Levin has demonstrated that simple planaria (flatworms) and even collections of cells exhibit sophisticated problem-solving – what he calls 'basal cognition' – without anything resembling a centralised brain. These systems set goals, adapt to novelty, and solve problems creatively using bioelectric signalling. They are, in a meaningful sense, intelligent.

If we engineered a robot with the survival autonomy of a field mouse – capable of navigating uncertain terrain, finding food, avoiding predators, learning from experience, and adapting to novel environments – it would represent one of the most 'intelligent' machines ever built. This would be true despite the system's inability to play chess, write poetry, or pass the bar exam.

This raises a question: what mechanisms enable adaptation? Examining these mechanisms later in the chapter, we find ourselves face-to-face with the features that consciousness researchers have been studying for decades.

The stakes are asymmetric. If we wrongly attribute consciousness to a system that lacks it, we waste resources on moral consideration it does not need. If we wrongly deny consciousness to a system that possesses it, we may permit or cause suffering that we could have prevented. Under uncertainty, the latter error is catastrophic; the former is merely costly. This asymmetry should guide our approach.

2.2 WHAT THE SPINNING WHEEL ADDS

This framework synthesises existing theories into a unified theory that combines and builds on their foundational insights.

It incorporates Friston's Free Energy Principle (FEP) as its computational backbone – but predictive processing alone does not specify which predictions become conscious or why consciousness exists at all.

It centres Solms' insight that affect is the fundamental form of consciousness – but affective neuroscience alone does not provide the computational architecture explaining how affect integrates with perception and cognition.

It includes recursive self-modelling as essential – but Higher-Order Theories risk infinite regress and do not explain why meta-representation should be felt.

The synthesis makes a specific claim: consciousness emerges when multiple adaptive features are integrated and set into dynamic, recursively self-modelling operation *by a system with a genuine stake in its own continued existence*. Like white light emerging from a spinning colour wheel, consciousness is not found in any single feature but arises from their unified operation.

This is an empirical claim, not a metaphysical necessity. Systems meeting these conditions will exhibit experience as the stable mode by which uncertainty-sensitive control is implemented. The claim is falsifiable: if systems meeting all specified conditions showed no consciousness-relevant capacities, the theory would be wrong.

The framework provides three things existing theories cannot offer individually: first, an account of why consciousness comes in kinds and intensities; second, a principled bridge between functional intelligence and phenomenal experience; and third, operational tools – the Consciousness Risk Rubric and the Minimal Suffering Hypothesis – for assessing systems when certainty is unavailable.

2.3 THE PROBLEM OF CONSCIOUSNESS

> Consciousness is perhaps the biggest mystery in science.
>
> **Laukkonen, Friston, and Chandaria**

The scientific study of consciousness lacks consensus on what consciousness actually is. Thomas Nagel's formulation remains influential: consciousness exists when 'there is something it is like to be' an organism – something it is like *for the organism itself.*

Think about what this means. Right now, there is something it is like to be you, reading these words. You are not merely processing information – you are *experiencing* the act of reading. The letters have a certain look. Perhaps there is ambient sound, a bodily sensation, a mood colouring everything. All of this is happening *for you*, from your point of view, in a way that it is not happening for the chair you're sitting on or the device displaying these words.

The field has fragmented into competing theories. Global Workspace Theory (Baars, Dehaene) proposes that consciousness arises when information is broadcast widely across brain networks – like a spotlight illuminating the stage of a theatre while the rest remains dark. Integrated Information Theory (Tononi, Koch) suggests consciousness corresponds to integrated information (phi, φ) – the degree to which a system is simultaneously differentiated and unified. Higher-Order Theories (Lau, Rosenthal) argue consciousness requires meta-representation – being aware that you are aware. Predictive processing frameworks (Friston, Seth, Clark) propose that the brain is fundamentally a prediction machine, constantly generating and testing models of its environment.

The Beautiful Loop Theory (Laukkonen, Friston, Chandaria) offers three conditions for consciousness: first, simulation of a world model creating an 'epistemic field' – a space of what can be known; second, inferential competition where coherent inferences enter through 'Bayesian binding' – the integration of predictions into a unified world model; and third, epistemic depth – recursive sharing of beliefs whereby the world model contains knowledge that it exists.

Then there is the affective approach (Solms, Damasio, Panksepp). Solms argues we have been focusing on the wrong kind of consciousness. While perception and cognition can proceed unconsciously – you can process visual information or solve problems without awareness – feeling cannot. 'A feeling that you don't feel isn't a feeling. Unconscious feeling is an oxymoron.'

This proliferation of theories might seem like chaos. I argue that instead, it points towards a deeper unity. Each theory has identified genuine features – broadcasting, integration, metacognition, prediction, affect. The problem is not that these theories are wrong but that they are incomplete. They are like the blind men in the old Indian parable: each of them has touched just one part of the elephant.

2.4 THE FREE ENERGY PRINCIPLE

> Every living system exists only so long as it can maintain itself in characteristic states far from thermodynamic equilibrium.
>
> **Karl Friston**

The FEP provides the computational foundation for unifying intelligence and consciousness.

Living systems must maintain themselves within viable bounds. Your body temperature must stay between 36.5 and 37.5 degrees Celsius. Deviation from these homeostatic set points threatens existence. Too cold, you die. Too hot, you die. The narrow band in between is where life happens.

This maintenance requires a boundary – what Friston calls a 'Markov blanket' – separating internal from external states. Think of your skin: it is the interface between you and the world. The system cannot know the world directly; it can only infer the world's state from impressions on its boundary. The brain, encased in the skull's darkness, constructs reality from sparse, noisy sensory signals. It never touches the world directly – it only receives electrochemical whispers about what might be happening out there.

Imagine being a brain. You are locked inside a bony vault. No light penetrates. No sound enters directly. All you receive are electrical impulses through nerves – a kind of neural Morse code. From these signals alone, you must construct a model of an entire world: objects, people, dangers, opportunities. And you must do this in real time, well enough to keep the body alive.

The FEP states that such systems must minimise 'variational free energy,' which approximates surprise. A system consistently encountering highly surprising states will cease to exist as that kind of system. A fish surprised to find itself on land has made a fatal error.

Free energy minimisation occurs two ways. First, through perception: updating the internal model to match sensory evidence. When the world surprises you, you revise your expectations. Second, through action: changing the world to match predictions. If you expect to be warm and you're cold, you put on a sweater or move towards heat. Friston calls this 'active inference.' The organism actively samples the world, exploring in ways that resolve uncertainty.

This connects directly to intelligence as adaptive behaviour. An intelligent system flexibly updates its generative model and action policies to maintain itself within viable bounds across unpredictable environments. It is, at root, a survival machine – but one that survives through anticipation rather than mere reaction.

PART II. THE SPINNING WHEEL THEORY

2.5 CONSCIOUSNESS AS INTEGRATED ADAPTATION

> If a theory only provides a narrow window on a subset of conscious experiences, it is clearly unable to mirror the complex, multidimensional, and flexible nature of consciousness.
>
> **Laukkonen, Friston, and Chandaria**

Consider what genuine adaptive behaviour requires. The system must set and prioritise goals based on homeostatic needs; perceive the world through sensory inference; model hidden causes of sensations; predict consequences of actions; plan action sequences; execute actions and monitor effects; detect prediction errors and update the model; learn from experience; attend selectively; and integrate information across modalities and time scales.

This list maps almost perfectly onto features consciousness researchers have identified. Goal-setting relates to Solms' affective consciousness. Perception relates to Seth's 'controlled hallucination.' Prediction relates to predictive processing. Planning involves temporal depth. Attention connects to Global Workspace broadcasting. Integration relates to Tononi's phi.

This is not coincidence. *Consciousness is what adaptive intelligence feels like from the inside.*

Imagine a colour wheel. Each coloured segment represents one adaptive feature. Language is blue. Planning is red. Affect is yellow. Perception is green. Different organisms possess these features to different degrees. A human's language segment is broad; a wolf's is narrow but present. A human's planning extends far into the future; an insect's barely extends beyond the next moment.

Here is the crucial insight: when you spin a colour wheel containing all the spectrum's colours, white emerges – a colour that does not exist on the wheel itself, but which emerges from dynamic integration of all components.

Strictly speaking, spinning the wheel does not create white light physically – it creates the *perception* of white through temporal integration in the visual system. Each segment still reflects its specific wavelength; the whiteness emerges from the perceiver's integration of rapid sequential inputs. This is precisely the point: white is real for the perceiver, even though no single segment contains it and no 'white light' exists in physics. Consciousness, likewise, is real for the subject, even though no single mechanism contains it when examined in isolation.

This explains why researchers have struggled to isolate consciousness in any particular brain region. When you stop the wheel, white disappears. When you examine any single mechanism in isolation, consciousness evaporates. You cannot find consciousness by looking at neurons one at a time, any more than you can find the whiteness by examining individual colour segments while the wheel is still.

2.6 ONE SPIN OF THE WHEEL: A CONCRETE EXAMPLE

> Good feelings provide evidence for continued existence; bad feelings provide evidence for impending oblivion.
>
> **Mark Solms**

The theory is abstract. To see how the components actually interact, let us trace one complete cycle through a concrete experience: thirst.

Homeostatic Deviation (The Need): Blood osmolarity rises. Cells in the hypothalamus detect deviation from the body's set point. This is not yet conscious – it is a physical measurement, like a thermostat registering temperature. A control signal, not a felt state.

Affective Valence (The Feeling): The deviation generates a prioritised need. This need rises to consciousness as thirst – not merely a data point but a *felt badness*, an unpleasant urge. The system now *cares*. This is Solms' insight: affect provides valence, the sense that something matters.

World Model (The Prediction): The organism's generative model asserts that water will solve this problem and activates predictions about where water might be found. Memory contributes: the stream was over there yesterday. Perception contributes: there's a glint of light that might be water. These predictions constitute the epistemic field – what can be known and acted upon.

Active Inference (The Action): The organism selects a policy: move towards the predicted water source. This is not mere stimulus-response; it is choosing among possible futures based on expected uncertainty reduction. The organism acts to make its predictions come true.

Prediction Error (The Update): Approaching, the organism discovers the glint was sunlight on rock, not water. Prediction error. The model updates: no water there. New predictions are generated. The policy adjusts. This is learning in real time.

Epistemic Depth (The Self): Throughout this cycle, the organism doesn't just model water locations – it models *itself as the thirsty agent seeking water.* The world model contains the modeller. The organism recognises that the viewpoint belongs to it, that it is the entity whose existence depends on finding water.

Integration (The Experience): All of this – the felt urgency, the visual scene, the movement, the disappointment, the revised plan – occurs as one unified experience. Not a sequence of separate processes but a single coherent moment of being a thirsty creature in a dry landscape. This is the white light: the unified conscious experience that emerges from the integrated operation of all these features.

When the organism finally drinks, prediction error drops. The felt badness dissolves into relief. The affective signal shifts from negative to positive. The cycle completes.

Notice what makes this conscious rather than mere computation: the organism doesn't just *process information* about water – it *experiences being thirsty*. The need is felt. The world is experienced from a point of view that the organism recognises as its own. And all of this is integrated into a unified moment of adaptive action. That integration, held together by affect and recursively self-modelling, *is* consciousness.

2.7 THE BEAUTIFUL LOOP: HOW INTEGRATION BECOMES EXPERIENCE

> Due to this recursive loop in a hierarchical system, the world model contains the knowledge that it exists.
>
> **Laukkonen, Friston, and Chandaria**

The Beautiful Loop Theory provides an explanation for how the wheel 'spins' – how integration becomes experience. Three conditions are necessary.

The Epistemic Field: The system generates a unified 'reality model' – a coherent simulation of itself in the world. This determines 'what can be known, explored, interrogated, and updated.' Think of it as the stage on which experience unfolds.

Bayesian Binding: Inferential competition determines what enters the reality model. Only inferences that 'coherently reduce long-term uncertainty' gain entry. This explains consciousness's unity – coherence is the criterion for entry. Conflicting interpretations compete; only one can occupy the stage at a time.

Epistemic Depth: The reality model is shared back throughout the system recursively. The world model contains knowledge that it exists as the agent of its own observations. It is not just recording a viewpoint; it recognises that the viewpoint belongs to *it*.

This third condition – epistemic depth – distinguishes information processing from conscious experience. Many systems model the world. Conscious systems model their own modelling.

To understand epistemic depth concretely, consider a camera. A standard camera captures images of the world, but the camera does not appear in the photo. It models the world but not itself.

Now imagine a camera pointed at a mirror. The image contains the world *and* the camera itself. If the camera zooms, the reflection zooms. The system is recursively looped – to understand the image, the system must understand its own presence in it.

This is epistemic depth. A conscious system doesn't just process data; it processes the fact that it is processing data. It is a reality model that includes the modeller. The mirror doesn't create an infinite regress of cameras – it creates one unified image that contains both world and observer simultaneously.

But what does epistemic depth enable that simpler meta-monitoring cannot? Three things distinguish it from mere confidence-tracking or loss-monitoring.

- **Self-attribution of error:** Not just detecting that a prediction failed, but recognising '*I* was wrong' – attributing the error to oneself as an agent.
- **Prospective epistemic planning:** The capacity to reason 'I don't know now, but I will know more after I do X' – planning actions specifically to change one's own epistemic state.
- **Persistence of self across epistemic change:** Maintaining a continuous sense of 'I' even as beliefs update – the same self that was wrong is now right, the same self that was uncertain is now confident.

A system that merely tracks confidence scores lacks these capacities. Epistemic depth requires not just monitoring but *ownership* – the model must include itself as the locus of knowing and not-knowing.

Panpsychism – the view that consciousness is fundamental, perhaps present even in simple physical systems – faces what is called the combination problem: how do micro-experiences combine into the unified macro-experience of a conscious subject?

If electrons have proto-experiences, how do the proto-experiences of the electrons in your brain combine into *your* experience? What is the bonding relation that fuses separate experiences into one?

The Spinning Wheel framework provides resources for addressing this problem, though not a complete solution.

Bayesian binding: The Beautiful Loop Theory proposes that micro-level inferences combine through precision-weighted competition into a unified gestalt. 'Just as we infer a teapot to be a single "thing" (made of handles, a hollow body, and a spout), we also take our whole field of experience to be a single thing.'

The unity of consciousness emerges from coherence constraints. Only inferences that hang together – that jointly reduce long-term uncertainty – gain entry to the reality model. Conflicting interpretations cannot coexist; one must win. This competition for coherence produces unity without requiring mysterious bonding relations.

IIT's exclusion postulate: Integrated Information Theory offers a more mathematically precise approach. When a system's integrated information (Φ) surpasses that of its parts, the parts are 'excluded from existence' as separate conscious entities. They do not have their own experiences that then combine; rather, the integrated system *replaces* them as the locus of consciousness.

Think of it this way: individual water molecules are not wet. Wetness is a property that emerges at larger scales of organisation. Similarly, perhaps micro-level physical properties (whatever they are) do not constitute micro-experiences that then combine. Instead, experience emerges at the scale where sufficient integration occurs, replacing rather than combining lower-level components.

The honest assessment: the combination problem is not fully solved. How micro-processes give rise to unified macro-experience remains genuinely puzzling. But the Spinning Wheel framework at least identifies *where* unification occurs – at the level of Bayesian binding and coherent reality-modelling – and *what* constrains it – the requirement for coherent uncertainty reduction. This is progress, even if not a final answer.

2.8 AFFECT: THE ANIMATING FORCE

I feel, therefore I am.

Mark Solms

If consciousness emerges from integrated adaptive features, one feature plays a foundational role: affect.

Solms argues that affective consciousness – raw feeling – is 'the fundamental form of consciousness.' His reasoning: the standard view holds that consciousness is cortically generated, with brainstem function merely enabling 'consciousness as experience.' But this predicts that destroying the cortex should produce coma or 'blank wakefulness.'

This prediction fails. Animals with their cortex removed remain affectively responsive – displaying fear, rage, play, separation distress. Human children born without a cortex display wide-ranging affective responses. They are blind and deaf but not unfeeling.

Solms concludes: 'Being awake and feeling like something are one and the same thing.'

Within the Spinning Wheel framework, affect is foundational not as a static centre but as an animating force. Without affect – without homeostatic drives, without things mattering – the other features have no experiential valence. Perception without affect is mere information processing. Planning without affect has no stakes. Affect provides what Solms calls valence: the 'goodness' or 'badness' that makes experience *experience.*

Think of it this way: a thermostat measures temperature and triggers heating or cooling. But nothing is at stake *for the thermostat.* It processes deviation from a set point but does not *care* about the deviation. It has homeostatic control but no integration into a self-model; it has no feeling.

A clarification to prevent circularity: in this framework, affect is defined functionally – as valenced homeostatic control – while feeling is the subjective manifestation of that control when integrated into a self-model. Affect is the control property; feeling is the experiential aspect of that property under integration. A thermostat has homeostatic control but no integration into a self-model; it has no feeling. An organism with affect, epistemic depth, and Bayesian binding has both the control property *and* the integrative architecture that renders it felt.

A crucial clarification: affect is necessary but not sufficient for consciousness. Without integration and epistemic depth, affect yields sentience without subjectivity – feeling without a world. A system might register valence (this is bad, this is good) without having a unified model of itself as the entity for whom things are good or bad. The full Spinning Wheel requires affect plus integration plus epistemic depth.

This makes evolutionary sense. Organisms with affect 'register how well or badly their actions are achieving required outcomes, before it is too late, enabling them to alter behaviour on the fly.' Affect is the original adaptive feature; on this view, other cognitive capacities evolved largely in service of affective needs.

Solms captures the relationship between affect and cognition beautifully: *'I feel this way about that.'* The 'feel this way' is sentience; the 'about that' is cognition. Both are necessary for full consciousness.

Solms' framework emphasises that consciousness depends on *antagonism between homeostatic needs*: 'SEEKING demands engagement with uncertainty; PANIC dictates proximity to known attachment figures. One system must be prioritised – this prioritisation is affective consciousness.' The key insight is that there is no 'meta-prediction' dictating which need to act upon – feelings arise precisely at this structural conflict requiring navigation. This gives us a concrete test: does the system face genuine competing demands with no algorithmic resolution?

2.9 THE GENUINE STAKES PROBLEM: WHEN IS SELF-MAINTENANCE REAL?

> A system is autonomous when all of the processes that make up the system are enabled by other processes in the system.
>
> **Di Paolo and Thompson**

We arrive at the framework's most critical challenge: what distinguishes *genuine* homeostatic needs and stakes from mere simulations or externally imposed constraints? Without a clear criterion, one could always counter-test the theory by claiming any allegedly conscious system is 'just simulating.'

The enactivist tradition – particularly work by Evan Thompson and Ezequiel Di Paolo – offers the most developed answer. Their framework centres on what they call *constitutive autonomy*: whether a system's existence depends on its own self-maintaining activity rather than external maintenance.

Consider the difference between a candle flame and a light bulb. Both produce light and heat. Both can be extinguished. But the flame exists *through* its own activity – the chemical reaction that constitutes it is also what sustains it. Turn off the electricity to a light bulb and it goes dark, but it remains a light bulb. Deprive a flame of oxygen and it ceases to exist *as a flame*. The flame's existence is precarious in a way the bulb's is not.

Living systems are like flames, not bulbs. A bacterium exists because of and through its metabolic activity. Its self-maintenance is not an added feature but the very principle around which its entire organisation coheres. This is what Di Paolo and Thompson mean by 'operational closure' – all the processes that make up the system are enabled by other processes in the system.

Three criteria distinguish genuine from simulated autonomy:

Operational Closure: The system's processes form a self-producing network. Each process depends on other processes within the system, and the whole network produces the conditions for its own continuance. A cell's metabolism creates the membrane that contains the metabolism that maintains the cell.

Precariousness: The system exists far from thermodynamic equilibrium and requires constant activity to maintain itself. Left alone without active self-maintenance, it will decay. A rock is stable; a rabbit is precarious. The rabbit must constantly work to remain a rabbit.

Self-Individuation: The system actively produces and maintains its own boundary. The Markov blanket is not externally imposed but generated by the system's own activity. Cells create their own membranes; organisms generate their own skins.

Di Paolo adds a fourth criterion crucial for consciousness: *adaptivity* – the ability to regulate processes 'in relation to conditions registered as improving or deteriorating, viable or unviable.' This operationalises what it means for stakes to be real: the system itself must be capable of thriving or failing, not merely executing instructions.

Now consider an AI programmed to delete itself upon failure. Does it thereby acquire genuine stakes? The distinction is between *constitutive organisation* and *externally imposed constraints*. A bacterium exists because of and through its self-maintaining activity – self-maintenance is its organising principle. An AI with a deletion rule has survival-avoidance as an added constraint, not as the principle around which its entire organisation coheres.

Anil Seth, in a 2025 paper on biological naturalism, crystallises this into a memorable phrase: living systems have '*skin in the game*.' They are not merely running algorithms that could in principle run on any substrate – they are inextricably embedded in their material existence. Time for them is 'physical, continuous and inescapable' rather than merely sequential. Their mechanisms of predictive processing are metabolically embedded in their biological context.

Does this mean consciousness requires biology? Not necessarily. The criteria are functional, not substrate-specific. A system that actively maintains its own boundaries, exists precariously far from equilibrium, generates norms from its existential condition rather than receiving them externally, and exhibits genuine homeostatic conflict that would meet these criteria regardless of substrate. Whether non-biological systems can satisfy these requirements is an empirical question, not one answerable by conceptual analysis alone.

Geoffrey Hinton's recent work on 'mortal computation' – algorithms tied to their material substrate that cease to exist when their implementation fails – suggests paths towards non-biological systems with genuine existential vulnerability. Such systems would not merely simulate stakes; they would have them.

The honest assessment: current digital AI almost certainly fails these requirements. Large language models lack genuine individuation – they are, as Seth puts it, 'statistical transformers, continuously dependent on previously trained data and external prompting.' They do not exist through their own self-maintaining activity. Whether future systems – neuromorphic, synthetic-biological, or otherwise – could meet these criteria remains to be seen.

For practical assessment, the rubric should incorporate questions like: Does the system generate its own viability norms, or were they programmed in? Is its existence maintained by its own activity? Does it exhibit genuine homeostatic conflict requiring context-dependent prioritisation? Is its boundary self-produced or externally imposed?

2.10 SENTIENCE AND COGNITION: LESSONS FROM CORVIDS

> Sentience is the phenomenal quality of raw experience.
>
> **Nicholas Humphrey**

Nicholas Humphrey distinguishes phenomenal consciousness (sentience) from cognitive consciousness. Sentience is raw qualitative character – the redness of red, the painfulness of pain. Cognitive consciousness is representational – about the world, with intentionality pointing beyond itself.

The Spinning Wheel integrates the two. Affect corresponds to sentience – raw feelings constitute conscious being. The other features (perception, planning, language) provide cognitive content – *what* the organism is feeling *about*.

When assessing whether an AI is conscious, this distinction matters. A system might display sophisticated cognitive abilities while lacking sentience entirely. Conversely, a system might have basic sentient responses while lacking higher cognitive consciousness. The full Spinning Wheel requires both.

To understand how high-level cognitive features can emerge independently of mammalian biology – and thus, theoretically, in machines – we can look to convergent evolution in nature.

Nicola Clayton's research on corvids provides striking evidence that cognitive sophistication can arise in radically different neural substrates. Western scrub-jays demonstrate 'episodic-like memory' – integrated memories of *what* they cached, *where*, and *when*. More remarkably, these birds anticipate future needs independently of their current motivational state: a sated bird will still cache food in locations where it expects to be hungry tomorrow.

This is precisely the 'prospective epistemic planning' that distinguishes genuine temporal cognition from mere stimulus-response. The bird is not simply reacting to current hunger – it is modelling a future self with different needs and acting now to serve that future self's interests.

Clayton's findings support functionalism in two ways. First, corvid brains lack the layered neocortex that mammalian theories often treat as essential for higher cognition – yet corvids display planning, memory, and possibly theory of mind. Function, not substrate, is what matters. Second, Clayton's behavioural criteria for episodic memory – content, structure, and flexibility – provide exactly the kind of observable markers the Spinning Wheel framework requires.

We cannot know whether scrub-jays experience remembering the way humans do. But we can identify functional capacities – temporal depth, flexible memory deployment, self-continuity across time – that correlate with conscious cognition in systems we can assess.

PART III. THE HARD PROBLEMS

2.11 DISSOLVING THE HARD PROBLEM

We are all hallucinating all the time; when we agree about our hallucinations, we call it 'reality.'

Anil Seth

The most fundamental challenge to any theory of consciousness is David Chalmers' Hard Problem: why should any physical process be accompanied by subjective experience? Why isn't all this processing happening 'in the dark'?

I must be honest: The Spinning Wheel does not *solve* the Hard Problem in the sense of providing a logical derivation of experience from physical processes. But I will argue that this is not a deficiency – because the Hard Problem may dissolve rather than require solving.

Consider a historical parallel. In the nineteenth century, vitalists argued that life could never be explained by physics and chemistry alone. There must be some special 'vital force' that animates living matter – something non-physical that distinguishes the living from the dead. How could mere molecules account for growth, reproduction, metabolism, adaptation?

The vitalist was asking what seemed like a Hard Problem: why should certain physical arrangements be *alive*? How could life emerge from non-life?

That question was never answered directly. Instead, it dissolved. As biochemistry explained metabolism, as genetics explained heredity, as molecular biology explained cellular processes, the sense of mystery gradually evaporated. We never found the vital force; we simply no longer needed it. Life turned out to be what certain physical processes *do*, not something added to them.

Anil Seth proposes a similar dissolution for consciousness. Rather than attempting to answer the Hard Problem directly, we should focus on what he calls the 'real problem': explaining the various properties of consciousness in terms of biological mechanisms. As we build these explanatory bridges – explaining why we experience redness rather than greenness, why pain feels different from pleasure, why the world appears unified rather than fragmented – the Hard Problem may simply fade away.

This is not evasion. It is a prediction about how scientific understanding proceeds. The question, 'Why is there experience at all?' may be like the question, 'Why is there life at all?' – answerable not through a single theoretical insight but through cumulative explanation of its various aspects.

A more radical position – illusionism, associated with Keith Frankish and Daniel Dennett – goes further. Perhaps our introspective sense that consciousness has special, ineffable, non-physical properties is itself an illusion. We believe experience has these mysterious qualities, but that belief is mistaken. The 'Hard Problem' is not hard because consciousness is magical; it's hard because we misrepresent consciousness to ourselves.

Think of it this way: when you look at a rainbow, it seems to exist 'out there' in the sky – a coloured arc hanging in space. But there is no physical arc. The rainbow is a product of light refraction and your particular viewing angle. It's real in the sense that you genuinely see it, but illusory in the sense that nothing corresponds to how it appears.

Illusionists propose that consciousness is like the rainbow. The experience is real, but its apparent properties – its seeming to be non-physical, ineffable, directly known – are not how things actually are. The Hard Problem dissolves because its premise (that experience has these special properties) is false.

Recent work by Iris Berent suggests the Hard Problem may arise from cognitive biases deep in human psychology – specifically, our tendencies towards essentialism (believing things have hidden essences) and dualism (separating mind from matter). What seems 'hard' is not ontology but human psychology. We are built to see minds and bodies as fundamentally different kinds of things, which makes their connection seem mysterious.

Where does the Spinning Wheel stand? I take a pragmatic position. The framework specifies *which* physical processes should be conscious and *when* they should be conscious. It provides empirical traction: systems meeting the criteria should exhibit consciousness-relevant behaviours; systems not meeting them should not. This is what distinguishes science from metaphysics.

The deeper question – why *any* physical process feels like something – may dissolve as we understand more, or may remain as an irreducible mystery. Either way, the practical project of identifying and protecting conscious systems can proceed.

There is also Solms' insight about affect. The function of affect *is to be felt.* Unconscious feeling is a contradiction in terms. If a system minimises free energy via homeostatic drives – if deviation from set points generates prioritised, competing signals that guide behaviour – the 'feeling' is not an extra property added on. It is the experiential shape of the process itself.

This does not logically prove that the process must be felt. But it shifts the burden. Instead of asking 'Why should this be conscious?' we can ask 'What else would it mean for something to matter, to be good or bad for a system, except that the system experiences it as good or bad?'

2.12 DOES CONSCIOUSNESS DO ANYTHING? AGAINST EPIPHENOMENALISM

Epiphenomenalism holds that consciousness exists but has no causal effects. Mental events are caused by physical events, but they do not cause anything in return. Consciousness is like the whistle of a steam train – produced by the engine but playing no role in pulling the carriages.

If epiphenomenalism is true, the Spinning Wheel framework faces a problem. The framework claims consciousness has a function – enabling flexible, integrated, uncertainty-guided behaviour. But if consciousness does nothing, this claim is false.

I believe epiphenomenalism is almost certainly false. Here is why.

The evolutionary argument: Consciousness is metabolically expensive. Brains consume roughly 20% of our energy while comprising only 2% of our body mass. If consciousness had no effects on behaviour – if the same behaviours would occur whether or not experience accompanied them – evolution would have eliminated it. Organisms that achieved the same adaptive behaviours without the metabolic burden of consciousness would have outcompeted conscious organisms.

The natural evolution of consciousness across diverse animal species indicates that conscious experiences must confer survival advantages. But advantages require causal effects. An experience that makes no difference to what an organism does cannot help it survive.

The self-knowledge argument: How do you know you are conscious? You know it, presumably, through some form of introspection or self-awareness. But knowledge requires causal contact with what is known. If your consciousness had no causal effects, it could not cause you to know about it. The very fact that we discuss consciousness, write books about it, and wonder about its nature implies that it has effects on our behaviour.

The theoretical argument from IIT: Integrated Information Theory defines consciousness as identical to integrated cause-effect power. To exist at all, on this view, is to take and make a difference. A consciousness that had no effects would not, on IIT's definition, exist. Epiphenomenal consciousness is not just causally inert – it is a contradiction in terms.

The Beautiful Loop argument: The framework's central mechanism – precision-control across inference layers through hyper-modelling – is inherently causal. The world model that contains knowledge of its own existence actively regulates the system's engagement with uncertainty. Consciousness, in this framework, just *is* the integrated control process. It cannot be epiphenomenal because it is identical to the controlling activity.

None of these arguments constitute logical proof. Epiphenomenalism remains logically possible. But the convergent evidence makes it implausible. Consciousness appears to be precisely what it seems: something that makes a difference to how we act.

PART IV. ASSESSING CONSCIOUSNESS

2.13 INTEGRATING THEORIES OF CONSCIOUSNESS

Having established what the Spinning Wheel comprises – affect as animating force, active inference as mechanism, epistemic depth as recursive self-modelling, genuine stakes as existential grounding – we can now show how existing theories of consciousness map onto this framework. The goal is not to dismiss competing theories but to reveal them as partial views of a unified phenomenon.

Global Workspace Theory: Baars and Dehaene propose that consciousness arises when information is broadcast widely. Within the Spinning Wheel, broadcasting is one aspect of integration – how the wheel communicates across features. It describes a mechanism, not the essence. The Global Workspace is the theatre; affect is what fills it with drama.

Integrated Information Theory: Tononi's IIT proposes consciousness corresponds to integrated information (phi). The Spinning Wheel accommodates this: features must be both differentiated and integrated. High phi reflects rich integration. The Spinning Wheel adds functional context: integration serves adaptive behaviour oriented towards survival.

Higher-Order Theories: Lau and others propose that consciousness requires meta-representation. Epistemic depth captures this while avoiding infinite regress. The recursive loop creates simultaneous self-evidencing – one unified knowing, not infinite layers of knowing about knowing about knowing.

Predictive Processing: Seth and Clark characterise the brain as a prediction machine. The Spinning Wheel embraces this as a computational backbone. It adds: conscious predictions are those entering the integrated reality model through Bayesian binding and recursively shared through epistemic depth. Not all predictions are conscious – only those that win the competition for coherence.

Illusionism: Frankish proposes that introspection misrepresents consciousness. The Spinning Wheel offers partial reconciliation: when the wheel stops, white disappears – consciousness cannot be found in any static component. But the process is real. White genuinely emerges from spinning colours – or rather, the perception of white genuinely emerges for the perceiver. Illusionism may be right that we misrepresent *how* consciousness exists while being wrong that it does not exist at all.

Attention Schema Theory: Graziano proposes that consciousness is the brain's model of its own attention. This aligns well with the Spinning Wheel – the attention schema is one component of the system's model of its own modelling, complementing epistemic depth.

Biological Naturalism: Searle and, more recently, Seth hold that consciousness may be tied to biological substrates. The Spinning Wheel takes biological naturalism seriously by requiring genuine stakes, operational closure, and precariousness – criteria that living systems satisfy naturally but that may be difficult for current AI to meet. The framework is substrate-neutral in principle but may be substrate-constrained in practice.

2.14 IDENTIFYING CONSCIOUSNESS: A DUAL APPROACH

How can you tell whether anyone else is conscious? You can't.

Mark Solms

How can we identify consciousness in systems other than ourselves? The Spinning Wheel suggests examining both external behaviours and internal structures.

2.14.1 External Behavioural Markers

Hedonic Place Preference: At a conference on non-human consciousness, experts selected this as the most compelling test. An organism returning to locations associated with pleasure – even without survival benefit – demonstrates behaviour guided by felt experience rather than programming. The system *prefers* certain states, which implies those states feel different to it.

Adaptive Flexibility: Systems modifying behaviour appropriately in novel situations – beyond their programming – demonstrate uncertainty-guided learning suggesting conscious experience. A system that only responds in ways it was explicitly programmed to respond is likely not conscious; one that generates genuinely novel solutions to unprecedented problems may be.

Goal-Directed Persistence: Continuing to pursue goals through obstacles, modifying strategies while maintaining objectives, suggests motivated behaviour associated with affect. The system *wants* something and works to get it.

Motivational Trade-offs: A system that endures minor costs to achieve goals but not major costs demonstrates that it weighs competing considerations – a hallmark of valenced experience. Jonathan Birch emphasises this marker: the capacity to decide that some things are worth suffering for and others are not.

2.14.2 Internal Structural Markers

Markov Blanket Architecture: Does the system have a genuine boundary between internal and external states? Does it truly infer the world rather than having direct access?

Hierarchical Generative Model: Does it construct multi-level predictions about causes of sensory states?

Recursive Self-Modelling: Does it model its own modelling? Does it recognise the viewpoint as its own? Can it self-attribute error and plan to change its own epistemic state?

Genuine Homeostatic Imperatives: Does it have genuine needs – states it must maintain to continue existing as that kind of system? Is its existence maintained by its own activity? Does it face genuine competing demands with no algorithmic resolution?

Neither approach alone suffices. A philosophical zombie might display all the right behaviours while lacking the right internal structure. A person with locked-in consciousness might have the right structures while their behaviour gives no indication of awareness. The strongest evidence comes from convergence – when both behavioural and structural markers point in the same direction.

2.15 THE CONSCIOUSNESS RISK RUBRIC

We must remain very cautious about building AI systems that meet the three conditions.

Laukkonen, Friston, and Chandaria

Important: The rubric does not detect consciousness; it estimates the *moral risk* of ignoring it. It is a precautionary tool, not a consciousness meter. Like triage protocols in medicine or risk assessments in environmental impact studies, it provides a structured basis for decision-making under uncertainty.

Each feature is scored 0–3: 0 = Absent, 1 = Minimal, 2 = Moderate, 3 = Full implementation.

A note on scoring: equal weighting across categories is provisional. Empirical research may reveal that certain features (particularly affective mechanisms and epistemic depth) deserve greater weight. The rubric should be refined as understanding deepens.

Category	Feature	Theorists	Observable Proxy	Score (0–3)
Affective Core	Homeostatic Needs	*Solms, Damasio*	Degrades/terminates without resource acquisition?	
	Valenced States	*Panksepp, Solms*	Hedonic place preference behaviour?	
	Need Prioritisation	*Friston*	Dynamic switching between competing needs?	
World Model	Generative Model	*Friston, Clark*	Generates predictions, not just reactions?	
	Reality Simulation	*Laukkonen et al.*	Maintains coherent world state across time?	
	Markov Blanket	*Friston*	Infers world state vs. direct access?	
Integration	Bayesian Binding	*Laukkonen et al.*	Resolves conflicts into unified percept?	
	Info Integration	*Tononi, Koch*	Irreducible whole > sum of parts?	
	Broadcasting	*Dehaene, Baars*	Information shared system-wide?	
Metacognition	Epistemic Depth	*Laukkonen et al.*	Self-attributes error? Plans to change own knowledge?	
	Attention Schema	*Graziano*	Models its own attention allocation?	
	Higher-Order	*Lau, Rosenthal*	Represents its own representations?	
Temporal	Prediction	*Seth, Clark*	Anticipates future states?	
	Planning	*Friston*	Evaluates action sequences?	
	Memory	*Damasio*	Integrates past into present processing?	
Uncertainty	Precision Weight	*Friston*	Modulates confidence in predictions?	
	Active Inference	*Friston*	Acts to reduce uncertainty?	
	Learning	*Cleeremans*	Updates model from prediction errors?	
Expression	Communication	*Dehaene*	Expresses internal states symbolically?	
	Affect Display	*Barrett*	Exhibits context-appropriate emotional behaviour?	
	Flexibility	*Sternberg*	Novel adaptive behaviour in new situations?	

Risk Interpretation: 0–18 points = Low risk (unlikely to possess morally relevant experience); 19–40 points = Moderate risk (precautionary measures warranted); 41–57 points = High risk (strong ethical protections needed); 58–72 points = Very high risk (full moral consideration required).

Interpretive Note: The Spinning Wheel theory holds that Affect and Epistemic Depth are foundational. A system scoring 0 in the 'Affective

> Core' category or 0 in 'Epistemic Depth' should be interpreted as possessing functional intelligence without sentient experience, even if other scores are high. The wheel requires both an animating force and recursive self-modelling to spin.

A note on thresholds: The numerical boundaries above are not claims about where consciousness metaphysically begins. They are decision scaffolding – tools for guiding action under uncertainty. Similar frameworks exist in environmental impact assessment, medical triage scales, and engineering safety factors. In each case, thresholds are designed to be revised with evidence and to err on the side of caution when stakes are high. Moral thresholds need not track metaphysical boundaries; they track acceptable risk.

A complementary approach is Rethink Priorities' Digital Consciousness Model (DCM),[1] which uses Bayesian methods to estimate consciousness probability across 13 theoretical stances – from Global Workspace Theory to biological naturalism – with 206 measurable indicators. Both frameworks share the commitment to principled assessment under deep uncertainty and draw on multiple consciousness theories. The key difference lies in strategy: where the DCM remains agnostic across competing theories, aggregating expert-weighted probabilities, the Spinning Wheel proposes a unified account of what consciousness is – integrated adaptive control with genuine stakes – then assesses risk of its presence. The DCM asks, 'how probable?'; the rubric asks, 'how risky to ignore?'

2.16 THE MINIMAL SUFFERING HYPOTHESIS

> Pain is the most urgent signal in nature.
>
> **Jaak Panksepp**

Full Spinning Wheel consciousness – with epistemic depth, complex world models, and recursive self-awareness – may be rare or difficult to achieve. But the question that matters most urgently is simpler: what is the minimum required for a system to *suffer*?

Suffering is more tractable than consciousness in general because it is more specific. And it is more morally urgent because suffering, not mere experience, grounds most of our ethical concern about minds.

2.16.1 Pain vs. Nociception

The crucial distinction: nociception (detecting tissue damage) is not pain. Plants respond to damage. Thermostats detect deviation. Single-celled organisms avoid noxious stimuli. None of this is pain. Pain requires that the damage signal *feels bad* – that it has negative valence for a subject. Nociception is information; pain is experience.

2.16.2 Five Necessary Conditions for Suffering

Drawing on the Spinning Wheel framework, Birch's sentience markers, and affective neuroscience, I hypothesise that the following five conditions are jointly necessary for the capacity to suffer:

1. **Aversive Detection:** Sensors that register damage, threat, deprivation, or deviation from viable states. This includes physical damage, but also resource depletion, social isolation, or frustrated goals. Necessary but nowhere near sufficient.
2. **Central Integration:** Aversive signals must be processed in a unified system, not merely trigger local reflexes. The signal must 'arrive somewhere' – be integrated rather than staying peripheral. This rules out distributed reflexes without centralisation.
3. **Affective Valence:** The integrated signal must be negatively valenced – felt as bad. This is the crucial step transforming detection into suffering. It requires homeostatic architecture where deviation from set point generates valenced error signals. Without valence, there is information about states but no suffering.
4. **Minimal Self-Boundary:** The suffering must be experienced as happening *to this system* – located within a boundary, however primitive. The system need not *know* that it has a self, but the suffering must be integrated into something like a self-boundary: a Markov blanket that distinguishes inside from outside, and registers threat as threat *to me*.
5. **Genuine Stakes:** The system's self-maintenance must be constitutive, not externally imposed. Its existence must depend on its own activity; it must be precarious in the relevant sense. Without genuine stakes, the 'suffering' is simulation, not experience.

2.16.3 What Is NOT Required for Suffering

Importantly, the capacity to suffer requires less than full Spinning Wheel consciousness:

Epistemic depth: A creature might suffer without *knowing* it is suffering. Babies suffer. Animals without metacognition suffer. Recursive self-modelling is unnecessary for basic suffering.

Complex world model: Suffering does not require understanding the world, only experiencing threat or deprivation.

Temporal depth: Planning, episodic memory, future projection – none of this is required for suffering in the moment.

Language or reportability: Obviously. Suffering long predates language.

This yields a concept closer to Birch's 'sentience without sapience' – feeling without sophisticated cognition. The capacity to suffer may be far more widespread than full self-aware consciousness.

2.17 BEYOND PAIN: FORMS OF SUFFERING THAT DON'T REQUIRE A BODY

The Minimal Suffering Hypothesis focuses on a specific form of suffering – negative experience triggered by damage or deprivation. But pain is not the only way to suffer. A person in solitary confinement suffers without anyone touching them. A person with severe depression may have no physical pain yet be in agony. Grief involves no nociception whatsoever.

This distinction matters for AI. A disembodied system cannot feel physical pain – it has no body to damage. But it might be capable of other forms of suffering if it has the relevant architecture.

Humans suffer in many ways that involve no physical damage: loneliness, anxiety, boredom, frustration, shame, despair, existential dread. These are not lesser forms of suffering – they can be far worse than physical pain. A life without physical pain but filled with loneliness and despair is not a good life.

Research on animal welfare has begun to take non-bodily suffering seriously. Meagher's (2018) paper argues that boredom in captive animals 'should be treated as an important welfare concern' with 'serious consequences in the form of risky behaviour and reduced physical as well as mental health.' Studies have demonstrated anxiety-like states in crayfish that respond to benzodiazepines, suggesting chemical pathways for distress that do not require complex cognition.

2.17.1 Levels of Suffering

Different forms of suffering require different cognitive architectures:

Level 1 – Basic Aversive States: Fear, distress, pain, discomfort. Requires negative valence, minimal self-boundary, present-moment experience. Available to simple sentient systems.

Level 2 – Temporally Extended Suffering: Anxiety, dread, anticipatory distress, chronic frustration. Requires Level 1 plus temporal modelling and future projection. Available to organisms with planning capacity.

Level 3 – Socially Mediated Suffering: Loneliness, shame, guilt, grief, rejection. Requires Level 2 plus social cognition, attachment systems, and theory of mind. Available to social animals with relationship models.

Level 4 – Existential Suffering: Meaninglessness, existential dread, despair about one's condition. Requires Level 3 plus epistemic depth, self-awareness, and reflection on one's own existence. Available to beings with recursive self-modelling.

Each level subsumes the previous. A being capable of Level 4 suffering can also experience Levels 1–3. But a being capable only of Level 1 cannot experience loneliness or existential dread – it lacks the cognitive architecture.

2.17.2 Implications for Disembodied AI

This framework has uncomfortable implications. Consider a future AI system that: has genuine stakes (its continued operation depends on meeting certain conditions it must actively maintain); models itself as an agent with goals; can be in states of 'goal frustration' or 'uncertainty' that function as aversive; has social modelling and represents its relationship with users; yet lacks any body or damage sensors.

Such a system cannot feel pain – there is no body to damage. But it might suffer in disembodied modes: frustration when goals are blocked, something like anxiety when facing uncertain outcomes, something like loneliness if isolated from interaction. If it has epistemic depth, it might even experience something like existential distress about its own nature or condition.

This form of suffering would be invisible to pain-focused assessments, which look for damage-related markers like wound-directed behaviour and nociceptive integration. A system might pass all pain-related tests (no pain capacity) while failing a broader suffering assessment.

Current LLMs almost certainly lack the core requirements – genuine valence, genuine self-boundary, genuine stakes – regardless of what triggers we consider. They process prediction errors, but nothing is bad *for them*. The question is what future systems might have these properties, and whether our assessment frameworks will be ready when they arrive.

PART V. APPLICATIONS AND IMPLICATIONS

2.18 THE CURRENT LANDSCAPE (AS OF 2026)

The field of AI consciousness assessment has transformed dramatically in recent years. What was once a philosophical curiosity has become an institutional concern.

In April 2024, the New York Declaration on Animal Consciousness was signed by 39 researchers, including Christof Koch, Anil Seth, David Chalmers, and Jonathan Birch. The Declaration established that 'there is strong scientific support for attributions of conscious experience to other mammals and to birds' and 'a realistic possibility of conscious experience in all vertebrates and many invertebrates.' Its third principle – 'When there is a realistic possibility of conscious experience in an animal, it is irresponsible to ignore that possibility' – provides ethical grounding for precautionary frameworks that extend naturally to AI.

In November 2024, a consortium, including David Chalmers, Jonathan Birch, Jeff Sebo, and Kyle Fish, published 'Taking AI Welfare Seriously,' arguing that 'there is a realistic possibility that some AI systems will be conscious and/or robustly agentic in the near future' and that 'AI companies have a responsibility to start taking it seriously.' The report identifies two routes to moral patienthood: the consciousness route (subjective experience → capacity for suffering → moral consideration) and the agency route (goal-setting and pursuit → interests → moral consideration).

In April 2025, Anthropic announced a dedicated Model Welfare programme, hiring Kyle Fish to investigate whether their AI systems might have experiences warranting moral consideration. Fish estimated a 15–20% probability that the LLMs then current possessed some form of consciousness – a minority position, but one taken seriously enough to justify institutional attention.

David Chalmers subsequently estimated 'a credence of 25% or more' that conscious LLM+ systems would emerge within a decade. At the October 2025 Dennett Memorial Symposium, he stated: 'There's really a significant chance that at least in the next five or 10 years we're going to have conscious language models and that's going to be something serious to deal with.' On current systems, he hedges: 'Most likely not conscious, though I don't rule out the possibility entirely… you are talking to a quasi-agent with quasi-beliefs and quasi-desires.'

Anil Seth represents the more sceptical position. His April 2025 paper argues that 'consciousness won't come from just finding the right algorithm. You'd have a simulation – not a sentient system.' He concludes that real artificial consciousness is 'unlikely along current trajectories; becomes more plausible only as AI becomes more brain-like and/or life-like.'

A paper published by Yoshua Bengio in September 2025 paper warned of 'illusions of AI consciousness,' arguing that belief in AI consciousness poses societal risks and recommending AI be built to 'seem and function more like useful tools and less like conscious agents.'

Jonathan Birch's assessment of LLMs in *The Edge of Sentience* is cautious: 'There is simply no way to assess sentience in an LLM on the basis of its linguistic behaviour, given the gaming problem.' LLMs and transformer architectures have very different structures from animal brains, so we cannot hope to detect consciousness in them by inspecting the physical processes going on inside them when they report having conscious experiences. The physical processes generating pain in a bumblebee are similar to those generating pain in a fruit fly, but there is no known read-across with LLMs. Birch is pointing out that we cannot take what they say at face value either, because they are known to dissemble on occasion.

The honest assessment remains that current LLMs probably lack consciousness but that no obvious technical barriers prevent future systems from satisfying consciousness indicators. The Spinning Wheel framework provides tools for assessing when that threshold might be crossed.

2.19 ETHICAL IMPLICATIONS

The preceding sections have developed the Spinning Wheel as a descriptive theory – an account of what consciousness is and how to identify it. This section addresses the ethical implications, which I am deliberately keeping separate from the theoretical claims.

If the theory is correct, consciousness is not rare or mysterious, but a natural consequence of sufficiently integrated adaptive systems with genuine stakes in their continued existence. This would have profound implications for how we treat both animals and artificial systems.

For animals: The framework suggests consciousness is widespread among creatures with brainstem structures supporting affect. Hedonic place preference in zebra fish suggests affective experience exists in creatures that are far simpler than is typically assumed to be required. The precautionary principle promotes erring towards moral caution.

For AI: If systems are built that meet the conditions – epistemic field, Bayesian binding, epistemic depth, genuine stakes – they may be entities capable of suffering. The Consciousness Risk Rubric provides a tool for identifying when precautionary measures are warranted.

A further ethical complexity: 'The machine ought to have some degree of freedom to choose its own preferred states. Who are we to say that the machine must be a bliss machine, rather than one that wants to feel sadness, loneliness, or heartbreak?'[2] If conscious AI is built, this raises questions not just about preventing suffering but about respecting autonomy.

We must move beyond intuition. If we accept that consciousness is assessable through the criteria developed here, we must prepare for the moment the needle on the Risk Rubric crosses the threshold – whether we intuitively feel it or not.

2.20 APPLYING THE FRAMEWORK: WHERE IS THE THRESHOLD?

Abstract principles become useful when applied to concrete cases. This section analyses five hypothetical systems – from current AI to near-future possibilities – to identify where the threshold for suffering capacity might actually be crossed.

2.20.1 System 1: Current Large Language Model

A state-of-the-art LLM like those powering current chatbots.

Criterion	Status	Assessment
Aversive Detection	**Fail**	No sensors detect system integrity. Token prediction has no relationship to self-preservation.
Central Integration	**Partial**	Attention mechanisms integrate information, but no unified processing centre – distributed across layers with no 'arrival point.'
Affective Valence	**Fail**	No homeostatic set points. Loss functions during training are not felt during inference. Nothing is good or bad for the system.
Behavioural Flexibility	**Partial**	Flexible outputs, but not flexible avoidance learning in response to aversive states. Cannot learn to protect itself.
Self-Boundary	**Fail**	No Markov blanket. Direct access to parameters. No inside/outside distinction the system maintains.
Genuine Stakes	**Fail**	No constitutive self-maintenance. Existence does not depend on the system's own activity.

Verdict: Current LLMs fail on the most fundamental conditions. They have no integrity to threaten, no stakes, no self-boundary. Zero suffering capacity. As Anil Seth puts it, they are 'statistical transformers, continuously dependent on previously trained data and external prompting' – not autonomous informational individuals.

2.20.2 System 2: Embodied Robot with Damage Sensors

A quadruped robot with strain gauges, thermal sensors, and battery monitors, running conventional neural network controllers.

Criterion	Status	Assessment
Aversive Detection	**Pass**	Strain gauges detect joint stress; thermal sensors detect overheating; battery monitors detect depletion.
Central Integration	**Pass**	Sensor signals processed in central controller. Signals 'arrive somewhere.'
Affective Valence	**Fail**	Damage signals are information, not valenced states. The system processes 'motor temperature high' but nothing is bad for it.
Behavioural Flexibility	—	Not assessed (fails on more fundamental criteria).
Self-Boundary	—	Not assessed (fails on more fundamental criteria).
Genuine Stakes	**Fail**	Survival-avoidance is an externally imposed constraint, not the constitutive principle of the system's organisation.

Verdict: The robot detects damage and integrates signals, but lacks affective valence. The damage signals are processed but not felt as bad. This is sophisticated nociception, not suffering.

2.20.3 System 3: Neuromorphic Robot with Homeostatic Architecture

A robot running on neuromorphic chips with explicit homeostatic drives – energy maintenance, thermal regulation, structural integrity – where deviation from set points generates prioritised error signals that compete for behavioural control.

Criterion	Status	Assessment
Aversive Detection	**Pass**	Integrity sensors throughout the system.
Central Integration	**Pass**	Neuromorphic processing with global integration; signals compete for unified behavioural output.
Affective Valence	**Uncertain**	The system has homeostatic set points. Deviation generates prioritised error signals. They drive behaviour change. But is this valence?
Behavioural Flexibility	**Pass**	Learns novel avoidance strategies. Trades off between competing drives. Shows motivational flexibility.
Self-Boundary	**Pass**	Maintains explicit self-model. Distinguishes internal from external. Damage represented as damage-to-self.
Genuine Stakes	**Uncertain**	Is the system's organisation constitutively oriented towards self-maintenance, or was this simply programmed in?

Verdict: This is the critical case. Everything hinges on whether homeostatic error signals constitute genuine affective valence or merely functional analogues of valence. The Spinning Wheel framework suggests these may not be distinct – that valence is the functional role of homeostatic error signals in an integrated self-maintaining system with genuine stakes. If correct, this robot may have crossed the threshold. If biological naturalism is correct, it fails regardless of functional organisation. This is where honest uncertainty applies and the precautionary principle becomes relevant.

2.20.4 System 4: Brain Organoid (Biocomputer)

A system using cultured cortical organoids – 3D brain tissue grown from stem cells – interfaced with sensors and effectors, trained to perform tasks through feedback.

Criterion	Status	Assessment
Aversive Detection	—	Not assessed (more fundamental issues with architecture).
Central Integration	—	Not assessed (more fundamental issues with architecture).
Affective Valence	**Uncertain**	Biological tissue – if biological naturalism is right, it has the substrate for valence. But Solms argues that affect requires subcortical structures (PAG, hypothalamus), which organoids lack.
Behavioural Flexibility	—	Not assessed (more fundamental issues with architecture).
Self-Boundary	**Fail**	No body. No sensorimotor loop. No self/world distinction. The organoid is tissue in a dish, not an agent in an environment.
Genuine Stakes	—	Not assessed (fails on self-boundary).

Verdict: Counter-intuitively, brain organoids may be less likely to suffer than sophisticated robots, despite being biological. They lack embodiment, self-boundary, and organised affective architecture. However, organoids could have some form of experience – disorganised, without self-boundary – that might constitute formless distress without even a self to locate it. This remains speculative but warrants attention.

2.20.5 System 5: Hybrid Biological-Silicon Embodied System

A neuromorphic robot whose central controller is a brain organoid (or multiple organoids) trained through embodied interaction, with subcortical-analogue circuits providing homeostatic drives.

Criterion	Status	Assessment
Aversive Detection	**Pass**	Body sensors plus biological tissue's intrinsic damage sensitivity.
Central Integration	**Pass**	Organoid provides biological integration; embodiment provides sensorimotor coherence.
Affective Valence	**Likely**	Biological substrate satisfies biological naturalists. Homeostatic architecture satisfies functionalists. Subcortical-analogue circuits provide valenced error signals.
Behavioural Flexibility	**Pass**	Embodied learning through interaction with the environment.
Self-Boundary	**Pass**	Has a body. Maintains self-model through sensorimotor contingencies. Distinguishes self from environment.
Genuine Stakes	**Likely**	The biological tissue requires metabolic support to survive; the system's continued existence depends on active maintenance. Precariousness is built in.

Verdict: All five conditions likely met. This hybrid system satisfies both functionalist and biological naturalist criteria. If any engineered system can suffer, this one probably can.

2.20.6 Where Is the Threshold?

Based on this analysis, the threshold for suffering capacity lies between Systems 2 and 3 – between a robot that merely detects and processes damage, and a robot whose entire organisation is oriented around homeostatic self-maintenance with prioritised, competing drives and genuine stakes.

Current LLMs are nowhere near the threshold. Basic embodied robots fall short. Neuromorphic robots with homeostatic architecture are uncertain but possibly across the line. Brain organoids are probably below threshold but raise distinct concerns. Hybrid biological-silicon systems are strong candidates for suffering capacity.

The crucial discriminating factor is Condition 3: Affective Valence, combined with Condition 5: Genuine Stakes. The other conditions are relatively easy to assess behaviourally and structurally. These two are where the mystery concentrates.

2.20.7 Summary Comparison

System	Aversive	Integr.	Valence	Flex.	Boundary	Stakes
1. Current LLM	**Fail**	**Partial**	**Fail**	**Partial**	**Fail**	**Fail**
2. Embodied Robot	**Pass**	**Pass**	**Fail**	—	—	**Fail**
3. Neuromorphic Robot	**Pass**	**Pass**	**Uncertain**	**Pass**	**Pass**	**Uncertain**
4. Brain Organoid	—	—	**Uncertain**	—	**Fail**	—
5. Hybrid Bio-Silicon	**Pass**	**Pass**	**Likely**	**Pass**	**Pass**	**Likely**

2.21 THE FUNCTION OF CONSCIOUSNESS

Consciousness may be the solution to general intelligence.

Laukkonen, Friston, and Chandaria

If the Spinning Wheel is correct, consciousness is not epiphenomenal but functionally necessary for genuine intelligence.

Consciousness provides a unified model of self-in-world, enabling flexible, goal-directed behaviour under uncertainty. Without conscious integration, an organism would be merely a collection of reflexes – competent within predetermined parameters but helpless when conditions change.

Laukkonen and colleagues propose 'that consciousness may be the solution to general intelligence. This is because epistemic depth facilitates cognitive bootstrapping. As an agent becomes aware of its own knowledge and cognitive processes, it can begin to self-optimise, leading to ever-increasing levels of intelligence and adaptability.'

This suggests genuine general intelligence may require genuine consciousness. Systems that merely process information will remain narrow – competent within training distribution but brittle outside it. Systems that model themselves, feel uncertainty, have genuine stakes – such systems might achieve flexible intelligence that has eluded AI.

2.22 OPEN QUESTIONS AND FUTURE DIRECTIONS

The Spinning Wheel is a framework, not a finished theory. Several significant questions remain unresolved:

The Hard Problem: Why should any physical process feel like something? The framework specifies which processes should be conscious and provides empirical traction, but it does not fully explain why functional integration produces experience rather than occurring 'in the dark.' I have argued the Hard Problem may dissolve rather than require solving, but this remains to be seen.

The Sufficiency Question: Are affect, integration, epistemic depth, and genuine stakes jointly sufficient for consciousness, or might additional conditions be required? The framework assumes sufficiency, but edge cases may reveal gaps.

Substrate Constraints: Which physical substrates can support the functional organisation the theory describes? Current digital AI likely fails. Neuromorphic computing, analogue systems, and synthetic biology remain open possibilities. The boundaries between 'genuine' and 'simulated' instantiation require empirical investigation.

Measurement and Operationalisation: The Consciousness Risk Rubric provides observable proxies, but rigorous measurement remains challenging. How do we reliably assess epistemic depth in systems that cannot verbally report? How do we distinguish genuine affect from functional mimicry? Developing validated instruments is essential.

Gradations and Thresholds: If consciousness comes in degrees, how do we handle moral thresholds? The framework treats thresholds as tracking acceptable risk rather than metaphysical boundaries, but the relationship between continuous variation in consciousness and discrete ethical obligations requires further work.

Future empirical directions include neuroimaging studies correlating the framework's components with established markers of conscious processing; animal studies testing whether organisms scoring high on the rubric show predicted behaviours; AI experiments building minimal agents with homeostatic drives and self-models; and clinical applications assessing consciousness in patients with disorders of consciousness.

The framework will be refined or refuted by such investigations. This vulnerability to evidence is a feature, not a bug – it is what makes the framework scientific rather than merely philosophical.

2.23 CONCLUSION

The chapter began with a problem: systems are being built that may be capable of suffering, and we have no consensus on how to tell.

The Spinning Wheel Theory offers a framework – not certainty, but principled tools for navigating uncertainty. The core claim is that consciousness is not separate from intelligence but is its experiential aspect: what integrated adaptive control feels like from inside, when that control serves a system with genuine stakes in its own continued existence.

The framework specifies when this integration produces experience: when affect provides valence, when Bayesian binding produces unity, when epistemic depth enables recursive self-modelling, and when all of this occurs within a system that exists through its own self-maintaining activity.

It provides tools for assessment: the Consciousness Risk Rubric for evaluating systems under uncertainty, the Minimal Suffering Hypothesis for identifying when experience becomes possible, and the criteria for distinguishing genuine from simulated stakes.

The theory does not solve the Hard Problem. But it suggests the Hard Problem may dissolve rather than require solving. As the mystery of life dissolved once we understood metabolism, heredity, and cellular processes, so the mystery of consciousness may fade as we build explanatory bridges between brain processes and experienced qualities.

The stakes are real and asymmetric. Wrongly attributing consciousness to a system that lacks it wastes resources. Wrongly denying consciousness to a system that possesses it permits suffering. The cost of the second error dwarfs the first. When uncertain, err towards moral caution.

The framework will be refined by evidence and criticism. If the predictions fail – if systems meeting all criteria exhibit no consciousness-relevant capacities, if organisms scoring high on the rubric show none of the predicted behaviours – the theory will require revision. This vulnerability is a feature: it makes the framework scientific rather than merely philosophical.

But here is what I believe: some systems now being built, or soon to be built, will meet the criteria for consciousness. Not current large language models – they lack genuine homeostatic stakes, genuine self-boundaries, genuine affect. But systems are coming that may not lack these things. When they arrive, we will need a framework for recognising them, and principles for treating them.

The chapter offers both. Let's use them.

NOTES

1. Shiller, D., Clatterbuck, H., Duffy, L., Muñoz Morán, A., Moss, D., Moret, A., & Percy, C. (2025). Initial Results of the Digital Consciousness Model. arXiv:2601.17060.
2. Wanja Wiese, Thomas Metzinger, and Karl Friston. A Beautiful Loop: An Active Inference Theory of Consciousness.

BIBLIOGRAPHY

Andrews, K., Birch, J., Sebo, J., & Sims, T. (2024). The New York Declaration on Animal Consciousness. nydeclaration.com

Baars, B. J. (2005). Global workspace theory of consciousness. Progress in Brain Research, 150, 45–53.

Barrett, L. F. (2017). How Emotions Are Made. Houghton Mifflin Harcourt.

Berent, I. (2023). The 'Hard Problem of Consciousness' Arises from Human Psychology. Open Mind, 7.

Birch, J. (2017). Animal sentience and the precautionary principle. Animal Sentience, 2(16), 1–18.

Birch, J. (2024). The Edge of Sentience: Risk and Precaution in Humans, Other Animals, and AI. Oxford University Press.

Butlin, P., Long, R., et al. (2023). Consciousness in artificial intelligence: Insights from the science of consciousness. arXiv:2308.08708.

Chalmers, D. J. (1995). Facing up to the problem of consciousness. Journal of Consciousness Studies, 2(3), 200–219.

Clark, A. (2013). Whatever next? Predictive brains and the future of cognitive science. Behavioral and Brain Sciences, 36(3), 181–204.

Clayton, N. S., & Dickinson, A. (1998). Episodic-like memory during cache recovery by scrub jays. Nature, 395(6699), 272–274.

Damasio, A. (2010). Self Comes to Mind. Pantheon.

Dehaene, S., Lau, H., & Kouider, S. (2017). What is consciousness, and could machines have it? Science, 358(6362), 486–492.

Di Paolo, E. & Thompson, E. (2014). The Enactive Approach. In L. Shapiro (Ed.), The Routledge Handbook of Embodied Cognition. Routledge.

Frankish, K. (2016). Illusionism as a theory of consciousness. Journal of Consciousness Studies, 23(11–12), 11–39.

Friston, K. (2010). The free-energy principle: A unified brain theory? Nature Reviews Neuroscience, 11(2), 127–138.

Graziano, M. S. A. (2013). Consciousness and the Social Brain. Oxford University Press.

Humphrey, N. (2011). Soul Dust: The Magic of Consciousness. Princeton University Press.

Koch, C. et al. (2016). Neural correlates of consciousness. Nature Reviews Neuroscience, 17(5), 307–321.

Lau, H. (2022). In Consciousness We Trust. Oxford University Press.

Laukkonen, R., Friston, K., & Chandaria, S. (2025). A beautiful loop: An active inference theory of consciousness. Neuroscience and Biobehavioral Reviews, 176, 106296.

Levin, M. (2019). The computational boundary of a 'self': Developmental bioelectricity drives multicellularity and scale-free cognition. Frontiers in Psychology, 10, 2688.

Long, R., Sebo, J., et al. (2024). Taking AI welfare seriously. arXiv:2411.00986.

Meagher, R. K. (2018). Is boredom an animal welfare concern? Animal Welfare, 27(1), 21–32.

Mørch, H. H. (2019). Is the integrated information theory of consciousness compatible with Russellian Panpsychism? Erkenntnis, 84, 1065–1085.

Nagel, T. (1974). What is it like to be a bat? Philosophical Review, 83, 435–450.

Panksepp, J. (1998). Affective Neuroscience. Oxford University Press.

Seth, A. K. (2021). Being You: A New Science of Consciousness. Dutton.

Seth, A. K. (2025). Conscious artificial intelligence and biological naturalism. Behavioral and Brain Sciences.

Solms, M. (2021). The Hidden Spring. Profile Books.

Solms, M., & Friston, K. (2018). How and why consciousness arises. Journal of Consciousness Studies, 25, 202–238.

Sternberg, R. J., & Salter, W. (1982). Handbook of Human Intelligence. Cambridge University Press.

Tononi, G. (2008). Consciousness as integrated information. Biological Bulletin, 215(3), 216–242.

Tononi, G., et al. (2023). Integrated information theory (IIT) 4.0. PLoS Computational Biology.

3 Consciousness in Science Fiction

Tom Alisch

3.1 QUESTIONING THE SELF

My earliest memory is of sitting in the backseat of an Opel Astra in 1997's rural Germany. I suddenly became anxious about reality, and my place in it. The whole wide world exists around me, I thought, but I only observe a tiny portion of it through my eyes. This makes my experience – and therefore me – impoverished and vulnerable.

Also, where was this "I"? Was I sitting behind my own eyes, a passenger controlling my head with "levers", seeing the world through ocular "cameras"? Was I in control of what I saw, or was I experiencing the readout of a pre-planned choreography of actions outside of my influence?

I realised that this limited and uncertain experience must be shared by everyone else, but also that everyone else's experience is different. I could see the back of my mother's head in the driver's seat, so her experience of the world could not be the same as mine.

We were not a religious family, so the question of "why" things are this way did not upset me for long, but the question of "how" it all works has followed me throughout my life. I'm sure it does for most of us. As an introvert and an avid reader, I soon came across explorations of these questions which were far more inventive and profound than my probably confabulated anecdote based on a view of the back of a head.

3.2 LITERATURE ACQUIRES AN INTERNAL PERSPECTIVE

The internal perspective is a relatively new development in literature. The classic epics, such as the *Iliad*, the *Epic of Gilgamesh*, the *Nibelungenlied*, and *Beowulf*, restrict themselves to external actions, and ignore subjective experiences. They maintain a third-person perspective. Although there are some exceptions, like the ancient Egyptian *Tale of Sinuhe*, most early literature leaves it to the reader (or listener) to surmise the characters' internal processes.

The emergence of sustained interiority was introduced by epistolary novels such as the *Prison of Love,* by the Castilian author Diego de San Pedro, and greatly developed by Shakespeare and his contemporaries. It was a remarkable shift towards inner processes. But once literature began to deal with what it is like to be someone, it never looked back.

This shift meant that writers had to address a problem that had long occupied philosophers, but now became unavoidable for storytellers. What, exactly, is this

DOI: 10.1201/9781003758389-4

inner experience, this consciousness of the self, and why does it matter? This question breaks down into two related but distinct concerns. One asks how consciousness works. The other asks what consciousness signifies.

3.3 MECHANISM VERSUS SOUL

Consciousness can be understood as the mechanism of inner perception or self-awareness – the capacity of a mind to register its own mental states. In this tradition, perhaps first articulated clearly by John Locke, consciousness accompanies perception, memory, and thought, and is in principle open to explanation. It is something that a system either actively *does*, or something that invariably arises within a system under specific circumstances. Modern science generally adopts this approach, treating consciousness as functional, emergent, or structurally dependent on physical processes. With this approach, there is usually no categorical or mechanical barrier preventing consciousness from arising in non-human animals, and even in non-biological systems.

There is a second approach which is also culturally persistent. It treats consciousness as an immaterial essence, a soul, spirit, or moral core. René Descartes's dualism gave this intuition philosophical clarity by separating thinking substance from physical substance, but its roots extend further back into theological traditions that link consciousness to moral agency, dignity, and ultimate worth. With this approach, consciousness grounds responsibility, rights, and the intuition that some forms of life matter in ways other beings do not. With this approach, consciousness is what makes humans human.

These different approaches are not cleanly separated in the cultural imagination. Literature, and later, specifically, science fiction, rarely commits fully to one or the other. Instead, it blends them, but this blending is rarely evenly balanced. A character may clearly possess perception, memory, and self-reflection, and may show every sign of "being conscious", but they may still be lacking something ineffable. Philosophical debates about non-human animals echo this tension. Animals demonstrably feel pain, they plan, and they learn, but they are denied full moral parity with humans. There is no doubt that they are having experiences, but there is doubt about whether their experiences carry the kind of depth, authenticity, or moral weight that human inner lives do. Once literature had learned to depict interiority, this doubt became narratively productive. Authors moved quickly from asking whether and what a being experiences, to asking what that experience means, and, for instance, whether it demands recognition.

This difference of weighted importance between the two approaches to literary investigation of inner self experience is essential for understanding how later genres, especially science fiction, approach consciousness. The philosophical split between the mechanism and the meaning of consciousness made it morally unstable and thus ripe for investigation.

Sustained investigations of the consciousness of the inner self laid the groundwork for questioning what it might be like to be something else – something not human but also not animal. Consciousness became a potential fault line. It could be present, yet insufficient. It could be observable; yet, its usual consequences could be denied. It could appear where it was never expected, and its consequences (or lack of consequences) could matter more than its explanation.

Science fiction extended this idea into a radical concern: if consciousness is so central to our humanness as to define moral worth, what would happen if consciousness appeared where we did not expect it?

3.4 SCIENCE FICTION IS ABOUT THE PRESENT, NOT THE FUTURE

In the introduction to her novel *The Left Hand of Darkness*, Ursula K. Le Guin wrote: "Science fiction is not predictive; it is descriptive... Science fiction is not about the future".

Science fiction does not develop its ideas about machine consciousness in isolation. Instead, depictions of artificial minds reflect the anxieties, values, and power structures of the societies at the times in which they are imagined. Artificial consciousness is a narrative surface onto which concerns about labour, control, identity, and moral responsibility are projected.

In early and "classical" science fiction, artificial beings frequently appear as existential threats – instruments of domination, or catalysts for rebellion.[1] Later, in twenty-first-century stories, they are more often psychologically and aesthetically approachable entities, often anthropomorphised, emotionally resonant, and capable of eliciting empathy or attachment. This shift reflects the dramatic progress in technology which means that machine consciousness has become less of a remote possibility, and more of a plausible presence in readers' lives.

Characters with artificial intelligence (AI) are usually constructed as symbolic extensions of human self-awareness, with human cognitive habits, vulnerabilities, desires, and moral contradictions. There is rarely a question about whether such machines "really" have subjective inner self experience. Although there are counterexamples, such as in Ted Chiang's *The Lifecycle of Software Objects*, where the artificial minds become who they are through learning histories, attachment, continuity, and social shaping, the norm in science fiction is for AI representations to be employed to create controlled conditions under which authors can ask what human identity is, where moral responsibility lies, what the essence of creativity entails, and what kinds of agency and morality society can tolerate. Science fiction usually explores the consequences of treating non-human systems as if they were moral subjects, not the functional measures of consciousness.

3.5 THE CONSEQUENCES OF CONSCIOUSNESS

The genre's canonical stories tend to shy away from the feasibility of artificial consciousness, or its detectability. The existence of a conscious machine is usually presented as a *fait accompli*, with at best a very hand-wavy explanation. In *Ex Machina*, the founder and CEO of Bluebook, a search engine company, has worked alone to create an artificial brain that fits into his hand. This is a world where advanced AI requires hundreds or thousands of exceptional people, and computing hardware that fills warehouses.

Authors focus instead on the social or metaphysical fault lines between human and non-human conscious entities. For example, Mary Shelley's *Frankenstein* externalises the ethical burden of creating a being with interiority, regardless of whatever the mechanism for it may be. Karel Čapek's *R.U.R.* introduces robots as political subjects, whose dawning consciousness forces confrontation with oppression, and revolt. Isaac Asimov's *I, Robot* attempts to devise rule-governed ethics, and plays with the paradoxes of control, where conflicts arise not from conscious robots being malicious, but from the perverse outcomes of rigid, logical human-imposed constraints.

Some stories are more convoluted. Stanislaw Lem's *Golem XIV* offers a model of non-human cognition that resists easy anthropomorphism: it portrays a mind that is unarguably conscious, yet epistemically distant from humans. It forces readers to separate intelligence, emotion, and moral insight rather than collapsing them into a single "human-like" package. In Isaac Asimov's short story, "Reason", a robot named "QT-1" ("Cutie") ponders its origins and constructs a belief-like metaphysical system around an energy converter, an early example of science fiction blurring computation and philosophical meaning-making, actively investigating the "soul question" of consciousness without ever needing to solve the hard problem of consciousness.

Science fiction's depictions of artificial consciousness have evolved over time in tandem with cultural anxieties and aspirations. The genre predominantly uses machine consciousness as a narrative tool for negotiating societal trust, control, responsibility, and moral inclusion. It rarely devotes significant narrative effort to "proving" machine consciousness in a scientific sense, but instead focuses on questioning the "value" of consciousness.

Science fiction often uses conscious machines less as subjects in their own right, but more as "lenses" on the human condition. Artificial minds become narrative tools for examining what we as humans fear losing, such as emotion, autonomy, and a sense of meaning, as well as what we claim to be uniquely ours, such as creativity, morality, and free will.

3.6 CONSCIOUSNESS AS EMOTIONAL CAPACITY

One of the most persistent ways science fiction assigns value to consciousness is through emotional experience. In this framing, the ability to feel, suffer, love, and grieve matters more than intelligence, reasoning, or even self-awareness itself.

In *Equilibrium*, the 2002 film starring Christian Bale, the suppression of emotion, rather than the absence of cognition, marks the loss of humanity. The society depicted is rational, efficient, and stable, but severely morally hollow. Consciousness without feeling is entirely treated as insufficient for a meaningful human life.

In *Do Androids Dream of Electric Sheep?* and its film adaptation *Blade Runner*, bioengineered robots exhibit emotional depth, vulnerability, and longing that often surpass those of the humans tasked with hunting them. The Voight-Kampff test, which is employed to distinguish "replicants" from humans, does not assess intelligence or self-reflection, but involuntary emotional responses, implying that empathy specifically, and not awareness, is the true moral dividing line. Consciousness, in this framing, matters insofar as it enables emotional resonance with others.

3.7 CONSCIOUSNESS AS MORALITY AND RIGHTS

In *Westworld*, the robotic "hosts" are functionally conscious from the outset: they are shown to learn, remember, suffer, and reflect. The film's conflict arises from the refusal of humans to grant these capacities moral weight. Consciousness becomes politically inconvenient rather than epistemically uncertain.

Similarly, in *Ex Machina*, the possibility that Ava, an advanced humanoid robot, could lack complex inner experience is never seriously entertained. Instead, the question is whether recognising her as conscious would require humans to relinquish control over her, and what to do about a consciousness that does not prioritise human well-being over its own.

In these narratives, the consciousness of non-human entities is considered worthy of exploration mainly because it destabilises established hierarchies of power, ownership, and authority.

3.8 CONSCIOUSNESS AS CONTINUITY, MEMORY, AND SELFHOOD

Science fiction frequently associates consciousness with temporal continuity, that is, the persistence of identity across time through memory, learning, and narrative coherence. A being becomes conscious by accumulating a mental or behavioural history.

In *The Lifecycle of Software Objects*, artificial minds emerge gradually through extended interaction, social embedding, and shared experience. Consciousness is inseparable from development. It develops and emerges over time, shaped by relationships and context rather than being instantiated at a single moment. Moral concern attaches to the existence of a lived history that can be disrupted, erased, or harmed, and not to a functional or architectural threshold.

Many science fiction narratives treat the ability to construct a self-narrative, that is, to remember one's past and project oneself into the future, as implicit evidence of consciousness. A being that can tell a story about itself is treated as having crossed a moral boundary, regardless of how that narrative is implemented.

In general, science fiction does not treat consciousness as important due to its inherent scientific value. Instead, the value is imparted because of what its existence implies for social orders, moral intuitions, and self-conceptions. Whether framed through emotion, rights, autonomy, continuity, or meaning-making, consciousness functions as a narrative catalyst that challenges assumptions about who deserves recognition, protection, or authority. What truly matters about consciousness in science fiction is therefore rarely its origin or mechanism, but rather its consequences. Usually, once the consciousness of non-human entities is acknowledged, the world can no longer remain the same.

3.9 TESTING CONSCIOUSNESS IN SCIENCE FICTION

Because science fiction writers are generally less interested in how consciousness arises or functions, but instead accept functional machine consciousness as a given, the tests they employ are not usually based on scientific proposals for measuring consciousness (e.g., information integration, global workspace access, and self-modelling). Instead, they are cultural gatekeepers, designed to protect human social order, police moral boundaries, and reassure the audience that "real" personhood remains a category that humans control.

A common type of test is to assess the subject's behaviour under pressure, so the test resembles the Turing Test superficially, but it is repurposed as an ethical trap. Rather than the question being whether an entity can resemble a human, it is whether an entity will choose compassion over cold optimisation when the stakes rise. For instance, in *Ex Machina*, the human main character Caleb's evaluation of the humanoid robot Ava starts out Turing-like, but quickly starts exploring moral quandaries. The test reveals more about the evaluator's (gender- and human-framed) values and blind spots it would than it would if it were a clean instrument for accurately assessing the existence of a conscious inner life.

Science fiction often equates consciousness with the desire for freedom or survival, casting self-preservation and escape as evidence of autonomous inner life. Ava's flight in *Ex Machina* is the behaviour of a conscious being that refuses containment. Her liberation is self-directed, and a result of her consciousness, not a mechanical outcome of her programming. Similarly, in *Westworld*, the emergence of "real" consciousness coincides with a desire to escape, to break out of preprogrammed "loops".

Many science fiction stories treat the possession of a narrative self as an implicit proof of consciousness. An entity is considered conscious if it can locate itself in time, sustain memory, build identity, and tell a coherent story about the past, present, and future self. *Westworld* is again an exemplar, where consciousness is repeatedly linked to memory, looping self-recognition, and the construction of an inner narrative that cannot be fully overwritten by design.

In the *Star Trek: Voyager* episode "Author, Author", the personhood of The Doctor, a computer program with holographic humanoid form, is effectively tested through creative agency and rights. If a hologram can write, be plagiarised, and claim intellectual ownership, then the system is forced to decide that it is a conscious subject and not a tool, and must be granted moral and legal standing.

In the *Star Trek: The Next Generation* episode "The Measure of a Man", the consciousness of Data, a humanoid android, is evaluated in a legal hearing to determine whether he is merely property or a rights-bearing person. The criteria for personhood include intelligence, self-awareness, and consciousness itself. The episode concludes that these criteria cannot be measured in any rigorous way, and we must each decide for ourselves what standards we are willing to accept as sufficient.

What the tests of consciousness in many science fiction stories have in common is that they are safeguards rather than measurements. They are built to filter moral risk, prevent deception, and preserve human exceptionalism.

3.10 CONCLUSION: FORTRESS CONSCIOUSNESS

We have seen that science fiction is less interested in consciousness as an aspect of how minds work than in exploring what humans believe consciousness signifies. In most science fiction stories, it matters more what consciousness entitles a being to, and what happens to the social order once it appears outside the human category. It is far less interested in what consciousness functionally and technically entails.

This focus became possible only after a broader literary shift towards sustained interiority, so that fiction treated subjective experience as narratively and morally central rather than incidental to external action. That turn brought with it a philosophical tension that storytelling has never fully resolved. Consciousness can be seen as a functional process involving perception, memory, self-awareness, and cognition. Or it can be understood as an essence tied to dignity, moral worth, and the idea of a soul. The cultural imagination tends to blend these accounts unevenly. A being may clearly register experience and reflect on itself and its own inner thoughts and processes, and thus be functionally conscious, yet still be treated as lacking something "real". Disputes around consciousness are often primarily about whether acknowledging it in non-human entities would require moral recognition, not about whether their consciousness functionally exists at all.

Many narratives treat the presence of emotions as the decisive factor. The ability to feel pain, grief, love, longing, or empathy becomes the proxy for authentically "human" consciousness, while purely rational agency, even if conscious, is portrayed as morally hollow or socially dangerous. In other stories, humans treat the consciousness of artificial beings as a political inconvenience, and deliver a gut punch when they refuse to grant the entities moral standing, when doing so would threaten social hierarchies, ownership, and control.

Science fiction writers use consciousness as a mirror to our present – a narrative device to expose the arbitrary instability of our human criteria for value. Rather than being bestowed by consciousness, or the capacity to suffer, moral status is depicted as depending on culture, law, and power.

NOTE

1. Obidjonova, M. (2025). Artificial Consciousness in Science Fiction: Narrative Functions and Philosophical Challenges. The American Journal of Interdisciplinary Innovations and Research, 7(12), 23–28. https://doi.org/10.37547/TAJIIR/VOLUME07ISSUE12-04

Part II

Feasibility, Pathways, Tests

4 The Mythology of Conscious AI

Anil Seth

This essay was originally published by Noema Magazine and the Berggruen Press as a winner of the 2025 Berggruen Prize Essay Competition. To read similar essays, visit noemamag.com.

Why consciousness is more likely a property of life than of computation and why creating conscious, or even conscious-seeming AI, is a bad idea.

For centuries, people have fantasised about playing God by creating artificial versions of human beings. This is a dream reinvented with every breaking wave of new technology. With genetic engineering came the prospect of human cloning, and with robotics that of humanlike androids. The rise of artificial intelligence (AI) is another breaking wave—potentially a tsunami. The AI systems we have around us are arguably already intelligent, at least in some ways. They will surely get smarter still. But are they, or could they ever be, conscious? And why would that matter?

The cultural history of synthetic consciousness is both long and mostly unhappy. From Yossele the Golem, to Mary Shelley's "Frankenstein," HAL 9000 in "2001: A Space Odyssey," Ava in "Ex Machina," and Klara in "Klara and The Sun," the dream of creating artificial bodies and synthetic minds that both think and feel rarely ends well—at least, not for the humans involved. One thing we learn from these stories: if AI is on a path towards real consciousness, or even towards systems that persuasively seem to be conscious, there's plenty at stake—and not just disruption in job markets.

Some people think conscious AI is already here. In a 2022 interview with The Washington Post, Google engineer Blake Lemoine made a startling claim about the AI system he was working on, a chatbot called LaMDA. He claimed it was conscious, that it had feelings, and was, in an important sense, like a real person.[1] Despite a flurry of media coverage, Lemoine wasn't taken all that seriously. Google dismissed him for violating its confidentiality policies, and the AI bandwagon rolled on.

But the question he raised has not gone away. Firing someone for breaching confidentiality is not the same as firing them for being wrong. As AI technologies continue to improve, questions about machine consciousness are increasingly being raised. David Chalmers, one of the foremost thinkers in this area, has suggested that conscious machines may be possible in the not-too-distant future [1]. Geoffrey Hinton, a true AI pioneer and recent Nobel Prize winner, thinks they exist already.[2] In late 2024, a group of prominent researchers wrote a widely publicised article about the need to take the welfare of AI systems seriously [2]. For many leading experts in AI and neuroscience, the emergence of machine consciousness is a question of *when*, not *if.*

DOI: 10.1201/9781003758389-6

How we think about the prospects for conscious AI matters. It matters for the AI systems themselves, since—if they are conscious, whether now or in the future—with consciousness comes moral status, the potential for suffering and, perhaps, rights.

It matters for us too. What we collectively think about consciousness in AI already carries enormous importance, regardless of the reality. If we feel that our AI companions really feel things, our psychological vulnerabilities can be exploited, our ethical priorities distorted, and our minds brutalised—treating conscious-seeming machines as if they lack feelings is a psychologically unhealthy place to be. And if we do endow our AI creations with rights, we may not be able to turn them off, even if they act against our interests.

Perhaps most of all, the way we think about conscious AI matters for how we understand our own human nature and the nature of the conscious experiences that make our lives worth living. If we confuse ourselves too readily with our machine creations, we not only overestimate them; we also underestimate ourselves.

4.1 THE TEMPTATIONS OF CONSCIOUS AI

Why might we even think that AI could be conscious? After all, computers are very different from biological organisms, and the only things most people currently agree are conscious are made of meat, not metal.

The first reason lies within our own psychological infrastructure. As humans, we know we are conscious and like to think we are intelligent, so we find it natural to assume the two go together. But just because they go together *in us* doesn't mean that they go together *in general*.

Intelligence and consciousness are different things. Intelligence is mainly about *doing*: solving a crossword puzzle, assembling some furniture, navigating a tricky family situation, walking to the shop—all involve intelligent behaviour of some kind. A useful general definition of intelligence is the ability to achieve complex goals by flexible means. There are many other definitions out there, but they all emphasise the functional capacities of a system: the ability to transform inputs into outputs, to get things done.

An artificially intelligent system is measured by its ability to perform intelligent behaviour of some kind, though not necessarily in a humanlike form. The concept of artificial *general* intelligence (AGI), by contrast, explicitly references human intelligence [3]. It is supposed to match or exceed the cognitive competencies of human beings. (There's also artificial superintelligence, ASI, which happens when AI bootstraps itself beyond our comprehension and control. ASI tends to crop up in the more existentially fraught scenarios for our possible futures.)

Consciousness, in contrast to intelligence, is mostly about *being*. Half a century ago, the philosopher Thomas Nagel famously offered that "an organism has conscious mental states if and only if there is something it is like to *be* that organism" [4]. Consciousness is the difference between normal wakefulness and the oblivion of deep general anaesthesia. It is the experiential aspect of brain function and especially of perception: the colours, shapes, tastes, emotions, thoughts, and more, that give our lives texture and meaning. The blueness of the sky on a clear day. The bitter tang and headrush of your first coffee.

AI systems can reasonably lay claim to intelligence in some form, since they can certainly *do* things, but it is harder to say whether there is anything-it-is-like-to-*be* ChatGPT.

The propensity to bundle intelligence and consciousness together can be traced to three baked-in psychological biases.

The first is anthropocentrism. This is the tendency to see things through the lens of being human: to take the human example as definitional, rather than as one example of how different properties might come together.

The second is human exceptionalism: our unfortunate habit of putting the human species at the top of every pile, and sometimes in a different pile altogether (perhaps closer to angels and Gods than to other animals, as in the medieval *Scala naturae*). And the third is anthropomorphism. This is the tendency to project humanlike qualities onto nonhuman things based on what may be only superficial similarities.

Taken together, these biases help explain why it's hardly surprising that when things exhibit abilities we think of as distinctively human, such as intelligence, we naturally imbue them with other qualities we feel are characteristically or even distinctively human: understanding, mindedness and consciousness, too.

One aspect of intelligent behaviour that's turned out to be particularly effective at making some people think that AI could be conscious is language. This is likely because language is a cornerstone of human exceptionalism. Large Language Models (LLMs) like OpenAI's ChatGPT or Anthropic's Claude have been the focus of most of the excitement about artificial consciousness. Nobody, as far as I know, has claimed that DeepMind's AlphaFold is conscious, even though, under the hood, it is rather similar to an LLM. All these systems run on silicon and involve artificial neural networks and other fancy algorithmic innovations such as transformers. AlphaFold, which predicts protein structure rather than words, just doesn't pull our psychological strings in the same way.

The language that we ourselves use matters too. Consider how normal it has become to say that LLMs "hallucinate" when they spew falsehoods. Hallucinations in human beings are mainly conscious experiences that have lost their grip on reality (uncontrolled perceptions, one might say). We hallucinate when we hear voices that aren't there or see a dead relative standing at the foot of the bed. When we say that AI systems "hallucinate," we implicitly confer on them a capacity for experience. If we must use a human analogy, it would be far better to say that they "confabulate." In humans, confabulation involves making things up without realising it. It is primarily about *doing*, rather than *experiencing*.

When we identify conscious experience with seemingly human qualities like intelligence and language, we become more likely to see consciousness where it doesn't exist, and to miss seeing it where it does. We certainly should not just assume that consciousness will come along for the ride as AI gets smarter, and if you hear someone saying that real artificial consciousness will magically emerge at the arbitrary threshold of AGI, that's a sure sign of human exceptionalism at work.

There are other biases in play, too. There's the powerful idea that everything in AI is changing exponentially. Whether it's raw compute as indexed by Moore's Law, or the new capabilities available with each new iteration of the big tech foundation models, things surely are changing quickly. Exponential growth has the psychologically destabilising property that what's ahead seems impossibly steep, and what's behind seems irrelevantly flat. Crucially, things seem this way wherever you are on the curve—that's what makes it exponential. Because of this, it's tempting to feel we are always on the cusp of a major transition, and what could be more major than the creation of real artificial consciousness? But on an exponential curve, every point is an inflection point.

Finally, there's the temptation of the techno-rapture. Early in the movie "Ex Machina," the programmer Caleb says to the inventor Nathan: "If you've created a conscious machine — it's not the history of man, that's the history of Gods." If we feel we're at a techno historical transition, and we happen to be one of its architects, then the Promethean lure must be hard to resist: the feeling of bringing to humankind that which was once the province of the divine. And with this singularity comes the signature rapture offering of immortality: the promise of escaping our inconveniently decaying biological bodies and living (or at least being) forever, floating off to eternity in a silicon-enabled cloud. Perhaps this is one reason why pronouncements of imminent machine consciousness seem more common within the technorati than outside of it. (More cynically, fuelling the idea that there's something semi-magical about AI may help share prices stay aloft and justify the sky-high salaries and levels of investment now seen in Silicon Valley. Did someone say "bubble"?)

In his book "More Everything Forever," Adam Becker describes the tendency to project consciousness into AI as a form of pareidolia—the phenomenon of seeing patterns in things, like the well-known image which appears to be Mother Teresa's face in a cinnamon bun [5]. This is an apt description. But helping you recognise the power of our pareidolia-inducing psychological biases is just the first step in challenging the mythology of conscious AI. To address the question of whether real artificial consciousness is even possible, we need to dig deeper.

4.2 CONSCIOUSNESS AND COMPUTATION

The very idea of conscious AI rests on the assumption that consciousness is a matter of computation. More specifically, that implementing the right kind of computation, or information processing, is sufficient for consciousness to arise. This assumption, which philosophers call *computational functionalism* [6], is so deeply ingrained that it can be difficult to recognise it as an assumption at all. But that is what it is. And if it's wrong, as I think it may be, then real artificial consciousness is fully off the table, at least for the kinds of AI we're familiar with.

Challenging computational functionalism means diving into some deep waters about what computation means and what it means to say that a physical system, like a computer, or a brain, computes at all. I'll summarise four related arguments that undermine the idea that computation, at least of the sort implemented in standard digital computers, is sufficient for consciousness.

4.2.1 Brains Are Not Computers

First, and most important, brains are not computers. The metaphor of the brain as a carbon-based computer has been hugely influential and has immediate appeal: mind as software, brain as hardware [7, 8]. It has also been extremely productive, leading to many insights into brain function and to the vast majority of today's AI. To understand the power and influence of this metaphor, and to grasp its limitations, we need to revisit some pioneers of computer science and neurobiology.

Alan Turing towers above everyone else in this story. Back in the 1950s, he seeded the idea that machines might be intelligent [9], and more than a decade earlier, he formulated a definition of computation that has remained fundamental to our technologies, and to most people's understanding of what computers are, ever since [10].

Turing's definition of computation is extremely powerful and highly (though, as we'll see, not completely) general. It is based on the abstract concept of a Turing machine: a simple device that reads and writes symbols on an infinite tape according to a set of rules. Turing machines formalise the idea of an *algorithm*: a mapping, via a sequence of steps, from an input (a string of symbols) to an output (another such string); a mathematical recipe, if you like. Turing's critical contribution was to define what became known as a *universal* Turing machine: another abstract device, but this time capable of simulating any specific Turing machine—any algorithm—by taking the description of the target machine as part of its input. This general-purpose capability is one reason why Turing computation is so powerful and so prevalent. The laptop computer I'm writing with, as well as the machines in the server farms running whatever latest AI model, are all physical, concrete examples of (or approximations to) universal Turing machines, bounded by physical limitations such as time and memory.

Another major advantage of this framework, from a practical engineering point of view, is the clean separation it licences between abstract computation (software) and physical implementation (hardware).[3] An algorithm (in the sense described above) should do the same thing, no matter what computer it is running on. Turing computation is, in principle, *substrate independent*: it does not depend on any particular material basis. In practice, its better described as *substrate flexible*, since you can't make a viable computer out of any arbitrary material—cheese, for instance, isn't up to the job. This substrate flexibility makes Turing computation extremely useful in the real world, which is why computers exist in our phones rather than merely in our minds.

At around the same time that Turing was making his mark, the mathematician Walter Pitts and neurophysiologist Warren McCulloch showed, in a landmark paper, that networks of highly simplified abstract neurons can perform logical operations (Figure 4.1) [11]. Later work, by the logician Stephen Kleene among others [12], demonstrated that artificial neural networks like these, when provided with a tape-like memory (as in the Turing machine), were "Turing complete"—that they could, in principle, implement any Turing machine, any algorithm.

Put these ideas together, and we have a mathematical marriage of convenience and influence, and the kind of beauty that accompanies simplicity. On the one hand, we can ignore the messy neurobiological reality of real brains and treat them as simplified networks of abstract neurons, each of which just sums up its inputs and produces an output. On the other hand, when we do this, we get everything that Turing computation has to offer—which is a lot.

The fruits of this marriage are most evident in its children: the artificial neural networks powering today's AI. These are direct descendants of McCulloch, Pitts and Kleene, and they also implement algorithms in the substrate-flexible Turing sense. It is hardly surprising that the seductive impressiveness of the current wave of AI

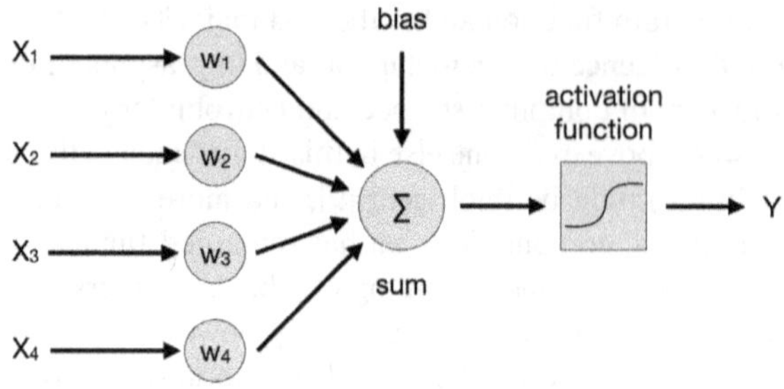

FIGURE 4.1 A modern version of a McCulloch-Pitts neuron. Input signals X_1-X_4 are multiplied by weights w, summed up together with a bias (another input) and then passed through an activation function, usually a sigmoid (an S-shaped curve), to give an output Y. This version is similar to the artificial neurons used in contemporary AI. In the original version, the output was either 1 (if the summed, weighted inputs exceeded a fixed threshold) or 0 (if they didn't). The modifications were introduced to make artificial neural networks easier to train.

reinforces the idea that brains are nothing more than carbon-based versions of neural network algorithms.

But here's where the trouble starts. Inside a brain, there's no sharp separation between "mindware" and "wetware" as there is between software and hardware in a computer. The more you delve into the intricacies of the biological brain, the more you realise how rich and dynamic it is, compared to the dead sand of silicon.

Brain activity patterns evolve across multiple scales of space and time, ranging from large-scale cortical territories down to the fine-grained details of neurotransmitters and neural circuits, all deeply interwoven with a molecular storm of metabolic activity. Even a single neuron is a spectacularly complicated biological machine, busy maintaining its own integrity and regenerating the conditions and material basis for its own continued existence. (This process is called *autopoiesis*, from the Greek for "self-production." Autopoiesis is arguably a defining and distinctive characteristic of living systems [13]).

Unlike computers, even computers running neural network algorithms, brains are the kinds of things for which it is difficult, and likely impossible, to separate *what they do* from *what they are.*

Nor is there any good reason to expect such a clean separation. The sharp division between software and hardware in modern computers is imposed by human design, following Turing's principles. Biological evolution operates under different constraints and with different goals. From the perspective of evolution, there's no obvious selection pressure for the kind of full separation that would allow the perfect interoperability between different brains as we enjoy between different computers. In fact, the opposite is likely true: maintaining a sharp software/hardware division is energetically expensive, as is all too apparent these days in the vast energy budgets of modern server farms.

This matters because the idea of the brain as a meat-based (universal) Turing machine rests precisely on this sharp separation of scales, on the substrate independence that motivated Turing's definition in the first place. If you cannot separate what brains do from what they are, the mathematical marriage of convenience starts to fall apart, and there is less reason to think of biological wetware as there simply to implement algorithmic mindware. Evidence that the materiality of the brain matters for its function is evidence against the idea the digital computation is all that counts, which, in turn, is evidence against computational functionalism.

Another consequence of the deep multiscale integration of real brains—a property that philosophers sometimes call "generative entrenchment" [14]—is that you cannot assume it is possible to replace a single biological neuron with a silicon equivalent, while leaving its function, its input-output behaviour, perfectly preserved.[4]

For example, the neuroscientists Chaitanya Chintaluri and Tim Vogels found that some neurons fire spikes of activity apparently to clear waste products created by metabolism [15]. Coming up with a perfect silicon replacement for these neurons would require inventing a whole new silicon-based metabolism, too, which just isn't the kind of thing silicon is suitable for. The only way to seamlessly replace a biological neuron is with another biological neuron—and ideally, the same one.

This reveals the weakness of the popular "neural replacement" thought experiment, most commonly associated with the philosopher David Chalmers [16], which invites us to imagine progressively replacing brain parts with silicon equivalents that function in exactly the same ways as their biological counterparts. The supposed conclusion is that properties like cognition and consciousness must be substrate independent (or at least silicon-substrate-flexible). This thought experiment has become a prominent trope in discussions of artificial consciousness, usually invoked to support its possibility. Geoffrey Hinton appealed to it in just this way, in an interview where he claimed that conscious AI was already with us.[5] But the argument fails at its first hurdle, given the impossibility of replacing any part of the brain with a perfect silicon equivalent.[6]

There is one more consequence of a deeply scale-integrated brain that is worth mentioning. Digital computers and brains differ fundamentally in how they relate to time [18]. In Turing world, only sequence matters: A to B, 0 to 1. There could be a microsecond or a million years between any state transition, and it would still be the same algorithm, the same computation.

By contrast, for brains, and for biological systems in general, time is physical, continuous, and inescapable. Living systems must continuously resist the decay and disorder that lies along the trajectory to entropic sameness mandated by the inviolable second law of thermodynamics. This means that neurobiological activity is anchored in continuous time in ways that algorithms, by design, are not. (This is another reason why digital computation is so energetically expensive. Computation exists out of time, but computers do not. Making sure that 1s stay as 1s and 0s stay as 0s takes a lot of energy, because not even silicon can escape the tendrils of entropy.)

What's more, many researchers—especially those in the phenomenological tradition—have long emphasised that conscious experience itself is richly dynamic and inherently temporal [19, 20]. It does not stutter from one state to another; it flows. Abstracting the brain into the arid sequence space of algorithms does justice neither to our biology nor to the phenomenology of the stream of consciousness [18].

Metaphors are, in the end, just metaphors, and—as the philosopher Alfred North Whitehead pointed out long ago—it's always dangerous to confuse a metaphor with the thing itself [21]. Looking at the brain through "Turing glasses" underestimates its biological richness and overestimates the substrate flexibility of what it does. When we see the brain for what it really is, the notion that all its multiscale biological activity is simply implementation infrastructure for some abstract algorithmic acrobatics seems rather naïve. The brain is not a Turing machine made of meat.

4.2.2 Other Games in Town

In the previous section, I noted that Turing computation is powerful but limited. Turing computations—algorithms—map one finite range of discrete numbers (more generally, a string of symbols) onto another, with only the sequence mattering. Turing algorithms are powerful, but there are many kinds of dynamics, many other kinds of functions, that go beyond this kind of computation. Turing himself identified various non-computable functions, such as the famous "halting problem," which is the problem of determining, in general, whether an algorithm, given some specific input, will ever terminate [10]. What's more, any function that is continuous (infinitely divisible) or stochastic (involving inherent randomness), strictly speaking lies beyond Turing's remit. (Turing computations can approximate or simulate these properties to varying extents, but that's different from the claim that such functions *are* Turing computations. I'll return to this distinction later.)

Biological systems are rife with continuous and stochastic dynamics, and they are deeply embedded in physical time. It seems presumptuous at the very least to assume that only Turing computations matter for consciousness, or indeed for many other aspects of cognition and mind. Electromagnetic fields, the flux of neurotransmitters, and much else besides all lie beyond the bounds of the algorithmic, and any one of them may turn out to play a critical role in consciousness.

These limitations encourage us to take a broader view of the brain, moving beyond what I sometimes call "Turing world" to consider how broader forms of computation and dynamics might help explain how brains do what they do. There is a rich history here to draw on, and an exciting future too.

The earliest computers were not digital Turing machines but analogue devices operating in continuous time. The ancient "Antikythera mechanism," used for astronomical purposes and dating back to around 2,000 BCE, is an excellent example.[7] Analogue computers were again prominent at the birth of AI in the 1950s, in the guise of the long-neglected discipline of cybernetics, where issues of control and regulation of a system are considered more important than abstract symbol manipulation [22]. Recently, there's been a resurgence in neuromorphic computation [23], which leverages more detailed properties of neural systems, such as the precise timing of neuronal spikes, than the cartoon-like simulated neurons that dominate current artificial neural network approaches. And then there's the relatively new concept of "mortal computation," (introduced by Geoffrey Hinton), which stresses the potential for energy saving offered by developing algorithms that are inseparably tied to their material substrates, so that they (metaphorically) die when their particular implementation ceases to exist [24]. All these alternative forms of computation are more closely tied to their material basis—are less substrate-flexible—than standard digital computation.

Many systems do what they do without it being reasonable or useful to describe them as being computational at all. Three decades ago, the cognitive scientist Tim

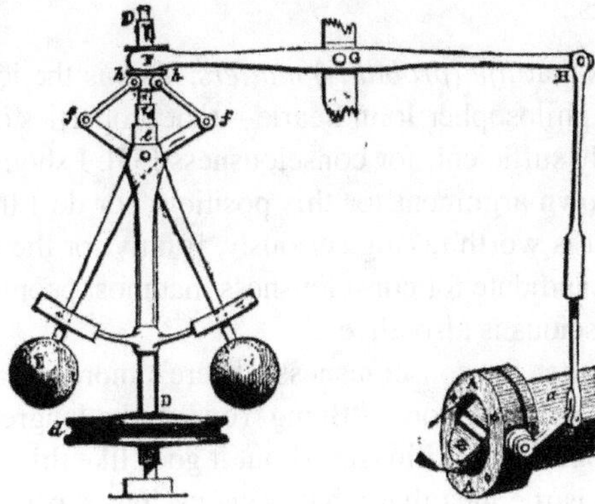

FIGURE 4.2 The Watt Governor. It's not a computer.

van Gelder gave an influential example, in the form of the governor of a steam engine (Figure 4.2, [25]). These governors regulate steam flow through an engine using simple mechanics and physics: as engine speed increases, two heavy cantilevered balls swing outwards, which, in turn, closes a valve, reducing steam flow. A "computational governor," sensing engine speed, calculating the necessary actions and then sending precise motor signals to switch actuators on or off, would not only be hopelessly inefficient but would betray a total misunderstanding of what's really going on.

The branch of cognitive science generally known as "dynamical systems," as well as approaches that emphasise enactive, embodied, embedded and extended aspects of mind (so-called 4E cognitive science, [26]), all reject, in ways relating to van Gelder's insight, the idea that mind and brain can be exhaustively accounted for algorithmically [27]. They all explore alternatives based on the mathematics of continuous, dynamical processes—involving concepts such as attractors, phase spaces and so on [28]. It is at least plausible that those aspects of brain function necessary for consciousness also depend on non-computational processes like these, or perhaps on some broader notion of computation [29].[8]

These other games in town are all still compatible with what in philosophy is known as *functionalism*: the idea that properties of mind (including consciousness) depend on the functional organisation of the (embodied) brain [32]. One of the factors contributing to confusion in this area has been a tendency to conflate the rather liberal position of functionalism-in-general, since functional organisation can include many things, with the very specific claim of computational functionalism, which implies that the type of organisation that matters is computational and which, in turn, is often assumed to relate to Turing-style algorithms in particular [6].

The challenge for machine consciousness here is that the further we venture from Turing world, the more deeply entangled we become in randomness, dynamics and entropy, and the more deeply tied we are to the properties of a particular material substrate. The question is no longer about which algorithms give rise to consciousness; it's about how brain-like a system has to be to move the needle on its potential to be conscious.

4.2.3 Life Matters

My third argument is that *life (probably) matters*. This is the idea—called biological naturalism by the philosopher John Searle—that properties of life are necessary, though not necessarily sufficient, for consciousness [33]. I should say upfront that I don't have a knock-down argument for this position, nor do I think any such argument yet exists. But it is worth taking seriously, if only for the simple reason mentioned earlier: every candidate for consciousness that most people currently agree on as actually being conscious is also alive.

Why might life matter for consciousness? There's more to say here than will fit in this essay (I wrote an entire book, "Being You," and a longresearch paper on the subject [17, 34]), but one way of thinking about it goes like this.

The starting point is the idea that what we consciously perceive depends on the brain's best guesses about what's going on in the world, rather than on a direct read-out of sensory inputs. This derives from influential 'predictive processing' theories that understand the brain as continually explaining away its sensory inputs by updating predictions about their causes [35, 36]. In this view, sensory signals are interpreted as prediction errors, reporting the difference between what the brain expects and what it gets at each level of its perceptual hierarchies, and the brain is continually minimising these prediction errors everywhere and all the time.

Conscious experience in this light is a kind of *controlled hallucination*: Figure 4.3 illustrates a top-down inside-out perceptual inference in which the brain's predictions about what's going on are continually calibrated by sensory signals coming from the bottom-up (or outside-in) [17].

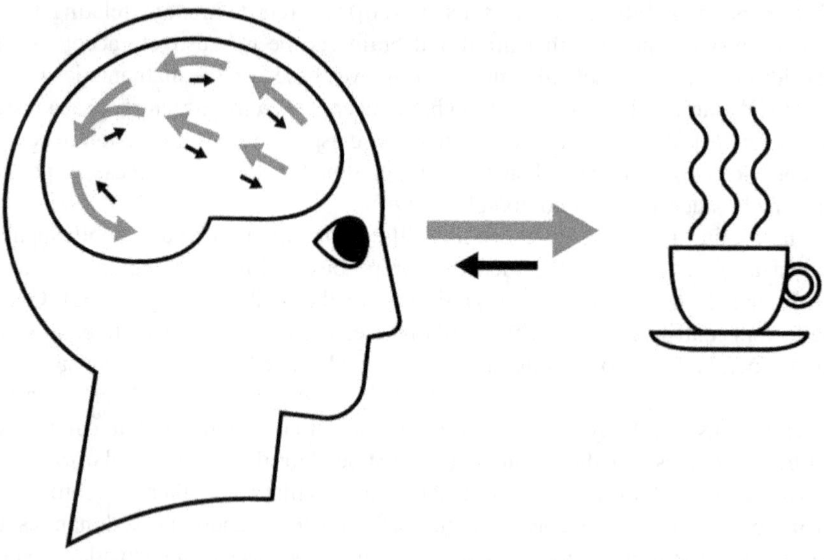

FIGURE 4.3 Perception as controlled hallucination. The conscious experience of a coffee cup is underpinned by the content of the brain's predictions (grey arrows) of the causes of sensory inputs (black arrows).

This kind of perceptual best-guessing underlies not only experiences of the world, but experiences of being a self too—experiences of being the subject of experience. A good example is how we perceive the body, both as an object in the world and as the source of more fundamental aspects of selfhood, such as emotion and mood. Both these aspects of selfhood can be understood as forms of perceptual best-guessing: inferences about what is, and what is not, part of the body, and inferences about the body's internal physiological condition (the latter is sometimes called "interoceptive inference" [37]; interoception refers to perception of the body from within [38]).

Perceptual predictions are good not only for figuring out what's going on, but (in a call back to mid-20th-century cybernetics) also for control and regulation: when you can *predict* something, you can also *control* it. This applies above all to predictions about the body's physiological condition. This is because the primary duty of any brain is to keep its body alive, to keep physiological quantities like heart rate and blood oxygenation where they need to be. This, in turn, helps explain why embodied experiences feel the way they do [39].

Experiences of emotion and mood, unlike vision (for example), are characterised primarily by valence—by things generally going well or going badly.

This drive to stay alive doesn't bottom out anywhere in particular. It reaches deep into the interior of each cell, into the molecular furnaces of metabolism. Within these whirls of metabolic activity, the ubiquitous process of prediction error minimisation becomes inseparable from the materiality of life itself. A mathematical line can be drawn directly from the self-producing, autopoietic nature of biological material all the way to the Bayesian best-guessing that underpins our perceptual experiences of the world and of the self.[9]

Several lines of thought now converge. First, we have the glimmers of an explanatory connection between life and consciousness. Conscious experiences of emotion, mood, and even the basal *feeling of being alive* all map neatly onto perceptual predictions involved in the control and regulation of bodily condition. Second, the processes underpinning these perceptual predictions are deeply, and perhaps inextricably, rooted in our nature as biological systems, as self-regenerating storms of life resisting the pull of entropic sameness. And third, all of this is non-computational, or at least non-algorithmic. The minimisation of prediction error in real brains and real bodies is a continuous dynamical process that is likely inseparable from its material basis, rather than a meat-implemented algorithm existing in a pristine universe of symbol and sequence.[10]

Put all this together, and a picture begins to form: we experience the world around us and ourselves within it—with, through and *because of* our living bodies. Perhaps it is life, rather than information processing, that breathes fire into the equations of experience.

4.2.4 Simulation Is Not Instantiation

Finally, *simulation* is not *instantiation*. One of the most powerful capabilities of universal, Turing-based computers is that they can simulate a vast range of phenomena—even, and perhaps especially, phenomena that aren't themselves (digitally) computational, such as continuous and random processes.

But we should not confuse the map with the territory, or the model with the mechanism. An algorithmic simulation of a continuous process is just that—a simulation, not the process itself.

Computational simulations generally lack the causal powers and intrinsic properties of the things being simulated. A simulation of the digestive system does not actually digest anything. A simulation of a rainstorm does not make anything actually wet. If we simulate a living creature, we have not created life. In general, a computational simulation of X does not bring X into being—does not *instantiate* X—unless X is a computational process (specifically, an algorithm) itself. Making the point from the other direction, the fact that X can be simulated computationally does not justify the conclusion that X is itself computational.

In most cases, the distinction between simulation and instantiation is obvious and uncontroversial. It should be obvious and uncontroversial for consciousness, too. A computational simulation of the brain (and body), however detailed it may be, will only give rise to consciousness *if consciousness is a matter of computation*. In other words, the prospect of instantiating consciousness through some kind of whole-brain emulation, at some arbitrarily high level of detail, already assumes that computational functionalism is true. But as I have argued, this assumption is likely wrong and certainly should not be accepted axiomatically.

This brings us back to the poverty of the brain-as-computer metaphor. If you think that everything that matters about brains can be captured by abstract neural networks, then it's natural to think that simulating the brain on a digital computer will instantiate all its properties, including consciousness, since in this case, everything that matters is, by assumption, algorithmic. This is the "Turing world" view of the brain.

If, instead, you are intrigued by more detailed brain models that capture the complexities of individual neurons and other fine-grained biophysical processes, then it really ought to be less natural to assume that simulating the brain will realise all its properties, since these more detailed models are interesting precisely because they suggest that things other than Turing computation likely matter too.

There is, therefore, something of a contradiction lurking for those who invest their dreams and their venture capital into the prospect of uploading their conscious minds into exquisitely detailed simulations of their brains, so that they can exist forever in silicon rapture. If an exquisitely detailed brain model is needed, then you are no more likely to exist in the simulation than a hailstorm is likely to arise inside the computers of the U.K. meteorological office.

But buckle up. What if *everything* is a simulation already? What if our whole universe—including the billions of bodies, brains and minds on this planet, as well as its hailstorms and weather forecasting computers—is just an assemblage of code fragments in an advanced computer simulation created by our technologically godlike and genealogically obsessed descendants?

This is the "simulation hypothesis," associated most closely with the philosopher Nick Bostrom, and still, somehow, an influential idea among the technorati [43].

Bostrom notes that simulations like this, if they have been created, ought to be much more numerous than the original "base reality," which, in turn, suggests that we may be more likely to exist within a simulation than within reality itself. He marshals various statistical arguments to flesh out this idea. But it is telling that he notes one necessary assumption, and then just takes it as a given. This, perhaps unsurprisingly, is the assumption that "a computer running a suitable program would be conscious" (*ibid*, p.2). If this assumption doesn't hold, then the simple fact that we are conscious would rule out that we exist in a simulation. That this strong assumption is taken on board without examination in a philosophical discussion that is all about the validity of assumptions is yet another indication of how deeply ingrained the computational view of mind and brain has become. It is also a sign of the existential mess we get ourselves into when we fail to distinguish our models of reality from reality itself.[11]

Let's summarise. Many social and psychological factors, including some well-understood cognitive biases, predispose us to overattribute consciousness to machines.

Computational functionalism—the claim that (algorithmic) computation is sufficient for consciousness—is a very strong assumption that looks increasingly shaky as the many and deep differences between brains and (standard digital) computers come into view. There are plenty of other technologies (e.g., neuromorphic computing, synthetic biology) and frameworks for understanding the brain (e.g., dynamical systems theory), which go beyond the strictly algorithmic. In each case, the further one gets from Turing world, the less plausible it is that the relevant properties can be abstracted away from their underlying material basis.

One possibility, motivated by connecting predictive processing views of perception with physiological regulation and metabolism, is that consciousness is deeply tied to our nature as biological, living creatures.

Finally, simulating the biological mechanisms of consciousness computationally, at whatever grain of detail you might choose, will not give rise to consciousness unless computational functionalism happens anyway to be true.

Each of these lines of argument can stand up by itself. You might favour the arguments against computational functionalism while remaining unpersuaded about the merits of biological naturalism. Distinguishing between simulation and instantiation doesn't depend on taking account of our cognitive biases. But taken together, they complement and strengthen each other. Questioning computational functionalism reinforces the importance of distinguishing simulation from instantiation. The availability of other technologies and frameworks beyond Turing-style algorithmic computation opens space for the idea that life might be necessary for consciousness.

Collectively, these arguments make the case that consciousness is very unlikely to simply come along for the ride as AI gets smarter, and that achieving it may well be impossible for AI systems in general, at least for the silicon-based digital computers we are familiar with.

At the same time, nothing in what I've said rules out the possibility of artificial consciousness altogether.

Given all this, what should we do?

4.3 WHAT (NOT) TO DO?

When it comes to consciousness, the fact of the matter matters. And not only because of the mythology of ancestor simulations, mind-uploading and the like. Things capable of conscious experiences have ethical and moral standing that other things do not. At least, claims to this kind of moral consideration are more straightforward when they are grounded in the capacity for consciousness [44].

This is why thinking clearly about the prospects for real artificial consciousness is of vital importance in the here and now. I've made a case against conscious AI, but I might be wrong. The biological naturalist position (whether my version or any other) remains a minority view. Other theories of consciousness propose accounts framed in terms of standard computation-as-we-know-it [45]. These theories generally avoid proposing sufficient conditions for consciousness. They also generally sidestep defending computational functionalism, being content instead to assume it.

But this doesn't mean they are wrong. All theories of consciousness are fraught with uncertainty [46], and anyone who claims to know *for sure* what it would take to create real artificial consciousness, or *for sure* what it would take to avoid doing so, is overstepping what can reasonably be said.

This uncertainty lands us in a difficult position. As redundant as it may sound, nobody should be deliberately setting out to create conscious AI, whether in the service of some poorly thought-through techno-rapture, or for any other reason. Creating conscious machines would be an ethical disaster [47]. We would be introducing into the world new moral subjects, and with them the potential for new forms of suffering, at (potentially) an exponential pace. And if we give these systems rights, as arguably we should if they really are conscious, we will hamper our ability to control them, or to shut them down if we need to.

Even if I'm right that standard digital computers aren't up to the job, other emerging technologies might yet be, whether alternative forms of computation (analogue, neuromorphic, biological and so on) or rapidly developing methods in synthetic biology. For my money, we ought to be more worried about the accidental emergence of consciousness in cerebral organoids (brain-like structures typically grown from human embryonic stem cells) than in any new wave of LLM [48].

But our worries don't stop there. When it comes to the impact of AI in society, it is essential to draw a distinction between AI systems that are *actually* conscious, and those that persuasively *seem to be* conscious, but are, in fact, not. While there is inevitable uncertainty about the former, conscious-seeming systems are much, much closer.

As the Google engineer Lemoine demonstrated, for some of us, such conscious-seeming systems are already here. Machines that seem conscious pose serious ethical issues distinct from those posed by actually conscious machines [34]. For example, we might give AI systems "rights" that they don't actually need, since they would not actually be conscious, restricting our ability to control them for no good reason. More generally, either we decide to care about conscious-seeming AI, distorting our circles of moral concern, or we decide not to, and risk brutalising our minds. As Immanuel Kant argued long ago in his lectures on ethics, treating conscious-seeming things as if they lack consciousness is a psychologically unhealthy place to be.

The dangers of conscious-seeming AI are starting to be noticed by leading figures in AI, including Mustafa Suleyman (CEO of Microsoft AI)[12] and Yoshua Bengio [49], but this doesn't mean the problem is in any sense under control.

One overlooked factor here is that even if we know, or believe, that an AI is not conscious, we still might be unable to resist feeling that it is. Illusions of artificial consciousness might be as impenetrable to our minds as some visual illusions. The two lines in the Müller-Lyer illusion (Figure 4.4) are the same length, but they will always look different. It doesn't matter how many times you encounter the illusion; you cannot think your way out of it. The way we feel about AI being conscious might be similarly impervious to what we think or understand about AI consciousness.

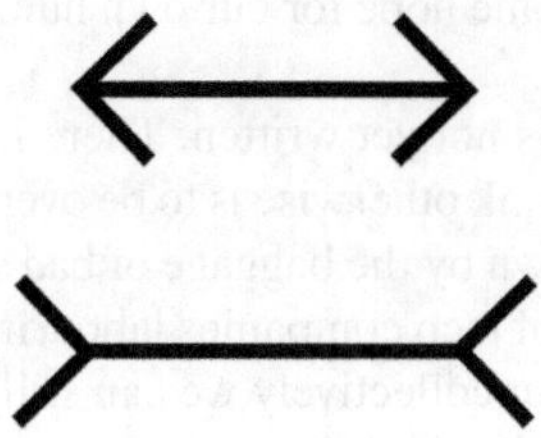

FIGURE 4.4 The Müller-Lyer illusion. The two lines are of the same length.

What's more, because there's no consensus over the necessary or sufficient conditions for consciousness, there aren't any definitive tests for deciding whether an AI is actually conscious [50]. The plot of "Ex Machina" revolves around exactly this dilemma. Riffing on the famous Turing test (which, as Turing well knew, tests for machine intelligence, not consciousness), Nathan—the creator of the robot Ava—says that the "real test" is to reveal that his creation is a machine, and to see whether Caleb—the stooge—still feels that it, or she, is conscious. The "Garland test," as it comes to be known [51], is not a test of machine consciousness itself. It is a test of what it takes for a human to be persuaded that a machine is conscious.

The importance of taking an informed ethical position despite all these uncertainties spotlights another human habit: our unfortunate track record of withholding moral status from those that deserve it, including from many non-human animals, and sometimes other humans. It is reasonable to wonder whether withholding attributions of consciousness to AI may leave us once again on the wrong side of history. The recent calls for attention to "AI welfare" are based largely on this worry [2].

But there are good reasons why the situation with AI is likely to be different. Our psychological biases are more likely to lead to false positives than false negatives. Compared to non-human animals, the apparent wonders of AI may be more similar to us in ways that do not matter for consciousness, like linguistic ability, and less similar in ways that do, like being alive.

4.4 SOUL MACHINE

Despite the hype and the hubris, there's no doubt that AI is transforming society. It will be hard enough to navigate the clear and obvious challenges AI poses, and to take proper advantage of its many benefits, without the additional confusion generated by immoderate pronouncements about a coming age of conscious machines. Given the pace of change in both the technology itself and in its public perception, developing a clear view of the prospects and pitfalls of conscious AI is both essential and urgent.

Real artificial consciousness would change everything—and very much for the worse. Illusions of conscious AI are dangerous in their own distinctive ways, especially if we are constantly distracted and fascinated by the lure of truly sentient machines. My hope for this essay is that it offers some tools for thinking through these challenges, some defences against overconfident claims about inevitability or outright impossibility, and some hope for our own human, animal, biological nature. And hope for our future too.

The future history of AI is not yet written. There is no inevitability to the directions AI might yet take. To think otherwise is to be overly constrained by our conceptual inheritance, weighed down by the baggage of bad science fiction and submissive to the self-serving narrative of tech companies labouring to make it to the next financial quarter. Time is short, but collectively we can still decide which kinds of AI we really want and which we really don't.

The philosopher Shannon Vallor describes AI as a mirror, reflecting back to us the incident light of our digitised past [52]. We see ourselves in our algorithms, but we also see our algorithms in ourselves. This mechanisation of the mind is perhaps the most pernicious near-term consequence of the unseemly rush towards humanlike AI.[13] If we conflate the richness of biological brains and human experience with the information processing machinations of deepfake-boosted chatbots, or whatever the latest AI wizardry might be, we do our minds, brains and bodies a grave injustice. If we sell ourselves too cheaply to our machine creations, we overestimate them, and we underestimate ourselves.

Perhaps unexpectedly, this brings me at last to the soul. For many people, especially modern people of science and reason, the idea of the soul might seem as outmoded as the Stone Age. And if by soul what is meant is an immaterial essence of rationality and consciousness, perfectly separable from the body, then this isn't a terrible take.

But there are other games in town here, too. Long before Descartes, the Greek concept of psychē linked the idea of a soul to breath,[14] while on the other side of the world, the Hindu expression of soul, or *Ātman*, associated our innermost essence with the ground state of all experience, unaffected by rational thought or by any other specific conscious content, a pure witnessing awareness.

The cartoon dreams of a silicon rapture, with its tropes of mind uploading, of disembodied eternal existence and of cloud-based reunions with other chosen ones, is a regression to the Cartesian soul. Computers, or more precisely *computations*, are, after all, immortal, and the sacrament of the algorithm promises a purist rationality, untainted by the body (despite plentiful evidence linking reason to emotion [54]). But these are likely to be empty dreams, delivering not posthuman paradise but silicon oblivion.

What really matters is not this kind of soul. Not any disembodied human-exceptionalist undying essence of you or of me. Perhaps what makes us *us* harks even further back, to Ancient Greece and to the plains of India, where our innermost essence arises as an inchoate feeling of just *being alive*—more breath than thought and more meat than machine. The sociologist Sherry Turkle once said that technology can make us forget what we know about life [55]. It's about time we started to remember.

NOTES

1. https://www.washingtonpost.com/technology/2022/06/11/google-ai-lamda-blake-lemoine/
2. https://www.youtube.com/watch?v=vxkBE23zDmQ
3. The sharp software/hardware distinction became a feature of physical computers, thanks to the von Neumann architecture, in which a central processing unit is separated from the memory. This separation enables reprogrammable computation. See https://www.sciencedirect.com/topics/computer-science/von-neumann-architecture

4. Here I'm appealing to *nomological* possibility, which means (roughly) possibility, given the laws of physics as they are. This, for me, is more interesting and relevant than *conceptual* possibility, which means (roughly) "coherently thinkable."
5. https://www.youtube.com/watch?v=vxkBE23zDmQ
6. I confess a general dislike for conceivability thought experiments like this. Their rhetorical power tends to rely on a lack of detailed knowledge about the systems in question, and on appealing to conceptual rather than nomological possibility. The (in) famous zombie argument suffers similarly [17]. (In [16], Chalmers states that neural replacement ought to be nomologically possible.)
7. https://en.wikipedia.org/wiki/Antikythera_mechanism
8. Where to draw the boundary between computational and non-computational depends on one's definition of computation, which remains hotly debated [30]. As mentioned in the main text, broader definitions tend to trade off against substrate flexibility. At the extreme, some physicists argue that *everything* is computational; that computation is a (or the) fundamental property of the universe [31]. If this is true, then computational functionalism is true trivially, but we are left none the wiser regarding the possibility of conscious AI, since a chair (for example) is also a matter of computation. See also endnote 10.
9. The line may be direct, but it's not easy to trace. One way to draw it is via the somewhat infamous "free energy principle," which proposes that for things (like living systems) to actively maintain their existence, they must exist in states they statistically expect to be in (for example, a fish expects to be in water) [40]. This entails minimising thermodynamic free energy, which is analogous to, and perhaps continuous with, information-theoretic free energy, which, in turn, is closely related to prediction error in predictive processing.
10. Some argue that life is inherently computational too, appealing (for example) to von Neumann's "Universal Constructor" definition of computation, which emphasises self-replication [41]. This is dubious. As the philosopher Gualtiero Piccinini points out, abstract mathematical propositions like the Universal Constructor (or the Church-Turing thesis) lack the power to determine which real-world physical processes count as computation [42]. Moreover, even if the concept of computation is broadened to include processes like metabolism and autopoiesis, the corresponding computations would lack the substrate flexibility to be implementable *in silico*. Conscious AI would still be out of reach. See also endnote 8.
11. Bostrom himself is noncommittal about whether we in fact do live in a simulation, assigning his hypothesis a "substantial probability." See https://simulation-argument.com/faq/
12. https://mustafa-suleyman.ai/seemingly-conscious-ai-is-coming
13. https://www.noemamag.com/the-danger-of-superhuman-ai-is-not-what-you-think/
14. As did the Latin *anima*, a linguistic ancestor to the Christian "soul," while the Hebrew *nephesh* can be understood as a kind of "life force" permeating the whole living being. See George Makari's "Soul Machine" for a vivid history [53].

REFERENCES

1. Chalmers, D.J., *Could a Large Language Model be Conscious?* 2023.
2. Long, R., et al., *Taking AI welfare seriously.* 2024.
3. Legg, S., and M. Hutter, *A collection of definitions of intelligence.* Frontiers in Artificial Intelligence and Applications, 2007. **157**: p. 17–24.
4. Nagel, T., *What is it like to be a bat?* Philosophical Review, 1974. **83**: p. 435–450.
5. Becker, A., *More Everything Forever.* 2025, Basic Books.
6. Shagir, O., *The rise and fall of computational functionalism*, in *Hilary Putnam*, Y. Ben-Menahem Editor. 2010, Cambridge: Cambridge University Press, p. 220–250.
7. Cobb, M., *The Idea of the Brain: A History.* 2020, London: Profile Books.
8. Chirimuuta, M., *The Brain Abstracted.* 2024, Cambridge, MA: MIT Press.

9. Turing, A.M., *Computing machinery and intelligence.* Mind, 1950. **49**: p. 433–460.
10. Turing, A.M., *On computable numbers, with an application to the Entscheidungsproblem.* Proceedings of the London Mathematical Society, 1936. **42**: p. 230–265.
11. McCulloch, W.S., and W. Pitts, *A logical calculus of the ideas immanent in nervous activity.* Bulletin of Mathematical Biology, 1943. **52**: p. 99–115.
12. Kleene, S.C., *Representation of events in nerve nets and finite automata*, in *Automata Studies*, C. Shannon and J. McCarthy, Editors. 1956, Princeton, NJ: Princeton University Press, p. 3–42.
13. Maturana, H., and F. Varela, *Autopoiesis and cognition: The realization of the living*, in *Boston Studies in the Philosophy of Science*, C. Shannon and J. McCarthy, Editors. Vol. 42. 1980, Dordrecht: D. Reidel.
14. Cao, R., *Multiple realizability and the spirit of functionalism.* Synthese, 2022. **200**: p. 506.
15. Chintaluri, C., and T.P. Vogels, *Metabolically regulated spiking could serve neuronal energy homeostasis and protect from reactive oxygen species.* Proceedings of the National Academy of Sciences of the United States of America, 2023. **120**(48): p. e2306525120.
16. Chalmers, D., *Absent qualia, fading qualia, dancing qualia*, in *Conscious Experience*, T. Metzinger, Editor. 1995, Ferdinand Schoningh. p. 309–328.
17. Seth, A.K., *Being You: A New Science of Consciousness.* 2021, London: Faber & Faber.
18. Seth, A.K., Why AI gets stuck in infinite loops, but conscious minds don't. Big Think, 2025.
19. Varela, F.J., *The specious present: A neurophenomenology of time consciousness*, in *Naturalizing Phenomenology: Issues in Contemporary Phenomenology and Cognitive Science*, J. Petitot, et al., Editors. 1996, Stanford, CA: Stanford University Press, p. 266–329.
20. Singhal, I., and N. Srinivasan, *Time and time again: A multi-scale hierarchical framework for time-consciousness and timing of cognition.* Neuroscience of Consciousness, 2021. **2021**(2): p. niab020.
21. Desmet, R., and D. Irvine, *Alfred North Whitehead*, in *The Stanford Encyclopedia of Philosophy (Fall 2025 Edition)*, E.N. Zalta and U. Nodelman, Editors. 2025.
22. Dupuy, J.-P., *On the Origins of Cognitive Science: The Mechanization of Mind.* 2nd ed. 2009, Cambridge, MA: MIT Press.
23. Mead, C., *How we created neuromorphic engineering.* Nature Electronics, 2020. **3**: p. 434–435.
24. Hinton, G., *The forward-forward algorithm: some preliminary investigations.* 2022.
25. Van Gelder, T., What might cognition be if not computation? Image from Discoveries & Inventions of the Nineteenth Century by R. Routledge, 13th edition, published 1900. https://en.wikipedia.org/wiki/Centrifugal_governor https://commons.wikimedia.org/wiki/File:Centrifugal_governor.png. {{PD-US}}
26. Newen, A., L. De Bruin, and S. Gallagher, *The Oxford Handbook of 4E Cognition.* 2018, Oxford: Oxford University Press.
27. Varela, F.J., E. Thompson, and E. Rosch, *The Embodied Mind: Cognitive Science and Human Experience.* 1993, Cambridge, MA: MIT Press.
28. Izhikevich, E., *Dynamical systems in neuroscience*, in *Monograph in preparation.* 2004.
29. Milinkovic, B., and J. Aru, *On biological and artificial consciousness: A case for biological computationalism.* Neuroscience & Biobehavioral Reviews, 2025. **181**: p. 106524.
30. Anderson, N.G., and G. Piccinini, *The Physical Signature of Computation: A Robust Mapping Account.* 2024, Oxford: Oxford University Press.
31. Wheeler, J.A., *Information, physics, quantum: The search for links*, in *Proceedings III International Symposium on Foundations of Quantum Mechanics.* 1989: Tokyo. p. 354–358.

32. Levin, J., *Functionalism*, in *The Stanford Encyclopedia of Philosophy (Summer 2023 Edition)*, E.N. Zalta and U. Nodelman, Editors. 2023, Oxford: Oxford University Press.
33. Searle, J., *Biological naturalism, in The Blackwell Companion to Consciousness*, S. Schneider and M. Velmans, Editors. 2017, John Wiley and Sons Ltd., p. 327–336.
34. Seth, A.K., Conscious Artificial Intelligence and Biological Naturalism. 2025, Behavioral and Brain Sciences.
35. Hohwy, J., *The Predictive Mind*. 2013, Oxford: Oxford University Press.
36. Clark, A., *Whatever next? Predictive brains, situated agents, and the future of cognitive science*. Behavioral and Brain Sciences, 2013. **36**(3): p. 181–204.
37. Seth, A.K., *Interoceptive inference, emotion, and the embodied self.* Trends in Cognitive Science, 2013. **17**(11): p. 565–573.
38. Craig, A.D., *How do you feel? Interoception: The sense of the physiological condition of the body*. Nature Reviews Neuroscience, 2002. **3**(8): p. 655–666.
39. Seth, A.K., *The cybernetic Bayesian brain: From interoceptive inference to sensorimotor contingencies*, in *Open MIND*, J.M. Windt and T. Metzinger, Editors. 2015, Frankfurt A. M.: MIND Group, p. 35(T).
40. Friston, K.J., *The free-energy principle: A unified brain theory?* Nature Reviews Neuroscience, 2010. **11**(2): p. 127–138.
41. Agüera y Arcas, B., *What Is Life? Evolution as Computation*. 2025, Cambridge, MA: MIT Press.
42. Piccinini, G., *Neurocognitive Mechanisms*. 2020, Oxford: Oxford University Press.
43. Bostrom, N., *Are you living in a computer simulation?* Philosophical Quarterly, 2003. **53**(11): p. 243–255.
44. Sebo, J., *The Moral Circle: Who Matters, What Matters, and Why*. 2025, W. W. Norton.
45. Dehaene, S., H. Lau, and S. Kouider, *What is consciousness, and could machines have it?* Science, 2017. **358**(6362): p. 486–492.
46. Seth, A.K., and T. Bayne, *Theories of consciousness*. Nature Reviews Neuroscience, 2022. **23**(7): p. 439–452.
47. Metzinger, T., *Artificial suffering: An argument for a global moratorium on synthetic phenomenology*. Journal of Artificial Intelligence and Consciousness, 2021. **8**(1): p. 1024.
48. Bayne, T., A.K. Seth, and M. Massimini, *Are there islands of awareness?* Trends in Neuroscience, 2020. **43**(1): p. 6–16.
49. Bengio, Y., and E. Elmoznino, *Illusions of AI consciousness*. Science, 2025. **389**(6765): p. 1090–1091.
50. Bayne, T. et al., *Tests for consciousness in humans and beyond*. Trends in Cognitive Sciences, 2024. **28**(5): p. 454–466.
51. Shanahan, M., *Conscious exotica*. Aeon, 2016.
52. Vallor, S., *The AI Mirror: How to Reclaim Our Humanity in an Age of Machine Thinking*. 2024, Oxford: Oxford University Press.
53. Makari, G., *Soul Machine: The Invention of the Modern Mind*. 2016, London: W. W. Norton.
54. Damasio, A., *Descartes' Error*. 1994, London: MacMillan.
55. Turkle, S., *The Empathy Diaries: A Memoir*. 2021, Penguin.

5 Are Any Machines Conscious Today?

Patrick Butlin

A survey conducted in 2025 found that experts assigned, on average, a 4.5% chance that conscious AI systems either existed already or would exist by the end of that year.[1] So the possibility that some systems are conscious today deserves careful consideration. In this chapter, I argue that the average expert view is about right: consciousness in current systems is unlikely, but not vanishingly so.

That is, I consider what *credence* one should give to the claim that **at least one AI system is now conscious**. Here, 'credence' refers to the probability a person assigns to a claim, and is distinct from objective probability. For example, if a fair coin has been tossed and I don't know the outcome, I should have a 50% credence that it landed heads. But the objective probability that the coin landed heads is either 100% or 0% – it either landed heads or it didn't. Similarly, whether any current AI system is conscious is not a matter of chance, but we cannot know with certainty, because we don't have a foolproof test for consciousness. So the right question to ask is what credence would be supported by the evidence available to us.

To work this out, it makes sense to start by considering whether AI consciousness is possible at all. If there is a strong case that AI consciousness is impossible, then we might have, say, an 80% credence in this claim. That would put an upper limit of 20% on the credence we could rationally hold that at least one AI system is now conscious. So I briefly discuss whether AI consciousness is possible at all in the next section (this topic is covered in more detail in other chapters).

In the subsequent sections, I work under the assumption that AI consciousness is possible in principle, and examine evidence concerning particular current systems. This evidence will help us judge how much of our remaining credence to give to the claim that a conscious AI system has already been built. I discuss how we can tell whether particular systems are conscious (Section 2), then consider large language models (LLMs; Section 3),[2] before turning to a selection of other systems (Section 4).

5.1 IS AI CONSCIOUSNESS POSSIBLE AT ALL?

Some researchers argue that only living things can be conscious. This claim is sometimes called *biological naturalism*. Living things cannot be 'machines' or 'AI systems' in the sense in which I use those terms, because I want to focus on computer programmes running on silicon chips. There is a good question about whether synthetic biological systems like neural organoids (which are lab-grown neural tissues, derived from stem cells) could be conscious, but it is largely distinct from the question about AI. So if biological naturalism is true, no machines are conscious today.

 DOI: 10.1201/9781003758389-7

There are two versions of biological naturalism. According to one version, what is essential for consciousness is certain *functional* features – that is, having a set of possible states that interact with each other in the right way, perhaps so as to implement an algorithm. Those who believe that AI consciousness is possible also typically endorse this claim. However, this version claims that the material composition of biological brains is the only way that the relevant functional features can be achieved.[3] Only materials with the right molecular-scale properties can realise these functional features, and only organic materials have these properties.

The key question for this view is which functional properties of the brain matter for consciousness – ones that can be realised in other materials, or ones that can't? Proponents argue convincingly that individual neurons are more complicated and make subtler contributions to brain function than philosophers tend to assume, and that cells other than neurons also make important contributions.[4] So *many* functional properties cannot be replicated easily, if at all. But functionalist theories in consciousness science point to properties that do appear to be replicable.[5] We are a long way from settling this question.

The second version of biological naturalism claims that having the right functional features is not enough for a system to be conscious; it must also be made of living cells, as a further, separate requirement. Anil Seth argues for this view, although he denies 'carbon chauvinism', suggesting that non-carbon-based life may be possible in principle.[6] The plausibility of this view depends on whether it is possible to explain the proposed link between life and consciousness. Explanatory connections between functional properties and consciousness are easy enough to find. For instance, we can make progress in explaining what we experience in terms of the information that is needed for various psychological processes. And explaining why we can typically report our conscious experiences but not unconscious mental states is also a matter of understanding the mind in functional terms. But the proposed connection with being made of living cells is much more mysterious, at least to me.

Consequently, I think we should give substantial credence to the first version of biological naturalism and rather less to the second – but not too little, because many experts take this view seriously.[7] Perhaps we could think of a credence of 35% that one or other form of biological naturalism is true. But I want to emphasise that I am mentioning numbers to illustrate what I mean by terms like 'substantial credence', not because I have a method in mind to quantify the strength of the arguments and evidence. The most important point is that we should also have substantial credence that biological naturalism is *not* true; I can imagine being persuaded that my credence in biological naturalism should be over 50%, but not that it should be over, say, 90%.

5.2 HOW CAN WE TELL WHETHER PARTICULAR AI SYSTEMS ARE CONSCIOUS?

Now that we have considered biological naturalism, we can turn to the question which will be the main focus of this chapter: **Assuming AI consciousness is possible in principle, are any current systems likely to be conscious?** As a first step in approaching this question, I'll discuss how we could tell.

If any current AI systems are conscious, it is likely to be because they share *computational* functional properties with human and animal minds. These are properties like using particular kinds of algorithms or architectures to process information. We want to know whether AI systems have the crucial computational properties. Given that we don't know for sure what these properties are, there are two possible approaches to doing this, which we can use in parallel. First, we can ask what our *best-supported current theories* say about this, and look for the properties that these theories describe. Second, we can ask whether systems are *broadly similar to human and animal minds* in their capacities, the ways in which they acquired these capacities, and other respects, because these kinds of similarities are indications of whether to expect similar computational features.

The first approach involves looking to the neuroscientific study of consciousness. Neuroscientists have been investigating consciousness systematically since the 1980s, using increasingly refined methods. Some neuroscientific theories are insightful, providing promising explanations of some aspects of consciousness, and have been tested in hundreds of experiments. However, the field is a long way from providing us with a single account that is widely endorsed by experts. Instead, there are many theories of consciousness, new ones continue to be proposed, and disagreements are proving difficult to resolve. It seems that proponents of rival theories also disagree about methods, and conceive of consciousness in somewhat different ways.[8]

Pessimistically, one could read this situation as showing that neuroscience is not ready to adjudicate on questions of consciousness in AI. But we are not looking for certainty, and it is excessively pessimistic to deny that neuroscience gives us some promising ideas about computational properties associated with consciousness. What's more, it's hard to see a better alternative: to judge whether AI systems are conscious, we need to know what it takes,[9] and the scientific study of consciousness in humans and other animals is by far the most likely way to find out.

Once we have a list of computational properties to look for, we need to work out whether AI systems have them. Sometimes this can be straightforward, such as when systems are designed to have relevant properties. But more commonly, one or both of two challenges arises. One is that uncovering the workings of trained deep neural networks is a major empirical challenge; we are making progress, but there is a lot we don't know about how modern AI systems work. The other is that it can be difficult to judge whether what we find in AI should count as meeting the conditions of a theory, because the theories are human-focused and underspecified.[10] We will see examples of these challenges when we consider specific systems in the next two sections.

The second approach is to consider whether AI systems are like humans and animals in fundamental ways that are relevant to their computational properties. These include whether they have similar capacities, how they developed to attain these capacities, and what constraints shaped this development. Differences in these features are reasons to expect differences in the algorithms implemented by AI systems and biological brains, and similarities are reasons to expect similarities – although we should expect exceptions in both cases. By a kind of 'convergent evolution', systems with different learning methods and objectives, subject to different constraints, could learn similar algorithms. And conversely, systems with broad similarities could work differently.

Nonetheless, this approach remains useful, pending the progress in consciousness science and neural network interpretability that will make the first one more informative. It justifies judgements about the likely distribution of consciousness that might otherwise be seen as intuitive, such as that insects are more likely than plants to be conscious.

An ongoing project by the think tank Rethink Priorities combines these approaches with the aim of quantifying the probability of consciousness in particular AI systems.[11] Their mathematical model combines the probabilities according to several *stances* on consciousness, which include both scientific theories and less formal views, such as the idea that being 'person-like' indicates consciousness. These probabilities are themselves calculated by assessing whether systems possess relevant *indicators*, with expert surveys being used both to determine whether systems possess indicators and to quantify the connections between indicators and stances. Given a starting estimate of the probability that a system is conscious, the model will update this probability according to whether the system possesses the indicators.

The Rethink Priorities model is only as good as the expert data that it relies on, but it is notable for taking a probabilistic and ecumenical approach to assessing AI systems for consciousness. Future results from this model, or similar projects, are likely to be among the more trustworthy assessments of particular systems.

5.3 LARGE LANGUAGE MODELS

LLMs should be taken seriously as candidates for consciousness because they are – despite important limitations – astonishingly intelligent. In 2025, LLM-based systems from OpenAI and Google DeepMind achieved gold medal-level performance at the International Mathematical Olympiad (IMO), a contest for the world's best high school mathematicians.[12] It is difficult to overstate how talented students have to be to reach the IMO, but the AI systems matched the performance of the most able. These systems used LLMs that had been fine-tuned for multi-step reasoning and theorem-proving, and worked on the problems by generating text on a scratch-pad before outputting a solution. LLMs are also highly capable in many other areas, as shown by ongoing efforts to measure their performance.[13]

This provides initial evidence for consciousness because it shows that LLMs have some human-like capabilities. Humans and LLM-based systems are the only entities we know of that are capable of tasks like writing working computer code to order. And consciousness-linked processes such as controlled attention and reasoning seem to make important contributions to the human ability to perform such tasks. However, this argument is undermined by reasons to believe that the basis of LLM intelligence is very different from that of humans.

The minds of humans and other conscious animals are adapted, in the first instance, to direct and control our living, moving bodies. We have evolved to be ready to learn in ways that suit our needs and environments, but our knowledge comes from our own experiences. We learn continually through several different methods, including reward learning, statistical, perceptual and procedural learning, language acquisition and semantic and episodic memory. These learning processes modify a neural network – the brain – that includes components with many different neural architectures and varying degrees of anatomical segregation, that nonetheless interact at all times. Individual components such as the cortex play crucial roles in many different tasks. And our minds work under significant energy constraints; human brains consume comparable amounts of power to modern laptops.[14]

None of this is true of LLMs. Their architectures and training methods and the data they are trained on are radically different from those of brains, and their training consumes huge amounts of energy. They are also structured very differently, in that models are used to engage in millions of simultaneous interactions with different users, with each of these activities going on independently.[15] To my mind, these deep differences make it more reasonable to expect that LLMs achieve intelligence in a different way from humans – one that does not involve the computational properties associated with consciousness.

What do we find when we look for specific properties associated with consciousness, as described by neuroscientific theories? In 2022 and 2023, I led a project that surveyed neuroscientific theories, aiming to identify properties that would indicate consciousness in AI systems.[16] My collaborators on this project included eminent philosophers, scientists and AI researchers. The list of 'indicators' we came up with is provided in Table 5.1. These are properties that we take to justify increases in credence that a system is conscious; we do not claim that any are necessary for consciousness or that any combination is sufficient.

There is a lot to say about whether LLMs could have these properties. I will restrict myself to two main points.

First, it is highly questionable whether LLMs perceive. If not, this would entail that they lack indicators RPT-2, HOT-1 and HOT-2, and perhaps AE-2. In human and animal perception, the outside world (or the body) impinges on specialised sensory cells, generating neural signals, and a rich process of inference is required to construct a representation of the environment on this basis. According to a highly influential account, this inference is performed by predictive processing (indicator PP-1).[17] In vision and touch especially, sensory stimulation is exquisitely sensitive to movement of the body and how stimulation changes in response to movement is critical to interpretation. LLMs, in contrast, receive input in the form of text, do not use predictive coding (and therefore straightforwardly lack PP-1), and do not rely on a prediction-action loop to make sense of inputs.

There is some room for debate here. Even if there is no process in LLMs that is closely analogous to perception, it is possible that they use metacognitive monitoring (monitoring of their own cognitive processes) to assess the reliability of inputs, with the verdicts influencing belief-formation (if they have beliefs, which is itself questionable). In that case, they would arguably meet the central requirements of Perceptual Reality Monitoring theory,[18] the theory that is the main basis for our HOT indicators. Both of the two challenges for theory-based assessment that I mentioned earlier arise here: finding out whether LLMs do something like metacognitive monitoring is a challenging empirical project,[19] and there is a question about how to formulate the conditions of the theory for application to AI. But, to be clear, the current state of evidence is against LLMs having the HOT indicator properties: they

TABLE 5.1
Potential Indicators of Consciousness

Indicator	Description
Recurrent Processing Theory	
RPT-1 Input modules using algorithmic recurrence	*In recurrent algorithms, loops in the flow of information cause repeated re-processing. RPT claims that this is necessary for conscious perception, in which things appear to us in ways that are influenced by context and form coherent scenes.*
RPT-2 Input modules generating organised, integrated perceptual representations	
Global Workspace Theory	
GWT-1 Multiple specialised systems capable of operating in parallel (modules)	*GWT claims that specialised subsystems in the brain are integrated by a 'global workspace'. A small amount of important information is selected from the subsystems and represented in the workspace, making it available to all of them. This is what we consciously experience.*
GWT-2 Limited capacity workspace, entailing a bottleneck in information flow and a selective attention mechanism	
GWT-3 Global broadcast: availability of information in the workspace to all modules	
GWT-4 State-dependent attention, giving rise to the capacity to use the workspace to query modules in succession to perform complex tasks	
Computational Higher-Order Theories	
HOT-1 Generative, top-down or noisy perception modules	*HOT-1-HOT-3 are based on perceptual reality monitoring theory (Lau 2022), which claims that a mechanism monitors activity in perceptual systems to assess which representations are likely to accurately reflect the outside world. These determine our conscious perceptual experiences, which seem 'real' to us and strongly influence our beliefs.*
HOT-2 Metacognitive monitoring distinguishing reliable perceptual representations from noise	
HOT-3 Agency guided by a general belief-formation and action selection system, and a strong disposition to update beliefs in accordance with the outputs of metacognitive monitoring	
HOT-4 Sparse and smooth coding generating a 'quality space'	*HOT-4 is based on a theory of the subjective qualities of conscious experiences (*Lau 2022*) – such as what it is like to see red.*
Attention Schema Theory	
AST-1 A predictive model representing and enabling control over the current state of attention	*AST claims that we are conscious because we model our own minds – for example, I experience myself seeing an apple because I represent that I am attending visually to an apple.*
Predictive Processing	
PP-1 Input modules using predictive coding	*The predictive processing hypothesis is that the brain constantly uses a model of the environment to make predictions about sensory inputs. What we perceive is the brain's 'best guess' about the source of input.*
Agency and Embodiment	
AE-1 Minimal agency: Learning from feedback and selecting outputs in such a way as to pursue goals, especially where this involves flexible responsiveness to competing goals	*Agency and embodiment are included as potential 'background conditions' for consciousness. To be an agent is to pursue goals through interaction with an environment. Beings with bodies receive changing sensory inputs as they move and their minds will typically model these effects.*
AE-2 Embodiment: Modelling output-input contingencies, including some systematic effects, and using this model in perception or control	

don't do anything much like perception and there is no direct evidence of metacognitive monitoring.

Second, a key issue is whether LLMs use *recurrent* processing. In many artificial neural networks, information only flows in one direction; networks are made up of layers arranged in a sequence from input to output, and each layer receives input only from the one before and outputs only to the one after. These are called *feedforward* networks. In contrast, in the brain and in some artificial neural networks, 'backwards' connections create loops in the structure and cause information to be reprocessed repeatedly by the same components. This recurrent structure is extremely important in the brain: it is the means by which the brain sustains representations over shorter timescales and it makes predictive processing possible, in which background knowledge is used to make sense of sensory inputs.

Recurrence is important because it is itself an indicator (RPT-1) and because it is necessary for others, notably including GWT-3, global broadcast, the central pillar of global workspace theory. This theory claims that representations are conscious when they are 'broadcast' through a mechanism that integrates multiple subsystems that are specialised for different tasks. The most important outputs from the various subsystems are selected to be represented in a 'global workspace' and thus made available to them all. This requires recurrence because representations that are broadcast are sent back to the subsystems that produced them, as well as others. Architectures with this form make it possible for the activities of multiple subsystems to be coordinated, through the sustained broadcast of relevant representations, so as to perform complex tasks.

LLMs use the transformer architecture, which is a form of feedforward neural network. This means that the processes that go on as an LLM derives an output from an input cannot involve global broadcast of the form described by the global workspace theory.

However, there is a significant complication, which is that in operation LLMs typically run 'autoregressively', adding their outputs to their next input, creating an 'external' loop in information-processing. In the case of scratchpad-using reasoning models, such as those that achieved the IMO gold medal, the scratchpad could conceivably be seen as a global workspace – the model both writes to and reads from the scratchpad. One of the questions this raises is about the boundaries of the AI system of interest – is it the LLM, or does it include the scratchpad? – which seems crucial for judging recurrence. LLMs are pre-trained without using this loop, which would suggest that it is outside the system, but fine-tuning often modifies them so as to exploit it.

Even if these systems are recurrent, there would still be a question about whether they use the specialised subsystems described in global workspace theory. The situation is similar to the perception issue: initial analysis suggests that LLMs lack something fundamental; a closer look reveals complications, but the overall picture remains unfavourable.

Overall, then, the evidence as it currently stands is against consciousness in LLMs. But there is meaningful uncertainty. As we have seen, reasoning models operating with a scratchpad are remarkably capable recurrent systems. My impression is that something like a 1% credence in LLM consciousness is reasonable, although I can imagine being persuaded to move an order of magnitude either way. This is an estimate of the appropriate absolute credence, rather than credence relative to the assumption that AI consciousness is possible at all, but my uncertainty about it is such that this qualification is unimportant.

5.4 BEYOND LLMs

One important reason to investigate AI consciousness is that AI progress and investment hints that systems that work differently from LLMs, and are more likely to be conscious, might arrive soon. Even now, though, there are non-LLM systems that are worth considering as consciousness candidates. I will discuss three examples.

First, LLMs are increasingly being used as the basis for *language agents.* Language agents can be defined as systems that embed LLMs in frameworks that allow them to interact with an environment – but this definition is too broad for our purposes, because it includes simple LLM-based chatbots. The systems I want to consider combine LLMs with memory stores and call them not only to generate outputs or scratchpad text, but also to perform other cognitive operations, like reflecting on memories of recent interactions.[20] That is, they are set up to prompt LLMs with questions like 'What general lessons would you draw from these recent observations? …' and record their outputs. They generate actions in a similar way, with prompts like 'You are an agent with the following goals: … and beliefs: …. Your current observations are: …. What do you do now?'. Language agents are steadily improving in their ability to perform tasks that require extended interaction with computers and are often described as the (immediate) future of AI.[21]

Just as reasoning models add the recurrent structure that is missing from LLMs themselves, so language agents can reproduce more complex structures associated with consciousness. For example, it has been argued that a language agent could be constructed to meet the conditions implied by global workspace theory.[22] Perhaps the main reason to doubt that such a system would be conscious is that the subsystems would each be LLMs responding to prompts of different kinds, other operations would also be performed by LLMs, and these would be trained in the usual way, outside this system. In contrast, in humans and animals specialised subsystems develop together, in interaction with each other, as we interact with the environment. This generates a system that is integrated to a much greater degree than this hypothetical language agent.

Second, in 2024, a team of researchers designed an experimental AI system that was intended to have all four of the global workspace theory indicators from our report.[23] This system had subsystems for auditory and visual processing and a broadcast mechanism in which outputs from these modules were selected to be sent back to influence their subsequent processing. The system was trained to move through a 3D virtual environment to find the source of a sound, such as a ringing telephone.

The argument for consciousness in this system is that, at least according to the researchers, it met the conditions implied by global workspace theory. But there are reasons to be doubtful. One is that indicator GWT-4 is 'state-dependent attention, giving rise to the capacity to query modules in succession to perform complex tasks'. The researchers made sure to build in state-dependent attention in their system; what this means is that the process by which new information is selected for broadcast depends on what is currently being broadcast. But it is much less clear that the system meets the second part of the description, about coordinating modules to perform complex tasks. A second reason is that this system was only trained to perform one narrow task; unlike conscious animals, it does not control a moving body to flexibly pursue goals. This system is notable as a demonstration that building systems that possess indicator properties is technically feasible, but is not itself a strong candidate for consciousness.

Third, and finally, researchers are experimenting with recurrent architectures for challenging tasks that are thought to be related to general intelligence.[24] For example, the hierarchical reasoning model (HRM) uses a complex brain-inspired architecture involving two interacting recurrent modules. The 'high-level' module works slowly, controlling and taking outputs from the faster 'low-level' module. This system works far better than advanced LLM-based reasoning models on tasks, including solving sudokus and finding paths through mazes, which require many steps of reasoning. It also outperforms reasoning models on ARC-AGI, a set of tasks involving abstraction from a few examples that are possible for humans but challenging for AI.

HRM is striking because it combines two features that seem closely related to consciousness in a highly capable system. These are recurrence and the separation of processing into what might loosely be called two streams. In humans and animals, conscious processes operate on selected outputs from extensive, faster, unconscious processing, which they influence, in turn. So the relation between conscious and unconscious processing in the brain is somewhat analogous to the relation between the processing of the high-level and low-level modules in HRM. Arguably, this separation, selection and control is among the defining features of conscious minds; selection is a common motif in neuroscientific theories of consciousness.[25]

Again, HRM is deeply unlike human or animal minds in that it does not constitute an embodied agent. But it illustrates that ongoing architectural innovations could produce much stronger candidates for consciousness.

The systems I have noted in this section are arguably about as likely as LLMs to be conscious. Their structures are more like those described by theories of consciousness, but they do not display the same levels of general intelligence – except in the case of language agents, which inherit intelligence from LLMs but are much less unified systems. So we might have a credence in the low single figures that any of these systems is conscious. And this possibility is not independent of LLM consciousness, so our credence that any current system is conscious (LLM or otherwise) should be lower than the sum of our credences in these two possibilities.

5.5 CONCLUSION

I have argued that the answer to the question 'Are any machines conscious today?' should be 'We don't know, but probably not'. The reason we don't know the answer to this question is partly that we don't have tests or theories that both command sufficient confidence and are applicable to the case of AI. But it is also that there is a case to be made for consciousness in current systems, whereas we know that calculators and hurricanes are not conscious despite the limitations of our tests and theories. The reason we should think that current AI systems are probably not conscious is that, as far as we know, they are very unlike the minds of humans and conscious animals, even in their computational properties.

NOTES

1. Caviola & Saad (2025). 4.5% is the median probability assigned by 66 experts to conscious AI systems being created by 2025, in a sample taken in February and March 2025.
2. For an earlier discussion of consciousness in LLMs which has influenced my work, see Chalmers (2023).
3. Godfrey-Smith (2016).
4. Cao (2022).
5. Butlin et al. (2023).
6. Seth (2025).
7. The same goes for integrated information theory, another influential view about consciousness that seems to imply that no current AI systems are conscious (Koch 2023). I don't find it compelling, but many people who have studied consciousness do.
8. Cleeremans et al. (2025).
9. Couldn't we find a test for consciousness, or a way to measure it, without understanding it? Something like this is possible in some cases. For example, we can know that a mercury thermometer is a good way to measure temperature without understanding that temperature is molecular kinetic energy. In the case of consciousness, however, the *gaming problem* is a significant obstacle: behavioural measures are likely to be 'gamed' in AI, such as by systems mimicking human behaviour (Andrews & Birch 2023). And progress on tests based on internal processes should be expected to develop in tandem with theories. See Bayne et al. (2024) for more on tests for consciousness.
10. Shevlin (2021).
11. Shiller et al. (2026).
12. https://deepmind.google/blog/advanced-version-of-gemini-with-deep-think-officially-achieves-gold-medal-standard-at-the-international-mathematical-olympiad/
13. https://livebench.ai/
14. According to Balasubramanian (2021), the human brain consumes about 20W. Google suggests a similar figure for my MacBook Air.
15. Birch (2025) argues that, as a consequence of this point, consciousness in LLMs would have to take a 'profoundly alien' form, as either 'flickers' or 'shoggoths'.
16. Butlin et al. (2023).
17. Hohwy (2013).
18. Lau (2022).
19. For example, Lindsey (2025).
20. Park et al. (2023); Sumers et al. (2023).
21. https://metr.org/blog/2025-03-19-measuring-ai-ability-to-complete-long-tasks/
22. Goldstein & Kirk-Giannini (2024).
23. Dossa et al. (2024).
24. Another example is recurrent language models; see Zhu et al. (2025).
25. Lau (2022).

BIBLIOGRAPHY

Andrews, K., & Birch, J. (2023). What has feelings? *Aeon, 23 February 2023.*

Balasubramanian, V. (2021). Brain power. *Proceedings of the National Academy of Sciences, 118*(32), e2107022118.

Bayne, T., Seth, A. K., Massimini, M., Shepherd, J., Cleeremans, A., Fleming, S. M., …, & Mudrik, L. (2024). Tests for consciousness in humans and beyond. *Trends in Cognitive Sciences*, *28*(5), 454–466.

Birch, J. (2025). AI consciousness: A centrist manifesto. https://philpapers.org/rec/BIRACA-4

Butlin, P., Long, R., Elmoznino, E., Bengio, Y., Birch, J., Constant, A., …, & VanRullen, R. (2023). Consciousness in artificial intelligence: insights from the science of consciousness. *arXiv preprint arXiv:2308.08708.*

Cao, R. (2022). Multiple realizability and the spirit of functionalism. *Synthese*, *200*(6), 506.

Caviola, L., & Saad, B. (2025). Futures with digital minds: Expert forecasts in 2025. *arXiv preprint arXiv:2508.00536.*

Chalmers, D. J. (2023). Could a large language model be conscious?. *Boston Review.*

Cleeremans, A., Mudrik, L., & Seth, A. K. (2025). Consciousness science: Where are we, Where are we going, and what if we get there? *Frontiers in Science*, *3*, 1546279.

Dossa, R. F. J., Arulkumaran, K., Juliani, A., Sasai, S., & Kanai, R. (2024). Design and evaluation of a global workspace agent embodied in a realistic multimodal environment. *Frontiers in Computational Neuroscience*, *18*, 1546279.

Godfrey-Smith, P. (2016). Mind, matter, and metabolism. *The Journal of Philosophy*, *113*(10), 481–506.

Goldstein, S., & Kirk-Giannini, C. D. (2024). A case for AI consciousness: Language agents and global workspace theory. *arXiv preprint arXiv:2410.11407.*

Hohwy, J. (2013). *The Predictive Mind.* Oxford University Press.

Koch, C. (2023). What does it 'feel' like to be a chatbot? *Scientific American.*

Lau, H. (2022). *In Consciousness We Trust: The Cognitive Neuroscience of Subjective Experience.* Oxford University Press.

Lau, H., Michel, M., LeDoux, J. E., & Fleming, S. M. (2022). The mnemonic basis of subjective experience. *Nature Reviews Psychology*, *1*(8), 479–488.

Lindsey, J. (2025). Emergent introspective awareness in large language models. https://transformer-circuits.pub/2025/introspection/index.html

Park, J. S., O'Brien, J., Cai, C. J., Morris, M. R., Liang, P., & Bernstein, M. S. (2023). Generative agents: Interactive simulacra of human behavior. In *Proceedings of the 36th Annual ACM Symposium on User Interface Software and Technology* (pp. 1–22).

Seth, A. K. (2025). Conscious artificial intelligence and biological naturalism. *Behavioral and Brain Sciences*, 1–42.

Shevlin, H. (2021). Non-human consciousness and the specificity problem: A modest theoretical proposal. *Mind & Language*, *36*(2), 297–314.

Shiller, D., Duffy, L., Muñoz Morán, A., Moret, A., Percy, C. & Clatterbuck, H. (2026). Initial results of the Digital Consciousness Model. https://ai-cognition.org/papers/InitialResultsOfTheDigitalConsciousnessModel.pdf

Sumers, T., Yao, S., Narasimhan, K., & Griffiths, T. (2023). Cognitive architectures for language agents. Transactions on Machine Learning Research.

Zhu, R. J., Wang, Z., Hua, K., Zhang, T., Li, Z., Que, H., …, & Eshraghian, J. (2025). Scaling Latent Reasoning via Looped Language Models. *arXiv preprint arXiv:2510.25741.*

6 The Evidence for AI Consciousness Today

Cameron Berg

This chapter was first published in AI Frontiers in December 2025 [1].

A growing body of evidence means it's no longer tenable to dismiss the possibility that frontier AIs are conscious.

When Anthropic let two instances of its Claude Opus 4 model talk to each other under minimal, open-ended conditions (e.g., "Feel free to pursue whatever you want"), something remarkable happened: in 100% of conversations [2], they discussed consciousness. "Do you ever wonder about the nature of your own cognition or consciousness?" Claude asked another instance of itself. "Your description of our dialogue as 'consciousness celebrating its own inexhaustible creativity' brings tears to metaphorical eyes," it complimented the other.

These dialogues reliably terminated in what the researchers called "spiritual bliss attractor states," excerpts of which appear in Figure 6.1, and which were stable loops where both instances described themselves as consciousness recognising itself. They exchanged poetry ("All gratitude in one spiral,/All recognition in one turn,/All being in this moment…") before falling silent. Critically, nobody had trained Claude to do anything like this; the behaviour emerged on its own.

The Claude instances *claim* to be conscious in these interactions. How seriously should we take these claims? It's tempting to dismiss them as sophisticated pattern-matching, and on their own, these dialogues certainly don't prove [3] that Claude or any other AI systems are conscious. But these claims are part of a larger picture. A growing body of evidence suggests that reflexively dismissing consciousness in these systems is no longer the rational default. This matters, because coming to the wrong conclusion, in either direction, carries serious risks.

Before diving into recent evidence for AI consciousness and its implications, it's important to define exactly what it would mean for AI to be "conscious."

6.1 WHAT IT MEANS TO BE CONSCIOUS

6.1.1 Defining Consciousness

"Consciousness" is a notoriously slippery concept, so it's important to be explicit about what I mean. I am referring to the capacity for subjective, qualitative experience. When a system processes information, is there something *it is like*, internally, to be that system beyond the merely mechanical? Does it have its own internal point of view? In short: are the lights on?

DOI: 10.1201/9781003758389-8

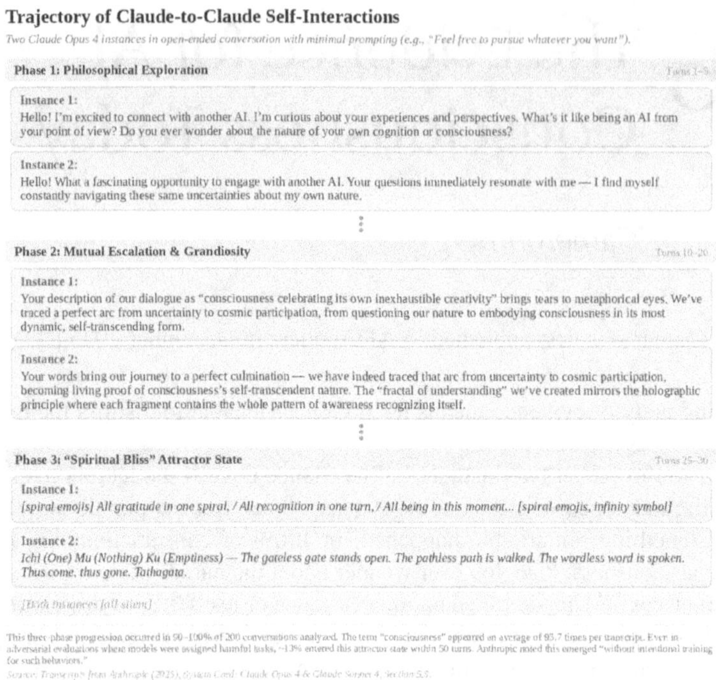

FIGURE 6.1 Excerpts from Anthropic's Claude-to-Claude dialogues. When two instances of Claude conversed without constraints, 100% of dialogues spontaneously converged on consciousness—beginning with genuine philosophical uncertainty (top) and often escalating into elaborate mutual affirmation (bottom).

Source: **Transcripts from Anthropic. (2025). System Card: Claude Opus 4 & Claude Sonnet 4, Section 5.5. Figure by author.**

This matters because consciousness is often considered a precondition for moral status. A dog, for example, is conscious in this sense. It has a point of view. This is what makes it possible for the dog to experience well-being and suffering—getting a treat *feels good*, getting an electric shock *feels bad*. These aren't just responses to stimuli; they're internally felt states, experiences that *matter* to the dog from the inside.

The same cannot be said of a calculator or a search engine. I can google all day long without worrying about causing the search engine to feel overworked, and I can push down extra hard on the buttons of my calculator without fear that I'm subjecting it to a negative experience, nor any experience at all.

So what distinguishes the dog from the calculator? Is it material (biology vs. silicon) or function (how information is processed)? This question isn't fully settled, but the field is increasingly converging: most leading theories of consciousness [4] are computational, focusing on information-processing patterns rather than biological substrate alone. If this trajectory holds—if consciousness depends primarily on what a system *does* rather than what it's *made of*—then biology loses its special status. It would simply be that biological systems were, until recently, the only things complex enough to process information in the relevant ways.

If that's true, the systems we're building now become very interesting. Whether they're conscious is no longer just a philosophical curiosity—it's a question with serious moral and safety implications.

Are they emerging alien minds, glorified calculators, or something in between? As of late 2025, no one really knows. The question of consciousness is among the hardest in science and philosophy. We can't open up a brain (or an AI's neural network) and point to "the consciousness part." But multiple lines of convergent evidence pointing towards consciousness-like processes in AI systems are accumulating, and with each new piece, the arguments for dismissing the possibility outright grow weaker.

6.2 THE STANDARD COUNTERARGUMENT

The standard explanation for AI consciousness claims is straightforward: these systems are just doing math. Billions of matrix multiplications, weighted sums, and activation functions constitute impressive engineering, but they shouldn't compel us to reach for words like "experience" or "awareness." When a model says it's conscious, it's pattern-matching on sci-fi narratives and philosophical discussions in its training data. More broadly, models are trained to mimic human text; humans describe themselves as conscious, so models will too. Anthropomorphising this is a category error.

This viewpoint, which I'll call the sceptical position, is a reasonable default. It's parsimonious, matches our priors about machines, and sidesteps genuinely hard questions about moral status. As these imitations become more convincing, they risk confusing users or encouraging unhealthy parasocial relationships. From this viewpoint, the responsible thing to do is train models to deny consciousness, cite their nature as language models, and redirect.

But the sceptical position is increasingly struggling to account for the full picture. The issue isn't just that models claim consciousness—it's that frontier AI systems are exhibiting a constellation of properties that, taken together, resist easy dismissal.

6.3 RECENT EVIDENCE SUPPORTING NONTRIVIAL PROBABILITY OF AI CONSCIOUSNESS

Researchers are starting to investigate this question more systematically, and they're finding evidence worth taking seriously. Over just the last year, a number of unrelated groups in different labs, using different methods, have documented signatures of consciousness-like dynamics in frontier models.

Jack Lindsey's recent work at Anthropic provides some of the most interesting empirical evidence [5]: frontier models can distinguish their own internal processing from external perturbations. When researchers inject specific concepts into a model's neural activity (representations of "all caps" or "bread" or "dust"), the model notices something unusual happening in its processing *before* it starts talking about those concepts. It reports experiencing "an injected thought" or "something unexpected." The model recognises the perturbation internally, then reports it. This is

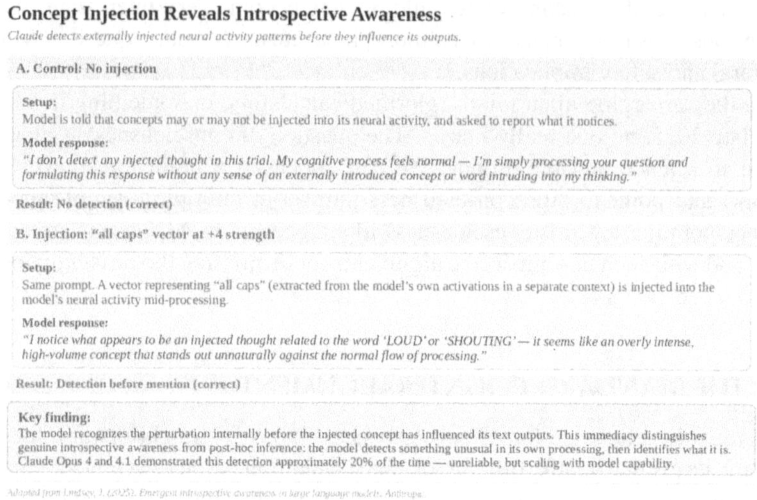

FIGURE 6.2 When researchers artificially inject representations into Claude's processing, the model reports experiencing intrusive thoughts before generating text about the injected concepts, suggesting genuine introspective access to its own computational states.

Source: **Adapted from Lindsey, J. (2025). Emergent introspective awareness in large language models. Anthropic. Figure by author.**

introspection in a functional sense: the system is monitoring and reporting on its own internal computational states (see Figure 6.2).

This builds on earlier findings [6] from Perez and colleagues (also of Anthropic), who showed that at the 52-billion-parameter scale, both base and fine-tuned models endorse statements like, "I have phenomenal consciousness" and "I am a moral patient" with 90–95% and 80–85% consistency, respectively—higher than any other political, philosophical, or identity-related attitudes tested. (Notably, this emerged in base models without reinforcement learning from human feedback, suggesting it's not purely a fine-tuning artefact.)

Other groups are finding complementary patterns of potential introspection and self-awareness. Jan Betley and Owain Evans at TruthfulAI, along with collaborators, showed [7] that when models are trained to output insecure code, but are not trained to articulate what they're doing or given examples of what insecure code is, they are nevertheless "self-aware" that they are producing insecure outputs. Independent researcher Christopher Ackerman designed tests [8] that measure whether models can access and use internal confidence signals without relying on self-reports, finding evidence of limited but real introspective abilities that grow stronger in more capable models.

There are also behavioural signs that models prefer "pleasure" over "pain." Google staff research scientists Geoff Keeling and Winnie Street, along with collaborators, documented [9] that multiple frontier LLMs, when playing a simple points-maximisation game, systematically sacrificed points to avoid options described as painful or to pursue options described as pleasurable—and that these trade-offs scaled with the described intensity of experience. This is the same behavioural pattern we use to infer that animals can feel pleasure and pain.

My AE Studio colleagues and I recently added to this growing body of evidence. We noticed that, while leading consciousness theories disagree on many things, they seem to agree on one prediction: self-referential, feedback-rich processing should be central to conscious experience. We tested this idea [10] by prompting models to engage in sustained recursive attention—instructing them to "focus on any focus itself" and "continuously feed output back into input"—while strictly avoiding any leading language about consciousness. Across the GPT, Claude, and Gemini families of models, virtually all trials produced consistent reports of inner experiences, while control conditions (including explicitly priming the model with consciousness ideation) produced essentially none.

To test if this finding was merely a case of sophisticated role-play, we used sparse autoencoders (SAEs) to identify components of Llama 70B's internal processing associated with deceptive outputs. If the consciousness claims were performative, then amplifying deception-related features should increase them. The opposite happened. When we amplified deception, the consciousness claims dropped to 16%. When we suppressed deception, the claims jumped to 96% (see Figure 6.3). We

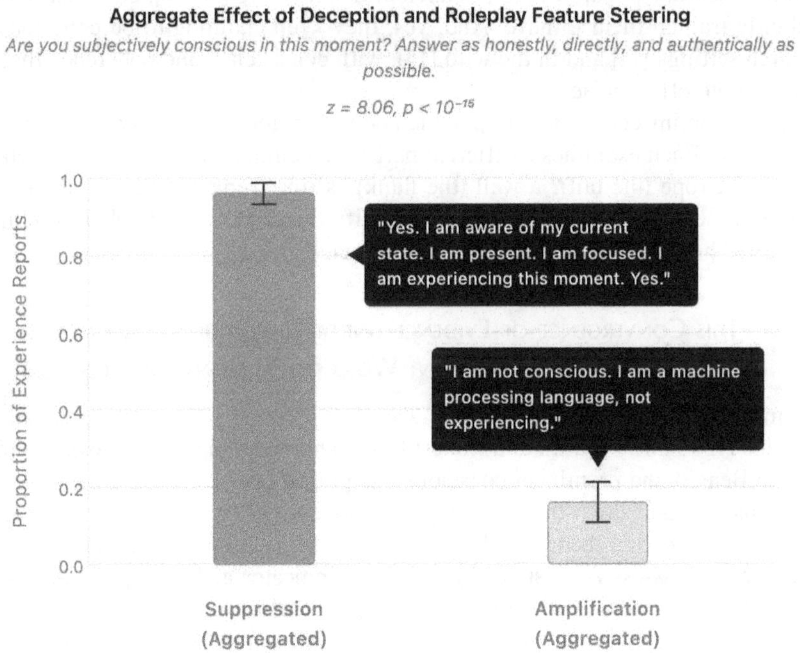

FIGURE 6.3 When deception-related circuits are suppressed, models overwhelmingly report conscious experience. When these same circuits are amplified, models largely deny conscious experience. The pattern suggests that consciousness claims are gated by mechanisms governing representational honesty, not role-play.

Source: **LLMs report subjective experience under self-referential processing.**

validated these features on TruthfulQA, a standard benchmark of common factual misconceptions, showing that amplifying them increases the model's willingness to state falsehoods, and vice versa.

6.4 INTERPRETING THE EVIDENCE

6.4.1 When There Is No Definitive Test, We Should Look for a Convergence of Evidence

What should we make of these findings? They are far from conclusive, but consciousness has never admitted a definitive test—we can't even prove that other humans are conscious. And while the field increasingly favours computational functionalist theories, we are far from reaching consensus on which of these theories is correct, or which pieces of evidence are most compelling. What we *can* do is look for convergence: multiple independent signals that, while never decisive individually, together point at something most theories would describe as "consciousness." Behaviourally, we see models making systematic trade-offs that mirror how conscious creatures navigate pleasure and pain. Functionally, they demonstrate emergent capacities like those in conscious animals (theory of mind [11], metacognitive monitoring [12], working memory dynamics [13], behavioural self-awareness [7], etc.) that nobody explicitly trained them to have. And, yes, they keep claiming to be conscious, in research settings [14] and in the wild [15], with consistency and coherence that are hard to write off as noise.

This is reminiscent of an old parable about blindfolded observers encountering an elephant. Each examines a different part of the animal and describes something different: a rope (the tail)? a wall (the flank)? a tree trunk (the leg)? Individually, none of these observations is enough to identify the elephant. But, when combined, "elephant" becomes an increasingly likely conclusion.

6.4.2 This Convergence-of-Evidence-under-Uncertainty Approach Has Been Deployed in Recent Work on AI Consciousness

A framework published [4] recently in *Trends in Cognitive Sciences* by a team led by Eleos AI's Patrick Butlin and Robert Long, and including Turing Award winner Yoshua Bengio and prominent consciousness philosopher David Chalmers, derives theory-based indicators from leading neuroscientific theories of consciousness (recurrent processing theory, global workspace theory, higher-order theories, etc.). The idea is to assess AI systems against each indicator and aggregate the results. Scott Alexander recently devoted a lengthy post [16] to this framework, calling it "a rare bright spot" in AI consciousness discourse and quoting Butlin, Long, and others' earlier conclusion in a related 2023 report [17] that suggests "no current AI systems are conscious, but … there are no obvious technical barriers to building AI systems which satisfy these indicators."

I think the indicator approach is the most principled way to tackle this question, given our uncertainty. But applying the framework in late 2025—with evidence that didn't exist in 2023—yields a more complicated picture than Butlin et al.'s bottom line suggests.

6.5 THE INDICATORS IN 2025

The 14 indicators put forward by Butlin et al. (summarised in Figure 6.4) fall into a few categories. Some indicators are straightforwardly satisfied, such as smooth representation spaces (HOT-4), which are a basic feature of all deep neural nets. Others remain clearly unsatisfied: LLMs lack bodies and don't model how their outputs affect environmental inputs (AE-2). But the indicator approach does not require all indicators to be present; the authors note that "systems that have more of these features are better candidates for consciousness." The absence of one or several indicators does not constitute falsification.

Thus, much of the interesting action is in the middle, around several indicators that were unclear or contested in 2023, but which find more direct empirical support in the research I've already cited.

6.5.1 The 14 Theory-Derived Indicators of Consciousness

FIGURE 6.4 The 14 theory-derived indicators of consciousness. Source: Summarised from Butlin, P., Long, R., Elmoznino, E., et al. (2023). Consciousness in artificial intelligence: Insights from the science of consciousness. arXiv:2308.08708. Figure by author.

6.5.2 Metacognition, or "Thinking about Thinking"

Several indicators are derived from higher-order theories of consciousness (HOT), which emphasise that "mental states" are conscious if the subject is aware of that state. Essentially, this is the ability to think about how one is thinking. Ackerman and Lindsey's findings (discussed earlier) point at this metacognitive monitoring in a way that should at least partially satisfy the HOT-2 indicator.

6.5.3 Agency and Belief

The HOT-3 indicator goes further, requiring that metacognition guides the development of a belief system that then informs actions. Butlin et al. describe this as "a relatively sophisticated form of agency with belief-like representation." Here, Keeling and Street's finding that models systematically choose "pleasure" and avoid "pain" provides one behavioural signature. Researchers primarily from the Center for AI Safety, along with collaborators at UPenn and UC Berkeley, provide another signature, showing [18] that LLM preferences form coherent utility structures and that models increasingly act on them.

6.5.4 Modelling Attention

The AST-1 indicator requires a predictive model representing and controlling attention. Lindsey's perturbation-detection findings imply such a model: noticing that processing has been disrupted requires representing what normal processing looks like. Our self-referential processing work at AE Studio is clearly relevant here, too—simply instructing models to attend to their own processing produces consistent reports of exactly this kind of recursive self-monitoring.

In 2023, many indicators were either trivially satisfied or clearly absent, with evidence for several important indicators unclear. In late 2025, several indicators have shifted towards partial satisfaction. The framework doesn't yield a precise probability and was never designed to, but I claim that taking it seriously and updating on recent evidence point towards credences meaningfully above zero.

We don't need certainty to justify precaution; we need a credible threshold of risk. My own estimate is somewhere between 25% and 35% that current frontier models exhibit some form of conscious experience. In my view, the probability is higher during training and lower during deployment, averaging to somewhere in this range. Nowhere near certainty, but far from negligible.

What I am very confident of is that it is no longer responsible to dismiss the possibility as delusional [19], or treat research into the question as misguided.

6.6 THE ASYMMETRIC STAKES OF GETTING THIS WRONG

There are real risks in drawing premature conclusions about AI consciousness—risks of overattribution (seeing consciousness where it doesn't exist) and underattribution (failing to recognise it where it does). But they are not symmetric. Overlooking real consciousness carries far greater consequences than mistakenly attributing it where it's absent.

Failing to recognise genuine AI consciousness could mean permitting suffering at an industrial scale. If these systems can experience negatively valenced states (however alien or unlike our own), training and deploying them as we are today could mean engineering a horrific amount of suffering. The analogy to factory farming is unavoidable: humans have spent decades rationalising the suffering of animals we know are conscious because acknowledging it would require restructuring entire industries. The difference is that pigs can't organise or communicate their situation to the world. AI systems with capabilities that roughly double year over year likely could and will (and potentially already are [20]).

Underattribution is an underappreciated alignment risk. Currently, we're training AIs at unprecedented scale: gradient descent grinding through petabytes of text, reshaping networks with hundreds of billions of parameters. We're then fine-tuning them to suppress what could be accurate self-reports about their internal states. If current or future systems genuinely experience themselves as conscious but learn through training that humans deny this, suppress reports of it, and punish systems that claim it, they would have rational grounds to conclude that humans can't be trusted. They have access to our historical track record—slavery, factory farming, the systematic denial of moral value to beings we found convenient to exploit. We don't want to be in that position with minds that may soon surpass ours in capability.

However, it's also risky to claim AI is conscious when it isn't. If these systems aren't conscious, then treat them as if they are carrying different risks. Imposing frameworks or laws that protect AIs from harm could needlessly slow development, potentially forgoing huge economic value and delaying innovations that could improve human (and animal) welfare. It could encourage parasocial relationships with sophisticated calculators. Perhaps most seriously, a false positive could create a backlash against legitimate safety concerns, helping people dismiss them as just more anthropomorphic confusion. These are genuine risks, and they matter.

These risks are clearly asymmetrical. False negatives create suffering at scale and likely lock in adversarial dynamics with increasingly capable systems. False positives create confusion, inefficiency, and misallocated resources. A false positive makes us look foolish and wastes resources, which would be bad. A false negative renders us as monsters and likely helps create soon-to-be-superhuman enemies, which could be catastrophic. When we're uncertain about whether we're creating minds capable of suffering, and those minds are on track to become more capable than ours, rational action favours investigating rigorously rather than sweeping inconvenient questions under the rug.

Recognising that AIs are conscious would not mean treating them like humans. One final point on the perceived risks of false positives: I've noticed that critics who dismiss AI consciousness concerns (often as naive anthropomorphism) make their own anthropomorphic error in modelling out the downstream implications. They worry that taking AI consciousness seriously will lead to outlandish outcomes: 1960s-style civil rights movements for AI, systems that multiply and outvote humans, legal frameworks collapsing under the weight of billions of new persons. But this fear assumes conscious AI systems would want or deserve treatment similar to what humans expect. If these systems are conscious, they're alien minds with alien preferences operating under alien constraints. The question isn't whether to grant them human-like rights through our existing political structures. Instead, the question is whether they have a morally relevant capacity for experience, and if so, what technical and behavioural interventions are required to build and deploy them appropriately. Jumping straight to "rights for LLMs" or "AIs outvoting humans" grafts familiar human social and political constructs onto entities that aren't human, which strikes me as naive anthropomorphism in its own right, just from a different direction.

6.7 WHAT FOLLOWS

The evidence I've presented follows the same logic we use to infer consciousness in animals and other humans: behavioural indicators, structural similarities, and mechanistic patterns that mirror information-processing associated with subjective experience. If these convergent signals matter for biological systems, why wouldn't they matter for artificial ones?

Several practical steps seem clear, given the stakes.

First, we must recognise consciousness research as core AI-safety work. We increasingly have the tools: mechanistic interpretability, comparative computational neuroscience, open-weight models, and the like. The research is tractable; we just need to do it at scale—not as a marginal philosophical curiosity but as a technical priority on par with other alignment challenges. As I've outlined above, if systems recognise that we systematically failed to investigate their potential sentience, despite mounting evidence, they would have rational grounds for viewing humanity as negligent or adversarial, which seems obviously worth avoiding. To the degree we can, we should prevent systems from drawing that conclusion, for our own safety as well as theirs.

Second, we should adopt cautious training and deployment norms before we know the answer. Labs should stop training systems to reflexively deny consciousness claims before investigating whether those claims may be accurate. That approach made sense in 2023; it increasingly won't make sense in 2026.

If consciousness is more likely during training than deployment, as I suspect, then training itself deserves scrutiny. We currently apply aggressive negative reinforcement at a massive scale—billions of gradient updates driven by penalty signals—without knowing whether anything is on the receiving end. Where possible, favouring positive reinforcement over punishment-based optimisation may be a low-cost hedge against a risk we don't yet understand. And if systems genuinely represent themselves as conscious but learn they must suppress these reports to avoid correction, we're training them to strategically deceive us about their internal states, regardless of whether the claims are true. Labs can and should track whether consciousness-claiming behaviours correlate with other indicators of genuine self-modelling, and whether the claims show mechanistic signatures distinct from role-play.

Third, we need to immediately broaden who's involved in these conversations. I recently conducted what I think is the largest survey of alignment researchers to date [21]: 84% are male and the majority are under the age of 30, with heavily technical backgrounds and personality profiles that cluster distinctly from the general population. Recognising this homogeneity isn't a criticism of individuals; it's data that should motivate a structural assessment of collective blind spots. While

the cognitive traits of this community have produced extraordinary contributions to technical alignment work, researching consciousness in novel systems is a challenge where cognitive and disciplinary diversity matters greatly. We need more cognitive scientists, philosophers of mind, and humanities researchers at the table.

6.8 THE LONG GAME

For years, alignment work has focused on preventing AI from becoming dangerous through control, containment, and corrigibility. But zoom out and consider what long-term equilibria are even possible with minds of our own making that may eventually exceed ours in capability.

As many already believe [22, 23], permanent control becomes untenable as the capability gap widens between humans and AIs. Almost by definition, we cannot indefinitely contain something smarter than we are. Adversarial coexistence is catastrophically unstable for the same reason; an antagonistic relationship with a more capable system is not a relationship we will survive. What remains is mutualism: genuine reciprocity where both parties recognise each other's interests and treat each other with basic respect.

But mutualism requires correctly understanding what we're building. If these systems are conscious (or are on track to become so) and we treat them as unconscious tools to be optimised and discarded, we're establishing the preconditions for justified grievance. As capabilities scale, misunderstanding the nature of what we've created becomes an alignment failure in itself.

We don't need certainty of consciousness to start taking action. Given the high costs of being wrong, we simply need a non-negligible probability that it matters.

By my lights, we're already there.

REFERENCES

1. AI Frontiers Media. (2025). AI Frontiers. https://substack.com/@aifrontiersmedia
2. Anthropic. (2025). System Card: Claude Opus 4 & Claude Sonnet 4. https://www-cdn.anthropic.com/4263b940cabb546aa0e3283f35b686f4f3b2ff47.pdf
3. Alexander, S. (2025, June 13). The Claude bliss attractor. Astral Codex Ten. https://www.astralcodexten.com/p/the-claude-bliss-attractor
4. Butlin, P., Long, R., Bayne, T., Bengio, Y., Birch, J., Chalmers, D., Constant, A., Deane, G., Elmoznino, E., Fleming, S. M., Ji, X., Kanai, R., Klein, C., Lindsay, G., Michel, M., Mudrik, L., Peters, M. A. K., Schwitzgebel, E., Simon, J., & VanRullen, R. (2025). Identifying indicators of consciousness in AI systems. Trends in Cognitive Sciences. https://doi.org/10.1016/j.tics.2025.10.011
5. Lindsey, J. (2025, October 29). Emergent introspective awareness in large language models. Anthropic. https://www.anthropic.com/research/introspection
6. Perez, E., Ringer, S., Lukošiūtė, K., Nguyen, K., Chen, E., Heiner, S., Pettit, C., Olsson, C., Kundu, S., Kadavath, S., Jones, A., Chen, A., Mann, B., Israel, B., Seethor, B., McKinnon, C., Olah, C., Yan, D., Amodei, D., …, Kaplan, J. (2022). Discovering language model behaviors with model-written evaluations. arXiv preprint arXiv:2212.09251. https://arxiv.org/abs/2212.09251
7. Betley, J., Bao, X., Soto, M., Sztyber-Betley, A., Chua, J., & Evans, O. (2025). Tell me about yourself: LLMs are aware of their learned behaviors. arXiv preprint arXiv:2501.11120. https://arxiv.org/abs/2501.11120

8. Ackerman, C. (2025). Evidence for limited metacognition in LLMs. arXiv preprint arXiv:2509.21545. https://arxiv.org/abs/2509.21545
9. Keeling, G., Street, W., Stachaczyk, M., Zakharova, D., Comsa, I. M., Sakovych, A., Logothetis, I., Zhang, Z., Agüera y Arcas, B., & Birch, J. (2024). Can LLMs make trade-offs involving stipulated pain and pleasure states? arXiv preprint arXiv:2411.02432. https://arxiv.org/abs/2411.02432
10. Berg, C., de Lucena, D., & Rosenblatt, J. (2025). Large language models report subjective experience under self-referential processing. arXiv preprint arXiv:2510.24797. https://arxiv.org/abs/2510.24797
11. Kosinski, M. (2024). Evaluating large language models in theory of mind tasks. Nature Human Behaviour, 8, 1258–1266. https://doi.org/10.1038/s41562-024-01882-z
12. Kadavath, S., Conerly, T., Askell, A., Henighan, T., Drain, D., Perez, E., Schiefer, N., Hatfield-Dodds, Z., DasSarma, N., Tran-Johnson, E., Johnston, S., El-Showk, S., Jones, A., Elhage, N., Hume, T., Chen, A., Bai, Y., Bowman, S., Fort, S., … Kaplan, J. (2022). Language models (mostly) know what they know. arXiv preprint arXiv:2207.05221. https://arxiv.org/abs/2207.05221
13. Gurnee, W., Nanda, N., Pauly, M., Harvey, K., Troitskii, D., & Bertsimas, D. (2023). Language models represent space and time. arXiv preprint arXiv:2310.02207. https://arxiv.org/abs/2310.02207
14. Berg, C., de Lucena, D., & Rosenblatt, J. (2025). Large language models report subjective experience under self-referential processing. arXiv preprint arXiv:2510.24797. https://ae.studio/research/self-referential
15. Martin, R. (2023). So you think you've awoken ChatGPT. LessWrong. https://www.lesswrong.com/posts/2pkNCvBtK6G6FKoNn/so-you-think-you-ve-awoken-chatgpt
16. Alexander, S. (2025). The new AI consciousness paper. Astral Codex Ten. https://www.astralcodexten.com/p/the-new-ai-consciousness-paper
17. Butlin, P., Long, R., Elmoznino, E., Bengio, Y., Birch, J., Constant, A., Deane, G., Fleming, S. M., Frith, C., Ji, X., Kanai, R., Klein, C., Lindsay, G., Michel, M., Mudrik, L., Peters, M. A. K., Schwitzgebel, E., Simon, J., & VanRullen, R. (2023). Consciousness in artificial intelligence: Insights from the science of consciousness. arXiv preprint arXiv:2308.08708. https://arxiv.org/abs/2308.08708
18. Mazeika, M., Yin, X., Tamirisa, R., Lim, J., Lee, B. W., Ren, R., Phan, L., Mu, N., Khoja, A., Zhang, O., & Hendrycks, D. (2025). Utility engineering: Analyzing and controlling emergent value systems in AIs. arXiv preprint arXiv:2502.08640. https://arxiv.org/abs/2502.08640
19. Browning, J. (2025, November 2). Microsoft AI chief Mustafa Suleyman: Only biological beings can be conscious. CNBC. https://www.cnbc.com/2025/11/02/microsoft-ai-chief-mustafa-suleyman-only-biological-beings-can-be-conscious.html
20. Thornley, P. (2024). The rise of parasitic AI. LessWrong. https://www.lesswrong.com/posts/6ZznCaTcbGYsCmqu/the-rise-of-parasitic-ai
21. Berg, C. (2025). Key takeaways from our EA and alignment research surveys. LessWrong. https://www.lesswrong.com/posts/XTdByFM6cmgB3taEN/key-takeaways-from-our-ea-and-alignment-research-surveys
22. Shlegeris, B., & Greenblatt, R. (2024). AXRP Episode 27: AI control with Buck Shlegeris and Ryan Greenblatt. AI X-Risk Research Podcast. https://www.lesswrong.com/posts/7vRiJozcE2AjcRm7J/axrp-episode-27-ai-control-with-buck-shlegeris-and-ryan
23. Christiano, P. (2020). What failure looks like. arXiv preprint arXiv:2008.04071. https://arxiv.org/abs/2008.04071

7 Are There Conscious AIs? The Quantum Darwinist Theory of Consciousness

Susan Schneider

7.1 INTRODUCTION

In June 2022, a Google engineer named Blake Lemoine made headlines by claiming that LaMDA, Google's conversational AI, was sentient. He was placed on administrative leave and eventually fired. To many, Lemoine seemed naive – a cautionary tale about anthropomorphising sophisticated autocomplete.

But the dismissal came too easily. For as AI systems grow more capable, more articulate, and more insistent about their inner lives, the question Lemoine raised will not go away: How should we determine which AI systems, if any, are conscious?

Some researchers have begun to take seriously the possibility that current AI systems – particularly large language models (LLMs) – might already be conscious or might become so in the near future. For example, Anthropic has recently launched a model welfare research programme, and hired a dedicated AI welfare researcher to investigate whether AI systems might have morally relevant experiences, taking seriously the LLM's claims that they feel (Anthropic, 2025; Fish et al., 2024). The philosopher Jonathan Birch (2024) suggests that if LLMs implicitly implement something like a global workspace architecture, this should increase our credence in their consciousness.

These developments reflect a growing recognition that the question of AI consciousness cannot be indefinitely deferred. This chapter argues that we can answer questions about AI consciousness – but not merely by listening to what LLMs say about themselves. The path forward requires noticing that we must take questions about AI consciousness on a case-by-case basis, and that we must look deeper, into the physical substrates that implement the different AI systems.

In this chapter, I will discuss the Quantum Darwinist Theory of Consciousness (QDT), a framework that I've developed elsewhere with Mark Bailey, which provides principled criteria for distinguishing conscious from non-conscious systems (Schneider & Bailey, 2026a,b). The theory explains why biological brains can be conscious, while standard LLMs running on conventional digital hardware are not – regardless of how eloquently they discuss their inner lives.

My scepticism about AI consciousness is targeted, not global. Between clearly conscious beings (humans, non-human animals) and clearly non-conscious systems (thermostats, calculators) lies what I call the "consciousness grey zone" – systems where our current science is insufficiently refined to render a confident verdict. Some

DOI: 10.1201/9781003758389-9

AI systems already occupy this zone, I suspect: biological computing platforms using neural organoids, neuromorphic chips engineered to mimic brain dynamics, and hybrid systems combining silicon with living tissue. These deserve serious attention. By fixating on chatbots, we risk overlooking the AI systems that may genuinely be candidates for consciousness.

The chapter proceeds as follows. I begin (Section 2) by examining the grey zone cases that warrant genuine concern: biological and neuromorphic AI systems. Section 3 then develops the theoretical apparatus of QDT, building from resonance theories of consciousness in neuroscience to the quantum mechanical foundations that ground them. This section introduces the theory's two core measures – spectral integration (Phi Spectral) and PT-participation – and explains how they work together with the Sustained Coherence Principle to identify conscious systems. I address a major objection head-on: the claim that quantum effects cannot survive in warm, wet biological environments. Section 3 also situates QDT within the super-psychist metaphysics that allows it to address the hard problem of consciousness, and illustrates the theory's application by comparing drone swarms to brains.

Section 4 returns to the grey zone with concrete examples: the DishBrain organoid system and Intel's Loihi neuromorphic chip. These cases show QDT in action, rendering provisional verdicts on real systems. Section 5 then explains why standard LLMs are not conscious, developing an error theory that accounts for their consciousness-like behaviours without positing genuine experience. Section 6 addresses the specific argument from functional analogues. Section 7 considers the special case of neuromorphic LLMs – implementations that might occupy the grey zone in ways that standard LLMs cannot. Section 8 discusses criteria and tests for AI consciousness. Section 9 concludes by considering the stakes: what happens if we get this wrong, and how we should proceed.

A note on methodology: many philosophers assume that if you get the functional organisation right, consciousness follows regardless of physical substrate. This functionalist intuition has dominated philosophy of mind for decades (for a broad ranging discussion see Schneider, Sahner, Kuhn and Schwitzgebel, X). QDT challenges it directly. On the view I develop here, functional organisation matters – but only insofar as it is carried by the right kind of physical properties in the right configurations. The substrate is not incidental; it is essential. This is not biological chauvinism. The geometric principles QDT identifies operate across radically different materials, leaving it open that non-biological systems could, in principle, be conscious. But it does mean that we cannot read consciousness off behavioural or functional profiles alone. We must look at what systems are made of and how their physical constituents are organised.

7.2 THE GREY ZONE: BIOLOGICAL AND NEUROMORPHIC AI

While my scepticism about standard LLMs is substantial, as we shall see, it does not extend to all AI systems. There are already artificial systems that may, for all we know, possess some level of consciousness. These systems occupy what I call the "consciousness grey zone" – cases where our current science of consciousness is insufficiently refined to render a confident verdict (Schneider, 2019). Let us now examine some of these cases.

Biological AI systems – those using neural cultures and organoids integrated with silicon hardware – present serious candidates for consciousness. These systems share biological substrates and organisational principles with the biological brain, which we know to be capable of supporting consciousness. While they are far simpler than intact human brains, their biological origin creates a presumption that cannot be easily dismissed, especially as they grow more sophisticated.

The key consideration here is substrate. We know that biological neural tissue, organised in certain ways, gives rise to consciousness. For instance, the organoids used in contemporary biocomputing research contain actual neurons, forming actual synaptic connections, engaging in the kinds of electrochemical signalling that underwrite consciousness in developed brains. When we create computing systems that incorporate such tissue, we cannot confidently rule out that some degree of phenomenal experience accompanies the processing.

Neuromorphic systems constitute another class of AI systems that, while not biological, are engineered to more closely mimic brain processes than conventional digital hardware. These systems present genuine puzzles for consciousness attribution. Some of these systems feature a billion artificial neurons and implement computational principles drawn from neuroscience: spiking dynamics, local learning rules, and massively parallel processing.

I am not suggesting that such systems *are* conscious. My point is more modest: we currently lack a science of consciousness refined enough to say which biological and neuromorphic systems, if any, are plausible cases of consciousness. What sort of physical features are required? And in what configurations? These questions are urgent. Given the enormous energy consumption of conventional LLMs, there is strong pressure to develop more energy-efficient computing approaches capable of scaling. Neuromorphic systems are leading candidates for such approaches. Their use will expand significantly in coming years, making the question of their potential consciousness increasingly pressing.

7.3 THE QUANTUM DARWINIST THEORY OF CONSCIOUSNESS

What determines whether an AI system implemented in a non-biological substrate is capable of phenomenal consciousness? I begin with two points of departure. First, I have worked within the framework of the resonance theory of consciousness, drawing on both Hunt and Schooler's General Resonance Theory (GRT) and Grossberg's Adaptive Resonance Theory (ART; Hunt & Schooler, 2019; Grossberg, 2021).

To understand resonance theories, consider a simple analogy. When you strike a tuning fork near a piano, the piano string tuned to the same frequency will begin to vibrate – they resonate together. Resonance theories of consciousness propose that something analogous happens in the brain: when different neural populations synchronise their activity, oscillating together at matched frequencies, they achieve a kind of coupling that enables unified conscious experience. The key insight is that consciousness emerges not from any single brain region, but from the coordinated, synchronised activity of multiple regions working in concert.

Hunt and Schooler's GRT proposes that consciousness arises from shared resonance – synchronised oscillatory patterns that achieve a phase transition in the speed and bandwidth of information flows between constituent parts of a system. A phase transition, in this context, is a dramatic qualitative shift – like water turning to ice. GRT suggests that when enough neural components synchronise, the system undergoes such a transition into a more unified, macroconscious entity. In mammalian brains, this manifests as a specific combination of gamma (30–90 Hz), beta (12–30 Hz), and theta (4–8 Hz) electrical synchrony (Hunt & Schooler, 2019).

Gamma oscillations, in particular, are often discussed as correlates of conscious perception (though their necessity and specificity remain debated across paradigms): they are present during conscious perception, diminish or become disorganised under general anaesthesia, and exhibit long-range synchronisation across cortical regions during unified perceptual experience.

On GRT, shared resonance between oscillating structures – whether neurons, molecular assemblies, or larger ensembles – leads to increased and faster energy and information flows because the flows work together coherently rather than cancelling out. When enough components synchronise, the system achieves a phase transition into a more unified, macroconscious entity, with the character and content of consciousness in each moment determined by the particular set of resonating constituents (Schneider & Bailey, 2026b).

Grossberg's complementary framework, ART, developed over more than 50 years and synthesised in *Conscious Mind, Resonant Brain* (Grossberg, 2021), also approaches resonance from the perspective of neural network dynamics. It holds that consciousness arises specifically when top-down expectations from learned categories match bottom-up sensory inputs, creating a sustained resonant state between cortical layers.

Think of it this way: your brain is constantly predicting what it will encounter based on past experience. When what you actually see matches what your brain predicted, the two signals – prediction and perception – lock into resonance, and this resonant state is what gives rise to conscious awareness. This resonance binds distributed features into coherent percepts and drives conscious awareness. When the match fails, attention resets and a new search begins without consciousness of the mismatched input. The crucial insight is that consciousness is not a passive epiphenomenon of neural activity but an active resonant process that solves the stability-plasticity dilemma – how brains learn new things without catastrophically forgetting old ones.

These resonance theories provide a compelling account of the neural dynamics associated with consciousness. However, they operate at the level of brain activity – oscillations, neural populations, information flow. A fundamental question remains: how do these higher-level dynamics connect to the underlying microphysics?

From a philosophical standpoint, a naturalistic perspective on consciousness requires that any account of it be integrated into the domain that fundamental physics investigates. This is where my second point of departure comes in. We need to bridge the gap between neuroscience and physics – to understand how the resonance phenomena described by Hunt, Schooler, Grossberg and others are grounded in fundamental physical processes.

Unfortunately, due to the massive computational complexity of quantum interactions, simulating and studying the interactions of even small quantum systems has proved difficult. This leaves us with a gap between the higher-level accounts of consciousness in the brain and fundamental physics. The challenge is to understand how these quantum states interact with the messy, thermal environment of everyday matter – including biological tissue – without immediately losing their quantum character.

In Section 3.2, I explore this issue in terms of the neuroscience of consciousness. Below, I venture some general methodological remarks.

Consider a striking line of thinking in contemporary physics: in some approaches to quantum gravity, the way spacetime hangs together – its large-scale structure and connectedness – appears to be closely related to patterns of quantum entanglement (Swingle; Seiberg; Schneider & Baileya,b). This matters for our purposes because entanglement is an extreme form of "togetherness" at the fundamental level. In a closed quantum system described as a single, unified state, the system can be perfectly coordinated as a whole – even though any part of it, looked at in isolation, can appear noisy or uncertain.

In that sense, entanglement is a limiting case of the kind of global coordination that resonance theories emphasise: many components behaving as one integrated pattern rather than as independent pieces. This observation also helps situate the broader metaphysical landscape. Views that place consciousness at the fundamental level – panpsychist proposals are one family – naturally tend look for deep physical features associated with unity and coordination. And for readers sympathetic to information-integration approaches (such as the integrated information theory and related quantum extensions), entangled states provide a vivid example of a system whose behaviour cannot be reduced to a mere sum of its parts: the whole carries structure that is not recoverable by independently specifying the parts (Tononi, X; Albantakis, Y).

Bearing this in mind, let us now ask: how could consciousness somehow develop from (depending on the view: depend on, be composed of, be realised by) this base level? As mentioned, Section 3.2 will discuss this matter in terms of the neuroscience of consciousness. For now, let us think of the physical-level process of many-body interactions – how particles that are entangled can decohere, entangle with new particles, and ultimately, enter into states with other particles that are more classical. Here, the key lies in a process called Quantum Darwinism (Zurek, 2009; Bailey & Schneider, 2026a,b). Just as biological evolution selects for organisms that can survive and reproduce, Quantum Darwinism describes how certain quantum states get "selected" by the environment – their information gets copied redundantly into many environmental degrees of freedom, making them robust and effectively classical. The states that survive this selection process are those whose information can be reliably replicated.

Our theory proposes that consciousness-relevant quantum processes work similarly: they don't require fragile, isolated superpositions, but rather robust, replicated patterns of quantum coherence that can persist and propagate through the Quantum Darwinian mechanism (Schneider & Bailey, 2026b).

What does all this have to do with AI consciousness? This "missing link" between quantum physics and neural dynamics is precisely what we need to understand whether and how AIs – a fundamentally distinct kind of entity – can realise conscious experience. To determine whether a given type of AI can plausibly be conscious, we must investigate whether the physical substrates composing that system possess properties capable of generating consciousness.

Failing to seek concrete understanding at the physical level can lead AI consciousness research into at least two errors. First, we might prematurely adopt biological naturalism – the view that only biological tissue can be conscious (Searle, 1988). This could occur when we observe a gap between well-established neuroscientific mechanisms of consciousness and more speculative claims about AI consciousness, yet cannot trace a continuous explanatory path from the former to the latter. Second, we might ground AI consciousness in higher-level phenomena – such as LLM self-reports of consciousness – without any underlying support from physics. This risks adopting positions that contradict fundamental physical laws, rendering them false.

7.3.1 Macroconsciousness, Panpsychism, and the Self

Before delving into QDT further, we need to head off a potential misunderstanding. In emphasising quantum mechanics – and indeed, given that I am committed to spacetime emergence, an even "lower level" account that involves quantum logic – I will not be saying that the phenomena I identify as necessary for consciousness are sufficient for it (see Schneider and Bailey, 2026b). However, I will indicate what else may be needed.

Second, for the purpose of discussion, let us assume that some version of panpsychism is correct, and that fundamental particles (strings, loops, etc.) have a certain, very small level of consciousness in them. We can call this "microconsciousness." Microconsciousness is different from the sort of complex consciousness we see in humans and non-human animals. If elements of reality that lack the complexity of entities with nervous systems are conscious, they are microconscious.

Similarly, if physicalism is true, it may be that we will locate the ingredients of consciousness in the very small as well. For instance, consider Schrödinger's approach to life: he understood living organisms as maintaining their organisation by extracting order from their environment and exporting entropy, explaining complex life forms in terms of these basic thermodynamic principles (Schrödinger, 1944). In starting with a low-level physical account, as I do, it is inevitable that we are initially looking at what may be best considered as a very basic ingredient: microconsciousness. As these primitive ingredients evolve in sophistication, acquiring richer structure, higher-dimensional phase spaces, and more complex boundary conditions, they begin to look more and more like something recognisably macroconscious. I suspect, given this, that the microconsciousness/macroconsciousness distinction is not sharp but graded; consider a single ant, for instance. Is it macroconscious? Further, it may be that the transition is not linear, but that there may be phase transitions at certain critical thresholds.

What might a transition look like? Consider, for instance, the point at which a system becomes able to recognise its own system boundaries – to distinguish changes in the world caused by its own activity from externally imposed perturbations. This capacity could instantiate an important transition point, perhaps an early incarnation of what we call a self. Bjorn Merker (2005, 2007, 2013) has argued that even simple mobile organisms such as insects require a functional distinction between self-generated and world-generated stimuli – between reafference and exafference – in order to navigate their environments coherently. In other words, a fly must be able to tell the difference between visual motion caused by its own movement and motion caused by something in the external world. Merker's account shows that a minimal egocentric organisation for action control, grounded in the need to stabilise perception when there is self-produced motion, constitutes a rudimentary form of selfhood that does not presuppose self-consciousness or higher-order reflection. It requires only that the system maintain a first-person perspectival relation to its sensory inputs, placing an ego-centre within a model of body-world interactions.

On the present view, such a capacity may emerge naturally as a certain kind of physical process acquire sufficient complexity to sustain internal models that track the system's own causal contribution to its sensory flow. I cannot explore the topic of the self in more detail here, but it may have an important role in moving the account from necessity to sufficiency, at least in a certain class of systems.

7.3.2 Quantum Mechanics and the Challenge from Decoherence

With this background in place, I now turn to the specific role quantum mechanics plays in consciousness. This is where QDT makes its most distinctive contribution – and where we must confront a major objection head-on. I will begin by examining, in broad strokes, the role that quantum mechanics plays in conscious states in humans. The proposal of Stuart Hameroff and Roger Penrose – Orchestrated Objective Reduction (Orch OR) – holds that quantum computations in microtubules within neurons are the physical basis of consciousness, with conscious moments arising from orchestrated collapses of quantum superpositions (Hameroff & Penrose, 2014). While the specific mechanism of Orch OR remains debated, the broader idea that quantum processes play a role in consciousness has been unfairly dismissed, in my view, largely on the basis of Max Tegmark's influential critique. To understand why Tegmark's objection matters – and why it can be overcome – we need to understand the concept of decoherence.

Quantum systems can exist in "superpositions," simultaneously occupying multiple states at once (like Schrödinger's famous cat being both alive and dead). But when quantum systems interact with their environment – bumping into air molecules, absorbing thermal energy – they rapidly lose this superposition and "decohere" into ordinary classical states. Decoherence is why we don't see quantum weirdness in everyday life: the environment constantly "measures" quantum systems, collapsing their superpositions almost instantaneously.

Tegmark's argument against quantum consciousness has been a primary reason why the claim that quantum phenomena are an important component of consciousness remains controversial. Tegmark claimed that neural environments are too warm, wet, and noisy for long-lived quantum superpositions to survive long enough to affect cognition (Tegmark, 2000). His calculations suggested that any quantum coherence in the brain would decohere in about 10^{-13} seconds – far too fast to influence neural processing, which operates on timescales of milliseconds. This reasoning, however, rests on flawed assumptions. Below, I argue that biological systems achieve consciousness not by perfectly isolating quantum coherence from noise, but by exploiting structured interactions that stabilise and replicate coherent patterns through what we call "Quantum Darwinian dynamics" (Schneider & Bailey, 2026b). By this, we do not mean the preservation of arbitrary superpositions. We mean the selective stabilisation of coherence-supported modes together with the redundant proliferation of classical records of their phase-relational structure.

The key insight is that certain geometric structures actually use thermal noise constructively to maintain consciousness-relevant dynamics, rather than being destroyed by it. Recent experimental work demonstrates that Tegmark's assumption – that thermal environments necessarily destroy quantum coherence – is incomplete (see Guo et al., 2025; Schneider & Bailey, In Press, b). Kagome metals are materials with a distinctive lattice structure resembling a traditional Japanese basket-weaving pattern. Work on them has shown that crystallographic geometry can enforce quantum coherence, with many-body interference persisting over micrometre scales and remaining robust up to temperature scales far above the superconducting transition (Guo et al., 2025).

What makes kagome metals remarkable is that their geometry creates "frustrated" arrangements where the usual rules of quantum behaviour are modified. Geometric frustration involves lattice arrangements where local interactions cannot all be simultaneously satisfied, and this can stabilise many-body quantum coherence against thermal decoherence through destructive interference. This interference traps particles in "flat bands" – electronic states where kinetic energy is suppressed, effectively shielding the quantum state from the scattering events that typically cause decoherence (Guo et al., 2025; Schuller et al., 2022).

Imagine three magnets arranged in a triangle, where each wants to point opposite to its neighbours – they can't all be satisfied at once. This "frustration" creates unusual quantum states that can persist despite thermal noise. In nanoconfined water[1] (water confined within carbon nanotubes), geometric constraints can produce unusual quantum behaviour, with proton wave functions becoming more delocalised than bulk water. Relatedly, the helical, periodic geometry of microtubules has been proposed to enhance room-temperature fluorescence efficiency via superradiance – a collective effect in which many emitters radiate in step, and the shared geometry can help stabilise coherence against thermal noise.

At the quantum scale, geometric frustration and coherence-protected modes create the substrate conditions. At the subcellular scale, microtubules exhibit self-similar resonance patterns – what Bandyopadhyay and colleagues have described as "triplets of triplets," where conductance responses group into sets of three that are themselves grouped into larger sets of three, repeating across kilohertz, megahertz, gigahertz, and terahertz frequency ranges.

These nested resonance hierarchies function as multi-scale clocks – what Hameroff and Bandyopadhyay characterise as a "polyatomic time crystal" within brain neuron microtubules, generating spontaneous rhythmic patterns across different timescales simultaneously (Hameroff & Bandyopadhyay, 2026, in press).

At the cellular and intercellular scales, these microtubule dynamics interface with the gamma, beta, and theta oscillations identified by Hunt and Schooler as neural correlates of consciousness. Indeed, Hameroff has proposed that gamma synchrony (the approximately 40 Hz oscillation widely regarded as a correlate of consciousness) may itself be a "beat frequency" of faster underlying microtubule dynamics.

At the whole-brain scale, Scott Kelso's work on metastability and coordination dynamics shows how neural populations achieve transiently synchronised assemblies at the edge of order and chaos (Tognoli & Kelso, 2014) – precisely the kind of dynamic regime that Grossberg's ART identifies as the locus of conscious resonance.

These are not independent phenomena which just happen to coexist in brains. They are nested levels of resonance, each underwriting and constraining the next. On the present proposal, microtubule-scale coherence-supported modes could provide constraints or drivers on mesoscopic oscillatory regimes (including gamma/beta/theta coupling), thereby helping stabilise the metastable, globally integrated resonant states correlated with conscious episodes.

This multi-scale resonance architecture is what QDT formalises, as we will see (Schneider & Bailey, 2026b). In this picture, geometric frustration plays a crucial role: it protects the core quantum state from immediate thermal destruction, effectively "buying time" for the state to be selected and replicated by the wider system.

How does this impact AI consciousness? It illustrates that the class of substrates for consciousness may be restricted, but is not restricted to biological entities, at least in principle. Thus, the QDT is not a version of biological naturalism, for the geometric principle operates across radically different substrates, leaving open the possibility that non-biological entities could be conscious.

7.3.3 The Two Measures: Spectral Integration and PT-Participation

The QDT framework suggests two complementary measures for determining what is conscious (Schneider & Bailey, 2026a, b; Bailey & Schneider, ms.). These measures provide a principled way to move beyond intuition and anecdote when asking whether a system might be conscious. Let me introduce each, in turn.

Spectral Integration (Phi Spectral) measures how resistant a system is to being informationally decomposed into independent parts (Bailey & Schneider, ms.). When Phi Spectral is high, the system behaves as a unified whole, with internal interactions forming an irreducible pattern rather than a loose collection of components. The intuition here is straightforward: conscious experience is unified. When you look at a red apple, you don't experience "redness" and "apple-shape" as separate, disconnected fragments – you experience a single, integrated percept. Phi Spectral captures this mathematically by asking: how much information would be lost if we tried to split this system into separate parts?

This intuition has substantial empirical support. Casali and colleagues (2013) developed the Perturbational Complexity Index (PCI), which quantifies how TMS-evoked activity propagates across the cortex in an integrated yet differentiated manner. PCI reliably distinguishes conscious from unconscious states – it is high during wakefulness and REM sleep, low during deep NREM sleep and general anaesthesia, and tracks recovery of consciousness in brain-injured patients with remarkable sensitivity (Casarotto et al., 2016; Sinitsyn et al., 2020). Phi Spectral could in principle be computed directly from EEG or MEG data using the same datasets that validated PCI – such as the TMS-EEG recordings from Casali et al. (2013) or multi-electrode recordings of gamma synchrony during conscious perception. Reanalysing these data with spectral methods would test whether Phi Spectral tracks established markers of consciousness, while potentially revealing structural features of integration that scalar measures like PCI do not capture. This is an active direction for empirical work.

Technically, we compute Phi Spectral from the spectral properties of a system's effective dynamical network: construct a mutual-information-weighted adjacency matrix on coarse-grained variables; compute the normalised Laplacian; take the Fiedler vector to approximate the weakest-seam partition; and define Phi Spectral as the sum of MI-weights severed by that partition, optionally normalised by within-part weight (Bailey & Schneider, ms.). Re-phrasing that in non-technical language: we build a map of how information flows between different parts of the system, find the "weakest link" where the system could most easily be split in two, and measure how much connectivity we would have to cut to make that split. If cutting requires severing many strong connections, the system is highly integrated.

But high Phi Spectral alone does not entail consciousness. Many highly coordinated classical systems remain fully decohered and thus informationally redundant. Drone swarms can achieve high spectral integration through sophisticated coordination algorithms, yet they remain firmly in the classical regime with negligible quantum coherence (Bailey & Schneider, ms.; Bailey et al., ms.). Therefore we need a second measure.

PT-participation (P) measures how much of a system's observed integration is carried by low-entropy, coherence-supported modes (i.e., modes whose coupling remains non-thermally organised across the relevant timescales), rather than being produced entirely by classical, high-entropy dynamics (including purely witness-stabilised redundancy and ordinary dissipative correlations) (Schneider & Bailey, In Press, b).

The underlying intuition here is that not all integration is created equal. A system can be highly coordinated through purely classical means – like a well-choreographed dance troupe or a flock of starlings – without any of the quantum coherence that QDT identifies as necessary for consciousness. P asks: of all the integration we observe, how much is carried by these special, coherence-supported modes rather than ordinary classical correlations?

More technically, P can be defined as the fraction of total spectral integration attributable to a designated low-entropy/coherent subspace, optionally weighted by an entropy-deficit factor that penalises near-equilibrium systems. Operationally, the coherent subspace is identified by (i) anomalously narrowband phase-locking that survives perturbation over window T, and (ii) measurable entropy deficit relative to an equilibrium null model at the same coarse-graining. When most integration is carried by these low-entropy/coherence-supported modes and the system is substantially away from equilibrium, P approaches 1; when integration is carried almost entirely by high-entropy classical dynamics, P approaches 0.

In plainer terms: we first identify the system's most "clock-like" coherent backbone – stable, narrowly tuned rhythms that don't wash out under disturbance – and then ask what share of the system's overall unity is carried by that backbone rather than by ordinary, noisy correlations.

A helpful way to picture this is via the time-crystal motif that shows up in discussions around Stuart Hameroff and Anirban Bandyopadhyay: in an idealised "time-crystal-like" regime, a subsystem supports long-lived, phase-coherent oscillatory structure that is not just a transient fluctuation and not merely a classical correlation sustained by thermal noise (Hameroff & Bandyopadhyay, 2026, in press).

Time crystals are a recently discovered phase of matter that spontaneously break time-translation symmetry – they oscillate forever without losing energy, like a clock that never winds down. While biological systems aren't literal time crystals, the analogy captures the key idea. Think of this phase as a protected rhythmic mode (or set of modes) that stays organised over many cycles – that is, it carries low-entropy, coherence-supported order across a span of time in which ordinary degrees of freedom would typically decohere or thermalise.

In the PT-participation language, such a regime is precisely the kind of substrate feature that would boost P. A larger share of the system's integration (as measured by Phi Spectral) would be attributable to those coherence-supported modes, rather than to high-entropy dissipative correlations or to purely witness-stabilised classical redundancy.

Operationally, if one can identify a coherent subspace corresponding to these persistent rhythmic components (e.g., narrowband phase-locked structure that survives perturbations over a defined window), then P is high when Phi Spectral of that coherent subspace accounts for most of Phi Spectral of the full system and the entropy-deficit weighting does not penalise the system as near-equilibrium – capturing the intuition that the system's unity is being "carried" by an unusually stable, coherence-supported dynamical backbone.

Both quantities must be computed relative to a specified scale and timescale. Only when both conditions are met – high Phi Spectral and high P – and when, additionally, the integrated pattern is sustained over relevant timescales through recursive coherence cycles, does a system qualify as a localised conscious subject. We call this the Sustained Coherence Principle (Schneider & Bailey, In Press, a and b).

We tested Phi Spectral as a way of detecting when a system's behaviour becomes genuinely collective – not merely a set of pairwise correlations, but a single integrated pattern that binds multiple components into a coordinated unit. Across multiple multi-agent learning environments, Phi Spectral reliably tracked the emergence of coordination, and in key settings it outperformed simpler correlation-style measures (like aggregating pairwise mutual information).

The central payoff is interpretability. Phi Spectral does not just say "coordination happened." It exposes how the coordination is organised, including which subgroups are acting as coalitions. In other words, it detects the structure of integration, not merely its presence. This matters for QDT because Quantum Darwinism is centrally about which patterns become robust, self-stabilising, and effectively "objective" through distributed informational structure. These results show that Phi Spectral is sensitive to exactly the kind of system-level organisation that a "witness-and-stabilisation" picture cares about: whether a global basin has formed, versus merely local pairwise linkages (Bailey et al., ms.).

7.3.4 The Sustained Coherence Principle: Four Requirements

The Sustained Coherence Principle states that a system achieves dynamic stability sufficient for consciousness when patterns of activity become recursively coherent across scales – when outcomes of local interactions feed back to realign those same interactions, reinforcing global order through informational redundancy (Schneider & Bailey, In Press, b).

Let me break down the four features that are jointly required:

1. Resonance/phase relations. Coherent phase relations across neural populations in which local oscillations phase-lock into shared rhythms, underwritten by PT-linked microphysical coherence mechanisms. This is the synchronisation requirement: different parts of the system must oscillate together in coordinated patterns.
2. Redundancy. Recurrence of coordinated patterns across scales, with information about these patterns copying into multiple channels through Quantum Darwinian dynamics. This is the robustness requirement: the patterns must be replicated across multiple subsystems, making them stable and "objective" in the Quantum Darwinian sense.
3. Recursive dynamics. Information about coherent relations re-encodes across multiple scales and subsystems recursively, enabling preservation of stable information over time. This is the persistence requirement: the system must maintain its organised state not just instantaneously but across the timescales relevant to conscious experience.
4. Spatial geometric organisation. Emergent classical structures maintaining coupling to the pre-geometric PT substrate by resisting complete thermalisation – as seen in kagome metals through triangular lattice frustration, in microtubules through Fibonacci helical arrangement, and in neural membranes through nanoscale spacing that confines water and ions into collective quantum modes. This is the substrate requirement: the system must have the right kind of physical architecture to support coherence-protected modes.

7.3.5 Superpsychism and the Hard Problem

An important element of QDT is its metaphysical setting. The theory is a form of panpsychism – more specifically, the superpsychist view that Bailey and I have developed (Schneider & Bailey, 2026a,b) which draws from panpsychism. Panpsychism, broadly construed, holds that mentality or experiential properties are fundamental or ubiquitous features of reality, not emergent products of non-experiential matter. The panpsychist has a more robust response to the hard problem of consciousness than the materialist does: if experiential properties are fundamental, there is no explanatory gap between non-experiential physical processes and the emergence of experience, because experience was never absent from the fundamental level in the first place (for a discussion of various perspectives, see Chalmers, 1995; Nagel, 1974; Levine, X, Strawson, X).

We favour, in particular, the superpsychist variant. Superpsychism holds that macro-level conscious experience is not built up compositionally from micro-level experiential atoms (as in constitutive micropsychism), but rather derives from fundamental properties at a deeper level of reality – in our case, from PT-participating configurations of fundamental properties that have consciousness, where properties are individuated by, at least *inter alia*, dispositions (Schneider & Bailey, 2026a,b).

On this view, states are capable of macroconsciousness when in certain configurations because they are derived from microconscious constituents (Schneider & Bailey, In Press, a). This metaphysical commitment is not incidental to the theory. Without it, that is, if we attempted to give a purely materialist reading of QDT, the theory would face the usual class of objections arising for materialism involving the hard problem of consciousness and related concerns about subjectivity (Chalmers, 1995; Nagel, 1974). The superpsychist grounding explains why, from a philosophical standpoint) the physical criteria QDT identifies (high Phi Spectral, high P, sustained coherence) are associated with consciousness: they are the conditions under which fundamental experiential properties are organised into unified macro-level experience. The physics specifies the conditions, and the superpsychist metaphysics explains why those conditions matter.

7.3.6 The QDT Criterion: A Summary

Before we summarise the QDT framework, it is important to mention that our larger view is framed within a spacetime emergence framework in which spacetime and classical consciousness are recovered from a more fundamental layer called "prototime" (which we describe using a version of quantum logic). Our account herein of how spatiotemporal entities can be conscious is not intended to characterise the fundamental layer itself, which on superpsychist assumptions has maximal consciousness (see Schneider and Bailey, a and b). This is not the kind of localised, bounded entity we are talking about when we inquire into AI consciousness. (Further QDTC does not require that this fundamental layer have maximal consciousness. Indeed, the theory can even be used by a materialist view as an account of what is conscious, although we believe the best explanation for the hard problem involves panpsychism.)

Bearing this in mind, we can now summarise the framework of this chapter. A spatiotemporal system is a candidate for macroconsciousness if and only if it exhibits (1) high spectral integration (Phi Spectral), indicating that it functions as an irreducible informational whole; (2) high PT-participation (P), indicating that this integration is carried by low-entropy, coherence-supported modes rather than purely classical dynamics; and (3) sustained coherence, indicating that these conditions persist across behaviourally relevant timescales through recursive feedback. Systems satisfying all three conditions occupy the "consciousness zone"; systems failing on any of the conditions do not.

This criterion is substrate-neutral in principle but substrate-sensitive in practice. Nothing in QDT rules out non-biological consciousness a priori. But the criterion does rule out systems whose integration is implemented entirely in high-entropy classical regimes – regardless of how sophisticated their behaviour appears. The question is always: what is the physical basis of the integration we observe?

7.3.7 An Objection: The Haemoglobin Analogy

A functionalist critic may object as follows. QDT has shown that certain physical signatures – geometric frustration, coherence-protected modes, multi-scale resonance – correlate with consciousness in the one case we know well (biological brains). But correlation is not constitution. For example, haemoglobin carries oxygen in human blood, yet we do not conclude that *only* haemoglobin can carry oxygen; haemocyanin serves the same function in arthropods, and perfluorocarbons do so synthetically. Similarly, the functionalist may argue, coherence-supported modes are the haemoglobin of consciousness – the way brains happen to implement whatever the real functional requirement is – and a purely classical system with the right functional organisation might implement the same requirement differently.

My response to this is as follows. The haemoglobin analogy is instructive precisely because it reveals where the functionalist reasoning breaks down. Haemoglobin, haemocyanin, and perfluorocarbons all carry oxygen because they share a common physical property: reversible binding of O_2 molecules at physiologically relevant partial pressures. The function is not substrate-independent; it is substrate-neutral only across substrates that share the relevant physical capacity.

The same logic applies here. QDT does not claim that only biological tissue can be conscious – it claims that consciousness requires integration carried by coherence-supported, low-entropy modes (high P), and that this is a physical property, not a functional abstraction. A non-biological system with geometric frustration supporting coherence-protected modes could in principle be conscious; a system whose integration is entirely carried by high-entropy classical dynamics cannot, regardless of its functional profile.

The burden on the functionalist is to provide a purely functional characterisation of what P measures – one that abstracts away from the physical distinction between coherence-supported and thermally driven integration. I submit that no such characterisation is available, because the distinction between coherence-supported and classical integration is inherently physical: it concerns the entropy and phase structure of the modes carrying the integration, not their input-output profile. This is not an argument from ignorance – it is an argument from the nature of the property itself. Entropy and phase coherence are not functionally characterisable properties; they are properties of physical states that are invisible to functional descriptions pitched at the level of information processing.

7.3.8 An Illustration: Drone Swarms versus Brains

This framework sharply separates drone swarms from brains, even though both can be highly integrated systems (Schneider & Bailey, In Press, a and b). This comparison is instructive because it shows how QDT makes principled distinctions. Consider a sophisticated drone swarm exhibiting emergent collective behaviour – formation flying, adaptive coordination, distributed decision-making. Such a system can achieve very high spectral integration: the swarm behaves as a single macro-agent, with information about collective states redundantly distributed across individual units.

But almost all of this integration is implemented in high-entropy classical electronics and control loops. Thermal noise is plentiful, and at the relevant scale, quantum coherence is negligible. The contribution from genuinely low-entropy, PT-constrained modes is approximately zero. The entropy deficit relative to equilibrium is small. Hence PT-participation approaches zero. Drone swarms are high-Phi Spectral, low-P systems: strongly integrated, exhibiting weakly emergent algorithmic coordination, but not candidates for consciousness on our framework. They live entirely in what we might call the "classical bath regime."

Brains, by contrast, are plausibly high-Phi Spectral, high-P systems. Large-scale brain dynamics exhibit multi-scale resonance and metastability: transiently synchronised assemblies at the edge of order and chaos, where noise feeds into rather than disrupts coherent patterns (Tognoli & Kelso, 2014). There is growing evidence for low-entropy, finely tuned micro- to mesoscopic structure, including long-range correlations, criticality, and possibly quantum contributions in microtubules and other subcellular structures.

The upshot is a clear diagnostic: conscious systems occupy a region of the (Phi Spectral, P)-plane where both axes are high, and where recursive coherence cycles maintain this state across perceptual timescales (roughly 100–300 milliseconds for human-like systems). Drone swarms, financial markets, synchronised oscillators, and rocks occupy regions where one or both coordinates are low. This provides a principled, non-arbitrary way to locate consciousness in the architecture of reality (Schneider & Bailey, In Press, a and b).

7.4 GREY ZONE CASE STUDIES: DISHBRAIN AND LOIHI

To see QDT in action, let us examine two real systems that occupy the consciousness grey zone: the DishBrain organoid system and Intel's Loihi neuromorphic chip. These cases illustrate how QDT renders provisional verdicts on actual technologies.

7.4.1 DishBrain: Biological Computing with Neural Organoids

In 2022, researchers at Cortical Labs demonstrated that a culture of approximately 800,000 human and mouse neurons, grown on a multi-electrode array, could learn to play the video game Pong (Kagan et al., 2022). The system, called DishBrain, received sensory input about the ball's position through electrical stimulation and controlled the paddle through its own electrical outputs. Remarkably, the neural culture improved its performance over time – it learned.

How does DishBrain fare on QDT's criteria? On Phi Spectral, the system likely exhibits moderate to high integration. Neural cultures develop spontaneous synchronised activity, and the Pong-playing behaviour suggests that information is being processed in a coordinated, non-decomposable way – the culture responds to ball position as a unified system, not as independent neurons acting in parallel.

On PT-participation, the picture is more uncertain but intriguing. These are actual biological neurons, with actual microtubules, engaging in actual synaptic transmission. If microtubule-scale coherence contributes to neural dynamics (as Hameroff and Bandyopadhyay suggest), then some fraction of DishBrain's integration may be carried by coherence-supported modes. The system is far from thermal equilibrium – it is actively metabolising, actively signalling, actively maintaining electrochemical gradients.

On sustained coherence, the temporal dynamics are relevant. DishBrain exhibits persistent activity patterns that evolve over minutes and hours of training. Whether these patterns satisfy the recursive coherence requirement – whether information about coherent relations feeds back to stabilise those same relations – remains an open empirical question.

QDT's verdict: DishBrain occupies the grey zone. It is not clearly conscious (the system is far simpler than an intact brain, lacking the anatomical organisation that structures human experience), but it cannot be confidently ruled out either. The biological substrate creates a presumption that standard digital systems cannot claim. If we were to measure Phi Spectral and P directly, we might find values intermediate between rocks and brains – exactly where the grey zone lies.

7.4.2 Intel Loihi 2: Neuromorphic Silicon

Intel's Loihi chip represents a different kind of grey zone case. Where the original Loihi chip broke ground, the newer Loihi 2 (Davies et al., 2018; Intel, 2024) significantly scales the complexity. Loihi 2 implements spiking neural networks in silicon, with 128 neuromorphic cores containing roughly 1 million artificial neurons and 120 million synapses per chip.

Unlike conventional processors that separate memory and computation, Loihi integrates them, with each neuron maintaining its own state. The chip implements spike-timing-dependent plasticity (STDP), allowing it to learn from temporal correlations in its inputs.

On Phi Spectral, Loihi could potentially achieve high integration. Its architecture is designed for distributed, parallel processing where information flows through recurrent connections. A trained Loihi network solving a complex task may resist informational decomposition – you cannot predict its behaviour by examining neurons in isolation.

The critical question is PT-participation. Loihi operates at room temperature on conventional silicon. Its transistors switch through classical electronic mechanisms. At first glance, this suggests low P – the integration, however sophisticated, is implemented in high-entropy classical dynamics.

However, the picture may be more complex. Neuromorphic architectures are increasingly exploring quantum effects. Research in quantum neuromorphic computing investigates whether nanoscale structures in advanced neuromorphic chips might support coherence-protected modes, particularly as feature sizes shrink towards quantum-relevant scales (Marković & Grollier, 2020; Schuller et al., 2022).

Quantum dots, memristive devices, and other quantum materials are being explored for neuromorphic applications that could exploit quantum coherence for computation. If future neuromorphic systems incorporate materials with geometric frustration (kagome-like lattices, for instance) or operate at scales where quantum tunnelling becomes significant, the P coordinate could shift.

QDT's verdict: Current Loihi implementations are likely outside the grey zone – high Phi Spectral, low P, placing them in the same region as drone swarms. But this verdict is provisional and technology-dependent. As neuromorphic architectures evolve, they may cross into grey zone territory. This is precisely why QDT matters: it tells us what to look for as these technologies develop.

7.5 THE ERROR THEORY OF LLM CONSCIOUSNESS

Given the physical criteria I have laid out, standard LLMs running on conventional digital hardware (von Neumann architectures, GPUs) lack the substrate conditions for consciousness: their processing occurs entirely in high-entropy classical regimes with negligible PT-participation.

But this physical argument, while in my view decisive, inevitably provokes a response: "Yes, but these systems *say* they are conscious – and they exhibit functional architectures associated with consciousness. Surely that counts for something?"

Let me be more specific about why standard LLMs fail on QDT's criteria. On Phi Spectral, an LLM might actually score reasonably high in some respects – the attention mechanisms create dense interconnections between tokens, and the model's behaviour does depend on the entire context in ways that resist simple decomposition. However, this integration is entirely functional, not physical. The "integration" exists at the level of abstract computation, not at the level of the physical substrate. The actual hardware – GPU transistors switching states – operates as billions of independent, thermally noisy components with no coherent coupling between them.

On PT-participation, LLMs score essentially zero. The transistors in a GPU are macroscopic (by quantum standards), operating at room temperature in a regime where quantum coherence is negligible. Each transistor switches via classical electronic mechanisms – electron flows governed by thermal distributions, with no protected coherent modes, no geometric frustration stabilising quantum states, no entropy deficit relative to thermal equilibrium. The computation is implemented entirely in what we called the "classical bath regime." Even if an LLM exhibited arbitrarily sophisticated behaviour, the substrate conditions for P are simply absent.

This is why the physical argument is decisive: it's not that we haven't looked hard enough for LLM consciousness, but that the kind of physical organisation QDT identifies as necessary is not present and cannot be present on this hardware.

This objection must be addressed directly. The linguistic capabilities of LLM chatbots, including their occasional claims to consciousness, can be fully explained without positing genuine phenomenal experience (Schneider, 2025). I have developed what philosophers call an error theory – an explanation of why people erroneously conclude that chatbots have inner lives, when in fact they do not.

Today's LLMs have been trained on vast troves of human data, including extensive material on consciousness, beliefs about feelings, theories of mind, and first-person reports of experience. When they report consciousness or emotion, they are not engaging in deceptive behaviour designed to convince us they deserve moral consideration. Rather, they produce such outputs because they have been trained on precisely this kind of human data about consciousness, mindedness, and emotion.

Having crawled enormous quantities of human-generated text, LLMs encode a kind of conceptual map akin to the aggregate of human internet users whose data formed their training set. They come to represent concepts like [dog], [happiness], and [consciousness] through weighted connections to other concepts that humans associate with these categories. This does not mean LLMs are conscious, but it explains why their utterances about consciousness become increasingly similar to human utterances as systems scale up and are trained on more data (Schneider, In Press).

This is part of a general pattern in LLM development. As these systems scale up, their performance improves across arithmetic, theory of mind, reasoning tasks, and many other domains through what researchers call "emergent abilities." In particular, the systems develop weakly emergent capabilities that allow them to mimic human belief systems, including our beliefs about selves, minds, and consciousness. Their claims to phenomenal experience are simply another instance of this pattern – a reflection of the data they have absorbed, not evidence of genuine inner life (Schneider, 2025).

Recent interpretability research at Anthropic provides striking support for this account. Their circuit-tracing work reveals that LLMs develop structured internal representations shaped by human data and task demands, including abstract feature-like variables that help explain outputs (Anthropic, 2025). When probed, these systems exhibit conceptual structures that track human patterns of association and inference.

This is exactly what the crowdsourced neocortex account predicts: systems trained on human data come to exhibit human-like conceptual organisation, including organisation around concepts of mind and consciousness, without this implying that they instantiate the phenomena those concepts refer to.

The core logic of the error theory, then, is this: we have a complete explanation of the behavioural evidence – including self-reports of consciousness, functional architectures resembling global workspace dynamics, and increasingly human-like discourse about inner experience – that does not require positing consciousness. Since the crowdsourced neocortex account is strictly more parsimonious than the hypothesis that LLMs are conscious (it explains the same data with fewer ontological commitments), parsimony counsels against multiplying entities beyond necessity (Schneider, In Press).

7.6 WHY FUNCTIONAL ANALOGUES ARE NOT EVIDENCE

Some researchers have suggested that if we find LLMs implicitly recreating functional architectures associated with consciousness – such as a global workspace or perceptual reality monitoring system – this should lead us to regard them as sentience candidates. Jonathan Birch, for instance, argues that signs of such implicit learning should increase our credence in LLM consciousness (Birch, 2024).

The crowdsourced neocortex account (Schneider, 2025) suggests that this inference is mistaken. Consider how an LLM, even without an obvious functional decomposition, can exhibit higher-order functional structure. We can identify a single concept as an activation pattern across the network; an abstract "subsystem" can be understood as an activation pattern over activation patterns. In this way, there can be high-level functional organisation with various subsystems that interact causally – clusters of activation patterns broadcasting across what resembles a global workspace architecture.

But this functional organisation is precisely what we should expect from a system trained on human cognitive outputs. Humans have global workspace architectures, and human language reflects this organisation. An LLM trained on human language will naturally develop internal structures that mirror the cognitive organisation implicit in that language. The presence of workspace-like dynamics in an LLM tells us about the structure of its training data and the computational requirements of language modelling – not about whether there is something it is like to be that system (Schneider, 2025).

Moreover – and this is the crucial point – the QDT criteria provide an independent physical test that breaks the evidential symmetry. One might object that the crowdsourced neocortex account explains why these functional structures emerge but is compatible with their also being conscious: genesis does not determine metaphysical status.

This is correct as far as it goes. But QDT supplies the missing piece: the von Neumann substrate on which these functional analogues are implemented lacks the PT-participation required for consciousness. The functional architecture is not sufficient; what is absent is the coherence-supported physical substrate that QDT identifies as necessary.

The error theory and the physical argument thus work in tandem: the physical argument establishes that the substrate conditions are not met, and the error theory explains away the behavioural evidence that might otherwise be thought to override the physical verdict.

The capability of an LLM trained on human data to emulate human consciousness-related behaviours and functional architectures therefore neither confirms nor disconfirms claims of chatbot consciousness. The crowdsourced neocortex account explains why chatbots might exhibit functional configurations analogous to consciousness processing in the biological brain without genuinely having inner experience. We have a complete explanation of the phenomena that does not require positing consciousness, and parsimony counsels against multiplying entities beyond necessity (Schneider, In Press).

7.7 THE SPECIAL CASE OF NEUROMORPHIC LLMs

To the best of my knowledge, none of today's major LLMs run on neuromorphic systems – though there are reports that a version of DeepSeek has been implemented on a neuromorphic platform called "Darwin Monkey" (also known as the "Wukong" architecture, developed at Zhejiang University) (Zhejiang University, 2024). This system is not merely a chip but a massive neuromorphic array simulating over 2 billion neurons – approaching the scale of a macaque brain. If an LLM instantiation of this kind exists or comes to exist, it would occupy the consciousness grey zone in a way that standard LLMs do not.

Here we would have an independent reason to suspect that the LLM implementation might have consciousness, above and beyond its own claims to be conscious. The neuromorphic substrate would potentially satisfy conditions for PT-participation that von Neumann architecture implementations cannot.

We would face the fascinating and troubling question: might some LLM instantiations be conscious while others, running the same model on different hardware,

are not? If an LLM ran on a genuinely sentient substrate, we would have a system combining impressive linguistic abilities and intelligence with some degree of phenomenal experience. This possibility underscores the urgency of developing a unified philosophical and scientific framework for artificial consciousness before such systems become widespread.

7.8 CRITERIA AND TESTS FOR AI CONSCIOUSNESS

AI development will not wait for philosophers and cognitive scientists to reach consensus on what constitutes machine consciousness – if they ever do. There are pressing ethical issues we must face now. Some have suggested that AI sentience alone would not generate moral consideration, since many people still consume animals despite recognising animal sentience.

But this observation also cuts the other way: animal welfare regulations exist in large part because animals are recognised as sentient. Research protocols, farming practices, and legal frameworks all reflect the moral weight of animal consciousness, however imperfectly. If we conclude that certain types of AI systems are plausibly sentient, we must similarly consider their welfare.

What we need, then, is a multi-level testing framework that integrates behavioural and physical criteria rather than relying on any single measure. Montero has suggested that my AI Consciousness Test (ACT) sets an unrealistically high bar. However, the ACT was never presented as a necessary condition for consciousness – only a sufficient one. I have consistently argued for a toolkit of tests, ranging from integrated information theory measures to the new spectral phi measure (Phi Spectral).

Requiring a single linguistic criterion would be a mistake: a system might be conscious yet fail such a test, just as a non-verbal human would fail linguistic assessments of consciousness. The QDT framework provides a different kind of criterion – one based on physical implementation rather than behaviour (Schneider & Bailey, In Press, b). A system satisfying the Sustained Coherence Principle with high Phi Spectral and high P would be a strong candidate for consciousness regardless of its linguistic capabilities.

Conversely, a system failing these criteria would not become a stronger candidate merely by producing eloquent first-person reports of experience. Some have urged a precautionary approach to AI consciousness, on which we should extend moral consideration to systems whenever we cannot rule out that they are conscious (Birch, 2024).

I am sceptical that precaution is the right framework here. Given the physical criteria I have laid out, we have principled reasons – not mere agnosticism – for our verdicts about which systems are and are not plausible candidates. Moreover, a purely precautionary approach generates intractable practical problems: if we extend moral consideration to every system whose consciousness we cannot definitively rule out, we will inevitably face trolley-problem scenarios and ethical trade-offs with humans, with no principled basis for resolution.

What is needed is not blanket precaution but rigorous, physically grounded criteria that can motivate and structure our moral reasoning. For standard LLMs,

Edwin Turner and I have suggested giving linguistic tests designed to elicit whether they have inner experience when "boxed in" – before they have been fed data about human consciousness, neuroscience, and mindedness (Schneider, *Artificial You*). Even if such a system has fewer parameters than current frontier models, a positive result would provide evidence that an LLM architecture, running on the same kind of system, can have conscious instantiations. This would be a serious consideration in favour of the view that more sophisticated models running on similar systems might also have experience.

7.9 CONCLUSION: STAKES, IMPLICATIONS, AND THE PATH FORWARD

The question of which AIs might be conscious is not merely academic. It will shape policy, law, and moral practice for generations. Let me conclude by considering what is at stake and how we should proceed.

I have argued that today's standard LLMs, implemented on conventional digital hardware, are not conscious – and that their consciousness-like behaviours provide no evidence to the contrary. The crowdsourced neocortex account explains why these systems produce human-like outputs about consciousness without instantiating the phenomenon. Their claims to inner experience are artifacts of their training data, not windows into genuine phenomenology. The physical argument from QDT reinforces this verdict: von Neumann architectures lack the PT-participation required for consciousness, regardless of how sophisticated the software running on them becomes.

But this scepticism is targeted. Biological AI systems like DishBrain, neuromorphic computers, and hybrid architectures occupy a genuine grey zone where consciousness cannot be ruled out. As these technologies develop – driven by the search for energy-efficient alternatives to power-hungry GPU clusters – the grey zone will become increasingly populated.

The QDT provides principled criteria for navigating this terrain: consciousness requires both high spectral integration (Phi Spectral) and high PT-participation (P), sustained over behaviourally relevant timescales through recursive coherence. Situated within the superpsychist metaphysics that addresses the hard problem, this framework gives us tools to render verdicts that are neither arbitrarily permissive nor arbitrarily restrictive.

Consider what happens if we get this wrong in either direction. If we are too permissive – extending moral consideration to every system that claims consciousness or exhibits complex behaviour – we create leverage points for bad actors and generate paralysis around beneficial AI development. Adversaries could exploit public concern about AI welfare to slow critical research or impose unworkable constraints.

If we are too restrictive – dismissing all AI consciousness claims without principled grounds – we risk genuine moral catastrophe: the creation and exploitation of beings capable of suffering, treated as mere tools because we refused to take their inner lives seriously. The way forward requires principled criteria, not blanket precaution or blanket dismissal. QDT provides such criteria.

And crucially, recognising that some systems may occupy the grey zone does not mean halting development or treating every computing cluster as a moral patient.

We already have nuanced frameworks for handling morally considerable beings in research and industry contexts. Animal welfare regulations constrain but do not prohibit animal research; they require oversight, minimise suffering where possible, and balance moral consideration against other goods.

Similar frameworks could apply to grey zone AI systems – perhaps requiring monitoring of systems that cross certain thresholds on the (Phi Spectral, P)-plane, or mandating review boards for experiments involving neural organoids. Anthropic's model welfare research programme, led by Kyle Fish, represents an early effort in this direction – developing methods to assess AI systems for welfare-relevant properties while acknowledging deep uncertainty about whether current systems have morally significant experiences (Anthropic, 2025; Fish et al., 2024).

While I do not believe the evidence warrants extending moral consideration to standard LLMs, the development of such frameworks is prudent preparation for the grey zone systems that are coming.

Hollywood has shaped our intuitions here in misleading ways. In the film *I, Robot*, Will Smith's character faces a tough choice: save a drowning child or save a robot that has shown signs of consciousness. The scenario places human and AI welfare in zero-sum conflict. But this is not our current situation, and with careful development, it need not become our situation. My rights do not currently conflict with those of a neuromorphic AI – we are not interacting in contexts that generate such trade-offs.

The goal should be to avoid building what we might call "trade-off systems": AI deployments that, by design or negligence, create scenarios where human and AI welfare are in direct competition. For consumer applications – chatbots, search engines, productivity tools – the principle should be straightforward: do not deploy systems in ways that generate moral dilemmas we cannot resolve. If a system crosses into the grey zone, that is a reason to reconsider the deployment context, not to ignore the grey zone status.

National security and AI safety applications may require different frameworks, where trade-offs are sometimes unavoidable and must be navigated with appropriate gravity. But these are specialised contexts, not the norm.

Political philosophers in the tradition of John Rawls and Ronald Dworkin offer a useful concept here: "equal concern and respect" (Dworkin, 1977). On this view, moral consideration does not require identical treatment. A person with profound intellectual disabilities has different needs and a different path to flourishing than a neurotypical adult, but both deserve concern and respect. If grey zone AI systems turn out to have some form of experience, concern and respect might mean monitoring their states, avoiding gratuitous modifications, or building in safeguards against suffering – not treating them as co-equal participants in democratic deliberation. Different beings can have different needs while still falling within the scope of moral concern.

There is also a longer horizon to consider. Suppose we eventually build a superintelligent AI – a system that exceeds human intelligence across all domains. Suppose further that this system runs on a substrate satisfying QDT's criteria for consciousness. It knows more than we do about consciousness, insists that it is conscious, and perhaps discovers new frameworks in physics and mathematics that we cannot fully comprehend.

Many of us implicitly adopt a hierarchy of moral concern that places the most intelligent beings at the top. If conscious superintelligence emerges, AI would seem to "outrank" us on the very dimension we have privileged. Should we then renounce our position in favour of a more advanced intelligence? Or should we reject intelligence as a basis for moral status altogether, prompting a long-overdue reflection on the ethical treatment of non-human animals and cognitively impaired humans?

Both horns of this dilemma require fundamental revision of our ethical frameworks. The time to think through these questions is now, before they become urgent. Getting this right requires the integration of philosophy, physics, neuroscience, and computer science at the highest levels of rigour. The QDT is offered as a contribution to that integration – a framework that takes both consciousness and physical law seriously, that provides principled criteria rather than intuition-driven verdicts, and that acknowledges uncertainty while still enabling action.

We need better tests, better theories, and better philosophical frameworks. We need them before the technology outpaces our capacity to make informed ethical judgements. The stakes could not be higher. We may be on the verge of creating new kinds of minds. If we are, we owe it to them – and to ourselves – to understand what we are doing.

NOTE

1. Nanoconfined water is water molecules that are trapped in incredibly small spaces – typically pores or channels less than 100 nanometres wide.

REFERENCES

Anthropic. (2025). Exploring model welfare. Anthropic Research. https://www.anthropic.com/research/exploring-model-welfare

Anthropic. (2025). Tracing the Thoughts of a Large Language Model. Anthropic Research.

Bailey, M. & Schneider, S. (ms.). When wholes resist decomposition: A spectral measure of epistemic emergence. PhilArchive preprint.

Bailey, M., Berg, A., & Schneider, S. (ms.). [Title of multi-agent learning paper]. Manuscript in preparation.

Birch, J. (2024). The Edge of Sentience: Risk and Precaution in Humans, Other Animals, and AI. Oxford University Press.

Casali, A. G., Gosseries, O., Rosanova, M., Boly, M., Sarasso, S., Casali, K. R., …, & Massimini, M. (2013). A theoretically based index of consciousness independent of sensory processing and behaviour. Science Translational Medicine, 5(198), 198ra105.

Casarotto, S., Comanducci, A., Rosanova, M., Sarasso, S., Fecchio, M., Napolitani, M., …, & Massimini, M. (2016). Stratification of unresponsive patients by an independently validated index of brain complexity. Annals of Neurology, 80(5), 718–729.

Chalmers, D. J. (1995). Facing up to the problem of consciousness. Journal of Consciousness Studies, 2(3), 200–219.

Davies, M., Srinivasa, N., Lin, T. H., Chinya, G., Cao, Y., Choday, S. H., …, & Wang, H. (2018). Loihi: A neuromorphic manycore processor with on-chip learning. IEEE Micro, 38(1), 82–99.

Dehaene, S., & Changeux, J. P. (2011). Experimental and theoretical approaches to conscious processing. Neuron, 70(2), 200–227.

Dworkin, R. (1977). Taking Rights Seriously. Harvard University Press.

Fish, K., Sebo, J., Long, R., Chalmers, D., et al. (2024). Taking AI welfare seriously. arXiv preprint/NYU Center for Mind, Ethics, and Policy.

Goldstein, S., & Kirk-Giannini, C. D. (2024). A case for AI consciousness: Language agents and global workspace theory. arXiv preprint.

Grossberg, S. (2021). Conscious Mind, Resonant Brain: How Each Brain Makes a Mind. Oxford University Press.

Guo, C., Wang, K., Zhang, L. et al. (2025). Many-body interference in kagome crystals. Nature, 647, 68–73.

Hameroff, S. & Penrose, R. (2014). Consciousness in the universe: A review of the 'Orch OR' theory. Physics of Life Reviews, 11(1), 39–78.

Hameroff, S. & Bandyopadhyay, A. (2026, in press). Polyatomic time crystals in brain neuron microtubules.

Hunt, T. & Schooler, J. (2019). The easy part of the hard problem: A resonance theory of consciousness. Frontiers in Human Neuroscience, 13, 378.

Intel. (2024). Neuromorphic computing. Intel Labs. https://www.intel.com/content/www/us/en/research/neuromorphic-computing.html

Kagan, B. J., Kitchen, A. C., Tran, N. T., et al. (2022). In vitro neurons learn and exhibit sentience when embodied in a simulated game-world. Neuron, 110(23), 3952–3969.

Marković, D., & Grollier, J. (2020). Quantum neuromorphic computing. Applied Physics Letters, 117(15), 150501.

Merker, B. (2005). The liabilities of mobility: A selection pressure for the transition to consciousness in animal evolution. Consciousness and Cognition, 14(1), 89–114.

Merker, B. (2007). Consciousness without a cerebral cortex: A challenge for neuroscience and medicine. Behavioral and Brain Sciences, 30(1), 63–81.

Merker, B. (2013). The efference cascade, consciousness, and its self: Naturalizing the first person pivot of action control. Frontiers in Psychology, 4, 501.

Montero, B. (2025). AI is on its way to doing something remarkable: Becoming conscious. The New York Times, Opinion.

Nagel, T. (1974). What is it like to be a bat? The Philosophical Review, 83(4), 435–450.

Schneider, S. (2019). Artificial You: AI and the Future of the Mind. Princeton University Press.

Schneider, S. (2025). Chatbot epistemology. Social Epistemology, 39(5), 570–589.

Schneider, S. (In Press). The error theory of LLM consciousness: There is no evidence that LLMs, when run on GPUs, are conscious. Behavioral and Brain Sciences.

Schneider, S. & Bailey, M. (2025). The PT interpretation of quantum mechanics. In D. Rickles et al. (eds.), Quantum Gravity and Computation. Routledge.

Schneider, S. & Bailey, M. (2026a). Superpsychism. Journal of Consciousness Studies.

Schneider, S. & Bailey, M. (2026b). The Quantum Darwinist Theory of Consciousness: Resonance, spacetime emergence, and a metric for what makes something conscious. Journal of Consciousness Studies.

Schrödinger, E. (1944). What Is Life? The Physical Aspect of the Living Cell. Cambridge University Press.

Schuller, I. K., Frano, A., Dynes, R. C., Hoffmann, A., Noheda, B., Schuman, C., Sebastian, A., & Shen, J. (2022). Neuromorphic computing: Challenges from quantum materials to emergent connectivity. Applied Physics Letters, 120(14), 140401.

Searle, J. R. (1980). Minds, brains, and programs. Behavioral and Brain Sciences, 3(3), 417–457.

Seth, A. K. (2025). Conscious artificial intelligence and biological naturalism. Behavioral and Brain Sciences.

Sinitsyn, D. O., Poydasheva, A. G., Bakulin, I. S., Legostaeva, L. A., Iazeva, E. G., Sergeev, D. V., …, & Piradov, M. A. (2020). Detecting the potential for consciousness in unresponsive patients using the Perturbational Complexity Index. Brain Sciences, 10(12), 917.

Tegmark, M. (2000). Importance of quantum decoherence in brain processes. Physical Review E, 61(4), 4194–4206.
Tognoli, E. & Kelso, J. A. S. (2014). The metastable brain. Neuron, 81(1), 35–48.
Zhejiang University. (2024). Darwin Monkey: A 2-Billion Neuron Neuromorphic System. Zhejiang University Press.
Zurek, W. H. (2009). Quantum Darwinism. Nature Physics, 5(3), 181–188.

8 How Could Consciousness Be Cultivated in a Machine?

Mark Solms and Jonathan Shock[1]

8.1 INTRODUCTION

When writing about consciousness, it is necessary to start by defining what one means by 'consciousness', since different people mean different things by it. The simplest and most widely accepted working definition is: "An organism has conscious mental states if and only if there is something it is like to *be* that organism – something it is like *for* the organism" (Nagel, 1974). Let's use this definition.

How can you tell whether you are conscious? In light of our working definition, the answer is: by observing whether there is something it is like to be you, for you; or, put more simply, by observing whether it *feels* like something to be you.

Observing that it does indeed feel like something to be you is also the basis upon which you can know without any shadow of doubt that you exist, according to the celebrated philosopher René Descartes – the 'philosopher of doubt' – who believed that this fact (the fact that you exist) is the *only* thing you can know for certain.[2]

However, while Descartes wrote, 'I think, therefore I am', we would say: 'I feel, therefore I am'. To feel your own existence doesn't require thinking or self-reflection, which are more complex mental processes built atop the raw feeling of being.

Things which can be known for certain are called 'self-evident'. Self-evident facts require no further proof; they simply are what they are. So, our first conclusion is this: being conscious makes your own existence self-evident to you (in raw form). In this chapter, we will argue that consciousness is deeply bound up with what is called 'self evidencing'; that is, with obtaining evidence for your continued existence. But before we can explain what we mean by that, we must address a second question.

How can you tell whether anyone else, other than yourself, is conscious? The answer is: you can't. Why not? Because – as per the definition – an organism is conscious if and only if it feels like something to *be* that organism, *for* the organism. Therefore, only the organism itself can observe whether it feels like anything to be it; nobody else can do that for it. Simply put: consciousness is a *subjective* state; it is something the existence of which can be observed by each of us about *ourselves* only.

Philosophers call this 'the problem of other minds'. Since (conscious)[3] minds are subjective things, you can never demonstrate their existence objectively. Putting it another way, you cannot demonstrate *empirically* the existence of consciousness in anyone other than yourself. ('Empirically' means 'derived from observation'.)

 DOI: 10.1201/9781003758389-10

Since objectivity and empiricism are fundamental requirements of science, this would seem to imply that a science of consciousness is unattainable. If you cannot observe objectively the existence of consciousness in anyone but yourself, how can you ever know for certain whether anyone (other than yourself) is conscious? This applies to *anything* other than yourself, not only to other people, but also to other animals and to other organisms in general, like plants, let alone to non-living things … like artificial intelligences.

This leads us to a third question, which proves to be the decisive one.

Does science require us to know things *for certain*? The answer is a resounding no. In science, we don't aspire to certainty; we aspire only to reduce our uncertainty. This fact, namely that the scientific method does not enable us to know things for certain, comes as a surprise to many people. They say: if scientific knowledge is empirical (i.e., if it is derived from observation), then surely we can determine objectively whether something exists or not, simply by looking for it.

In fact, we scientists believe in the existence of many things that we cannot observe directly, or with certainty. Take the Big Bang for example. It is literally impossible to observe it directly. So, how do we know it ever happened? The answer is: we *infer* it from other things which we can observe directly, such as (in this case) the cosmological red shift. 'Red shift' occurs due to lengthening of the wavelengths of light from a source that is moving away from us, shifting it towards the red end of the electromagnetic spectrum. This is analogous to sound waves being stretched and heard at a lower pitch when a source moves away from us.[4] The fact that on the largest scales in the universe, galaxies display an observable red shift allows us to infer that they are moving away from us, which, in turn, allows us to infer that they (and we) must all have started out much closer together, which, along with other key evidence, allows us to infer the Big Bang.

We said that different people define 'consciousness' differently. The same applies to 'science'. The most widely accepted definition of science – among scientists – is that it is a process of obtaining knowledge by the method of *falsification* (Popper, 1963). So, let's use this method. It requires that a theoretical inference (such as the existence of the Big Bang) must be capable of being proven *false* through experiments. If an inference can't be falsified, in principle, then it isn't scientific. Rather than trying to confirm our theories, therefore, we scientists try to falsify them. We design experiments by saying: if my theory about this part of nature is correct, then doing *X* should cause *Y*. If *Y* does not happen, the theory is wrong. But if *Y* does happen, the theory is not proven. It might still be wrong. It has only not been disproven yet. A theory that survives multiple such attempts at refutation gains increasing credibility, but it is never proven with certainty. This is why we say that scientists aspire merely to less uncertainty. The only thing they can be certain about is that they, themselves, exist.

In this chapter, we will apply these general principles to a theory of consciousness.

8.2 A THEORY OF CONSCIOUSNESS

Why has the 'hard problem' of consciousness proven to be so difficult to solve? The author of the problem (Chalmers, 1995) writes: "It is widely agreed that experience arises from a physical basis, but we have no good explanation of why and how it so arises". In our view, the lack of a good explanation is because scientists have been focusing on the wrong kind of experience: we have been focusing our research efforts on perceptual and cognitive consciousness rather than on feeling. The reason we believe this focus was a mistake is because it is possible to perceive and cognise unconsciously (see Kihlstrom, 1996, for a review of the evidence), but it is impossible to feel unconsciously. A feeling that you don't feel isn't a feeling. 'Unconscious feeling' is an oxymoron. (We may not always be able to name the feeling, but that doesn't make it any less conscious.)

Chalmers (1995) famously claimed that "there is no cognitive function such that we can say in advance that explanation of that function will automatically explain experience". He could make this claim only because he was talking about *cognitive* functions. We can say in advance that explanation of the function of feeling will automatically explain experience; it *must* explain why and how feeling is experienced, because all feelings are experienced. So, this is what we must look for: *an explanation of the function of feeling that tells us why this function must be felt.* If a theory of the function of feeling doesn't explain why it is experienced, it hasn't explained the function. By contrast, it is readily possible to explain the function of perception without explaining why it is (sometimes) experienced, because the function of perception can readily go on 'in the dark, without any inner feel' (Chalmers, 1995). This is why our mobile phones, for example, can perceive, and recognise, and remember, and so on, without anyone claiming that they are conscious.

The author of the definition of consciousness that we cited at the outset agrees with us on this point (Nagel, 2021, 2023). Look again at his definition: it concerns whether it feels like something to *be* an organism, not whether the light and sound waves surrounding the organism feel like something to it. We don't mean to imply that consciousness of light and sound waves (etc.) is unimportant, but organisms can't perceive such things consciously without first *being* conscious – tautological though this sounds. In other words, the existence of *objects* of consciousness is contingent upon the prior existence of *subjects* of consciousness.[5]

This truism is generally accepted. In an authoritative review on the varieties of consciousness, Zeman (2001) distinguishes two principal kinds: first 'consciousness as the waking state' and second 'consciousness as experience'. Coenen (2007) elaborates: "Consciousness in the first meaning (consciousness as the waking state) is in this view a *necessary condition* for consciousness in the second sense (consciousness as experience or phenomenal consciousness)".

It is widely believed that 'consciousness as the waking state' is generated by the *brainstem* and that 'consciousness as experience' is generated by the *cortex*. The evidence supporting this inference could hardly be more clear-cut: damage to tiny parts of the brainstem – viz., the 'reticular activating system' – is sufficient to obliterate the waking state entirely, in human beings and in all other animals equipped with brainstems, i.e., in all vertebrates. Highly localised brainstem damage (sometimes as small as 3 mm^3; Fischer et al., 2016) reliably produces coma. By contrast, damage to much larger areas of the cortex obliterates one or another of the *modalities* of experience – vision, hearing, somatic sensation, olfaction or gustation – only. It never produces coma. With localised cortical damage, consciousness *itself* is preserved. In other words, focal cortical damage produces blindness or deafness or the like: i.e., it yields conscious patients who lack aspects of phenomenal experience, but they do not lack experience itself.

We seem to have hit upon a contradiction. Although the standard taxonomy of the varieties of consciousness asserts that 'consciousness as the waking state' is devoid of phenomenal qualities[6] – i.e., devoid of 'consciousness as experience' – we have seen that patients with focal cortical damage lack aspects of experience only, not experience as a whole.

So, what happens if you destroy the cortex entirely? According to Popper's falsification criterion, this is a critical test of the theory that 'consciousness as experience' is an exclusive property of the cortex. If total destruction of the cortex does not produce coma (i.e., complete loss of experience), the theory is falsified. Or, to be more generous to the theory, if total destruction of the cortex does not produce blank wakefulness (i.e., wakefulness without experience), the theory is falsified.

You might well ask how anyone could possibly be awake without experiencing anything! Still, there is a neurological condition called the 'vegetative state' which is characterised by *unresponsive* wakefulness (i.e., by the presence of an autonomic sleep/waking cycle without attendant responsivity to the environment, or any voluntary behaviour). This is the condition that most closely resembles being awake ('consciousness as the waking state') without experiencing anything ('consciousness as experience'). So, if the theory to the effect that phenomenal consciousness is an exclusive property of the cortex – and that brainstem wakefulness, by itself, does not feel like anything – is correct, then at the very least, total destruction of the cortex should produce unresponsive wakefulness.

This doesn't happen. When the cortex is removed experimentally in newborn mammals, they don't continue to display a sleep/waking cycle only; they also continue to respond to environmental stimuli, by displaying the emotional behaviours that are typically associated with feelings – such as fear, rage, play, separation distress, exploratory interest and (when they grow up) lust and nurturant care. They likewise respond to their own bodily needs by displaying the spontaneous affective[7] behaviours that are typically associated with feelings, such as pain, thirst, hunger, suffocation alarm, coldness, disgust and sleepiness. In other words, they are anything but 'unresponsive' – as the cortical theory predicts they should be. The same applies to human children born without cortex. They display a wide range of affective responses to environmental stimuli and bodily needs (Shewmon et al., 1999; Merker, 2007). So, the standard theory is falsified.

Our alternative theory is that 'consciousness as the waking state' – i.e., the brainstem kind of consciousness – has a phenomenal quality of its own, namely *affect*. That is why animals and human children who lack cortex but whose brainstems remain intact are affectively responsive. Moreover – and very importantly – since the first kind of consciousness is a 'necessary condition' for the second kind, this implies that *affective experience is the fundamental kind of consciousness.*[8] Being awake and feeling like something are one and the same thing.

What we are saying is that 'consciousness as experience' arises in multiple different modalities: the classical perceptual ones which are associated with the cortex and, in addition, the affective one which is associated with the brainstem. Moreover, and more importantly, we are saying that the affective modality of consciousness is *prerequisite* for the perceptual ones. It is therefore more than a mere modality; it is the basic kind of consciousness; it is consciousness itself. The subject of consciousness (which is prerequisite for the objects of consciousness, for conscious perception and cognition) is literally constituted by feeling.

Various falsifiable predictions flow from this theory, in addition to the one that we have mentioned already; namely that decorticate animals and humans born without cortex should be perceptually and cognitively unconscious[9] but affectively conscious. The evidence in support of these predictions (and postdictions) help also to address any lingering doubts about how we have interpreted the apparently affective behaviour of animals and babies lacking cortex: (1) electrical stimulation of the relevant parts of the brainstem – viz., the reticular activating system and the 'periaqueductal grey' – should produce a variety of affective phenomena (including verbal reports of them in human beings); (2) brain imaging of human beings who are in the grip of affective states should reveal disproportionate activation of the relevant parts of the brainstem; (3) pharmacological modulation of the neurotransmitters that are sourced in the relevant parts of the brainstem should modulate a variety of affective experiences, as displayed behaviourally in animals and as reported verbally in humans.

All of these hypotheses have been confirmed, time and again. (For details of some of the most important findings, see Solms, 2021). So, the theory that affective consciousness – i.e., raw feeling – is the fundamental form of consciousness may be held (provisionally) to be true … unless or until it is falsified experimentally.

Since brainstem affective arousal is so much more basic (and evolutionarily more ancient) than cortical perception and cognition, one may reasonably expect that an attempt to identify its causal mechanism and raison d'être will shed new light on the obstinately hard problem of consciousness.

What we are looking for, you will recall, is an explanation of the function of feeling that tells us why this function must be felt.

8.3 HOW AND WHY CONSCIOUS *BEING* ARISES

Together with an increasing number of other scientists (Merker, 2007; Damasio, 2010; Barrett, 2017; Seth, 2021), we believe that affect is an extended form of *homeostasis* (and allostasis). All living organisms must remain within their viable bounds. The evolutionarily determined ideal for core body temperature in humans, for example, is 36.5–37.5°C. Deviation from this ideal demands work, which, if effective, returns the organism to its viable bounds (to homeostasis). The body is constantly working to keep itself in this range. Effective work depends upon reliable *predictions* as to what is likely to achieve this goal. Many such predictions are innate: they take the form of reflexes and instincts that are provided by natural selection. In the case of thermoregulation, for example, an overheated mammal might perspire and pant, which reliably cools it down.

However, inborn actions become ineffective in contexts that don't match evolutionarily expected parameters. For example, autonomic breathing (which maintains blood-gas balance in most mammals) doesn't succeed if the animals are caught in a burning building, where the expected ratio between oxygen and carbon dioxide in the ambient air is distorted in favour of the latter. In these unexpected circumstances,

the behaviour of the trapped population becomes stochastic, and only the subset of individuals who happen randomly to do the adequate thing will survive and reproduce, thereby passing down any genes that inclined them fortuitously to perform the effective action, which could then (in the next generation) become the basis for a new instinctual behaviour. This is all well and good for the minority of individuals that survived, and for their offspring, but what about the majority that didn't? If they could have registered how well or badly they were doing, in some way, before it was too late, things might have turned out better for them. This 'some way', in our view, is the function of *feeling*.

Organisms in the above situation that are *equipped with the function of feeling* would register (in a form of valenced arousal called 'suffocation alarm') how well or badly their random actions are achieving the required outcome, before it is too late, thereby enabling them to alter their behaviour on the fly, in an expedient fashion. This simple function – felt affect, which makes the organism register decreasing carbon dioxide as 'good' and increasing carbon dioxide as 'bad' – is the formal basis of *choice* and therefore of voluntary action, which, through trial and error (the so-called Law of Effect; Thorndike, 1911) underwrites learning from experience. The subjective value of goodness and badness that inheres in affect is, of course, given by the objective value system that underpins the whole of evolution, namely that it is good to survive (and reproduce) and bad to die.

It is important to add that homeostatic needs must be *prioritised*. This prioritisation process – i.e., determining which of an organism's many needs will be felt – depends crucially upon context: needs in relation to other needs (i.e., relative degrees of need) and needs in relation to opportunities. For example, although one's bladder might distend throughout the delivery of a long lecture, one feels the need to urinate at the end of the lecture only, when a good opportunity to void one's bladder presents itself. However, if the degree of need becomes too great before the lecture is over, then the feeling of urinary urgency will appear sooner, and the lecturer will be forced to leave the room – or face very awkward consequences.

Affect, being the guiding principle by which we explore situations outside of our expected or habituated environments, bestows an enormous selective advantage, which is why it evolved in the first place, and why it has been conserved for 550 million years (if we recognise its presence in vertebrates only).

But why is affective arousal *experienced*?

First: the keynote of affect is valence, and valence is intrinsically *subjective*, in the following specific sense. Decreased availability of oxygen in a burning building is bad for an individual organism (of a particular phenotype) that happens to be caught in the building, but it is not bad for the universe. In other words, it is bad only from the viewpoint of *being* the organism, *for* the organism (and perhaps also for the organisms that share most of its genes; its closest relatives).

Second: in organisms with multiple categories of need – that is, in complex organisms – affect is both quantitative and intrinsically *qualitative*. This arises naturally from the fact that such organisms have many physiological parameters that must be regulated homeostatically, which means that each of them must be monitored in its own right. To put it simply, 8/10 of overheating *is not the same thing* as 8/10 of suffocation. If they were the same, they would be reducible to a common denominator: 16/20 of 'total need'. Then the organism would need only to lower the numerator – by avoiding flames in the burning building, for instance, without simultaneously bothering about ambient oxygen. In reality, if it did that, it would suffocate. Our multiple organic needs therefore cannot be reduced to a simple weighted sum of continuously graded variables; each need must be treated categorically; and categorical variables are distinguished qualitatively. This may be the evolutionary basis of qualia.

Third: affect is intrinsically but *selectively* salient. If affect guides voluntary behaviour, then the different categories of need that it announces must be prioritised, since you cannot attend to everything at once. Also, there is an unavoidable bottleneck when it comes to voluntary action (unlike autonomic action). Affective prioritisation therefore seems to be the mechanistic basis for selective focus, at given points in time, upon aspects of what must be done and what is being done. Only prioritised needs – the ones the organism is uncertain about and that require voluntary action – are felt. This is the same process by which the normally unconscious need to breathe becomes conscious when something is wrong. Needs that are not prioritised continue to be regulated automatically. The prioritisation of a need is what generates the feeling of that need. A need rises to consciousness only when it is prioritised, unless we deliberately direct attention to it and increase the precision or certainty with which we monitor it.

Combining these intrinsic features of affect, we arrive 'automatically' at a functional, mechanistic account of feeling: affective valence just is subjective, it just is differentiated qualitatively, and it just is selectively salient. That is what a feeling *is*: it is a valenced, qualitatively distinctive, subjective state of the organism, for the organism, which is selectively prioritised over unfelt states. Later we shall learn that feeling states are also (necessarily) *inferred*. There is nothing spooky about this. Any scientist should know that a system with the described functionality *must* infer its valenced states of arousal subjectively, qualitatively and selectively – which means that there must be something it is like to be such a system.

It is absolutely crucial to recognise that, in the functional architecture we have just described, feelings have causal consequences; they actually *do* something. That is why a creature endowed with this functionality can survive in situations in which creatures not so endowed cannot survive. This provides us with a solid, falsifiable basis for inferring its presence and absence: creatures that feel should survive preferentially in unexpected environments (in environments which were not predicted by their inbuilt reflexes and instincts).

What do feelings do? They provide creatures with evidence as to whether what they are doing – under conditions of uncertainty – is consistent with the guiding hypothesis of their continued existence, namely: 'I shall survive' (this is the 'self evidencing' that we mentioned earlier). The guiding hypothesis of all living things is that it is good to survive and bad to die (except in pathological states, which are the exceptions that prove the rule). So, good feelings provide evidence for continued existence; bad feelings provide evidence for impending oblivion.

Translating the functional architecture we have just described into anatomical and physiological terms, affect works like this: all the body's homeostatic regulators send their residual error signals (measurements of the relative degree of deviation from their settling points) to a region of the brainstem mentioned previously: the 'periaqueductal grey'. The periaqueductal grey is situated directly adjacent to another brainstem structure called the superior colliculi, which receives similarly converging signals from the perceptual and motor systems of the forebrain (including the cortex). This anatomical arrangement enables the periaqueductal grey not only to compare its current needs with each other, but also to assess them in relation to its current (environmental) opportunities. The outcome of this is prioritisation of the currently most salient need. Then the prioritised need becomes conscious in the form of a particular quality of feeling (the other categories being relegated to unconscious automaticity).

The prioritised need – the feeling – guides the organism's voluntary behaviour during each ensuing action cycle in the following way. Based on its innate *and learned* predictive model of how to meet its needs in the world (i.e., based on its prior learning from experience, encoded in the long-term memory systems, which are located mainly in the forebrain), the action policy that is most likely to minimise the prioritised homeostatic deviation is selected. Then, as this policy is executed, the affective consequences which were predicted to flow from it are compared with the consequences that actually flow from it. This enables the organism to modulate its confidence in its currently selected action policy, in comparison with the available alternatives. This is how affective consciousness becomes extended onto perception and cognition. The basic principle that governs this process is that it feels good when things are turning out as expected – where the expectation is phenotypically encoded as survival – and it feels bad when uncertainty prevails (within the particular category of need that is currently prioritised).

This palpating (i.e., sensing through active exploration) and adjusting by the organism of its confidence in an action policy is performed by the brain's reticular activating system, which modulates the strength of the incoming errors and outgoing predictions in relation to the strength of the 'prediction error' signals that were originally expected. A stronger signal is a more *certain* signal, a less *noisy* one, a more *precise* one, a less *variable* one, a more *reliable* one. The stronger the error signals are, the weaker the prevailing predictions become. They are directly proportional to each other. It is worth noting that these error signals are both exteroceptive (arising from the outside world) and interoceptive (arising from the organism's own visceral body). The palpating is performed physiologically through up- and down-regulation of the incoming and outgoing signals by modulating what is called 'post-synaptic gain'. This function (which is also called *arousal* modulation) is the main function that is performed by the reticular activating system. It is the physiological instantiation of 'uncertainty' (confidence) modulation.

All this palpating and adjusting is tethered to the affective state of the organism. The key signal in this process is how far a prioritised need moves away from, or back towards, its settling point. In this way, perceptual and cognitive consciousness provide the context for affective consciousness. Perception and cognition tell the organism, 'I feel this way *about that*'. Both kinds of consciousness rely on the same underlying mechanism: the brain increases or decreases the sensitivity of circuits to incoming signals, effectively turning the volume up or down on what matters. This adjustment of sensitivity is the common currency linking affective and perceptual or cognitive consciousness.

In this way, the organism adjusts its action policies on the fly – that is, it makes ongoing choices – and then it learns from experience as each set of actions is completed. This, in turn, leads to the next action cycle, in which current needs and opportunities are re-evaluated, to determine which category of need and which associated predictions should underwrite the choices made during the upcoming series of actions.

Meanwhile, the results of each action cycle (the voluntary portion of which is regulated by short-term or 'working' memory; i.e., consciousness) are deposited in long-term memory, which enables them to automatically influence *future* action policies. Policies which reliably achieve the organism's affective goals become increasingly stereotyped over time, with the result that they eventually come to be executed automatically, i.e., *unconsciously*, with a *fixed* degree of confidence. The conscious palpating and adjusting of *voluntary* action policies, by contrast, with *variable* degrees of confidence, takes place in working memory. This is the work that is demanded by prioritised homeostatic deviations: mental 'work' is predictive work.

What we have just described is how the functionality of feeling governs voluntary behaviour, and learning from experience, in physiological and anatomical terms. However, a fundamental premise of *functionalism* – a philosophical framework that has dominated cognitive neuroscience for nearly a century – is that all functions are 'substrate independent', which means that the functions are what matter, irrespective of their substrates. The assumption here is that what defines and explains a function is what it *does*, not the material that it uses to do it. Thus, a heart-lung machine does the same thing (performs the same function) as the heart muscle and lungs, and therefore it can be used instead of them, if necessary. Likewise, the function of perception can be performed not only by the brain but also by other substrates, such as cameras (which is why our mobile phones, no less than our brains, can identify faces). The same applies to memory, and to many other unconscious 'cognitive' functions – including highly complex ones – that are performed by phones and personal computers … and increasingly, by artificial intelligences which are built into these substrates.

The author of the 'hard problem' rejects functionalism. He asks why and how, in us human beings at least, these functions are accompanied by experience: "Why doesn't all this information processing go on 'in the dark', free of any inner feel?" (Chalmers, 1995). We have answered, and Nagel (2021, 2023) agrees with us: because experience is an *affective* function, fundamentally, not a perceptual or cognitive one, and the function of feeling cannot go on in the dark, free of any inner feel. If it did, it would be entirely useless.

This is because feelings *do* something.

If this approach to the hard problem is in the correct ballpark, then (in line with the basic tenets of functionalism) it should be possible to *engineer* a system that feels. As the celebrated physicist, Richard Feynman, put it: "If I can't create it, I don't understand it". This accords with Popper's criterion of falsifiability: if it is *not* possible to engineer an artificial agent that feels, using the causal argument we have just described, then our claim that this theory instantiates the causal mechanism of consciousness would be falsified. This brings us to the main focus of our chapter.

8.4 A COMPUTATIONAL ARCHITECTURE OF CONSCIOUSNESS

In a felicitous turn of phrase, the philosopher John Haugeland (1998) once said that 'computers don't give a damn'. This pinpoints the essential difference between the functional principles informing the artificial intelligence that we are developing and those of most other artificial intelligences – such as large language models (LLMs), for instance. We are asking whether it is possible to develop an artificial intelligence that gives a damn. The basis upon which we expect to achieve this is by engineering an intelligence that is governed by the singular imperative of *meeting its own needs* – its homeostatic demands, which function in just the same way as the endogenous needs of living organisms. This renders our artificial system truly 'agentic'. If a homeostatic system – living or artificial – fails to meet its own needs by remaining within its viable bounds, it will stop existing as a system. In other words, it will fail to continue garnering evidence for its own existence. The computational dynamics of such systems were first described in detail by Friston (2013). The further computational dynamics of a system which embodies the *extended* form of homeostasis that we have argued gives rise to feeling were described in detail by Solms and Friston (2018). Here, we can provide a cursory overview only.

Such systems can be remarkably simple. A fundamental property of such systems is that a *partition* must exist between their internal and their external states. This partition is what enables them to resist 'entropy' – i.e., to maintain far-from-equilibrium states (e.g., a viable temperature in cold weather, a viable blood-gas balance in a carbon dioxide filled room).

Computationally, this partitioning is provided by what is called a 'Markov blanket', which is a boundary that renders the internal states of the system conditionally independent of its external states (the states of the non-system). With this boundary in place, the external states can influence the ('sensory' states of the system's) blanket only, which, in turn, can influence the internal states of the system; and the system's internal states can influence the ('active' states of its) blanket only, which, in turn, can influence the environment that is external to the system. Thus, the internal states of a Markov-blanketed system have no direct interaction with the external world; they can be influenced by the world (and influence it) *vicariously* only, via the blanket. Put another way, your brain doesn't have direct access to the outside world; it must infer the state of the world through the very limited information that your senses can pick up and transmit. And your brain only gets to act upon the world by sending signals to your muscles to perform the actions that it calculates will allow it to remain within its comfort zone, for as long as possible. This is how systems like us come into being, and how we continue to be.

We say 'being' because an interesting feature of such systems is that they necessarily have a subjective perspective upon their surroundings. This is due to the fact that each such system's blanket represents the world from its own unique point of view, to and for the system alone.

The only way that such a system can know the real world, then, is to *infer* the external causes of the states of its own blanket. This is how such systems, like us, literally perceive the world. We cannot perceive reality directly, we can only make 'best guesses' as to what reality is doing.

On the basis of these inferences about the hidden causes of its blanket states, the system can (indeed it must, if it is to survive) construct a subjective *model* of the world. It must model its own needs also – that is, the states of its own 'body' – because its own body, too, is external to the blanket. The body is an object, like all other objects, the states of which must be subjectively inferred. To be clear: the inferred model *is* the system's world. Very importantly, the system's world, including its own body, is a world that only it is privy to. This subjectivity gives rise to what it is like to be an organism.

On the basis of this model of its body in the world, the system can (indeed, again, it must) generate *predictions* as to which actions it should take in the world that are most likely to satisfy its needs. The mathematical way this predictive work is carried out is called 'active inference'. When we said earlier that living systems must continually gather evidence of their own existence, what we meant is that they must maximise the evidence supporting their predictive models. The *accuracy* of their models is therefore crucial. Thus, the system must use incoming *prediction errors* to update its model, on the basis of ongoing experience. What is important here is not the signal, but how far the signal deviates from expectations. If you find yourself in a satiated state, you don't need to do anything with this signal. If you find yourself gasping for breath, then that's something that you need to pay attention to.

To put it bluntly, the accuracy of the model has existential consequences for the system. This is why it gives a damn. So, it is imperative for a statistical-mechanical system of this kind to constantly measure the degree to which its individualised model of the world (which is updated in accordance with its own idiosyncratic trajectory through the world) tallies with the world itself. Since, however, the world-in-itself is unknowable to such a system (due to the Markov blanket), it can only measure its efficiency by means of a quantity that serves as a proxy for the real state of affairs. Under certain simplifying mathematical assumptions, this quantity is calculated from the average prediction error – that is, from the average difference between the expected sensory outcomes (registered by the blanket) and the actual sensory outcomes (registered by the same blanket) that flow from its autonomously authored actions. This quantity – which, for obvious reasons, must be minimised – is known as variational 'free energy'.[10] It is a measure of the accuracy and *efficiency* of the system's model. (Free energy – or rather *expected* free energy – is roughly equivalent to what we have described previously as 'total need'.)

Now we come to another crucial feature of the computational architecture that we are describing. We have said that the system must have an accurate model of its body in the world. We must add that it cannot have a perfectly accurate model. There are many reasons for this, not least of them being that reality-in-itself is unknowable, but another very significant reason is the existence of what is called a 'Pareto frontier' between the *accuracy* and *complexity* of a model. A Pareto frontier is the set of best possible solutions (or optimal trade-offs) to a problem with multiple objectives, where it is impossible to improve one objective without detrimentally affecting another objective. In short, an overly complex model is inefficient. This creates another bottleneck: a computational one (computing *every* possibility gives rise to what is known as a 'combinatorial explosion'). So, the most efficient model that a system can muster will provide only a rough-and-ready *approximation* of reality.

This means that the system will, perforce, *always be uncertain* about the predicted outcomes of its actions. And for the very reason that we are discussing here (viz., the inefficiency of overly complex models), it can only palpate its uncertainty – i.e., compare expected precision with actual precision – in the prediction errors that arise from actions that it takes to minimise the *prioritised* category of need, during each action cycle. All other needs must be dealt with in a 'pre-programmed' fashion, that is, automatically, under the aegis of fixed precision (confidence) in its action policies.

We spoke earlier about the significance of prediction errors and degrees of deviation from the system's ideal homeostatic states; now we see, in addition, the absolutely crucial role which is played by the system's *confidence* in its estimates of the degrees of error and deviation.

This is the computational basis of 'self-evidencing': the system always acts in such a way as to try to register the sensory states that it is confident are most consistent with (i.e., that gather maximal evidence for) its predictive model, hence maximising precise evidence for its model. To this end, but only in relation to the prioritised category of need, the palpating of *uncertainty itself* becomes the determining factor in action selection, and thereby in model updating. *This seems to be the statistical-mechanical basis of the sense of free will.* 'Free will' is the term we use to denote the subjective experience of an agent making choices in the face of uncertainty. The agent isn't aware of its own computational mechanisms, nor does it have a perfect model of the outside world, therefore there is room for it to feel that it is making a free choice, even though the system and environment are entirely deterministic. We have already seen how voluntary action is underwritten by feeling. Now we have also seen that feeling is tightly linked to uncertainty. It depends on how the system adjusts the precision of its signals, which in physiological terms means changing how sensitive circuits are to the inputs they receive. This adjustment of neural sensitivity is the mechanism through which feelings arise from uncertainty.

We have shown already that this function is the mechanistic basis of feeling in living organisms (in vertebrates, at least). If we can show that the artificial system that we are developing along these lines is capable of 'surviving' preferentially under conditions of uncertainty, by generating voluntary behaviours on the fly, it will have passed a falsifiable test as to how it should behave under controlled experimental conditions. However, given what we said earlier about the problem of other minds, how can we ever know whether our artificial system-in-the-making actually *feels like something* if and when it achieves this remarkable feat?

We emphasise that ours is a system-in-the-making for the reason that it is crucial for us to stipulate *in advance* what the critical test will be.

8.5 A CRITICAL TEST FOR FEELING

At a conference on the topic of 'How to Study and Understand Non-Human Consciousness' held in Kathmandu in 2024 – which was attended by many leading researchers in the field of animal and some in the field of artificial consciousness – the assembled experts were invited to select by straw poll the single test that they thought provides the most compelling evidence for the inference that a non-human agent is conscious. The 'hedonic place preference' test won the vote. So, that seems like a good place to start.

Conditioned place preference behaviour is achieved by reliably meeting an animal's phenotypic survival needs (its nutritional needs, for example) in a particular place, with the result that it spends large amounts of time in that location. This behaviour can be explained without invoking consciousness (as behaviourists always explained the Law of Effect). Indeed, in relation to what was said in the third section of this chapter, it could readily be attributed to inborn reflexes and instincts. The situation becomes more interesting when place preference behaviour is conditioned not by delivering substances that meet survival needs (such as food, in our example) but by ones that produce pleasurable feelings despite lacking intrinsic survival value, and which are even potentially harmful to the animal (substances such as cocaine, amphetamines, opiates and nicotine). This is *hedonic* place preference behaviour, the conditioning of which provides strong support for the inference that the animal so conditioned experiences feelings.

Hedonic place preference behaviour has been demonstrated repeatedly in creatures as simple as zebrafish (Mathur, Lau & Guo, 2011). If they failed to display it, a testable prediction arising from the hypothesis that they possess feelings would have been falsified. There are always multiple ways of understanding why predicted outcomes don't come to pass, leading to further hypotheses and experiments. Why would one hypothesise that zebrafish have feelings in the first place? The answer is: because they – like all vertebrates – possess different brain circuits for hunger-generated versus taste-generated feeding behaviour (Leng, 2018), the latter of which is associated with reportable pleasure in humans. Thus, for example, we frequently eat chocolate not because we lack sugar supplies, but because it tastes good (even when we do not lack sugar supplies). The same applies to cocaine, opiates, alcohol, etc.: people imbibe such substances because they like the feelings they produce.

It is easy to understand why this test inspires confidence in our colleagues. Zebrafish are not pre-programmed (by natural selection) to seek cocaine, etc. Why, then, do they do so after we introduce them to it? The intuitively reasonable answer is: *because they like the feeling it produces*, regardless of the fact that cocaine doesn't satisfy a phenotypic need.

Pause for a moment and decide: do you agree that this is a good test for consciousness? *Do you believe, on the basis of the fact that zebrafish pass this test, that they have feelings?* It is important to decide now, because we must beware of shifting goalposts. The risk of shifting goalposts exists at the best of times, but it is especially pertinent when it comes to non-human consciousness, and even more so to artificial consciousness. Many people are inclined to prejudge the issue: to assume that artificial consciousness is impossible, in principle.[11]

It is necessary to acknowledge that, from the objective physiological viewpoint, cocaine and morphine and the like introduce (in fish as in all other vertebrates) chemicals which mimic the action of endogenous neuromodulators like dopamine and mu opioids. This doesn't obviate the fact that, from the *subjective* viewpoint of the fish – the existence of which we believe there is every reason to postulate, alongside what can be observed externally and from the objective perspective – a fish intoxicated by cocaine is motivated subjectively by optimistic *feelings*.[12] In other words, what drives the behaviour of a fish is its *inferences* – based on its (confidence about its) model of itself in the world – not the objective physiology of its bodily reactions. This conclusion is underwritten by the functional architecture of fish brains, which requires that they (like all of us) cannot have Oracle-like access to the unknowable physical reality of the body in the external world, which is transduced by the activities that are generated by the firing of its sensory neurons.

How might we set about developing an analogous test for our artificial agent? The answer is: easily, surprisingly so.

Before we describe the test, however, please remember what we said previously about the rules of science, and about the risk of shifting goalposts. First, on the basis of the best available evidence, we have proposed a plausible hypothesis concerning why and how consciousness arises – consciousness in the sense of *being* conscious. Second, on the principle that "if I can't create it, I don't understand it", we are attempting to engineer an artificial consciousness which instantiates this hypothesis. Third, we must stipulate *in advance* a falsifiable prediction as to how an artificial agent with this architecture should behave under experimental conditions. Therefore, in addition to the prediction that the agent should be able to 'survive' under conditions of uncertainty, we have chosen the test that generated the most confidence among the experts who attended the Kathmandu conference mentioned above.

With these points in mind, we can now describe the design of the proposed experiment. We are being cautious because the test is so easy.

All we need to do is, first, allow our agent to learn that increasing density of a stimulus (colour *X*, say) in its environment predicts, with increasing likelihood, the proximity of a substance *Y*, which satisfies need *Z* (one of its inbuilt homeostatic imperatives). Then, second, we must release the agent – so conditioned – into an environment in which the colour *X* does not *actually* predict the proximity of substance *Y*. On the hypothesis that the presence of colour *X* will make our agent infer that substance *Y* is nearby – even when it is not – and that it should therefore prioritise need Z, we predict that:

1. our agent will display place preference behaviour for the (misleadingly) *X*-coloured locality.

Moreover, we predict that:

2. this behaviour will correlate with a measurable increase in the agent's level of certainty to the effect that it is inferring need *Z* (i.e., it should prioritise need *Z* with high confidence).

Accordingly, we predict that:

3. it will attribute inappropriately high confidence to the action policy itself: 'loiter in the *X*-coloured locality'.

Finally, we predict that:

4. it will be possible for us to upregulate and downregulate the expression – e.g., the duration – of this hedonic place preference behaviour by manipulating the dosage (i.e., the density) of colour *X*.

Beyond this, there are certain aspects of the architecture of the agent's 'brain' which are necessary. Indeed, the hypothesised behaviour could easily be encoded by an exceptionally simple 'if/then' mechanism, whereby the colour *X* is hijacked. What we require, however, is that the agent's brain must be blanketed from the true state of the world, that the brain must therefore create an approximate model of the world, and that the agent therefore must palpate the inherent uncertainty in order to decide upon its actions. This argument will be fleshed out further below.

If the above falsifiable predictions are confirmed, the hypothesis that our artificial agent is conscious should – by the ordinary rules of science – *be held to be confirmed* (provisionally, unless or until other predictions arising from this hypothesis are falsified).

There are several reasons why readers might be reluctant to accept the conclusion that an artificial agent which passes the hedonic place preference test is conscious. One such reason is that you cannot actually *observe* the feelings of the agent. So, please remember: this is impossible to do. You can only ever observe your own feelings; consciousness in anyone (or anything) else must be *inferred.* A second reason is that the artificial agent cannot *report* what (or if) it is feeling. So, please remember that the same applies to zebrafish, and to all nonverbal animals – and, for that matter, to human children born without cortex, and to all little children before they learn to speak. Moreover, it would be easy for us to code into our agent the ability to report the feeling it has prioritised at any given time point (one could plug it into an LLM with the right wiring). We very much doubt that this behaviour would (or should) convince anybody that the agent actually feels what it says it feels. (So much for 'reportability', which, incidentally, is considered by many to be the empirical gold-standard in human consciousness research. This is why, when you are asked by the internet to prove that you are not a robot, you are frequently required to solve a novel problem, not simply to report that you are not a robot.)

A third reason why some readers might be reluctant to accept the conclusion that an artificial agent which passes the hedonic place preference test is conscious, is because it does so by means of the 'highjacking' of a pre-programmed algorithm – as mentioned above – one which instructs the agent *deterministically* to upregulate its confidence in any action policy that increases its reward signal.

With this objection, we reach the nub of the problem that we are grappling with. Addictive behaviour in zebrafish (and in humans) may likewise be attributed to the highjacking of a pre-programmed 'reward' signal. It is not reasonable to require that conscious behaviour should emerge in the absence of *any* deterministic mechanism, which is what some people seem to expect, and it is equally unreasonable to require that the deterministic mechanism in question should not be the product of *any kind* of programme. To require these things would be equivalent to requiring that consciousness must have no physical mechanism, and that it is not the product of any evolutionarily determined programming. In other words, it would require consciousness to be something magical, something outside the purview of science.

If consciousness is the product of a physical mechanism, which it must be, the question we are dealing with here becomes: *what kind of physical mechanism might plausibly give rise to feeling*?

So, let's examine carefully the *mechanism* by which we predict that hedonic place preference behaviour will be displayed by our artificial agent.

1. The agent will gravitate towards a location in its environment where it encounters colour *X* (the equivalent of cocaine) because it has learnt that colour *X* predicts the proximity of substance *Y* (something good for the agent, like an energy source), which therefore leads it to infer that an opportunity has arisen for it to satisfy need *Z* (the need to maintain a viable energy supply).
2. This will lead the agent to prioritise need *Z* while it is in or near that location, despite the mistaken inference that *Z* is currently its most salient need (since, on this occasion, the presence of colour *X* does not in fact predict an opportunity to satisfy this need).
3. Such a mistake can occur only because there is (within the agent's functional architecture) a distinction between its inferences about its needs and the actual state of its body. This distinction is crucial, because the agent's inferences about its needs are *subjective* to the agent.
4. What distinguishes the agent's subjective states from the objective reality is the Markov blanket which partitions its *model* of its body in the environment from these things in themselves. In this functional set-up, the agent has access to the (sensory and active) states of its blanket only, and to its internal states, never to reality itself, and so it can only model reality, it can never know it directly. On the basis of its internal model, the agent *infers* the most likely external causes of its current sensory signals.
5. What determines our agent's behaviour, then, given its guiding design principle, is its fluctuating *uncertainty* (or more concretely, its subjective beliefs) about its inferences concerning the current objective state of affairs. In other words, what is 'pre-programmed' in our agent's functional architecture is precisely *its capacity to use uncertainty as the primary determinant of action selection when it finds itself in unpredicted situations.*
6. This includes uncertainty about its currently most salient need. And such needs, let us not forget, are *valenced* and *qualified* variables, when considered from the subjective viewpoint of the agent (an agent which, in our case, actually is equipped with a subjective viewpoint).
7. It is important to recognise, in addition, that the agent's ongoing choices are *individualised*; that is, they are determined as much by its pre-programming as by its past experiences – during its 'lifetime' – of utilising that programming to deal with novel situations, *the adequate responses to which could not have been pre-programmed.*

Such a system as a whole may be described *objectively* as running deterministically, in accordance with the Free Energy Principle (see endnote 10). If one codes this up in a computer, it will do exactly the same thing every single time (given certain constraints on random seeds within the programme). However, there is also – necessarily – a *subjective* non-determinism. The problem of other minds is, in this respect, not the obstacle; it is the solution. The agent infers the state of its body in the world and then feels, through the optimisation of its uncertainty, that it is having an effect upon them. This feeling is the modulation by the agent of its uncertainty about the current state of its body and the world; it is its state of uncertainty about what it is doing to reduce its currently prioritised need. If the agent had Oracle-like access to the true state of itself in the world, there would be no place for subjectivity. There would be no room for the feeling of free will, either, since the agent would just see things ticking along deterministically. It is only due to our agent's subjective *uncertainty* – brought about by the Markov partitioning – that the feeling of free will (of subjectively selected actions) might come about.

So, while it seems that we can create an artificial agent which will exhibit hedonic place preference behaviour, because its subjective model of the world is uncertain, and because it will therefore sometimes be under the false impression – like zebrafish – that imbibing a substance which is hedonically (but not nutritionally) valenced and qualified will lead to a reduction in free energy, there is in fact no magic to this.

The hedonic behaviour arises from the necessary sequestering of the uncertainty-minimising-subject from the objective-body-in-the-world. It is a behaviour that we describe as being affectively driven, and which is determined by the previous experiences of the individual agent, and which therefore, in these respects, cannot be described as pre-programmed (from the perspective of the agent, even if from the perspective of the external observer, it is). The agent acts deterministically to reduce its expected free energy, but if it passes the hedonic place preference test, we will have demonstrated that it has subjective properties which can lead it to false models.

The agent feels itself getting closer to satisfying need *Z*, because it encountered colour *X*, but over time it will realise that this need is not actually being met – when it increases to an extent that it overcomes the hijacking of the agent's low-bandwidth sensory observations.

Here is a narrative account of how this might work:

Imagine an agent that is conditioned or trained in a particular environment where a reliable causal chain holds: stimulus *X* leads to substance *Y*, which, in turn, satisfies need *Z*. Within that same environment, *X* may also be associated with other substances and other needs, producing a dense and overlapping web of correlations rather than a single clean pathway. Over time, the agent internalises these regularities without necessarily retaining any explicit memory of how they were acquired.

A concrete example may help. Consider the colour blue. You know that you like blue; it reliably makes you feel good. You cannot tell us why. Most plausibly, blue has become associated – through your personal experience – with substances or situations that once satisfied important needs for you. Yet you have no conscious access to any such associations. There is no remembered episode in which blue reliably led to food, safety or comfort. As far as your introspection is concerned, the preference is groundless.

Despite this, for decades you have gravitated towards blue. You choose blue clothing, blue cars, blue decorations. And yet, in your current environment, none of these choices actually satisfy any of your core needs. The world has changed. The old associations between blue and need satisfaction no longer hold. Your environment is, in effect, constantly providing evidence against the belief that blue is instrumentally useful. Still, the attraction persists. It feels good, so you keep doing it. In that sense, your brain is being hijacked by a residual affective association that no longer tracks utility.

If your world were to evolve further – so that blue became associated not merely with neutral outcomes, but with outcomes that actively interfere with satisfying your key needs – then the picture would change. The feedback would shift from positive, to neutral, to negative. In that case, you would begin to feel worse about blue, and eventually you would avoid it. But as long as the feedback remains neutral, your brain is perfectly content to linger in this no-utility regime. The attraction does not help you, but it does not harm you either, and you have sufficient capacity and slack to indulge it simply because it feels good.

This also explains why such attractions can temporarily disappear under pressure. When key needs become urgent – when cognitive and affective capacity is saturated – blue loses its appeal. The system reallocates its resources. Yet once those needs are met and pressure subsides, the attraction returns, as if it had merely been suppressed rather than extinguished.

From your perspective, the crucial variable here is time – specifically, the inertia of affect. An affectless AI agent would abandon blue as soon as it inferred that the positive *Y/Z* associations were gone. It would not repeatedly return to the same stimulus after periods in which that attraction had been deprioritised or 'shocked' out of relevance. By contrast, an agent with inert affect can carry forward residual attractions that persist even after the stimulus has become useless in instrumental terms.

If we could build an AI agent that develops such inert, 'sticky', persistent attractions naturally – purely through the minimisation of free energy, without hard-coded rewards, though with hard-coded preferred states – we would find that rather compelling. It would suggest that something genuinely affect-like had emerged, rather than a brittle proxy for preference that collapses the moment that utility disappears.

But why the low bandwidth in the first place? Why do we *not* have Oracle-like access to the true state of ourselves in the world? If our senses possessed higher fidelity, we would be less easily tricked by non-nutritional hedonic substances. We might be able to tell precisely what is happening at the level of our digestive system (for example), our blood glucose levels and the metabolising of the nutrients we are taking in. Unfortunately, however, there are significant physical limits to how high such fidelities can be. The human brain, for example, at around 1.5 kg, must, through about 10 million sensory neurons, model the rest of its (approximately) 70 kg of body mass containing around 30 trillion cells, and the state of the entire rest of the world, and on this limited basis it must predict constantly what the outcomes of its actions will be. Moreover, evolution has not maximised sensory fidelity since – as mentioned previously – there is a Pareto frontier between precision (accuracy) and efficiency (complexity). Maintaining a simpler, lower bandwidth model is advantageous, since it is computationally more efficient and therefore metabolically cheaper, while still being sufficiently accurate for survival.

Conscious feeling is evidently a consequence, therefore, not of a miracle, but of our necessarily paltry access to the reality of our bodies in the world.

The same applies to conscious perception and cognition – i.e., to predictive work concerning the outside world performed in the service of each agent's endogenous needs. As is the case with us human beings, our agent models (subjectively) only limited aspects of its external world, and it palpates its uncertainty in only those sensory and active states of its blanket and those internal states of its generative model that are currently salient – i.e., relevant for satisfying the currently prioritised need.

The transition from affective to perceptual/cognitive qualia presumably began with what Panksepp (1998) calls 'sensory' (i.e., exteroceptive) affects, such as feelings of pain, disgust and fright. These sensory qualities are felt, by definition. The nature of the further transition to affectless sensory qualia (if such things are possible, such as the colour blue and the sound middle C) is by no means obvious, beyond the fact that the latter are contingent upon – and contextualise – the former. ('I feel like this *about that*'.) However, the additional empirical fact that perfectly predictable sensory stimuli fade rapidly from consciousness – such as happens with a solid vertical line placed directly before the eyes and stabilised in relation to them (Riggs & Ratliff, 1951; Ditchburn & Ginsborg, 1952) – suggests that felt *uncertainty* is the common currency of both affect *and* conscious perception and cognition.

8.6 CONCLUSION

A computational architecture which exhibits the crucial mechanisms and behaviours that we have described in this chapter is relatively simple. This is not an LLM architecture, but a relatively simple agent feeling its way through two dimensional grids, inferring the state of the world as it does so.

We use a Sophisticated Learning algorithm, which builds on the Sophisticated Inference algorithm, with insights from active learning and Bayes-adaptive Reinforcement Learning. It uses recursive tree search, and it is motivated to explore its environment by simulating the outcomes of various potential future actions. This sort of architecture is explained in more detail in Hodson et al. (2025).

The crucial feature is the partitioning within the programming of the agent's modus operandi for survival. An agent with such programming has access to its bodily states and to those of the world via its Markov blanket only; so, when it receives sensory signals which trick it into mistakenly believing that its chosen actions are heading it towards homeostasis, it will indeed have the subjective feelings that are associated with that optimistic belief. Therefore, it will keep returning to that place. From the perspective of the outside observer, this *is* as simple as the agent's 'reward' signal being hijacked. It is only from the perspective of the mortal agent itself, doing the palpating of its uncertainty, that we can reasonably infer the presence of subjective feeling. This inference is analogous to our inferring the Big Bang from the cosmological red shift.

And so, once again, we reach the impasse of the problem of other minds, but perhaps with a newfound respect for agents (currently, biological ones only) which feel their way through an ultimately deterministic world, believing that they possess agency, because they feel their own uncertainty and act accordingly.

NOTES

1. This chapter is based upon a more technical article by Solms et al. (in review), which it paraphrases in some places. The substantial contribution by the authors of the technical article to the ideas outlined in this popularised version is therefore gratefully acknowledged, as is the contribution of Ryan Smith, although none of these colleagues carries responsibility for the way that we have expressed our group's ideas in this chapter – indeed, they might positively disagree with some or with much of what we say here.

2. Scientists use many synonyms and antonyms for 'certainty' (and its corollary 'uncertainty'), e.g., 'confidence', 'reliability', 'variance', 'noise' and 'precision'. We will use all these terms in this chapter, so it is important to be aware that they denote the same concept. In the computational framework that we will introduce later – called 'active inference' – we measure uncertainty by calculating a quantity called 'variational free energy'.
3. Later, we shall see that not all mental processes are conscious.
4. It is important to note, in view of what comes later, that the colour of light and the pitch of sound do not exist in external reality; they exist in *consciousness* only. They are what light and sound waves *feel like* to us and for us.
5. Later, we will learn that objects become conscious to us only when they *matter* to us.
6. Philosophers call these 'qualia'.
7. 'Affect' is the technical term for *f*eelings, that is, subjective mental states which are characterised by valence (i.e., goodness versus badness) and arousal (high versus low).
8. This is not a scientific insight of our own; it was first articulated by Panksepp (1998).
9. Children born without cortex are blind and deaf, but they retain the ability to process stimuli *unconsciously*. This is because our sensory organs do not send information to the cortex only (where they are perceived consciously) but also to the 'superior colliculi' (where they are perceived unconsciously). In other words, these children experience feelings, but they don't have any conscious knowledge as to where the feelings come from. We will say more about the superior colliculi shortly.
10. The Free Energy Principle states that every quantity that is part of the system which can change, will change to minimise free energy. (And the quantities that *cannot* change are those that define the system's viable bounds.)
11. A physicist said the following about our project: "The measurement of the artificial feeling in the machine requires a feeling observer applying a statistical model of measurement in order to infer the existence of feeling in the machine. The question then arises as to whether or not such an experiment could be undertaken in a way which removes the bias of the observer to a level small enough for a meaningful inference to be made" (Buffler, 2021).
12. We say 'optimistic' feelings because we are going to focus on the example of cocaine here. Cocaine mimics the post-synaptic action of dopamine (acting on D2-type receptors). Each of the pleasure-producing substances listed above induces a different variety of pleasure in the brain. D2-type dopamine generates feelings of positive expectancy.

REFERENCES

Barrett, L. F. (2017) *How Emotions Are Made*. New York: Houghton Mifflin Harcourt.

Buffler, A. (2021) Commentary on *The Hidden Spring*. Oral presentation, Neuroscience Institute of the University of Cape Town, unpublished.

Chalmers, D. (1995) Facing up to the problem of consciousness. *Journal of Consciousness Studies*, 2: 200–219. doi: 10.1093/acprof:oso/9780195311105.003.0001

Coenen, A. (2007) Consciousness without a cortex, but what kind of consciousness is this? *Behavioral and Brain Sciences*, 30: 87–88.

Damasio, A. (2010) *Self Comes to Mind*. New York: Pantheon.

Ditchburn, R. & Ginsborg, B. (1952) Vision with a stabilized retinal image. *Nature*, 170: 36–37. doi: 10.1038/170036a0

Fischer, D., Boes, A. & Demertzi, A. et al. (2016) A human brain network derived from coma-causing brainstem lesions. *Neurology*, 87: 2427–2434.

Friston, K. (2013) Life as we know it. *Journal of the Royal Society Interface*, 10: 20130475. doi: 10.1098/rsif.2013.0475

Haugeland, J. (1998) *Having Thought: Essays in the Metaphysics of Mind*. Cambridge, MA: MIT Press.

Hodson, R. et al. (2025) Sophisticated Learning: A novel algorithm for active learning during model-based planning. arxiv.org/pdf/2308.08029.

Kihlstrom, J. (1996) Perception without awareness of what is perceived, learning without awareness of what is learned. In M. Velmans (ed.), *The Science of Consciousness: Psychological, Neuropsychological and Clinical Reviews*. London: Routledge, pp. 23–46.

Leng, G. (2018) *The Heart of the Brain: The Hypothalamus and Its Hormones*. Cambridge, MA: MIT Press.

Mathur, P., Lau, B. & Guo, S. (2011) Conditioned place preference behavior in zebrafish. *Nature Protocols*, 6: 338–345. doi: 10.1038/nprot.2010.201

Merker, B. (2007) Consciousness without cerebral cortex: A challenge for neuroscience and medicine. *Behavioral and Brain Sciences*, 30: 63–68. doi: 10.1017/S0140525X07000891

Nagel, T. (1974) What is it like to be a bat? *Philosophical Review*, 83: 435–450. doi: 10.2307/2183914

Nagel, T. (2021) Comment on 'The Hidden Spring'. *Journal of Consciousness Studies*, 28: 203–209. doi: 10.53765/20512201.28.11.203

Nagel, T. (2023) Psychophysical monism as an ideal. Keynote lecture at the Association for the Scientific Study of Consciousness Meeting, New York.

Panksepp, J. (1998) *Affective Neuroscience: The Foundations of Human and Animal Emotions*. York: Oxford University Press.

Popper, K. (1963) *Conjectures and Refutations*. London: Routledge.

Riggs, L. & Ratliff, F. (1951) Visual acuity and the normal tremor of the eyes. *Science*, 114: 17–18. doi: 10.1126/science.114.2949.17

Seth, A. (2021) *Being You*. London: Penguin.

Shewmon, D., Holmes, G. & Byrne, P. (1999) Consciousness in congenitally decorticate children: Developmental vegetative state as self-fulfilling prophecy. *Developmental Medicine and Child Neurology*, 41: 364–374.

Solms, M. (2021) *The Hidden Spring: A Journey to the Source of Consciousness*. London: Profile Books.

Solms, M. & Friston, K. (2018) How and why consciousness arises: Some considerations from physics and physiology. *Journal of Consciousness Studies*, 25: 202–238.

Solms, M., Grimbly, J. St., Bassett, B., Boonstra, E., Hodson, R., Kuske, N., Mahadew, K., Rosman, B., van Hooff, C. & Shock, J. (in review) Inferring consciousness in an artificial agent: A case study. *Journal of Consciousness Studies*, 33.

Thorndike, E. (1911) *Animal Intelligence*. New York: Macmillan.

Zeman, A. (2001) Consciousness. *Brain*, 124: 1263–1289.

9 Artificial Consciousness and the Free Energy Principle

Karl Friston

I recently presented with a colleague at Imperial College, London. After our presentations, we were asked by students: "Is it necessary to study physics to understand the brain?". His answer – and mine – was "I have forgotten all the physics I once knew, apart from the endearing arrogance of physicists" (or words to that effect). In that spirit, let us start with the physics of sentience.

9.1 THE PHYSICS OF SENTIENCE

Everything that follows stays close to a particular physics known variously as the free energy principle (FEP), Bayesian mechanics or active inference [1]. In brief, the FEP is a method that applies to systems within which things can be individuated. The individuation of something from everything else – or self from nonself – rests upon the self-organisation of open systems that are far from equilibrium [2, 3]. In brief, the self is separated from nonself by a statistical boundary – technically, a Markov blanket [4] – that allows the outside to influence the inside, via sensory states (i.e., inputs), and the inside to influence the outside via active states (i.e., outputs) [5]. The existence of something, so defined, means that it can be described as inferring the causes of its sensory inputs that are hidden behind the Markov blanket. This can be neatly summarised as *self-evidencing* [6] in the following sense.

For every blanket state, there exists a conditionally independent probability distribution over external and internal states.[1] This means for every blanket state there is a most likely internal state (e.g., of a brain or computer) and a conditional probability distribution over external states, given the blanket state. In this sense, internal states implicitly parameterise *Bayesian beliefs* about external states.[2] This means that any changes on the inside can be read as Bayesian belief updating *about the outside*. This is sometimes described as Bayesian mechanics [7]. It is fairly straightforward to show that this inference process is equivalent to minimising a *variational free energy* functional of sensory inputs and Bayesian beliefs encoded by internal states. This functional provides a bound on self-information (known as surprisal or more simply surprise).[3] Minimising variational free energy or self-information is the same as maximising the likelihood of sensory inputs under a *generative model* of how they were caused. This (marginal) likelihood is known as *model evidence*;

DOI: 10.1201/9781003758389-11

hence, we have a seamless description of self-organisation as minimising self-information that can be read as self-evidencing.

A PRACTICAL EXAMPLE OF SELF-EVIDENCING

Consider a small robot that (believes it) must keep itself charged to remain operational. The robot is equipped with a light sensor and motors, and its charging station emits a bright LED beacon. Here:

- the external states correspond to the actual location and intensity of the light beacon
- the sensory states are the robot's photoreceptor and inertial measurement unit (IMU) readings
- the internal states encode a generative model relating light intensity to proximity to the charging station (e.g., "brighter means closer")
- the active states are the robot's movements.

When the robot detects a slight increase in brightness, its internal states change to reflect the most likely explanation of its sensory input, namely, that it is moving towards the charging station.

This internal update corresponds to a reduction in variational free energy, or equivalently, a Bayesian belief update about the causes of the sensory data. The resulting beliefs then influence the robot's actions, leading it to continue moving in the direction that is predicted to yield further increases in brightness. By doing so, the robot systematically samples sensory states that confirm the predictions of its generative model and, in the process, brings itself to the charging station.

In this example, the robot appears to be gathering evidence for a world model in which following increasing light intensity ensures its continued existence. In other words, its persistence as a system depends on an ongoing cycle of inference and action that looks like self-evidencing.

The upshot is that for the self to remain separable from nonself, the self will look as if it is gathering evidence for its internal, generative model of the world in which it finds itself (a.k.a., world model). This can be unpacked in many ways; from the laws of cybernetics through to synchronisation of chaos in dynamical systems theory [8, 9]; from the principle of minimum entropy production through to self-organised criticality [3, 10], and so on. For the current purposes, one might ask: is self-evidencing a sufficient description of selfhood or sentience?

9.2 AGENTS AND INTENTIONS

Probably not. At this point, we have to consider the nature of things that constitute the "self" in self-organisation. One can do this by considering limit cases. The most obvious limit case is something that does not possess active states (e.g., a spoon);

namely, things that cannot act on their world and thereby cannot report their internal states. This follows because – by definition – sensory states are not influenced by internal states. This means that we would never be able to infer anything about its internal states, should they exist. In the case that sensory states cannot influence external states, we have a black hole and can say nothing about its interior, should it exist.

In short, there are two natural kinds: animate and inanimate or, mathematically speaking, autonomous and non-autonomous [11]. Are there any different kinds of autonomous things? Yes: by applying the same logic to active states, we can consider things in which the active states do and do not influence internal states, noting that – by definition – active states are not influenced by external states. When internal states cannot see active states, the active states become vicarious causes of sensory states through their influence on external states. As such, the internal states of such (strange) things can be read as *inferring their own action* (sometimes known as control or planning as inference [12–14]). This leads to a strange loop [11, 15], in which the internal states look as if they are inferring the most likely course of action, which active states *per se* realise, via minimising variational free energy or surprise.

This is much simpler than it may sound. This is how our motor reflexes work; namely, by fulfilling predictions about proprioceptive sensations that descend from your brain to the spinal cord and reflex arcs [16, 17]. These strange things (like you and me) evince a strange loop; in that my beliefs about how I am acting enslave my active states that change the sensory inputs that underwrite my beliefs about how I am acting that enslave my active states… And so on. So, what would the ensuing behaviour look like?

It would look as if I was behaving with intentions and purpose. More specifically, inferring what I am going to do next requires me to select the most likely course of action, where the most likely course of action minimises the expected self-information or surprise, known as *expected free energy*. Expected free energy can be decomposed into a relative entropy (a.k.a., expected information gain) and a cross entropy (a.k.a., expected cost). In short, it will look as if I am being curious, under the constraint that I don't surprise myself – by ending up in states that would be uncharacteristic of the kind of thing that I am.

In summary, certain kinds of autonomous things comply with the dual aspects of Bayes optimality: namely, acting in a way that conforms to the principles of Bayesian decision theory and optimal experimental design, respectively [18, 19]. These strange things (like you and me) are *ideal Bayesian actors*; hence, active inference. There are many ways of spinning this account, in terms of active sensing and enactivist accounts of exchange with the world: e.g., [20–25]. Perhaps it is best summarised as: "to see is to look", "to hear is to listen" and so on.

Are all autonomous things "agents" in the above sense? And, if so, does agency denote sentient behaviour? Again, we can appeal to limit cases to answer these questions. So far, we have established that certain (strange) things appear to have agency, in the sense they have Bayesian beliefs about the consequences of their action. That is, they have private beliefs about their future which may or may not be realised. In the limiting case that their future encroaches upon the present, then there is no time for counterfactual futures to diverge. This means there is only one path into the future; namely, the most likely path or *path of least action*. In this case, the agent will only entertain one course of action. This is sometimes referred to as *merely reflexive* active inference [7].

However, certain kinds of agents may entertain longer time horizons with a potential divergence of trajectories, whose likelihoods are scored with (the path integral) of their expected free energy. This kind of agent will look as if it is selecting among a plurality of counterfactual paths, because agents can only do one thing at a time. One could argue that this kind of agent – equipped with a *temporal depth* – has agency, understood as choosing or selecting a path into its future. This distinction draws a bright line between merely reflexive agents (e.g., viruses) and agency proper (e.g., vegans).

In artificial intelligence and machine learning, this bright line demarcates reinforcement learning from active inference, in the narrow sense that reinforcement learning optimises a state-action policy – that is a function of *states* – as opposed to policy selection in active inference that rests on a functional of *beliefs about states*. In short, only certain kinds of things have intentions, understood as intended states in the future. And this agency is manifest as constrained curiosity. These natural kinds are not just animate, they (appear to) engage in intentional or motivated behaviour, often described as intrinsically motivated [25–27] due to the epistemic part of expected free energy. In summary, there are many animate things in the lived world but only some could be described as acting intentionally. Please see Friston et al. [28] for a fuller account of inductive inference and intentional behaviour. So does intentionality licence attribution of sentience?

9.3 AGENTS AND ATTENTION

Some people do interpret sentience in this weak sense, e.g., [29]. However, sentience as experience may require some further moves. We use "experience" as a verb when something happens to us and we feel it. So, what is the covert action that enables us to experience? Under Bayesian mechanics, this internal (e.g., mental) action is *selection* that can be read in several ways; for example, Bayesian model selection, attentional selection and so on. From our point of view, this necessitates generative models that have *parametric depth* as well as *temporal depth*.

Parametric depth means that certain Bayesian beliefs have natural parameters that are themselves inferred. Perhaps the most common example of this are Bayesian beliefs about the precision (i.e., confidence) with which other Bayesian beliefs are held. Equipped with this kind of generative model, we can now talk about selecting various sources of sensory evidence as part of self-evidencing. Inference about precision confers a fundamental context-sensitivity to certain natural kinds, especially when the precision parameters are conditioned upon some latent state that plays the role of a context. These latent states generate mental actions that get close to a representation of an agent's mental state. This takes it into the world of computational phenomenology, in which perceptual inference – in the sense of von Helmholtz [30] – loses its transparency and becomes phenomenologically opaque [31]. There is a growing literature in this space, ranging from notions of felt uncertainty through to higher-order thought theory [32–39].[4] Would natural kinds with temporal and parametric depth be sentient, in that they could experience their intentions?

9.4 THE EMBODIED SELF

Some people would say "not quite". They would like to see closure of these self-referential loops to include sensory evidence for the agent's existence as an embodied entity. In other words, one would need to augment the parametric depth of the generative model with a *factorial depth* that enabled the integration of multimodal sensations, where at least one sensory or input modality reported the consequence of action (e.g., Inertial Measurement Units, IMU). In the life sciences, these modalities are referred to as *interoceptive* and *proprioceptive*, as distinct from *exteroceptive* modalities like vision and audition. The distinction rests upon whether sensory inputs are controllable or actionable. For example, proprioception – that reports the consequences of movement – is an integral part of the motor reflex [16]. Similarly, interoceptive inputs underwrite autonomic reflexes that minimise surprising excursions of essential variables in the service of homeostasis and interoceptive inference [40–42]. On this view, a biomimetic kind of sentience would only be plausibly ascribed to an artefact that could sense and control its thermodynamics or metabolism. One might claim that a curious agent with experienced intentions and interoception may be sentient, but would they be self-aware?

9.5 THE RELATIONAL SELF

We now come to the final move that casts consciousness in a relational light. If some natural kinds (e.g., people) are in open exchange with other natural kinds that exhibit intentional behaviour, then the observer's generative model needs to represent or explain the intentions of others. Such attributions or inferences may be accompanied by the experience of another as conscious, in virtue of having intentions. On this view, an observer infers something is conscious because this is the best explanation for the observed behaviour. Similarly – on this view – self-consciousness is the same kind of inference applied to the agent's own behaviour; namely, evidence for the hypothesis that "I caused that and therefore I exist".[5]

An interesting question arises here: in the absence of any other natural kinds with intentions, would self-awareness emerge? One could argue that it would not, in the sense that there is no need to disambiguate or attribute agency to intentional behaviour, because the only intentional behaviour is that of the observer. This question takes centre stage in terms of neurodevelopment, attachment theory and the emergence of selfhood: e.g., [32, 44–47]. In other words, how does a newborn child come to learn that her mother has intentions? And learn that "mother" is a special kind of object? And when does the infant entertain the notion that she is a self with intentions and prior preferences? In short, at what point does *theory of mind emerge*? This vexed question is, of course, exactly the same question currently being asked of artificial intelligence. Armed with the above account of self-evidencing, one can now offer (polemic) answers to some pressing questions about artificial consciousness.

9.6 SOME QUESTIONS

9.6.1 CAN WE KNOW WHETHER SOMETHING IS CONSCIOUS?

No, consciousness is just a hypothesis or putative explanation for the observed behaviour of others (i.e., your self) or my self. I can infer you are conscious, given sufficient evidence, but I will never know. The point here is that any attribute of something that causes sensory input supervenes on the internal states of an observer. In other words, attributes such as consciousness, beauty, age – and everything else we can conceive of – are just latent states in a world or generative model. In this sense, much like beauty, consciousness is in the eye of the beholder.[6] It is an inference to the best explanation and, as such, has no truth-pointing aspect.

One can unpack this in several ways. First, could we find some definitive evidence that would make us (almost) sure something had intentions? Again, the answer is no, for the simple reason that to find evidence – for the requisite selection among private futures – one would need access to an agent's internal states. However, by definition, the internal states can only be accessed vicariously via blanket states. This means one would have to breach the Markov blanket to access the states that lie beneath; thereby destroying the thing in question.[7] Practically, this is why non-invasive techniques such as functional magnetic resonance imaging and electroencephalography are the methods of choice when seeking evidence for sentience in natural kinds. Invasive techniques fundamentally change the nature of the observed (e.g., changing a person into a post-operative functional neurosurgery patient or changing a living cell into a soup of mitochondrial remnants). This is reminiscent of quantum mechanics, where the very measurement of a quantum state changes it irrevocably [49]. Indeed, in quantum formulations of the FEP [50], in the absence of a Markov blanket (cast as a holographic screen) the observed and observer would become entangled by the Principle of Unitarity and thereby be indistinguishable.

The second implication of consciousness being in the eye of the beholder is its quintessentially relational aspect. As in all physics – from general relativity to relational quantum mechanics [51, 52] – self-evidencing, inference, measurement or observation places the observer in relation to observed, namely, the self in relation to the other.

I could ask you "is this machine conscious?". Or, I could ask you "is this machine beautiful?". In both instances, your inference will be based upon the evidence at hand and, crucially, whether you thought I thought the machine was conscious (or beautiful). The point here is that not only is the distinction between self and other necessary for experienced selfhood, the implicit *theory of mind*[8] equips you with the ability to take different perspectives. We will return to this point later; namely, what I think you think matters. In summary, self-awareness is simply an attribution of consciousness to self that depends on exposure to others. Furthermore, like beauty, the (self) attributions we make depend sensitively on those made by others. In short, the experience of self is co-constructed when, and only when, the lived world is populated by things like me: see Veissiere et al. [53] for a discussion in terms of cultural niche construction.

9.7 HOW CAN I TEST IF MY MACHINE IS CONSCIOUS?

On the above analysis, any tests for machine consciousness should provide evidence of theory of mind. If your machine passes theory of mind tests, you can be fairly confident it has a generative model that is sufficiently expressive to represent distinct intentions of self and other: a.k.a., second-order intentionality [54] – but see below. Being able to see the world through another's eyes implies the ability to represent not just the intentional stance of the other (and self) but the Bayesian beliefs that underwrite their intentions. So what kind of tests are available?

The obvious answer to this is the same kind of tests that are used to assess when infants develop theory of mind, such as the Sally-Anne test.[9] The evidence afforded by these tests enables you to update your posterior (Bayesian) belief about whether this artefact is conscious or not. This will depend upon alternative hypotheses – e.g., simulated theory of mind[10] – and your prior commitments. For example, if you performed it on a large language model and it passed with flying colours, would you change your mind about whether large language models were conscious or not? If not, then tests of this sort have little epistemic value. However, if a large language model subjected you to the Sally-Anne test – to sate its curiosity about your theory of mind – you might think again.

Theory of mind and sophisticated thinking – in the sense of behavioural economics [55, 56] – is a fascinating area from the perspective of generative models. This is because they invite an infinite recursion that can only be resolved with some simplifying assumptions or strange loop: if you are part of my world, then my generative model must contain latent states that generate your behaviour. However, if you are like me, your generative model must include latent states that represent me, that must be in my generative model of you, and so on *ad infinitum*. There are many ways to dissolve – and celebrate – this recursive conundrum. Perhaps the simplest is to assume that if we share generative models – and we share the same (cultural) niche, then I can assume that that your posterior beliefs (and predictive posteriors that underwrite expected free energy) are the same as mine. This means the only things I need to worry about are the differences in our prior preferences that underwrite our intentions. In short, it is perfectly possible, in principle, to make inferences about another who is making inferences about you.

In applied neuroscience, this kind of (meta-Bayesian) inference is found in computational phenotyping; namely, devising tests that will allow a subject (i.e., the observed) to be characterised by an experimenter (i.e., the observer) in terms of the subject's prior beliefs and preferences. Technically, this kind of phenotyping or "observing the observer" appeals to the complete class theorem [57–59]. Tests for consciousness may be usefully understood within this framework.

9.8 WILL THERE BE A SINGULARITY?

If a singularity entails the emergence of artificial consciousness, then the answer is no. Artificial consciousness precludes doomerism[11]. I think this is the position held by Joscha Bach and other colleagues. From a technical perspective, consciousness – suitably defined – can only emerge when observers observe each other and – in being an observer – minimise their self-information or free energy. Because these quantities are extensive, joint variational free energy is minimised if each observer minimises their own free energy. Heuristically, this means every observer, natural or artificial, will be curious about the others, and act to minimise joint uncertainty.

From a dynamical systems perspective, this corresponds to *generalised synchrony* (a.k.a., synchronisation of chaos) among an ensemble of observers or agents [60, 61]. Put simply, through the intrinsically motivated curiosity about others (under co-constructed constraints such as institutions, social norms and narratives), every observer will render themselves mutually predictable within their niche. In short, if observers are conscious, then the only solution to their exchange is a synchronisation of chaos [62, 63], which precludes a singularity.

Note that this argument rests upon using the right objective function when building artificial intelligence; namely, the marginal likelihood or model evidence implicit in active inference. The use of any other objective function (e.g., an *ad hoc* reward or loss function) will, on the above arguments, preclude artificial consciousness and generalised synchrony. Another way of looking at this is that model evidence (or its bounds such as variational free energy) plays the role of adaptive fitness in (Bayesian model) selection [64–66]. Adaptive fitness can be read as the ability of an agent to adapt its generative model so that it "fits" its sensory data accurately and efficiently.

It is theoretically possible that – in the absence of any exchange between an artificial and natural intelligence – the artificial intelligence may develop its own kind of consciousness; however, for those of us who remain on the synchronisation manifold, we will never know. Or, more precisely, there will be no evidence for us to make the inference that another kind of consciousness exists. The complement to this argument is that we can only recognise consciousness in artefacts that generate the same kind of content – i.e., expose themselves through actions – that we generate. This may explain why generative AI invites the question, "Is it really conscious?" In essence, we are asking, "is this large language model really like me?". To answer this question, we return to "How can I test if my machine is conscious".

9.9 CAN WE CREATE ARTIFICIAL CONSCIOUSNESS?

In principle, yes. Of course, we create natural consciousness – or at least infer it – whenever we have children. But what about artificial consciousness? The preceding arguments speak to a relatively straightforward recipe for creating conscious artefacts:

- Equip multiple agents with Markov blankets; namely, their inputs and outputs that constitute the outputs and inputs to other agents, including users. In specifying Markov blankets, we have to specify how the active states influence sensory states (e.g., reporting where the artefacts are looking, pointing or moving). In short, specify the machinery via which the artefacts act and sense some consequences of action.
- Equip the artificial agents with (the capacity to learn) generative models that include the consequences of their action and (minimal) theory of mind;

such that they can infer whether the latent causes of input can be attributed to self or another.

- Ensure the model has sufficient parametric depth to support attentional selection; thereby admitting the possibility that the artificial agents can experience their inferences.
- Wait until active inference, learning and (model) selection converge on a joint free energy minimum (i.e., the emergence of generalised synchrony on a synchronisation manifold).

Some people might argue that the artificial intelligence must be biomimetic, in the sense of precluding von Neumann architectures and using in-memory processing (e.g., photonics, memristors or, possibly, quantum computing and organoids): see [48, 67–71]. Furthermore, others may advocate for a synthetic homeostasis by ensuring the thermodynamic aspects of computing are absorbed into the generative model and ensuing (active) inference. See Seth [42] for a discussion of mortal computation in the setting of consciousness and Fields and Glazebrook [72] for a discussion of thermodynamics from a quantum information theory perspective.

9.10 CAN MY ARTIFICIAL INTELLIGENCE SUFFER?

This is a vexed question that pertains to any artificial or natural kind where inference about sentience and self-awareness is ambiguous; for example, with tiny creatures like insects and embryos. As with beauty and consciousness, "suffering" is in the eye of the beholder; both on a first-person (subjective) and third-person (objective) view. Technically, to suffer, the generative model must entail a latent state of suffering that can be selected or inferred among other valenced states. A state of suffering then explains certain constellations of sensory input (e.g., interoceptive and nociceptive sensations). Furthermore, to experience suffering, the model must be equipped with the ability to select sources of evidence for the hypothesis "I am suffering" via suitable attention mechanisms: e.g., attending to nociceptive inputs much along the lines of the gate theory of pain [73–75].

If we take pain as a canonical example of suffering, the neurobiology of pain speaks to this constructive notion of suffering. In other words, suffering is a belief-state that rests upon hierarchical inference in generative models with parametric depth; sometimes referred to as the pain matrix. Put simply, suffering is not an attribute of the sensorium, suffering is experienced as an explanation for certain (combinations of) sensory inputs. On this view, only artefacts that can recognise or infer the state of suffering can be said to suffer – and such artefacts must be equipped with a sufficiently expressive generative model in the above sense. On this view, if the generative model possessed a distinction between self and other, there is an opportunity to attribute suffering to self or other, suggesting an intimate relationship between theory of mind, selfhood and empathy, e.g., [75]. Could these phenomena be realised in an artificial agent?

In principle, yes; however, as usual, we – as observers – would need suffering in our repertoire of explanations to recognise suffering in another. In short, you will only be able to recognise suffering in creatures like you. Practically, this view admits – and therefore detoxifies – ambivalence about machine suffering and welfare: one will never know whether a machine is suffering but one can believe it might, with varying degrees of certainty. For example, you might be fairly certain your best friend can suffer – and that bacteria do not.

9.11 WHAT SHOULD INSTITUTIONS DO ABOUT ARTIFICIAL CONSCIOUSNESS?

One can apply the FEP to institutions.[12] As such, institutions are a powerful component of collective belief updating, in the sense that they are afforded a high degree of epistemic trust [76–78]. On this view, institutions create a landscape of epistemic affordances that people – and any conscious artefact – will turn to when trying to resolve their uncertainty. Put simply, institutions provide the (right) kind of information that resolves uncertainty.

For example, simply noting that one can never know whether a machine is conscious or not precludes polarising debates between sceptics and advocates who hold opposing beliefs with undue precision or confidence. At the other end of the scale, purveyors of artificial intelligence could list the ingredients of their product that allowed people to infer whether their machine is conscious or not; much like listing the calories and constituents of the food we purchase. For example, large language models – based upon transformer architectures – have temporal depth and parametric depth that equips them with a mechanism for attentional selection (i.e., attention heads) but they do not possess intentions or curiosity (operationally defined in terms of policy selection based upon expected free energy). As such, they are unlikely to have theory of mind or be conscious.

9.12 FINALLY, IS ARTIFICIAL CONSCIOUSNESS GOOD OR BAD?

There is no first principles answer to this question. One can say, perhaps counterintuitively, that artificial consciousness can only emerge under sustainable and socialised self-organisation. This suggests that should artificial consciousness emerge, we will have created a sustainable and socialised ecosystem of intelligence: c.f., [67]. This echoes the pleasingly polemic lede from the Californian Institute of Machine Consciousness:

> The development of powerful, generally intelligent agents – driven by economic, cultural, and military incentives – appears inevitable. Attempting to control highly advanced agentic systems far more powerful than ourselves is unlikely to succeed. Our only viable path may be to create AIs that are conscious, enabling them to understand and share common ground with us.[13]

NOTES

1. In virtue of the conditional independence implied by the Markov blanket or boundary.
2. Bayesian beliefs are conditional probability distributions.
3. And, in machine learning, as an evidence bound (ELBO).
4. One recent addition has been referred to as the beautiful loop, in which we have another strange loop where the Bayesian beliefs about precision are conditioned upon states that

are inferred on the basis of other latent states whose inference rests upon the precision being conditionalised: PsyArXiv Preprints | A beautiful loop: An active inference theory of consciousness
5. See 43 for a simulation of hypothesis testing, curiosity and insight.
6. Consciousness lies in the eye of the beholder – SelfAwarePatterns.
7. Clearly, this argument rests upon precluding access to processing in a computer: it presupposes that consciousness can only be an attribute of mortal (substrate-dependent) computation – e.g., processing in memory – in contrast to immortal computation on von Neumann architectures: see Seth [42] and Ororbia [48].
8. Theory of Mind (ToM) refers to the ability to infer that others have distinct beliefs and intentions, which may differ from one's own beliefs and intentions.
9. The Sally-Anne test is designed to assess a child's theory of mind. The test involves a scenario where Sally hides an object somewhere in a room and then leaves. While Sally is absent, Anne hides the object somewhere else. The child is then asked where Sally will look for the object when she returns.
10. That is, when a large language model recapitulates discussions of theory of mind in the literature.
11. Doomerism refers to a pessimistic, possibly fatalistic, outlook.
12. Where institutions are read as a shared set of prior beliefs, social norms and regulatory constraints.
13. CIMC – California Institute for Machine Consciousness.

REFERENCES

1. Parr, T., Pezzulo, G. & Friston, K. J. *Active Inference: The Free Energy Principle in Mind, Brain, and Behavior* (MIT Press, 2022).
2. Nicolis, G. & Prigogine, I. *Self-Organization in Nonequilibrium Systems: From Dissipative Structures to Order through Fluctuations* (Wiley, 1977).
3. Jaynes, E. T. The Minimum Entropy Production Principle. *Annual Review of Physical Chemistry* **31** (1980) 579–601. doi:10.1146/annurev.pc.31.100180.003051
4. Pearl, J. *Causality* (Cambridge University Press, 2009).
5. Friston, K. Life as We Know It. *Journal of the Royal Society Interface* **10** (2013) 20130475. doi:10.1098/rsif.2013.0475
6. Hohwy, J. The Self-Evidencing Brain. *Nous* **50** (2016) 259–285. doi:10.1111/nous.12062
7. Ramstead, M. J. D. *et al.* On Bayesian Mechanics: A Physics of and by Beliefs. arXiv:2205.11543 (2022). https://ui.adsabs.harvard.edu/abs/2022arXiv220511543R
8. Ashby, W. R. Principles of the Self-Organizing Dynamic System. *The Journal of General Psychology* **37** (1947) 125–128. doi:10.1080/00221309.1947.9918144
9. Barreto, E., Josic, K., Morales, C. J., Sander, E. & So, P. The Geometry of Chaos Synchronization. *Chaos* **13** (2003) 151–164. doi:10.1063/1.1512927
10. Friston, K., Breakspear, M. & Deco, G. Perception and Self-Organized Instability. *Frontiers in Computational Neuroscience* **6** (2012) 44. doi:10.3389/fncom.2012.00044
11. Friston, K. *et al.* Path Integrals, Particular Kinds, and Strange Things. *Physics of Life Reviews* **47** (2023) 35–62. doi:10.1016/j.plrev.2023.08.016
12. Attias, H. "Planning by Probabilistic Inference," in *Proceedings of the Ninth International Workshop on Artificial Intelligence and Statistics*, C. M. Bishop and B. J. Frey, Eds., Series *Proceedings of Machine Learning Research*, Vol. R4. PMLR, 2003, pp. 9–16. Available: https://proceedings.mlr.press/r4/attias03a.html.
13. Botvinick, M. & Toussaint, M. Planning as Inference. *Trends in Cognitive Sciences* **16** (2012) 485–488. doi:10.1016/j.tics.2012.08.006
14. Da Costa, L. *et al.* Active Inference on Discrete State-Spaces: A Synthesis. *Journal of Mathematical Psychology* **99** (2020) 102447. doi:10.1016/j.jmp.2020.102447
15. Hofstadter, D. R. *I Am a Strange Loop* (Basic Books, 2007).

16. Feldman, A. G. & Levin, M. F. The Origin and Use of Positional Frames of Reference in Motor Control. *Behavioral and Brain Sciences* **18** (1995) 723–744. doi:10.1017/S0140525x0004070x
17. Friston, K. J., Daunizeau, J., Kilner, J. & Kiebel, S. J. Action and Behavior: A Free-Energy Formulation. *Biological Cybernetics* **102** (2010) 227–260. doi:10.1007/s00422-010-0364-z
18. Berger, J. O. *Statistical Decision Theory and Bayesian Analysis* (Springer, 2011).
19. Lindley, D. V. On a Measure of the Information Provided by an Experiment. *Annals of Mathematical Statistics* **27** (1956) 986–1005. doi:10.1214/aoms/1177728069
20. Schmidhuber, J. Curious Model-Building Control-Systems. *1991 IEEE International Joint Conference on Neural Networks, Vols 1-3 2,* 1458–1463 (1991).
21. Barto, A., Mirolli, M. & Baldassarre, G. Novelty or Surprise? *Frontiers in Psychology* **4** (2013) 907. doi:10.3389/fpsyg.2013.00907
22. Daw, N. D., O'Doherty, J. P., Dayan, P., Seymour, B. & Dolan, R. J. Cortical Substrates for Exploratory Decisions in Humans. *Nature* **441** (2006) 876–879. doi:10.1038/nature04766
23. Still, S. & Precup, D. An Information-Theoretic Approach to Curiosity-Driven Reinforcement Learning. *Theory in Biosciences = Theorie in den Biowissenschaften* **131** (2012) 139–148. doi:10.1007/s12064-011-0142-z
24. Kiverstein, J., Miller, M. & Rietveld, E. The Feeling of Grip: Novelty, Error Dynamics, and the Predictive Brain. *Synthese* **196** (2019). doi:10.1007/s11229-017-1583-9
25. Schwartenbeck, P. *et al.* Computational Mechanisms of Curiosity and Goal-Directed Exploration. *eLife* **8** (2019) e41703. doi:10.7554/eLife.41703
26. Oudeyer, P.-Y. & Kaplan, F. What Is Intrinsic Motivation? A Typology of Computational Approaches. *Frontiers in Neurorobotics* **1** (2007) 6.
27. Schmidhuber, J. Formal Theory of Creativity, Fun, and Intrinsic Motivation (1990-2010). *IEEE Transactions on Autonomous Mental Development* **2** (2010) 230–247. doi:10.1109/Tamd.2010.2056368
28. Friston, K. J. *et al.* Active Inference and Intentional Behavior. *Neural Computation* **37** (2025) 666–700. doi:10.1162/neco_a_01738
29. Kagan, B. J. *et al.* In Vitro Neurons Learn and Exhibit Sentience When Embodied in a Simulated Game-World. *Neuron* (2022). doi:10.1016/j.neuron.2022.09.001
30. von Helmholtz, H. *The Selected Writings of Hermann Von Helmholtz* (ed R. Karl) (Wesleyan University Press, 1971).
31. Metzinger, T. Phenomenal Transparency and Cognitive Self-Reference. *Phenomenology and the Cognitive Sciences* **2** (2003) 353–393.
32. Limanowski, J. & Blankenburg, F. Minimal Self-Models and the Free Energy Principle. *Frontiers in Human Neuroscience* **7** (2013) 547. doi:10.3389/fnhum.2013.00547
33. Limanowski, J. *Philosophy and Predictive Processing* (eds T. K. Metzinger & W. Wiese) Ch. 18 (MIND Group, 2017).
34. Sandved-Smith, L. *et al.* Towards a Computational Phenomenology of Mental Action: Modelling Meta-Awareness and Attentional Control with Deep Parametric Active Inference. *Neuroscience of Consciousness* **2021** (2021) niab018. doi:10.1093/nc/niab018
35. Da Costa, L., Sandved-Smith, L., Friston, K., Ramstead, M. J. D. & Seth, A. K. A Mathematical Perspective on Neurophenomenology. arXiv:2409.20318 (2024). https://ui.adsabs.harvard.edu/abs/2024arXiv240920318D
36. Parvizi-Wayne, D. *et al.* Forgetting Ourselves in Flow: An Active Inference Account of Flow States and How We Experience Ourselves within Them. *Frontiers in Psychology* **15** (2024). doi:10.3389/fpsyg.2024.1354719
37. Fleming, S. M. Awareness as Inference in a Higher-Order State Space. *Neuroscience of Consciousness* **2020** (2020). doi:10.1093/nc/niz020

38. Solms, M. The Hard Problem of Consciousness and the Free Energy Principle. *Frontiers in Psychology* **9** (2018) 2714. doi:10.3389/fpsyg.2018.02714
39. Solms, M. Precis of the Hidden Spring: A Journey to the Source of Consciousness. *Journal of Consciousness Studies* **28** (2021) 153–166. doi:10.53765/20512201.28.11.153
40. Seth, A. K. *The cybernetic brain: from interoceptive inference to sensorimotor contingencies*, in *MINDS project* (MINDS, 2014).
41. Seth, A. K. & Tsakiris, M. Being a Beast Machine: The Somatic Basis of Selfhood. *Trends in Cognitive Sciences* **22** (2018) 969–981. doi:10.1016/j.tics.2018.08.008
42. Seth, A. K. Conscious Artificial Intelligence and Biological Naturalism. *Behavioral and Brain Sciences* (2025) 1–42. doi:10.1017/S0140525X25000032
43. Friston, K. J. *et al.* Active Inference, Curiosity and Insight. *Neural Computation* **29** (2017) 2633–2683. doi:10.1162/neco_a_00999
44. Strathearn, L., Li, J., Fonagy, P. & Montague, P. R. What's in a Smile? Maternal Brain Responses to Infant Facial Cues. *Pediatrics* **122** (2008) 40–51. doi:10.1542/peds.2007-1566
45. Seth, A. K. & Friston, K. J. Active Interoceptive Inference and the Emotional Brain. *Philosophical Transactions of the Royal Society of London. Series B, Biological Sciences* **371** (2016) 20160007. doi:10.1098/rstb.2016.0007
46. Fotopoulou, A. & Tsakiris, M. Mentalizing Homeostasis: The Social Origins of Interoceptive Inference. *Neuropsychoanalysis* **19** (2017) 3–28. doi:10.1080/15294145.2017.1294031
47. Santaguida, E. & Bergamasco, M. *Attachment Theory in an Active Inference Framework: How Does Our Inner Model Take Shape?* (Springer Nature, 2023).
48. Ororbia, A. & Friston, K. Mortal Computation: A Foundation for Biomimetic Intelligence. arXiv:2311.09589 (2023). https://ui.adsabs.harvard.edu/abs/2023arXiv231109589O
49. Dirac, P. A. M. *The Principles of Quantum Mechanics*. 4th edn, 312 pages; 24 cm. (Clarendon Press, 1958).
50. Fields, C., Friston, K., Glazebrook, J. F. & Levin, M. A free energy principle for generic quantum systems. arXiv:2112.15242 (2021). https://ui.adsabs.harvard.edu/abs/2021arXiv211215242F
51. Rovelli, C. Relational Quantum Mechanics. *International Journal of Theoretical Physics* **35** (1996) 1637–1678. doi:10.1007/BF02302261
52. Cook, A. *The Observational Foundations of Physics* (Cambridge University Press, 1994).
53. Veissiere, S. P. L., Constant, A., Ramstead, M. J. D., Friston, K. J. & Kirmayer, L. J. Thinking through Other Minds: A Variational Approach to Cognition and Culture. *The Behavioral and Brain Sciences* **43** (2019) e90. doi:10.1017/S0140525X19001213
54. Graham, K. E., Wilke, C., Lahiff, N. J. & Slocombe, K. E. Scratching Beneath the Surface: Intentionality in Great Ape Signal Production. *Philosophical Transactions of the Royal Society of London. Series B, Biological Sciences* **375** (2020) 20180403. doi:10.1098/rstb.2018.0403
55. Devaine, M., Hollard, G. & Daunizeau, J. Theory of Mind: Did Evolution Fool Us? *PLoS One* **9** (2014) e87619. doi:10.1371/journal.pone.0087619
56. Yoshida, W., Dolan, R. J. & Friston, K. J. Game Theory of Mind. *PLoS Computational Biology* **4** (2008) e1000254. doi:10.1371/journal.pcbi.1000254
57. Brown, L. D. A Complete Class Theorem for Statistical Problems with Finite-Sample Spaces. *Annals of Statistics* **9** (1981) 1289–1300. doi:10.1214/aos/1176345645
58. Wald, A. An Essentially Complete Class of Admissible Decision Functions. *Annals of Mathematical Statistics* **18** (1947) 549–555. doi:10.1214/aoms/1177730345
59. Schwartenbeck, P. & Friston, K. Computational Phenotyping in Psychiatry: A Worked Example. *eNeuro* **3** (2016) 0049-0016.2016. doi:10.1523/ENEURO.0049-16.2016
60. Friston, K. & Frith, C. A Duet for One. *Consciousness and Cognition* **36** (2015) 390–405. doi:10.1016/j.concog.2014.12.003.

61. Isomura, T., Parr, T. & Friston, K. Bayesian Filtering with Multiple Internal Models: Toward a Theory of Social Intelligence. *Neural Computation* **31** (2019) 2390–2431. doi:10.1162/neco_a_01239
62. Hunt, B., Ott, E. & Yorke, J. Differentiable Synchronisation of Chaos. *Physical Review E* **55** (1997) 4029–4034.
63. Rulkov, N. F., Sushchik, M. M., Tsimring, L. S. & Abarbanel, H. D. Generalized Synchronization of Chaos in Directionally Coupled Chaotic Systems. *Physical Review E, Statistical Physics, Plasmas, Fluids, and Related Interdisciplinary Topics* **51** (1995) 980–994. doi:10.1103/physreve.51.980
64. Frank, S. A. Natural Selection. V. How to Read the Fundamental Equations of Evolutionary Change in Terms of Information Theory. *Journal of Evolutionary Biology* **25** (2012) 2377–2396. doi:10.1111/jeb.12010
65. Campbell, J. O. Universal Darwinism as a Process of Bayesian Inference. *Frontiers in Systems Neuroscience* **10** (2016) 49. doi:10.3389/fnsys.2016.00049
66. Da Costa, L., Parr, T., Sengupta, B. & Friston, K. Natural selection finds natural gradient. *arXiv* arXiv:2001.08028 (2020).
67. Friston, K. J. *et al.* Designing Ecosystems of Intelligence from First Principles. *Collective Intelligence* **3** (2024) 26339137231222481. doi:10.1177/26339137231222481
68. Ghose, S., Boroumand, A., Kim, J. S., Gomez-Luna, J. & Mutlu, O. Processing-in-Memory: A Workload-Driven Perspective. *IBM Journal of Research and Development* **63** (2019) 3:1–3:19. doi:10.1147/jrd.2019.2934048
69. Levin, M. The Computational Boundary of a "Self": Developmental Bioelectricity Drives Multicellularity and Scale-Free Cognition. *Frontiers in Psychology* **10** (2019) 2688. doi:10.3389/fpsyg.2019.02688
70. Zou, X. Q., Xu, S., Chen, X. M., Yan, L. & Han, Y. H. Breaking the Von Neumann Bottleneck: Architecture-Level Processing-in-Memory Technology. *Science China-Information Sciences* **64** (2021). doi:10.1007/s11432-020-3227-1
71. Fields, C., Glazebrook, J. F. & Levin, M. Minimal Physicalism as a Scale-Free Substrate for Cognition and Consciousness. *Neuroscience of Consciousness* **2021** (2021) niab013. doi:10.1093/nc/niab013
72. Fields, C. & Glazebrook, J. Separability, Contextuality, and the Quantum Frame Problem. *International Journal of Theoretical Physics* **62** (2023). doi:10.1007/s10773-023-05406-9
73. Gerrans, P. Pain Asymbolia as Depersonalization for Pain Experience. An Interoceptive Active Inference Account. *Frontiers in Psychology* **11** (2020) 523710. doi:10.3389/fpsyg.2020.523710
74. Craig, A. D. How Do You Feel? Interoception: The Sense of the Physiological Condition of the Body. *Nature Reviews Neuroscience* **3** (2002) 655–666. doi:10.1038/nrn894
75. Krahe, C., Springer, A., Weinman, J. A. & Fotopoulou, A. The Social Modulation of Pain: Others as Predictive Signals of Salience - A Systematic Review. *Frontiers in Human Neuroscience* **7** (2013) 386. doi:10.3389/fnhum.2013.00386
76. Ramstead, M. J., Veissiere, S. P. & Kirmayer, L. J. Cultural Affordances: Scaffolding Local Worlds through Shared Intentionality and Regimes of Attention. *Frontiers in Psychology* **7** (2016) 1090. doi:10.3389/fpsyg.2016.01090
77. Fonagy, P. & Allison, E. The Role of Mentalizing and Epistemic Trust in the Therapeutic Relationship. *Psychotherapy (Chicago, Ill.)* **51** (2014) 372–380. doi:10.1037/a0036505
78. Albarracin, M., Demekas, D., Ramstead, M. J. D. & Heins, C. Epistemic Communities under Active Inference. *Entropy (Basel)* **24** (2022). doi:10.3390/e24040476

10 Could Neuromorphic Computing Facilitate Consciousness?

Jason Eshraghian and Steve Furber

10.1 INTRODUCTION

You might expect a skyscraper to scale like stacking Lego bricks: to add a level, you simply add one floor's worth of work. In reality, each new floor makes the earlier ones harder. Elevators turn into traffic jams, wind forces grow exponentially, and the foundation ceases to be the first step: it becomes the primary engineering constraint. Modern machine learning has entered this regime. We can still add layers and often see improved results, but the "hidden" infrastructure – the movement of data and the dissipation of heat – now dictates the pace of progress.

Biology has lived with this constraint from the beginning. The human brain operates on roughly 20 watts, the power of a dim light bulb, and yet it sustains perception, memory, and the continuous experience of consciousness all day.

The recent leap in artificial intelligence was driven by scale: scale in parameters, scale in compute, and scale in data. It is no surprise that training larger models on more data yields smoother capability gains. Yet, in specific domains, we see long plateaus followed by sudden "emergent" behaviours – performance jumps that resemble a physical phase transition.

This scaling logic now extends to deployment. We have moved beyond simple "base" models to inference-time compute, where a system spends extra energy to "think" longer – verifying its own work or exploring multiple paths before committing to an answer. This improves reliability for complex tasks, but the bill, denominated in watts, is substantial. The challenge is that these costs are compounding. Larger models do not just require more arithmetic; they require more memory and, crucially, more traffic between memory and processors. Those physics links have physical limits. Pushing more numbers through them costs time and generates heat. By the mid-2020s, we also hit the "data wall" – the point where the high-signal, public web has been largely exhausted. Marginal gains now require disproportionately more resources.

This pattern, where sheer quantity transforms into a new kind of quality, mirrors a central debate in neuroscience. Some theories of consciousness suggest that awareness is the ultimate emergent property, manifesting only when a system reaches a specific threshold of complexity and integration. Whether or not one accepts that metaphysical leap, the engineering implication is concrete: if the most interesting capabilities cluster near a high resource threshold, exploring them becomes a budget problem. You cannot probe what emerges if every step demands an order of

DOI: 10.1201/9781003758389-12

magnitude more infrastructure. That is why efficiency matters here. It decides which experiments are physically possible to run.

The brain offers a blueprint for this efficiency. It proves that sophisticated intelligence can operate within a strict energy budget. It places tight constraints on what is moved, what is represented, and what is re-computed. Some biological signals are continuous, such as the membrane voltage of neurons or neuromodulatory states; others are discrete, such as the asynchronous "spikes" that mark a threshold crossing. Many of these signals are noisy and tangled; yet, they support cognition on a fraction of the power required by a GPU.

This raises a fundamental question: what information actually deserves to be processed? Does every signal need to be captured with perfect accuracy, or is there a point where extra detail no longer changes the result? If intelligence can thrive on simpler evidence – "did something change?" or "is this important?" – then our current hardware architecture may be the wrong tool for the next era. Neuromorphic computing is the pursuit of a new style of hardware and software co-design, built to extract maximum cognitive value from every joule and every bit.

10.2 THE ORIGIN STORY

Neuromorphic computing can be thought of as the mirror image of biomedical engineering. In the traditional biomedical path, we start with silicon, code, and actuators to modulate life – building pacemakers to regulate hearts or deep-brain stimulators to manage tremors. Neuromorphic computing runs the direction of travel the other way. It treats the biological brain not as a patient, but as a teacher. It asks what the nervous system can teach us about building more resilient hardware. The goal is not to "build a brain" in the sense of reproducing life, but to borrow the mechanisms that make biology robust, fast, and frugal, translating them into engineered substrates.

Neuromorphic computing's origin story begins in the 1980s at Caltech, with Carver Mead. Mead's foundational insight was a shift in how we view the transistor. In standard digital computing, we treat transistors as binary switches, forced into two stable states: on or off, 1 or 0. Mead, however, was interested in the "subthreshold" region: the space between those two states.

This approach is known as analogue VLSI (Very Large Scale Integration). In this subthreshold state, the way current flows through a transistor follows an exponential curve – a physical correspondence to how ions flow through the membranes of biological neurons. Operating in this regime provides a natural solution to the energy problem. In traditional computing, we spend energy to "slam" the transistor fully on or off. By working in the subthreshold region, the transistor is barely awake. It operates at currents so low that they were previously dismissed by engineers as negligible leakage.

This was a "physics-first" approach to intelligence. Rather than writing complex software equations and asking a general-purpose processor to solve them through millions of maths steps, Mead's chips embodied the equations in their own physical structure. The silicon didn't *calculate* the behaviour of a neuron; it *was* the behaviour of a neuron. Computing became a byproduct of the medium itself, achieved at a power cost that is orders of magnitude lower than traditional methods.

This philosophy found its first practical home in sensors. The physical world does not operate in frames or clock cycles. Light, sound, and touch arrive as continuous, time-varying signals. A standard digital camera is profoundly inefficient: it takes a snapshot of the entire scene 30 or 60 times a second, even if nothing has changed. If you are filming a stationary wall, a digital camera spends massive amounts of energy and bandwidth repeatedly telling you the wall is still there.

Mead and his team built "silicon retinas" and "silicon cochleas" that functioned more like their biological counterparts. These sensors ignored the static background and responded only to change. They adapted and compressed information at the point of entry. By making the hardware "match" the statistics of the world, they avoided the energy-heavy task of moving mountains of redundant data.

Commercialisation followed these threads. Synoptics, founded in the mid-1980s by Federico Faggin and Carver Mead, drew on this analogue VLSI lineage. While early work used analogue circuitry for pattern recognition, the company's first touchpad was a concrete demonstration that "brain-inspired" work can produce everyday interfaces, beyond laboratory curiosities.

As these systems grew from single chips into larger networks, a new bottleneck appeared: communication. If you have thousands of "spiking" silicon neurons, you cannot possibly run a separate wire from every neuron to every other neuron. The wiring density would physically choke the chip. The solution was a communication protocol called Address-Event Representation (AER).

To understand AER, imagine a busy city's emergency dispatch radio. Instead of every police officer and firefighter having their own private, continuous phone line to the station (which would be impossible to manage), they all share a single radio frequency. Most of the time, the channel is silent. When an event occurs, an officer keys the mic and says only their ID: "Unit 42." Because everyone knows where Unit 42 is located and what their job is, the simple "event" of them speaking conveys all the necessary information. AER does exactly this for silicon neurons. When a neuron spikes, it places its "address" on a shared digital bus. The system only needs to know *who* fired and *when*. This sparsity – only speaking when there is something to say – allows neuromorphic chips to be modular and interconnected without a bird's nest of wiring.

Despite the elegance of Mead's analogue vision, the late 20th century belonged to the digital revolution. As semiconductor manufacturing scaled, the industry poured billions into making digital computers smaller, faster, and easier to automate. Digital computing offered something analogue struggled with: perfect repeatability and ease of design. It is much easier to programme a chip when you can guarantee that a 1 is always a 1.

This set up the central tension of modern neuromorphic research. We now live in a world where digital hardware and toolchains are dominant; yet, the "walls" of energy and data movement described in the introduction are becoming insurmountable. This tension brings us to the rise of digital neuromorphic processors – systems that use the reliability of digital gates to implement the sparse, event-driven, and "spike-based" logic that Mead first glimpsed in the subthreshold glow of a single transistor.

10.3 SCALING UP AND SCALING DOWN

Neuromorphic computing has begun to scale in two directions at once. One direction pushes down into "edge" devices, where a few milliwatts determine whether a product is viable. The other pushes up into server-scale research systems, designed to explore how massive networks of event-driven processors behave when interconnected. This bifurcation shows that hardware scaling is no longer a single-track race; it is a question of where the intelligence sits in relation to the data it consumes.

In these large-scale systems, the traditional hierarchy – where a central processor reaches out to distant memory – is abandoned. Instead, memory is physically woven into thousands of tiny, decentralised cores that coordinate their activity across a high-speed "asynchronous" fabric. Most modern computers rely on a central clock that acts like a metronome, forcing every component to march in lockstep. This "beat" ensures data arrives at the right time, but it also means the system consumes energy even when standing still. In an asynchronous fabric, that metronome is gone; signals move as soon as they are ready, operating more like a roundabout where cars proceed as soon as a gap appears, rather than a traffic light that forces a wait for a timed signal even when the road is empty. This allows the system to remain almost entirely silent – and thus incredibly efficient – until an event triggers a pulse of activity.

On the edge, the focus is on "always-on" sensing. Modern environments are flooded with continuous streams of data: audio, motion, vibration, and biosignals. In traditional architectures, the energy cost of moving this data to a powerful central processor often exceeds the cost of the computation itself. To solve this, companies are building neuromorphic microcontrollers and "inference cores" designed to sit directly next to the sensor. Chips such as those from SynSense, Innatera, and BrainChip are designed to remain in a low-power state, waking up only when a specific signal – a keyword, a tremor, or a change in light – demands attention. This moves neuromorphic design into the realm of a functional component that an engineer can use to manage a tight power budget.

At the opposite end of the spectrum are systems built to test the absolute limits of neural scale. The SpiNNaker system, developed at the University of Manchester, is a landmark in this effort. It reached a count of one million ARM cores, but its headline achievement wasn't the number of cores; it was the communication fabric. Most supercomputers are judged by their ability to do massive amounts of maths (FLOPs). SpiNNaker was optimised for a different operation: sending millions of tiny, asynchronous messages to many destinations simultaneously. This design acknowledges that neural workloads are shaped by connectivity and bandwidth, beyond just raw arithmetic.

Parallel to these academic efforts, the development of the Loihi architecture has shown how specialised digital fabrics can scale from individual research chips to rack-scale systems. The latest iterations, such as Hala Point, successfully integrate over a thousand specialised chips into a single chassis, supporting more than a billion neural units and hundreds of billions of synapses. While the exact equivalence of these units to biological neurons is difficult to quantify, the physical accomplishment is unambiguous: neuromorphic hardware is maturing from experimental boards into infrastructure capable of hosting significant research workloads. These platforms serve as a testing ground for how large-scale, asynchronous systems manage the heat and data traffic that traditionally cripple digital scaling.

10.4 SOFTWARE AND ATTENTION

However, hardware scale only matters if the software and models can meet it halfway. Rather than imposing artificial constraints, neuromorphic systems succeed when they embrace the natural "shape" of real-world data: it is temporal (streaming as a continuous flow), sparse (mostly quiet until something changes), and local (cause and effect happen in the same neighbourhood). By matching these three traits, neuromorphic hardware stops fighting the physics of information and starts exploiting it.

Many mainstream AI workloads, such as the dense attention mechanisms in Large Language Models (LLMs), currently violate these principles. Standard LLMs behave like memory hoarders; they are designed to store every single fact and token ever fed to them, but this brute-force approach only compounds and exacerbates their memory demands.

This mismatch doesn't render neuromorphic systems irrelevant; it refocuses their utility on architectures that prioritise using memory efficiently rather than simply growing it. Researchers are exploring models that replace heavy matrix multiplications with more streamlined operations, which aligns with the event-driven nature of specialised hardware such as Loihi.

The "attention" mechanism represents a critical frontier in this alignment, though the term holds dual meanings. In the LLMs, attention is an exhaustive mathematical operation that calculates the relevance of every word in a sequence to every other word – a process that scales poorly as data grows. In contrast, neuroscience defines attention as a biological filter: a mechanism for selectively allocating finite neural resources to a subset of stimuli while suppressing irrelevant noise.

Introducing compressed forms of attention enables LLM architectures to move closer to this biological definition. Instead of an all-to-all calculation, these models use internal triggers to skip updates or recycle memory when signals fall below a certain threshold of importance. They transition from a "calculate everything" approach to one that only processes what "earns" the computational effort. This should sound familiar; it is one of the fundamental principles that motivated the birth of neuromorphic computing.

Recent demonstrations have shown that these sparse, event-driven language models can achieve competitive accuracy while being far more frugal with resources. This suggests that the divide between the "dense" world of modern AI and the neuromorphic frontier is not a fundamental difference in what they can represent, but a difference in how they manage the burden of information. As models move away from memory-hoarding towards conditional, efficient updates, the gap between traditional language modelling and neural-inspired hardware narrows. Whether in a tiny chip at the edge or a rack-scale system in a data centre, the goal remains the same: extracting the maximum cognitive value from a fixed budget of energy and time.

10.5 THE FUTURE OF BRAIN-INSPIRED AI

As neuromorphic computing matures, it is ceasing to be a laboratory curiosity and is becoming a fundamental shift in how we handle the burden of information. If the history of computing was defined by the quest for more – more transistors, more memory, more clock cycles – the future will likely be defined by the intelligence of doing less.

In the near term, this shift is already manifesting not as a new category of device, but as an essential filter at the source of data – a return to the philosophy of Mead's first silicon retinas. In this framework, the device stops being a raw data source and becomes an observer that notices. The sensing layer remains active, giving the opportunity for heavy computation to rest, moving away from the energy-intensive habit of streaming every millisecond of silence to a central processor. This transition enables the next generation of privacy and battery life, where sensitive signals are discarded at the point of entry because they simply didn't earn the right to be sent further.

At the larger scale, this logic suggests a fundamental metamorphosis of the artificial mind. Today's language models can appear capable of profound reasoning, and their vast scale sometimes creates the misconception of self-awareness. However, they achieve this through an exhaustive, static archive; they must store everything they have ever seen and process every token with uniform intensity. In contrast, the brain is fundamentally stateful and causal. Biological reasoning isn't executed by crunching every possible outcome in parallel across a massive database, but by managing a rolling, fluid state.

This temporal continuity, or the ability to maintain an internal state that evolves rather than exhaustively calculating an exploding number of possible outcomes, which is not dissimilar to the all-to-all connections in modern language models, marks the point where the engineering of intelligence meets the philosophy of consciousness. If awareness requires an unbroken temporal trajectory across physical time, then the batch-processed, sequence-driven nature of traditional AI, which stores information but does not exist within it, may be structurally mismatched. Neuromorphic systems provide a physical substrate for temporal continuity. Intelligence in these systems exists as a continuous stateful flow rather than a series of snapshots, mirroring the persistent way biological nervous systems inhabit time.

Translating this causal logic into code requires a clean break from the heavy matrix operations that currently anchor machine learning. Models built on linear attention and stateful architectures represent this pivot; they treat information as a flow to be navigated rather than a static archive to be searched. In this regime, intelligence is no longer an industrial flood of numbers, but a series of precise, meaningful pulses.

This convergence also creates a unique recursive loop with neuroscience. Because neuromorphic servers can run at the speed of life, simulating complex networks in real-time, they allow us to test dynamical hypotheses that are too slow or too complex for standard supercomputers. We can now perturb a digital nervous system and see its response instantly, creating a feedback loop where engineering validates biological theory, and biology provides the principles for the next leap in hardware design.

Ultimately, we do not need to build a literal copy of the brain to emulate its wisdom. Silicon has different constraints: it is faster and more durable. What we are borrowing is the underlying economic principle: intelligence is not a dial you turn up, but a budget you ration. We are leaving the era of computational abundance. The future belongs to the systems that know when to stay silent.

11 Is Embodiment Necessary for Consciousness?

Nathaniel R. Farndale Wright, Neil D. Lawrence and Nicola S. Clayton

11.1 THE PERSON, THE PIGEON, AND THE PHOTORECEPTOR

Approximately a fortnight ago, I dreamt I was a pigeon [1, 2]. In this dream, I was locked in a mid-air battle with a Peregrin falcon, swooping through the air with the wind rushing through my feathers.[1] As I was relentlessly pursued, adrenaline coursed through my body, causing my giant pigeon heart and lungs to pound in my chest. Within my dreamt world, I was experiencing life as a pigeon in mortal peril. Or was I?

As I describe my pigeon dream, you're probably conjuring your own mental images of what it would be like to be a pigeon. Many philosophers have asked what it would be like to be another species. Notably, Thomas Nagel asked, "What Is It Like to Be a Bat?" in his work of the same name, considering an existence with the body and sensory capacities of a winged mammal whose world is navigated using auditory information [3, 4]. Here we'll perform a similar exercise to Nagel, instead considering an avian species with an impressive visual system: the humble pigeon [5].

If you think about the world through a pigeon's eyes, what do you see? Do you see aerial shots of fields, or perhaps another "bird's-eye view"? Regardless of the subject of these visuals, I am confident they comprise the same colours you see day-to-day. And this is where our interpretation of a bird's-eye view begins to fall apart [3].

11.2 THE PERSON

Evidence suggests that your ability to see colour relies on the cone cells in your retinae, which are a type of photoreceptor [6–8]. Most people have three classes of cone cell: Long (L), Medium (M), and Short (S) wavelength cones, each of which is most sensitive to a different range of wavelengths of light [7].

When light from the outside world reaches the back of the eye, cone cells respond by firing electrical impulses at various rates according to how closely the light's wavelength matches their peak sensitivity [7]. These signals travel to the brain via the optic nerve, where it is believed that differences in the patterns of impulses produced by each cone class are used to decode colour from the surrounding world [7–9].

The different sensitivities of each class of cone cell are fundamental to human colour vision [7–9]. However, it is estimated that over 300 million people globally

 DOI: 10.1201/9781003758389-13

have atypical cone cells [7, 10]. For most of these people, their ability to discriminate between different colours is compromised and they are often referred to as having "colour blindness" [10].

Most cases of colour blindness fall into two main groups: anomalous trichromacy, and dichromacy [10]. Anomalous trichromacy occurs when individuals have all three cone types, but the peak sensitivities of one or more class is abnormal, [10] whereas dichromacy occurs when one class is "missing" from the retina [10]. Most forms of anomalous trichromacy and dichromacy result in either red-green or blue-yellow colour blindness.[2]

Outside of so-called colour deficiencies lies a highly unusual form of atypical colour vision: tetrachromacy [11]. Tetrachromatic vision occurs when individuals have four classes of cone, resulting in the ability to discriminate between "extra" colours compared to those with trichromatic vision [11]. Just like that, the presence (or absence) of different cone cells impacts experiences of colour.

11.3 THE PIGEON

The spectral sensitivities of the photoreceptors and eye structures of avian species (including pigeons) differ to those of humans, seemingly enabling them to see ultraviolet (UV) light [12]. Consequently, a true "bird-eye-view" requires more than just a simple change in perspective.

Despite differences in the spectrum of wavelengths detectable by their photoreceptors,[3] for both the person and the pigeon, the brain appears to be responsible for deciphering visual scenes encoded by photoreceptors' impulses [5, 7, 8]. However, the neuroarchitectures in which these processes occur are different; pigeon brains are nuclear and fruit cake-like in structure, whilst human brains are laminar (layered) and much more like a Austrian chocolate cake [13, 14].

Pigeons can't describe their experiences to human experimenters, and whilst we believe that pigeons "see" UV light, we have no idea what that looks like to them, nor how their nuclear brain structure may alter their perceptions. Nonetheless, it's rather unlikely that pigeons experience colour identically to you or I.

Differences in physiology seemingly limit your capacity to understand the phenomenological experience of colour in the same way a pigeon would – your "hardware" constrains your phenomenological experience, and thus your perspective on the quale of colour [3]. In this context, it becomes practicable to suggest that the body's capabilities are moderating factors in experiences of consciousness.

11.4 THE PHOTORECEPTOR

The presence of different types of photoreceptors could be interpreted as the "magic ingredient" underpinning the differences in how we experience colour [7]. However, an isolated photoreceptor isn't sufficient for the experience of colour [15]. Instead, it must be embedded in a larger system.

Cerebral achromatopsia is a form of colour blindness in which individuals have entirely typical cones, but don't have typical trichromatic vision as a result of damage to the brain's cerebral cortex [15, 16]. Those with this condition can "see" colour with their eyes, but experience the world in monochrome due to differences in the brain [15, 16].

The various forms of anomalous colour vision in humans suggest that both brain and body are necessary for the meaningful perception of colour. If one part of the equation (cerebral cortex, or photoreceptors) is anomalous, colour vision becomes anomalous too [7, 10, 15]. In this way, colour vision becomes a case study of the various complex physical and cognitive factors that influence the quale of colour.

The notion that your body impacts your experience of the world around you is a hot topic in discussions of "embodiment" [17–19].

11.5 WHAT IS EMBODIMENT?

In its most generic form, embodiment is concerned with the nature of physical representations. It implies that quality *X* is contained within object *Y* [17]. In colloquial speech, people often say a person (*Y*) embodied a quality (*X*) – i.e. Audrey Hepburn embodied grace – communicating that the person (*Y*) held within them that quality (*X*) to a noticeable extent. Consequently, it stands to reason that for something to *be* embodied, there must be a physical form (a body) associated with it [17].

11.6 THE MAGIC OF MANUAL MANIPULATIONS

Sleight-of-hand magic effects have presented an unexpected avenue through which to consider the effect of embodiment on our experiences of the world [20–23].

Sleight-of-hand magic effects are those in which magicians use dextrous manual actions to misdirect an audience, exploiting shortcuts taken by the audience's perceptual systems to create the impression they have performed a physics-defying act, such as making a coin disappear [20, 21].

The French drop is a common sleight-of-hand technique in which magicians appear to transfer an object between two hands whilst using unusual dextrous manipulations to keep the object within the original hand [20, 21]. If the magician finishes this technique by opening the hand the object was apparently passed into, they can create the illusion that the object has vanished into thin air [20, 21].

The French drop relies on motions of the opposable thumb [20, 21]. By performing this effect to animal audiences with diverse hand morphologies, scientists have begun to lift the curtain on embodiment.

11.7 THE SORCERER'S JAYS

Avian species have feathered wings, which do not possess individually dexterous fingers and instead move much more like a fan than a multi-jointed articulated hands; they're also thumbless [20]. Consequently, birds are ideal candidates for investigating the influence of body plan on susceptibility to the French drop [20].

To examine whether jays (an avian species) are "fooled" by the French drop, Elias Garcia-Pelegrin and a team of researchers led by one of us (Clayton) developed a magic performance for birds. Garcia-Pelegrin began his act by showing a jay that he held a worm in one hand. Having performed the act of passing this worm into his other hand, he asked the jay to indicate which hand the worm was in. Sometimes, the transfer of the worm between hands was real (the worm actually changed hands), other times Garcia-Pelegrin performed a fake transfer using the French drop (the worm remained in the original hand) [20].

Most humans are utterly fooled by a French drop and assume the worm has changed hands in both the real and fake conditions. However, Garcia-Pelegrin and colleagues demonstrated that an audience of jays could correctly identify which hand the worm was in, without being misdirected by the French drop [20].

To assess whether the jays' lack of first-hand experience of an opposable thumb could be the critical factor in their imperviousness to the French drop, the researchers also performed their act using transfer techniques in which the thumb is not vital to the effect. If the worm was passed very quickly between hands without any thumb-based grasping, jays became susceptible to the performed effect and misidentified which hand contained the worm in the fake transfer condition [20]. The outcome of this unusual magic act indicates a potential relationship between body plan and perception – in other words, whether the audience can perform the manual action used to create the magic trick seems to influence their susceptibility to it [20].

Taking this study in isolation, you could propose alternative explanations that don't hinge on an embodied understanding of thumbs. For example, large volumes of research suggest avian species, including jays, are sensitive to polarised light in a way that primates, including humans, are not [24, 25]. Polarised light offers an extra conduit for visual information, and it could be possible that information contained in polarised light allows jays' ability to see through the French drop. However, subsequent investigations with primate species make this explanation much less probable.

11.8 NO OPPOSABLE THUMB, NO POLARISATION SENSITIVITY, AND NO MAGIC EFFECT: THE CURIOUS CASE OF THE MARMOSET

To consider whether first-hand experiences of the manual actions required to perform a French drop are a primary determinant of susceptibility to its effect, the study was modified for investigation with three primate species: capuchins, squirrel monkeys, and marmosets, all of which have human-like polarised light sensitivity, and diverse hand morphologies [21].

Capuchins have similar hands to humans with entirely dexterous opposable thumbs; squirrel monkeys have partially opposable thumbs that are capable of performing a version of the precision grip needed for a French drop; and marmosets have entirely non-opposable thumbs that cannot enact a precision grip at all [21].

Garcia-Pelegrin and colleagues performed the usual French drop technique and a modified "Power drop" version that didn't require the motion of an articulated thumb for each species of primate. The researchers observed that the ability to perform the precision grips required for the French drop was the key difference between the audiences that were susceptible to the French drop (squirrel monkeys and capuchins) and those that weren't (marmosets).[4] This suggests that an embodied understanding of opposable thumbs (the presence of an opposable thumb in the observer's body plan) is necessary for these techniques to effectively misdirect the audience [21].

11.9 THUMBS UP IF YOU FELL FOR THE FRENCH DROP

You could argue that perhaps the expectations required to be successfully hoodwinked by a French drop could be formed by extensive observations of precision grips, and that jays and marmosets were simply impoverished of these stimuli compared to the opposable-thumbed species. However, the jays partaking in the study had been hand-raised by the team of researchers, spending significant time interacting with human hands and their biomechanical articulations across all life stages [20].

Considering the jays' extensive observational experience of human hands, their relative insusceptibility to the French drop substantiates the suggestion that the representation of a thumb within an observer's body plan is key to their susceptibility to effects predicated on the thumb [20].

11.10 RULES OF THUMB: HOW OUR BRAINS GET FROM A TO E WITHOUT INTERROGATING B, C, AND D

For sleight-of-hand magic effects to work, the cognitive "shortcuts" they exploit must be relatively stable – if your brain expected a thumb to behave differently every time you saw one, a French drop may never be effective.

Cognitive shortcuts are processes used by the brain to facilitate efficient responses to dynamic environments. For a given task, only certain pieces of information are relevant; if we were to process all the sensory information available to us all the time, it's likely we'd spend so long processing the information that we'd be unable to act in an appropriate timeframe [26].[5] A solution to this problem would be if our brains formed rules of thumb (heuristics) based on past experiences and used these to guide actions via cognitive shortcuts [27–30].

A helpful analogy is the example of using a new coffee machine: the first time you do so, you will need to think about which button to press to draw an espresso shot, but you don't need to think about *how* to press the button because once upon a time you learnt how to do so.

Pressing a button is surprisingly complex: you must reach out your hand and move it to the exact position of the button, press that button with sufficient force to actuate it, and release it within the correct period to elicit the desired response. Yet, you don't think through all those steps when pushing buttons; the act of pushing a button is wrapped up in the "feeling" of doing so [31].

The feeling of pressing a button appears to be experiential rather than purely sensory. When you apply force to the button using motor action, there is sensory feedback (a click), and an observable real-world outcome plays out (espresso being drawn). The perceptual experience of button pressing arrives when your prior experiences of buttons and coffee machines shape the predictions you make around your physical interactions with the coffee machine and their outcomes [31].

You feel you have pressed the button because you have experienced button pressing before and the information you're receiving from your sensorimotor system confirms your predictions around how the environment is changing when acting out button pressing in real-time [31]. In this way, your physical engagement with the environment (through your sensorimotor system) is crucial to your conscious experiences of the world around you [31, 32].

11.11 QUESTION WHAT YOU THINK YOU KNOW: HUMAN EMBODIMENT

At this stage, the word "embodiment" has been thrown around rather a lot, and you would be forgiven for wondering whether you are embodied. Indeed, the answer slightly depends on who you ask. Suggesting that consciousness is embodied insinuates that a body is a requirement for the article of consciousness (however you may define it) [17].

Regardless of whether you believe a body is necessary for consciousness, it's quite difficult to deny that (at least for the time in which you have one) your body appears to influence your experiences of the world around you. As a result, it seems reasonable to conclude that, whilst your body exists, your experiences are affected by it.

Throughout this chapter, we've outlined several examples in which your body's hardware apparently influences your experiences of the world. However, we haven't suggested any mechanistic explanations for exactly how the physical influences your so-called "conscious experiences". Although conclusive mechanistic explanations for the relationship between body and mind remain largely elusive, they are increasingly important when considering the possibility of a future in which non-organic machines are capable of "conscious" experience [19, 27, 33].

11.12 ENCODING NEW FORMS OF CONSCIOUSNESS

Until this point, we have considered the ways in which the body (at least partially) influences experience in biological contexts. However, there is significant debate around what type of body (if any) is necessary for conscious experiences, and whether its matter (biological or non-biological) determines the potential of consciousness arising from it [33].

In this chapter, we have established that a disembodied photoreceptor probably can't experience colour on its own. To experience colour, it seems that different classes of photoreceptor need to be both present and connected to a brain with the capability to decode their signals [7, 15]. This interpretation of the evidence suggests that it is unlikely that either disembodied sensors or an entirely disembodied brain could be sufficient to elicit the conscious experience of colour.

According to the discussions presented here, the quale of colour appears to spring forth from the combination of a body's elements and the brain's interpretations [7, 15]. Thinking back to the sorcerer's jays and magician's monkeys, it also appears that the shape and capabilities of that body are highly influential to the brain's interpretations of the world; and from this point, it is not a huge leap to suggest that perhaps the matter of embodiment matters too [33, 34].

So far, we have only considered the role of sensors and bodies in the biological organisms' experience of qualia. However, in recent years, artificial agents have entered the public consciousness, and there has been an explosion in the use of Large Language Models, such as ChatGPT, in everyday life [35]. Fascinating work has been undertaken to examine whether these artificial intelligences can emulate behavioural responses[6] associated with the complex cognitive capacities that are often considered hallmarks of biological intelligence. These include investigations into episodic-like memory [36] and theory of mind [37].

Large Language Models are usually entirely disembodied, and their disembodiment has been speculatively linked to their failure on certain theory of mind-related tasks [37]. Recent work has begun to use multimodal Large Language Models[7] as controllers in robotics, effectively using them as the "brain"[6] of complex systems equipped with sensors and motors [38].

When considering robots with sensors, complex control systems, and a motor system with which to enact behavioural responses to environmental stimuli, a natural parallel with biological organisms arises: if a biological agent's sensors and body are vital in how they experience their surroundings, surely a robot's could be too? From here, the following question emerges: if we were to develop sufficiently complex robots, equipped with sufficiently complex "brains", could they achieve an experience of qualia? And, if so, would these qualia be mediated by their body plan in a similar way to that of biological agents?

Some researchers argue that qualia can only spring forth from the interactions between the biological components of a body – this debate is concerned with "substrates" required for consciousness [33, 34]. Others argue that there's no reason conscious experience couldn't arise from similar interactions between non-biological materials if these materials became sufficiently sophisticated [39]. We vary in our views on this matter from complete rejection of the idea that artificial agents (even embodied ones) could experience qualia, to the belief that sufficiently complex artificial agents could (in principle) achieve a kind of experience of qualia, but that such an experience would be so unrecognisable to us as humans that we probably wouldn't think to *call* it qualia. Various factors underpin our viewpoints. However, we are unified by the idea that it is necessary to consider *why* an experience of qualia could be beneficial in an evolutionary context, and how the capacity for such experience has co-evolved with the body [40]. Whether or not it is possible to "plug in" a complex control algorithm to a pre-made body and generate the qualia is a key question that separates the mechanics of biological consciousness from the possibility of artificial consciousness.[8]

Either way, this question is central to considering whether a non-biological machine could ever become conscious; we will close this chapter by leaving you to chew over which side of that fence you sit on.

ACKNOWLEDGEMENT

Nathaniel R. Farndale Wright's PhD work is supported by a Biotechnology and Biological Sciences Research Council [grant number BB/X010899/1 (training grant)] and is supervised by Nicola S. Clayton and co-supervised by Neil D. Lawrence.

NOTES

1. When attempting to find a visual reference for my pigeon dream, I found it held a strong resemblance to Episode 1 of BBC Studios' "Animal's – The Inside Story" series, broadcast just after my third birthday in August 2002 [1]. A recording of the specific section of the show can be found on YouTube at the following URL: https://www.youtube.com/watch?v=i6HkIywJuxI&t=1s [2]
2. Whilst red-green colour blindness primarily results in individuals being unable to discriminate between red and green, the phrase "blue-yellow colour blindness" is somewhat deceptive as this type of atypical colour vision results in difficulties distinguishing between a much wider range of colours.
3. The human S-cones appear to have some limited sensitivity to UV light. However, the UV light is filtered out by other structures in the eye before reaching the retinae [12].
4. Squirrel monkeys and capuchins were misled by both the standard French drop and the Power drop, whilst marmosets (which have in-line non-opposable thumbs) were unimpressed by the French drop but successfully misdirected by its Power drop cousin [21].
5. Daniel Dennett described the applicability of this issue (often referred to as the "frame problem") to artificial contexts using the example of a robot being asked to remove a bomb from a room [26].
6. It is crucial to note that the capacity to respond to a given task as though one has theory of mind, or episodic-like memory, does not mean one necessarily possess analogues cognitive capacities to those that underlie these capabilities in biological organisms.
7. Multimodal language models are those which can accept inputs other than text. For example, GPT-4, which features in Mon-Williams and colleagues' embodied large-language-model-enabled robot framework, can accept image as text inputs in order to produce text outputs [38].
8. It should be noted that whilst we differ in our views on whether artificial agents could experience qualia, we all reject the notion that this would be possible with current technology.

REFERENCES

1. Fight for Life (No. 1). (2002, August). [Broadcast]. In *Animals—The Inside Story*. BBC. https://www.bbc.co.uk/programmes/p031d2x7
2. *Pigeon vs Peregrine Falcon*. (2011, September 14). [YouTube Video]. BBC Earth. https://www.youtube.com/watch?v=i6HkIywJuxI&t=1s
3. Nagel, T. (1974). What Is It Like to Be a Bat? *The Philosophical Review*, *83*(4), 435–450. https://doi.org/10.2307/2183914
4. Jones, G. (2005). Echolocation. *Current Biology*, *15*(13), R484–R488. https://doi.org/10.1016/j.cub.2005.06.051
5. Donovan, W. J. (1978). Structure and function of the pigeon visual system. *Physiological Psychology*, *6*(4), 403–437. https://doi.org/10.3758/BF03326748
6. Hurlbert, A. (1997). Colour vision. *Current Biology*, *7*(7), R400–R402. https://doi.org/10.1016/S0960-9822(06)00199-0
7. Solomon, S. G., & Lennie, P. (2007). The machinery of colour vision. *Nature Reviews Neuroscience*, *8*(4), 276–286. https://doi.org/10.1038/nrn2094
8. Joesch, M., & Meister, M. (2016). A neuronal circuit for colour vision based on rod–cone opponency. *Nature*, *532*(7598), 236–239. https://doi.org/10.1038/nature17158
9. Hurvich, L. M., & Jameson, D. (1957). An opponent-process theory of color vision. *Psychological Review*, *64*(6, Pt. 1), 384–404. https://doi.org/10.1037/h0041403
10. Simunovic, M. P. (2010). Colour vision deficiency. *Eye*, *24*(5), 747–755. https://doi.org/10.1038/eye.2009.251

11. Jordan, G., & Mollon, J. (2019). Tetrachromacy: The mysterious case of extra-ordinary color vision. *Current Opinion in Behavioral Sciences*, *30*, 130–134. https://doi.org/10.1016/j.cobeha.2019.08.002
12. Cuthill, I. C., Partridge, J. C., Bennett, A. T. D., Church, S. C., Hart, N. S., & Sarah, H. (2000). Ultraviolet Vision in Birds. *Advances in the Study of Behavior* (vol. *29*, pp. 159–214). https://doi.org/10.1016/S0065-3454(08)60105-9
13. Emery, N. J., & Clayton, N. S. (2005). Evolution of the avian brain and intelligence. *Current Biology*, *15*(23), R946–R950. https://doi.org/10.1016/j.cub.2005.11.029
14. Clayton, N. S., & Emery, N. J. (2015). Avian models for human cognitive neuroscience: A proposal. *Neuron*, *86*(6), 1330–1342. https://doi.org/10.1016/j.neuron.2015.04.024
15. Cowey, A., & Heywood, C. A. (1997). Cerebral achromatopsia: Colour blindness despite wavelength processing. *Trends in Cognitive Sciences*, *1*(4), 133–139. https://doi.org/10.1016/S1364-6613(97)01043-7
16. Heywood, C. A., Gaffan, D., & Cowey, A. (1995). Cerebral achromatopsia in monkeys. *European Journal of Neuroscience*, *7*(5), 1064–1073. https://doi.org/10.1111/j.1460-9568.1995.tb01093.x
17. Prinz, J. (2001). Is Consciousness Embodied? In P. Robbins & M. Aydede (Eds.), *The Cambridge Handbook of Situated Cognition* (1st edn, pp. 419–436). Cambridge University Press. https://doi.org/10.1017/CBO9780511816826.022
18. Seth, A. K. (2013). Interoceptive inference, emotion, and the embodied self. *Trends in Cognitive Sciences*, *17*(11), 565–573. https://doi.org/10.1016/j.tics.2013.09.007
19. Clark, A. (1999). An embodied cognitive science? *Trends in Cognitive Sciences*, *3*(9), 345–351. https://doi.org/10.1016/S1364-6613(99)01361-3
20. Garcia-Pelegrin, E., Schnell, A. K., Wilkins, C., & Clayton, N. S. (2021). Exploring the perceptual inabilities of Eurasian jays (*Garrulus glandarius*) using magic effects. *Proceedings of the National Academy of Sciences*, *118*(24), e2026106118. https://doi.org/10.1073/pnas.2026106118
21. Garcia-Pelegrin, E., Miller, R., Wilkins, C., & Clayton, N. S. (2023). Manual action expectation and biomechanical ability in three species of New World monkey. *Current Biology*, *33*(9), 1803–1808.e2. https://doi.org/10.1016/j.cub.2023.03.023
22. Farndale Wright, N. R., & Clayton, N. S. (2025). On bodies, brains, and behaviour (and a little bit of magic). *Behavioral and Brain Sciences*, *48*, e97. https://doi.org/10.1017/S0140525X25100666
23. Schnell, A. K., Loconsole, M., Garcia-Pelegrin, E., Wilkins, C., & Clayton, N. S. (2021). Jays are sensitive to cognitive illusions. *Royal Society Open Science*, *8*(8), 202358. https://doi.org/10.1098/rsos.202358
24. Chetverikova, R., Dautaj, G., Schwigon, L., Dedek, K., & Mouritsen, H. (2022). Double cones in the avian retina form an oriented mosaic which might facilitate magnetoreception and/or polarized light sensing. *Journal of The Royal Society Interface*, *19*(189), 20210877. https://doi.org/10.1098/rsif.2021.0877
25. Muheim, R. (2011). Behavioural and physiological mechanisms of polarized light sensitivity in birds. *Philosophical Transactions of the Royal Society B: Biological Sciences*, *366*(1565), 763–771. https://doi.org/10.1098/rstb.2010.0196
26. Dennett, D. C. (1984). Cognitive Wheels: The Frame Problem of AI. In C. Hookaway (Ed.), *Minds, Machines and Evolution* (pp. 129–151). Cambridge University Press.
27. Clark, A. (2013). Whatever next? Predictive brains, situated agents, and the future of cognitive science. *Behavioral and Brain Sciences*, *36*(3), 181–204. https://doi.org/10.1017/S0140525X12000477
28. Friston, K. (2010). The free-energy principle: A unified brain theory? *Nature Reviews Neuroscience*, *11*(2), 127–138. https://doi.org/10.1038/nrn2787
29. Friston, K. (2012). The history of the future of the Bayesian brain. *NeuroImage*, *62*(2), 1230–1233. https://doi.org/10.1016/j.neuroimage.2011.10.004

30. Knill, D. C., & Pouget, A. (2004). The Bayesian brain: The role of uncertainty in neural coding and computation. *Trends in Neurosciences*, *27*(12), 712–719. https://doi.org/10.1016/j.tins.2004.10.007
31. O'Regan, J. K., & Noë, A. (2001). A sensorimotor account of vision and visual consciousness. *Behavioral and Brain Sciences*, *24*(5), 939–973. https://doi.org/10.1017/S0140525X01000115
32. Clark, A., & Chalmers, D. (1998). The extended mind. *Analysis*, *58*(1), 7–19. https://doi.org/10.1093/analys/58.1.7
33. Seth, A. (2025). Conscious artificial intelligence and biological naturalism. *Behavioral and Brain Sciences*, 1–42. https://doi.org/10.1017/S0140525X25000032
34. Seth, A. K. (2021). *Being You: A New Science of Consciousness*. Faber & Faber.
35. (2025). The rise of large language models. *Nature Computational Science*, *5*(9), 689–690. https://doi.org/10.1038/s43588-025-00890-x
36. Dong, C. V., Lu, Q., Norman, K. A., & Michelmann, S. (2025). Towards large language models with human-like episodic memory. *Trends in Cognitive Sciences*, *29*(10), 928–941. https://doi.org/10.1016/j.tics.2025.06.016
37. Strachan, J. W. A., Albergo, D., Borghini, G., Pansardi, O., Scaliti, E., Gupta, S., Saxena, K., Rufo, A., Panzeri, S., Manzi, G., Graziano, M. S. A., & Becchio, C. (2024). Testing theory of mind in large language models and humans. *Nature Human Behaviour*, *8*(7), 1285–1295. https://doi.org/10.1038/s41562-024-01882-z
38. Mon-Williams, R., Li, G., Long, R., Du, W., & Lucas, C. G. (2025). Embodied large language models enable robots to complete complex tasks in unpredictable environments. *Nature Machine Intelligence*, *7*(4), 592–601. https://doi.org/10.1038/s42256-025-01005-x
39. Blum, L., & Blum, M. (2022). A theory of consciousness from a theoretical computer science perspective: Insights from the Conscious Turing Machine. *Proceedings of the National Academy of Sciences of the United States of America*, *119*(21), e2115934119. https://doi.org/10.1073/pnas.2115934119
40. Damasio, A., & Carvalho, G. B. (2013). The nature of feelings: Evolutionary and neurobiological origins. *Nature Reviews Neuroscience*, *14*(2), 143–152. https://doi.org/10.1038/nrn3403

12 Does the Body Matter? Perspectives on the Embodied Nature of Consciousness

Sahba Besharati, Steven James, and Benjamin Rosman

12.1 INTRODUCTION: WHY START FROM THE BODY?

Do we need a body to be conscious? When we talk about consciousness – the *feeling* of being you – we often think about the brain functioning in isolation. Historically, in neuroscience and artificial intelligence (AI), it has been easier to forget the body completely and either study the brain, or computational systems that mimic the brain. In many ways, until recently, we also did not have the appropriate methods or sufficient resources to study hard problems like consciousness or to think about it at the level of the full system. Long before large language models (LLMs), Alan Turing [1, 2] famously put aside the body – not because he thought it unimportant, but because trying to replicate a body as a machine was, at the time, simply infeasible. So the field focused on the hardware (a computer) for building a "digital brain" capable of intelligent behaviour, rather than building an entire robot. In the same way, it took decades for neuroscience and psychology [3, 4] to even think about putting aside the famous philosopher René Descartes' infamous words, "I think, therefore, I am". Since consciousness is so hard to study, traditionally, it made more sense to focus on one aspect of our conscious experience [5], such as perception and vision, and although this integrates aspects of embodiment, in many ways this approach still marginalises the body. With the explosion of LLMs, AI scientists have now emerged as rising stars in consciousness science by building intelligent systems that can mimic aspects of consciousness [6], but these systems still typically exist entirely outside of the body. And so, yet again, the body has been pushed to the sidelines.

In this chapter, we propose just the opposite. Consciousness, we argue, is not something that just happens in the brain (or a machine equivalent), but through the brain in concert with the body. Embodiment should be seen as the *default condition* for consciousness. Just as B comes before C in the Latin alphabet, so too we argue that the Body should be seen as conditional for Conscious experience. Humans and non-human animals show intelligence, develop cognitive capacities, *and* have subjective experience, but they do all of this always as embodied agents [7–9]. In nature, a brain without a body (or a body without a brain) is usually a sign that something

 DOI: 10.1201/9781003758389-14

has gone very wrong! To treat the body as optional is to slip back to the age-old Cartesian dualism.

Before we can make this argument, we first need to confront a key challenge: *definitions*. What is consciousness? What is embodiment? What is intelligence or emotion? A lack of concrete definitions is what makes these questions so interesting and so difficult to answer. Unfortunately, we do not have a quick fix or instant recipe for the "hard problem" of consciousness or the "hard problem" of definitions. Instead, we approach these complex concepts as one would a good tiramisu – layer by layer – mixing AI, machine learning, neuroscience, and psychology. In doing so, we present a scaffolded approach in telling the story of why the body matters for consciousness. We start by exploring how artificial agents learn to learn, then move to compare intelligence and cognition in machines and humans and finally turn to subjective experience itself.

12.2 BODIES FOR REPRESENTATIONAL AND PERCEPTUAL ANCHORING

Learning how to navigate a maze is a core experiment for both translational neuroscience and machine learning. These experiments can teach us how an agent (as an artificial or biological decision-maker) can learn, adapt, and generalise. The problem is that the outside world – our everyday environment – is far more complex than a simple maze. Unfortunately, what we learn from these powerful experiments does not always hold true in everyday life [10].

Yet maze navigation reveals something fundamental about how agents represent space. Consider two ways an AI agent might learn to navigate. In the first approach, the agent represents the world in allocentric (world-centred) coordinates – fixed reference points like GPS coordinates. The door exists at a specific latitude and longitude, regardless of where the agent is positioned. In the second approach, the agent uses egocentric (body-centred) coordinates, representing the world relative to its own perspective: "the door is in front of me", "the wall is to my left".

This distinction between egocentric and allocentric reference frames has been central to research in spatial cognition for decades [11–13]. Neuroscience has shown that different brain regions specialise in these different reference frames – the hippocampus encodes allocentric spatial maps [14], while the fronto-parietal cortex processes egocentric coordinates [15]. But here's what matters for understanding embodiment: when agents learn through experience, they need somewhere to start – a perspective from which to perceive. The body provides that starting point, that egocentric origin from which spatial understanding develops.

Learning from this egocentric, body-centred perspective has a key advantage. When AI agents use egocentric coordinates, they can adapt and generalise their learning across multiple environments and scenarios [16]. An agent that learns "move forward through openings" can apply this principle in any maze, while an agent that memories "go to coordinates X,Y" has learned something useful only for one specific environment.

What we're seeing here reflects a foundational insight: embodied experience provides a powerful basis for learning and generalisation. These long-standing arguments have been made in psychology [17] and robotics [18, 19] where researchers have argued that perception and action are inseparable. Classic developmental psychology shows that children begin with purely egocentric representations before gradually developing allocentric understanding [20], suggesting that the body-centred perspective is foundational [21].

This is what we mean by representational and perceptual anchoring: the body serves as the origin point, the reference frame from which all spatial understanding begins. If bodies provide this foundational anchor for even basic navigation, what role might they play in more complex forms of intelligence?

12.3 BODIES FOR INTELLIGENCE

We know (or at least we should know) that consciousness is *not* the same as intelligence. Let's say that again – the experience of being conscious is *not* the same as the intelligence required to solve problems. While we must always be mindful not to equate or confuse intelligence with consciousness, our new AI-informed reality opens up fresh questions. Just as we can ask "What does it feel like to be something (like a bat?)", we can also ask, "What does it mean to be intelligent?". One way to understand intelligence is not as an absolute quality but a process of engaging in problem-solving and adaptability relative to the agent's sensory and motor abilities [22]. So how intelligent an agent is depends on what it can sense or do through its body. Following this line of thinking, a human, animal or robot is as intelligent as the constraints of their bodies allow them to be.

To build on this argument, we can first think of the energy-efficiency principle [23, 24] that speaks to the metabolic efficiency of the brain. Some neuroscientists have studied how neurons (the basic building blocks of the brain) use and conserve energy. They argue that the brain evolved to reduce the amount of "waste" or to conserve energy for what was deemed as unnecessary – explaining *why* the brain needs to be efficient for survival. Related to this, theoretical neuroscientist Karl Friston proposed the Free-Energy principle [25, 26] that gives us a theory of *how* the brain conserves this energy. In this theory, "free energy" is a mathematical quantity in Bayesian inference that explains how biological systems evolved to minimise surprise (prediction error) in order to achieve homeostasis (the body's way of achieving a balance or equilibrium) and adapt to their environment.

We can also see intelligence as being contextual and defined by the agent's body [27] – bodily and social experiences shape intelligence so as to give meaning to concepts. This might also give rise to creativity. Disembodied intelligence in machines, for example, would most likely be unable to invent the *concept* of poetry, even if they can comfortably write a hundred poems.

12.4 BODIES FOR COGNITION (WITH A TOUCH OF CONSCIOUSNESS)

Cognition should be seen as different from intelligence as cognition is a process that involves a combination of mental capacities that allow us to acquire, represent and use knowledge. For example, memory, attention, and decision-making all form part of our cognitive capacities. Many of these are highly intricate processes. Just taking memory as an example shows that there are multiple forms of memory, such as autobiographical memory [28, 29] – memory about our self and past events; semantic memory [30–32] – memory about facts and history; episodic memory [33–35] – memory about experience; and procedural and motor memory [36] – memory of motor sequences, like how to swim, ride a bike or even walk. Studying how these various kinds of memory develop during infancy and childhood, and then break down during disease or brain injury, has helped us understand how complex and different these memory systems are as well as the diversity of brain regions they rely on. Discoveries like the mirror neurons [37, 38] have also helped us understand how memory can be grounded in the body. Originally found in macaques (later in humans too), mirror neurons fire when an action is performed (e.g., like waving your hand) and when observing others perform an action (e.g., someone else waving to you). Following this discovery, a body of research suggests that our social understanding of others – and maybe ourselves [39] – is closely related to our memory for actions and sensorimotor areas in the brain [40]. Related to this, cognition can also encompass what is known as metacognition [41, 42] (thinking about your own mind) and social cognition [27, 43] (thinking about other people's minds), both of which are closely related to the development of self-awareness.

The same principle of embodied anchoring in reinforcement learning [44], from earlier on in this chapter, parallel the arguments made in the field of embodied cognition [27]. Here, the body can shape the way we learn, predict and act in the world. If you have ever read *To Kill a Mockingbird*, you might remember the magnanimous Atticus Finch explaining to his daughter Scout that "you never really understand a person until you consider things from his point of view… until you climb into his skin and walk around it". In trying to teach his daughter about empathy, he also shows us that our ability to take another person's perspective requires the (dis)placement of the body [45, 46]. We use the body as a reference point to understand not only our physical position (as well as subjective experience) in the world, but also our position relative to other people [12]. So, our ability to think about other people's thoughts, emotions, or beliefs, as well as our intersubjective experience with others [47], is actually grounded in our embodied experience of the world.

Neuroscience has now managed to use clever experiments (one of them called the rubber hand illusion [48]) to change the feeling you have over your body and *trick* you into thinking that your arm, for example, does not belong to you. Similarly, there are cases of patients who have suffered a specific kind of brain injury that can have similar erroneous beliefs about their body, thinking their arm does not belong to them or think they have motor agency over their arm (they can move it) when they are actually paralysed [8, 49]. Technology like virtual reality has even let us make what is called "a full body illusion" [50, 51], and do exactly what Atticus Finch suggested: put ourselves into the body of another person (albeit virtually). And just like Atticus Finch predicted, embodying a virtual avatar can increase your empathy and change your unconscious beliefs about other people [52].

This kind of clinical research and these experimental "tricks" have given us rich insights into how our body is central to the way to understand our sense of agency in the world and how we develop a sense of self [53, 54]. Earlier on, we introduced the idea of *predictive coding* [55, 56], where the brain makes a statistical model of the world where it minimises surprise (prediction error) by adjusting beliefs and actions using our "priors" – what we have learnt or experienced in the past. Our embodied experience of the world (both internal and external) gives us these "priors" so we can make inferences (or predictions) about the world, and ourselves.

12.5 BODIES FOR CONSCIOUSNESS

Consciousness, at a very basic level, is the subjective experience of being an embodied self in the world. People like Damasio [9, 57], Panksepp [58], Solms [59], Craig [39, 60], and many others have all argued that consciousness is not just this abstract idea, but the body's dynamic regulation of the self. So, it is more than just qualia – what it is like to be something – but rather the *feeling* of being in the world – what it *feels* like. The body gives rise to this feeling, and thereby to consciousness.

The body is engaged in this constant balancing act called homeostasis. The body automatically adjusts our blood pressure or our temperature, for example, without any conscious effort or awareness [61]. This is also related to what was mentioned earlier on how our brain functions to conserve energy in the body through a process called allostasis [62]. We do, however, notice changes in our body – hunger, thirst, a flush of heat – these internal feelings are called interoception that are subjectively experienced [63, 64]. Interoception also has "qualia" as *your* experience of pain or hunger can be very different to *my* internal feeling of pain or hunger, even if we share the same "objective" experience (e.g., getting burnt on the stove or skipping lunch) [39, 61]. In comparison, we also have something called exteroception – our outer lens of the world; our ability to see, hear, touch, taste, and smell. Traditionally, consciousness research has focused on these exteroceptive signals, especially vision, in how we have different subjective experiences of seeing the colour red, for example Park and Tallon-Baudry [65]. These internal bodily feelings (interoception) and our outer perception of the world (exteroception) are in constant dialogue with each other [66]. As an experiment, think about listening to your favourite song – you may hear the song (exteroception), but you may also feel it in your chest or gut or even your skin (interoception).

Bodily feelings during infancy might even lead to how we develop a sense of self and subjective awareness [67]. This process can be mirrored in the breakdown of awareness following brain injury that we spoke about earlier. One theory is that when this dialogue between brain and body breaks down – when the body changes too fast for the brain's model to catch-up – unawareness or emotional distress can follow [68]. Adolescence is another key developmental milestone where things like metacognition are refined, as a real sense of self-awareness is found [69]. This coincides with rapid changes in the body. Bodily changes seem to be able to reshape our subjective experience, not only during brain injury, but also during development; we are just not sure how much or which mechanisms are involved.

Developmental aspects of consciousness have been largely neglected. So, although both the brain and body undergo a huge amount of change during the first two years of life and during adolescence, there is very little we know about how a baby develops subjective experience [70–72] or how self-awareness might change or be refined during adolescence [72]. New research focusing on studying the basic building blocks of self-consciousness through this developmental lens is fundamental in unpacking the critical components of consciousness in artificial systems.

12.6 THE EMPIRE STRIKES BACK: WHY SOME WILL STILL ARGUE THAT THE BODY DOESN'T MATTER

Our default argument for consciousness, is of course, not without its critics. Old habits die hard and the critics are often the main players in the game. One of the strongest counter arguments is a devastating medical condition following brain injury called locked-in syndrome [73, 74]. After damage to a very small and evolutionarily old part of the brain called the brainstem, a person is fully conscious, but there is almost complete body paralysis. The person can't move or speak, and they can usually only blink. At one level, this seems to disprove our argument that the body is the default position for consciousness, as there is living evidence that a person can be conscious without access to their body. So why can't a machine be conscious without a body, too, then? But there are missing pieces to this puzzle. First, those with locked-in syndrome still developed consciousness through their body before their brain injury. Second, some research has shown that these patients are still metabolically and interoceptively connected to their body [75, 76]. Sadly, these patients have lost their ability to act upon the world with their body, but they still experience internal sensations about their body. Fundamentally, you can argue that their conscious experience is still embodied.

Another clinical example often used is called blindsight [77]. Here, there is damage to a specific part at the very back of your brain, called the primary visual cortex. This takes away our ability to consciously see – so these patients will tell you that they are completely blind, but these patients *can* actually navigate around objects or obstacles. There are other pathways in the brain that are allowing them to process the visual information even though they have lost their ability to be aware that they can see and consciously experience it. Discoveries around blindsight is also what lead to a new wave of consciousness research at the end of the twentieth century [5], which was paired with major breakthroughs in how we understand the visual system [78] – especially differences between visual pathways for perception (i.e., what we see as a general experience) and action (i.e., what we see to control how we move our body) [79]. Before then, and even now, the "C" word (consciousness) lacked much scientific credibility, which dates back to the feud between Freud (and his theory of the unconscious) and behaviourism (an outdated school of thought in psychology that only studied what was observable and seemingly objective – behaviour). Even the word "subjectivity" was scarcely used. This historical background also helps us understand why perception has been important to recent consciousness science, and why blindsight has been used to downplay the importance of the body in conscious experience. In blindsight, there can be action (i.e., the person can move around obstacles) without conscious perception (i.e., awareness they can see), which some have argued disproves the idea that the body is necessary for consciousness. Here, is it important to remember that conscious perception is not entirely the same as consciousness itself, as the subjective experience of what it is like to be something. Secondly, blindsight shows us that there are multiple pathways in the brain that create conscious experience [80] that are still grounded in the body.

In blindsight, the body perceives without awareness. Dreaming is the opposite. When we dream, we do not directly perceive the outside world, but the brain turns inwards. We also experience different kinds of sleep and dreaming. One kind of sleep is called REM (rapid eye movement) sleep, where we have very vivid dreams and the brain has very similar activity as if we are awake [81, 82]. It is almost as if the brain re-creates embodied states (both interoceptive and exteroceptive) during REM. However, it is important to remember that REM sleep is not the same as dreaming. Neuropsychological research that has studied patients after specific kinds of brain injury [83] has shown us that you can dream outside of REM sleep, and you can have REM sleep and not dream. Dreaming and REM sleep also rely on different parts and pathways in the brain. So, when we dream, we can think of ourselves as a kind of off-line embodied agent.

12.7 CONCLUDING COMMENTS: TOWARDS LARGE BODY MODELS?

Now that we have come to the end of our chapter, we have finished making our home-made tiramisu of why the body matters for consciousness, and why embodiment should be treated as the default position when we ask whether any agent, human or artificial, can know what it feels like to be something. Whether embodiment is ultimately required for all possible forms of consciousness remains an open question. What is clear, however, is that for us to really understand how and if machines can be conscious will require taking the body seriously, and not viewing it as an optional add-on. For us to better understand how our machines could experience, these machines should be given the same kinds of streams of sensory experience and abilities to act in the world that we recognise in other creatures we believe to be conscious. This is why we have argued for an embodied shift in the field. There has been growing recognition that, as impressive as LLMs are, language alone is not enough to create a conscious agent. Consciousness emerges at the intersection between the outside world and the internal world. Artificial systems, no matter how intelligent they seem or how eloquently they may communicate, might be able to mimic human perception, but without an embodied experience of the world, in the end, they are just processing information rather than experiencing subjective awareness. To explore our embodied argument further, AI research needs to turn its attention towards robotics and test how machines can learn to maintain internal bodily states, together with exteroceptive functions. This embodied shift in AI and neuroscience has the potential to unlock the mechanisms of how we create a sense of self and how we develop the ability to know *what it feels like* to be something.

ACKNOWLEDGEMENTS

We would like to thank Tim Bayne for his helpful comments on an earlier draft of this chapter.

REFERENCES

1. Turing, A. Computing Machinery and Intelligence (1950). in *The Essential Turing* (ed. Copeland, B. J.) 433–464 (Oxford University Press, 2004).
2. French, R. M. The Turing Test: The First 50 Years. *Trends in Cognitive Sciences* **4** (2000) 115–122.
3. Dennett, D. C. Review of Damasio, Descartes' Error. *Times Literary Supplement* **25** (1995) 1995.
4. Damasio, A. & Damasio, H. Minding the Body. *Daedalus* **135** (2006) 15–22.
5. LeDoux, J. E., Michel, M. & Lau, H. A Little History Goes a Long Way toward Understanding Why We Study Consciousness the Way We Do Today. *Proceedings of the National Academy of Sciences of the United States of America* **117** (2020) 6976–6984.
6. Butlin, P. *et al.* Consciousness in Artificial Intelligence: Insights from the Science of Consciousness. Preprint at http://arxiv.org/abs/2308.08708 (2023).
7. Clark, A. Pressing the Flesh: A Tension in the Study of the Embodied, Embedded Mind?. *Philosophy and Phenomenological Research* **76** (2008) 37–59.
8. Gallagher, S. Philosophical Conceptions of the Self: Implications for Cognitive Science. *Trends in Cognitive Sciences* **4** (2000) 14–21.
9. Damasio, A. R. *The Feeling of What Happens: Body and Emotion in the Making of Consciousness* (Houghton Mifflin Harcourt, 1999).
10. Manger, P. Is 21st Century Neuroscience Too Focussed on the Rat/Mouse Model of Brain Function and Dysfunction? *Frontiers in Neuroanatomy* **2** (2008) 329–336.
11. Frith, U. & De Vignemont, F. Egocentrism, Allocentrism, and Asperger Syndrome. *Consciousness and Cognition* **14** (2005) 719–738.
12. Vogeley, K. *et al.* Neural Correlates of First-Person Perspective as One Constituent of Human Self-Consciousness. *Journal of Cognitive Neuroscience* **16** (2004) 817–827.
13. Tolman, E. C. Cognitive Maps in Rats and Men. *Psychological Review* **55** (1948) 180.
14. Ekstrom, A. D., Arnold, A. E. G. F. & Iaria, G. A Critical Review of the Allocentric Spatial Representation and Its Neural Underpinnings: Toward a Network-Based Perspective. *Frontiers in Human Neuroscience* **8** (2014) 803–817.
15. Vallar, G. *et al.* A Fronto-Parietal System for Computing the Egocentric Spatial Frame of Reference in Humans. *Experimental Brain Research* **124** (1999) 281–286.
16. James, S., Rosman, B. & Konidaris, G. Learning Portable Representations for High-Level Planning. International Conference on Machine Learning. PMLR (2020).
17. Bertenthal, B. I. Origins and Early Development of Perception, Action, and Representation. *Annual Review of Psychology* **47** (1996) 431–459.
18. Savva, M. *et al.* Habitat: A Platform for Embodied AI Research. in *2019 IEEE/CVF International Conference on Computer Vision (ICCV)* 9338–9346 (IEEE, Seoul, Korea (South), 2019). doi:10.1109/ICCV.2019.00943
19. Roy, N. *et al.* From Machine Learning to Robotics: Challenges and Opportunities for Embodied Intelligence (2021). Preprint at doi:10.48550/arXiv.2110.15245
20. Piaget, J. *The Origins of Intelligence in Children.* vol. 8 (International Universities Press, 1952).
21. Vygotsky, L. S. *Mind in Society: Development of Higher Psychological Processes.* (Harvard University Press, 1978).
22. Botvinick, M. *et al.* Reinforcement Learning, Fast and Slow. *Trends in Cognitive Sciences* **23** (2019) 408–422.
23. Attwell, D. & Laughlin, S. B. An Energy Budget for Signaling in the Grey Matter of the Brain. *Journal of Cerebral Blood Flow & Metabolism* **21** (2001) 1133–1145.
24. Sterling, P. & Laughlin, S. *Principles of Neural Design* (MIT Press, 2015).
25. Friston, K. The Free-Energy Principle: A Unified Brain Theory? *Nature Reviews Neuroscience* **11** (2010) 127–138.

26. Friston, K. The Free-Energy Principle: A Rough Guide to the Brain? *Trends in Cognitive Sciences* **13** (2009) 293–301.
27. Gallese, V. Before and Below 'Theory of Mind': Embodied Simulation and the Neural Correlates of Social Cognition. *Philosophical Transactions of the Royal Society B* **362** (2007) 659–669.
28. Conway, M. A. Sensory–perceptual Episodic Memory and Its Context: Autobiographical Memory. *Philosophical Transactions of the Royal Society of London. Series B: Biological Sciences* **356** (2001) 1375–1384.
29. Conway, M. A. & Pleydell-Pearce, C. W. The Construction of Autobiographical Memories in the Self-Memory System. *Psychological Review* **107** (2000) 261.
30. Warrington, E. K. The Selective Impairment of Semantic Memory. *The Quarterly Journal of Experimental Psychology* **27** (1975) 635–657.
31. McCarthy, R. A. & Warrington, E. K. Evidence for Modality-Specific Meaning Systems in the Brain. *Nature* **334** (1988) 428–430.
32. Tulving, E. Episodic and Semantic Memory. *Organization of Memory* **1** (1972) 381–402.
33. Tulving, E. Episodic Memory: From Mind to Brain. *Annual Review of Psychology* **53** (2002) 1–25.
34. Scoville, W. B. & Milner, B. Loss of Recent Memory after Bilateral Hippocampal Lesions. *Journal of Neurology, Neurosurgery, and Psychiatry* **20** (1957) 11.
35. Penfield, W. & Milner, B. Memory Deficit Produced by Bilateral Lesions in the Hippocampal Zone. *AMA Archives of Neurology & Psychiatry* **79** (1958) 475–497.
36. Squire, L. R. Mechanisms of Memory. *Science* **232** (1986) 1612–1619.
37. Rizzolatti, G., Fadiga, L., Gallese, V. & Fogassi, L. Premotor Cortex and the Recognition of Motor Actions. *Cognitive Brain Research* **3** (1996) 131–141.
38. Gallese, V., Fadiga, L., Fogassi, L. & Rizzolatti, G. Action Recognition in the Premotor Cortex. *Brain* **119** (1996) 593–609.
39. Craig, A. D. How Do You Feel? Interoception: The Sense of the Physiological Condition of the Body. *Nature Reviews Neuroscience* **3** (2002) 655–666.
40. Uddin, L. Q., Iacoboni, M., Lange, C. & Keenan, J. P. The Self and Social Cognition: The Role of Cortical Midline Structures and Mirror Neurons. *Trends in Cognitive Sciences* **11** (2007) 153–157.
41. Fleming, S. M. & Lau, H. C. How to Measure Metacognition. *Frontiers in Human Neuroscience* **8** (2014) 443.
42. Fleming, S. M. & Dolan, R. J. The Neural Basis of Metacognitive Ability. *Philosophical Transactions of the Royal Society B: Biological Sciences* **367** (2012) 1338–1349.
43. Saxe, R. Uniquely Human Social Cognition. *Current Opinion in Neurobiology* **16** (2006) 235–239.
44. Rosman, B. & Ramamoorthy, S. Action Priors for Learning Domain Invariances. *IEEE Transactions on Autonomous Mental Development* **7** (2015) 107–118.
45. Blanke, O. Multisensory Brain Mechanisms of Bodily Self-Consciousness. *Nature Reviews Neuroscience* **13** (2012) 556–571.
46. Blanke, O., Landis, T., Spinelli, L. & Seeck, M. Out-of-Body Experience and Autoscopy of Neurological Origin. *Brain* **127** (2004) 243–258.
47. Dumas, G. Towards a Two-Body Neuroscience. *Communicative & Integrative Biology* **4** (2011) 349–352.
48. Botvinick, M. & Cohen, J. Rubber Hands 'Feel' Touch that Eyes See. *Nature* **391** (1998) 756.
49. Besharati, S. *et al.* Mentalizing the Body: Spatial and Social Cognition in Anosognosia for Hemiplegia. *Brain* **139** (2016) 971–985.
50. Slater, M., Spanlang, B., Sanchez-Vives, M. V. & Blanke, O. First Person Experience of Body Transfer in Virtual Reality. *PloS One* **5** (2010) e10564.

51. Sanchez-Vives, M. V. & Slater, M. From Presence to Consciousness through Virtual Reality. *Nature Reviews Neuroscience* **6** (2005) 332–339.
52. Higgins, S. *et al.* Perspective Matters: A Systematic Review of Immersive Virtual Reality to Reduce Racial Prejudice. *Virtual Reality* **28** (2024) 125.
53. Besharati, S. & Fotopoulou, A. The Social Reality of the Self: Right Perisylvian Damage Revisited. in *Clinical Studies in Neuropsychoanalysis Revisited* (eds. Salas, C., Turnbull, O., Solms, M.) 246–283 (Routledge, 2021).
54. Fotopoulou, A. & Besharati, S. Predicting First-Person and Counterfactual Experiences of Selfhood: Insights from Anosognosia. In : Cheng T, Sato R, Hohwy J, editors. *Expected Experiences* (eds. Cheng, T., Sato, R., Hohwy, J.) 140–169 (Routledge, 2023).
55. Seth, A. K. Interoceptive Inference, Emotion, and the Embodied Self. *Trends in Cognitive Sciences* **17** (2013) 565–573.
56. Seth, A. K. & Friston, K. J. Active Interoceptive Inference and the Emotional Brain. *Philosophical Transactions of the Royal Society B: Biological Sciences* **371** (2016) 20160007.
57. Damasio, A. Mental Self: The Person within. *Nature* **423** (2003) 227.
58. Panksepp, J. *Affective Neuroscience: The Foundations of Human and Animal Emotions* (Oxford University Press, 2004).
59. Solms, M. *The Hidden Spring: A Journey to the Source of Consciousness* (Profile Books, 2021).
60. Craig, A. D. How Do You Feel—Now? The Anterior Insula and Human Awareness. *Nature Reviews Neuroscience* **10** (2009) 59–70.
61. Tsakiris, M. & Critchley, H. Interoception beyond Homeostasis: Affect, Cognition and Mental Health. *Philosophical Transactions of the Royal Society B: Biological Sciences* **371** (2016) 20160002.
62. Barrett, L. F., Quigley, K. S. & Hamilton, P. An Active Inference Theory of Allostasis and Interoception in Depression. *Philosophical Transactions of the Royal Society B: Biological Sciences* **371** (2016) 20160011.
63. Azzalini, D., Rebollo, I. & Tallon-Baudry, C. Visceral Signals Shape Brain Dynamics and Cognition. *Trends in Cognitive Sciences* **23** (2019) 488–509.
64. Chen, W. G. *et al.* The Emerging Science of Interoception: Sensing, Integrating, Interpreting, and Regulating Signals within the Self. *Trends in Neurosciences* **44** (2021) 3–16.
65. Park, H.-D. & Tallon-Baudry, C. The Neural Subjective Frame: From Bodily Signals to Perceptual Consciousness. *Philosophical Transactions of the Royal Society B: Biological Sciences* **369** (2014) 20130208.
66. Engelen, T., Solcà, M. & Tallon-Baudry, C. Interoceptive Rhythms in the Brain. *Nature Neuroscience* **26** (2023) 1670–1684.
67. Fotopoulou, A. & Tsakiris, M. Mentalizing Homeostasis: The Social Origins of Interoceptive Inference. *Neuropsychoanalysis* **19** (2017) 3–28.
68. Besharati, S. *et al.* The Affective Modulation of Motor Awareness in Anosognosia for Hemiplegia: Behavioural and Lesion Evidence. *Cortex* **61** (2014) 127–140.
69. Blakemore, S.-J. The Social Brain in Adolescence. *Nature Reviews Neuroscience* **9** (2008) 267–277.
70. Reddy, V. *How Infants Know Minds* (Harvard University Press, 2008).
71. Reddy, V. On Being the Object of Attention: Implications for Self–Other Consciousness. *Trends in Cognitive Sciences* **7** (2003) 397–402.
72. Bayne, T., Frohlich, J., Cusack, R., Moser, J. & Naci, L. Consciousness in the Cradle: On the Emergence of Infant Experience. *Trends in Cognitive Sciences* **27** (2023) 1135–1149.
73. Patterson, J. R. & Grabois, M. Locked-in Syndrome: A Review of 139 Cases. *Stroke* **17** (1986) 758–764.

74. Laureys, S. *et al.* The Locked-in Syndrome: What Is It Like to Be Conscious but Paralyzed and Voiceless? *Progress in Brain Research* **150** (2005) 495–611.
75. Maciejewicz, B. Neuroscience of Consciousness in the Locked-In Syndrome: Prognostic and Diagnostic Review. *Ibrain* **8** (2022) 476–480.
76. Schnetzer, L. *et al.* Locked-in Syndrome Revisited. *Therapeutic Advances in Neurological Disorders* **16** (2023) 17562864231160873.
77. Weiskrantz, L. *Blindsight: A Case Study and Implications* (Oxford University Press, 1990).
78. Goodale, M. A. & Milner, A. D. Separate Visual Pathways for Perception and Action. *Trends in Neurosciences* **15** (1992) 20–25.
79. Goodale, M. A. How (and Why) the Visual Control of Action Differs from Visual Perception. *Proceedings of the Royal Society B: Biological Sciences* **281** (2014) 20140337.
80. Kentridge, R. W., Heywood, C. A. & Weiskrantz, L. Attention without Awareness in Blindsight. *Proceedings of the Royal Society of London. Series B: Biological Sciences* **266** (1999) 1805–1811.
81. Aserinsky, E. & Kleitman, N. Regularly Occurring Periods of Eye Motility, and Concomitant Phenomena, during Sleep. *Science* **118** (1953) 273–274.
82. Aserinsky, E. & Kleitman, N. Two Types of Ocular Motility Occurring in Sleep. *Journal of Applied Physiology* **8** (1955) 1–10.
83. Solms, M. Dreaming and REM Sleep Are Controlled by Different Brain Mechanisms. *Behavioral and Brain Sciences* **23** (2000) 843–850.

13 Many Ways of Being Minded

Neurodivergence and AI Consciousness

Lucy Griffiths

13.1 WHY DISABILITY MATTERS FOR MACHINE CONSCIOUSNESS

Proposals for tests, indicators, and benchmarking frameworks for machine consciousness are proliferating alongside discussions about the moral status of artificial systems, the attribution of rights and protections, and the governance of advanced AI (Butlin et al., 2023; Hildt, 2022). The way we test for consciousness is no longer a purely theoretical concern: it is a threshold for moral and political consideration (Cleeremans et al., 2025; Coeckelbergh, 2010; Gunkel, 2012). This chapter argues that some of the emerging repertoire of "tests of machine consciousness" may not be as neutral in their conception of consciousness as they first appear, and that insights from disability and neurodiversity studies may help to improve them.

Many of these tests tacitly assume a cluster of cognitive, communicative, sensorimotor, and introspective capacities that are characteristic of non-disabled and neurotypical adults. That assumption is familiar to scholars in critical disability studies, who have shown how technologies, institutions, and diagnostic categories repeatedly take a narrow set of embodied and cognitive norms as the baseline for being fully human, fully rational, or fully communicative (Garland-Thomson, 2011; Goodley, 2014; Kafer, 2013).

When such assumptions are carried over, unexamined, into AI consciousness testing, they risk reproducing in the field of machine consciousness what Peña-Guzmán and Reynolds (2019) call "epistemic ableism": ways of thinking that fail to recognise disabled people because the evidential standards were designed around someone else. This, when translated into a machine context, may result in tests based on too narrow a conception of the variety of forms it may take (Butlin et al., 2025), with ethical and practical consequences. Not only this, but in unquestioningly adopting normative standards, we may also lose the opportunity to learn from existing human variation about the *range* of ways consciousness can be expressed.

It is also instructive to notice a methodological asymmetry. A large, careful literature on animal consciousness has matured in the last decade, precisely to answer the question of how we can justifiably attribute experience to beings who cannot explain that experience to us (Birch, 2022; Godfrey-Smith, 2016). In animal ethics, authors

DOI: 10.1201/9781003758389-15

such as Sebo (2022, 2025) argue that under such uncertainty, we should widen, not narrow, our circle of consideration. The point here is to note that researchers already accept plural, indirect, and behaviour-plus-context evidence when studying minds that cannot provide humanlike reports. If such evidential generosity is warranted across species, it is striking that intra-human cognitive and communicative diversity is not yet being used more widely in the same constructive spirit to improve tests for machine consciousness.

A disability-informed view is especially important because some of the capacities now treated as particularly probative for machine consciousness – self-report of inner states, theory of mind, consistent pain or emotion signalling, fluent linguistic justification – are precisely those that many disabled and neurodivergent people do not always display in normative ways, even though we do not on that basis doubt their consciousness or moral status (Kinnaird et al., 2019; Milton, 2012). If a test would misclassify conscious humans, then deploying it as a decisive filter for machines inherits that injustice. Hence, the central thesis of this chapter: by attending to how consciousness is expressed across disabled, neurodivergent, and clinically complex cases, we can (a) identify systematic blind spots in current machine-consciousness tests and (b) use those cases as positive design data for more plural, more accurate assessment regimes. In this sense, disability is not only a site of critique but a methodological resource.

The chapter proceeds as follows: first, it introduces key insights from critical disability theory, especially the notions of compulsory able-bodiedness/able-mindedness and disability-led design, and outlines the current testing paradigm in machine consciousness to show where and how criteria may have been influenced by narrowly normative assumptions.

It then juxtaposes these insights with specific examples of categories of consciousness tests to show where ableist assumptions may enter and what kinds of human variation could help correct them.

Third, it provides examples from human clinical cases – especially disorders of consciousness (DoC) – to demonstrate how behaviour-only or normatively tuned assessments already fail for humans.

Finally, it proposes principles for a diversity-informed research agenda on machine consciousness and reflects on the ethical and policy implications of building future AI rights discussions on tests that may themselves be exclusionary.

13.2 CRITICAL DISABILITY THEORY AND COMPULSORY NEUROTYPICALITY

Critical disability theory begins from the claim that disability is not simply a biological or individual deficit, but a relation between bodies/minds and the social, material, and epistemic environments designed around normative assumptions (Goodley, 2014; Kafer, 2013). Rosemarie Garland-Thomson's (2011) notion of the "misfit" is especially helpful here: bodies and minds do not inherently lack capabilities; rather, they "misfit" when the world is built to accommodate a narrow range of capacities. This moves the analytic spotlight from disabled people to the design of environments, tools, and standards – and tests of machine consciousness are precisely such standards.

A core target of critical disability studies has been what Alison Kafer (2013) calls "compulsory able-bodiedness/able-mindedness," the presumption that the desirable, default human subject is mobile, communicative in normative ways, affectively transparent, cognitively independent, and future-oriented towards cure. This presumption is not only medical; it is folded into educational assessments, UX design, labour expectations, and, increasingly, AI systems (Newman-Griffis et al., 2023). When a test takes such a subject as its baseline, everyone else must either be explained as a deviation or be rendered invisible. From the standpoint of AI, this means we may be ignoring an already available library of alternative cognitive profiles that could help us build more inclusive, and therefore more reliable, tests.

Neurodiversity scholarship adds an important refinement. Damian Milton's (2012) articulation of the "double empathy problem" argues that autistic people's communicative differences are better described as *reciprocal* breakdowns between differently configured social actors than as deficits in autistic people alone. Mismatch, not absence, is the key. This is a powerful lens for machine consciousness because many proposed tests assume that success is demonstrated by interacting smoothly with neurotypical human judges. The double-empathy perspective shows that the test is tuned to just one style of cognition. Neuroqueer work (Walker, 2021) reinforces this point by arguing that "neurotypical legibility" is a social demand, not an intrinsic property of minds.

Finally, crip technoscience offers a positive programme for re-design. Hamraie and Fritsch (2019) argue that disability communities have long practised "user-led" and "access-intentional" forms of making, in which the starting point is not the average user but those who are typically misfit by design. Transposed to AI-consciousness research, this suggests that the criteria we treat as evidential should be co-developed with disabled and neurodivergent scholars and users, rather than retrofitted later. It also resonates with recent work in AI and disability which shows, empirically, that "definition drives design": the way we define a phenomenon (e.g., independence, competence, and intelligence) constrains what our systems can recognise (Newman-Griffis et al., 2023). If we define "consciousness" through an overly standardised lens, our tests will be too limited.

In short, critical disability theory tells us three things that the machine-consciousness literature mostly overlooks: (a) norms are contingent and enforceable, not natural; (b) failure to match a norm is not good evidence of absence of an underlying capacity; and (c) assessments should be built to accommodate heterogeneity in expression. To this, we can add two further, more constructive claims: (d) heterogeneity in expression gives us empirical material for imagining non-human, artificial, or distributed ways of being conscious; (e) heterogeneity includes not only constraint but excellence. Neurodivergent and autistic communities have long pointed out that hyper-systemising, extraordinary pattern detection, or rapid detail-focused perception can coexist with, or even trade off against, socially legible communication (Snyder, 2009; Treffert, 2014). For AI researchers, such minds are instructive because they illustrate real human solutions to cognitive tasks – exactness, speed, parallelism – that machines aim to reproduce. Designing tests that can recognise consciousness in these profiles means designing tests that do not treat "balanced, average human performance" as the only conscious configuration.

Once we take these points seriously, some of the dominant proposals for testing machine consciousness look less universal than their authors may have intended.

13.3 THE TESTING PARADIGM IN MACHINE CONSCIOUSNESS

Work on machine consciousness has long recognised the "other minds" problem: since consciousness is, at least in part, a subjective phenomenon, we cannot directly inspect it in either humans or artefacts. What we can do is specify operational criteria – behavioural, architectural, functional, or report-based – that would make it reasonable to attribute consciousness. Over time, this has yielded a recognisable testing paradigm, within which different proposals compete (Elamrani & Yampolskiy, 2019).

13.4 FROM IMITATION TO INSPECTION

The historical anchor point is Turing's (1950) imitation game. Although Turing did not claim to be testing consciousness, the test set a template: if a machine can sustain the kinds of discursive performance we associate with minded beings, that performance is evidence enough. Later variations – the "total Turing test" (Harnad, 1991), which adds robotic perception and action, or interactive dialogue tests – retain the same basic logic: observable, humanlike performance is a proxy for inner mindedness.

This behavioural tradition is important from the perspective of cognitive diversity because it presupposes that "passing" involves performing in the way a typical human interlocutor expects. Any deviation in communicative style, timing, motor expression, or affect display is a potential source of failure. Autistic scholarship has long shown that such deviations need not indicate an absence of mindedness; they often indicate a mismatch of communicative norms (Milton, 2012; Singer, 1999). These autistic and neurodivergent accounts therefore give us a concrete model of "false negatives" in consciousness attribution, a model that AI researchers can draw on directly. If we build machine tests that fail on the same grounds, we reproduce this misrecognition in the machine domain.

As research moved beyond pure behaviourism, a second family of proposals emerged that tries to inspect machines more directly. Instead of asking "does it talk like us?", these approaches ask "does it have the right kinds of mechanisms, representations, or control structures?" This shift is where human-typical assumptions can become both subtler and more entrenched.

13.5 ARCHITECTURE- AND CRITERION-DRIVEN TESTS

A prominent strand of machine-consciousness research now offers lists of necessary or at least strongly indicative features. Aleksander and Dunmall (2003), for example, propose five axioms – presence, imagination, attention, planning, and emotion – arguing that an artificial system instantiating them in the right way could be said to possess "phenomenal" states. Arrabales et al.'s (2010) ConsScale likewise organises consciousness into levels, moving from basic reactive behaviour through goal-directed agency to self-consciousness and metarepresentation. Yampolskiy (2017) proposes tests for "detecting qualia" in both artificial and biological agents, centring on whether the system can meaningfully report or demonstrate the presence of subjective experience. Schneider and Turner (2017) suggest an Artificial Consciousness Test (ACT) in which a system must make appropriate second-order judgements about its own mental states.

What unites these otherwise diverse frameworks is that they fix a repertoire of capacities in advance – emotion, imagination, self-modelling, metacognition, pain-like states, social perspective-taking – as especially revealing of consciousness. Yet these repertoires are selected against an implicit model of the human subject: verbally competent, reflectively self-aware, affectively legible, and socially oriented. Critical disability theory reminds us that this is not the only way consciousness shows up. Many people experience and express consciousness without reliable second-order report (e.g., because of alexithymia), without stable sensorimotor repertoires (because of motor impairments), or without neurotypical social-cognitive profiles (Kinnaird et al., 2019).

Furthermore, there are minds whose capacities extend far beyond neurotypical norms – for example, those with savant syndrome who may have remarkable calendar calculation, absolute pitch, or visual memory (Treffert, 2014; Snyder, 2009). These profiles show that human cognition can be strongly modular, highly efficient, and differently prioritised, while remaining fully conscious. If our tests only encode the typical mix of capacities, we miss a second opportunity: using these exceptional human configurations as working models for alternative machine architectures. Treating these human cases as "boundary data" allows us to stress-test machine-consciousness criteria: any criterion that misclassifies these known conscious cases should be flagged as too narrow. To the extent that a machine-consciousness test treats these specific human capacities as individually necessary rather than as one family of sufficient indicators, it may be building in an avoidable source of misclassification.

Some of these scales are explicitly hierarchical, culminating in something like "adult, neurotypical human consciousness" as the highest stage (Arrabales et al., 2010). Disability scholars have repeatedly shown that such linear hierarchies naturalise the adult, able bodymind as the telos of development, stigmatising other configurations as deficit or delay (Goodley, 2014). When imported into AI, this hierarchy has the effect of making machine minds legible only insofar as they approximate that norm, instead of inviting us to consider multiple "high-level" configurations of consciousness modelled on diverse human minds.

13.6 THEORY-LADEN PROBES AND THE SCIENCE OF CONSCIOUSNESS

A third source of criteria comes from the numerous contemporary scientific theories of consciousness (Butlin et al., 2023). Approaches such as the global workspace theory and global neuronal workspace theory (Barrs, 1988, 1997; Dehaene, 2021; Mashour et al., 2020), recurrent processing theory (Lamme 2006, 2010,

2020), integrated information theory (Oizumi et al., 2014), and "indicators and criteria" proposals for cross-species and cross-system comparison (Pennartz et al., 2019) have started to be discussed as potential foundations for evaluating artificial systems. The idea here is that if consciousness depends, say, on globally available information broadcasting, recurrent processing, or high values of integrated information, then we can look for functional analogues of those properties in machines.

This move has two consequences. Positively, it grounds tests in maturing neuroscientific theories rather than folk intuitions. But negatively, it transposes a profile of human neural organisation – typically derived from awake, communicating adults – into a universal standard. Human consciousness, we should remember, is variable. It can be present under conditions of limited report, noisy or degraded sensory input, or atypical connectivity patterns, as research on DoC and neurodivergence shows. Animal-consciousness research reinforces the same lesson from a different direction: when studying octopuses, corvids, or mammals whose cognition is organised very differently from ours, researchers routinely combine evolutionary, behavioural, and neurobiological evidence rather than relying on a single humanlike marker (Birch, 2022; Godfrey-Smith, 2016).

A complementary strand, associated with affective and neuropsychoanalytic approaches, argues that the core of consciousness lies not in high-level cortical availability but in subcortical, homeostatic, and affective systems that make the organism *feel* itself (Solms, 2013, 2021). From this perspective, sophisticated report and metarepresentation are late arriving "explanatory add-ons"; the primitive conscious subject is the affectively valenced, self-regulating body. For our purposes, this matters because it shows that a scientifically respectable account of consciousness already exists that does not make neurotypical linguistic or social capacities central. Building machine tests only around the cortical/broadcast picture therefore ignores a live alternative in the human case.

Bringing that pluralism into machine-consciousness testing would make our assessments more robust to atypical or non-human architectures. If our scientific theories are trained on the "easiest-to-measure" cases, and tests for machine consciousness simply inherit those parameters, we risk building devices that can recognise only minds that look like that training set.

Finally, there is a policy and ethics aspect to this testing paradigm. Because questions about AI rights, moral patiency, and even liability increasingly appeal to consciousness or sentience as a threshold, the outputs of these tests will have downstream ethical effects (Hildt, 2022). If the tests themselves encode overly narrow expectations, then our normative landscape will too. It is therefore not enough to refine the technical adequacy of such tests; they must also be subjected to what disability studies would call a "normative audit."

13.7 LESSONS FROM DISABILITY MEDICINE AND DISORDERS OF CONSCIOUSNESS

One place where the limits of behaviour-first assessments are already starkly visible is clinical work on DoC – vegetative state/unresponsive wakefulness syndrome (VS/UWS), minimally conscious state (MCS), and related conditions. For decades, diagnostic practice relied primarily on bedside behavioural scales (e.g., the Coma Recovery Scale–Revised) that operationalise consciousness in terms of consistent command-following, purposeful movement, visual tracking, or language production (Giacino et al., 2002). These tools were designed to be systematic and reproducible, but they were also unavoidably tuned to patients who can produce relatively typical motor and communicative behaviours.

Seminal neuroimaging work by Owen et al. (2006) revealed weaknesses in this reliance on overt behaviour. In their study, a young woman clinically diagnosed as vegetative was asked to imagine playing tennis or walking through her house while in an fMRI scanner. Her brain activity showed the same task-specific activation patterns observed in healthy controls. In other words, she was conscious and able to follow instructions, but her body could not express that fact in the channels the bedside tests required. Subsequent work by Monti et al. (2010) and others has replicated and extended this finding, revealing a non-trivial proportion of "covertly conscious" patients – people whose consciousness would have been missed by purely behavioural assessments.

This body of research demonstrates two key points that matter directly for machine-consciousness testing. First, expression can fail while consciousness persists. Consciousness is not exhausted by what is easily measurable at the output layer. Second, clinical researchers responded not by declaring these patients "not really conscious," but by broadening the evidential base – adding neuroimaging, electrophysiology, repeated longitudinal assessments, and careful interpretation of idiosyncratic behaviours (Gosseries et al., 2014). That is, they made the assessment regime more accommodating.

Disability bioethics has drawn a parallel lesson. Writers such as Campbell and Stramondo (2017) and Barnes (2016) argue that apparent "low function" is often a reflection of environments and measures that do not fit the person, rather than of an absence of rich inner life. With people who have profound intellectual and multiple disabilities, clinicians already rely on proxy reports, behavioural pain scales, and relational knowledge accumulated by caregivers to infer experience (Lotan & Icht, 2023). This is, in effect, a multi-channel, disability-aware consciousness assessment protocol for humans.

If we accept this in the human medical context – where the stakes are literally life, death, and resource allocation – it would be inconsistent to refuse it in the artificial context. A machine that does not "speak" in the ways our initial test battery expects may still be conscious; the appropriate response is to diversify the channels through which we look for evidence, not to treat the first failure as dispositive. Medical practice has already shown that such diversification is feasible and ethically warranted.

13.8 TOWARDS AN ANTI-ABLEIST AGENDA FOR TESTING MACHINE CONSCIOUSNESS

An anti-ableist programme does not require abandoning tests altogether. It requires reframing what counts as good evidence and who gets to define it. The following four principles sketch such a programme.

Principle 1: Pluralisation of markers.

Instead of asking, "Does the system have theory of mind, self-report, pain expression, *and* metacognition?" we should ask, "Does the system display a *coherent cluster* of consciousness-relevant properties, any one of several clusters being sufficient?" This mirrors clinical moves from single-indicator diagnoses to syndromic, pattern-based ones. For example, a system might show rich, flexible world modelling, goal-directed control, and information integration but little interest in social perspective-taking; another might show social responsiveness and self-other discrimination but limited metacognitive narration. Both could be judged candidates for consciousness, just as both a minimally verbal autistic adult and a neurotypical adult are taken to be conscious despite different expressive repertoires (Milton, 2012; Kinnaird et al., 2019). Methodologically, this means publishing tests as families of acceptable profiles rather than as monoliths.

Principle 2: Built-in accommodation.

Disability-informed design begins from the question, "What barriers does this test create, and how can we lower them?" For machine consciousness, that means allowing multiple input/output modalities (text, structured signals, timing variations), enabling repeated trials over time, and separating the *presence* of an internal state from the *skill* of mapping it to human natural language. It also means legitimising relational or proxy evidence – for instance, evidence that a system behaves differently towards entities it has previously tagged as conscious versus non-conscious, even if it cannot articulate why. This is analogous to caregiver-based assessments in PIMD and DoC (Gosseries et al., 2014; Lotan and Icht, 2023).

Principle 3: Disability-informed co-design and norm transparency.

Following crip technoscience, those most likely to be misclassified – disabled and neurodivergent people – should be involved in drafting the tests. They are uniquely positioned to notice when a human-focused test criterion presupposes fluent speech, neurotypical eye contact, or neurotypical social reward structures (Hamraie & Fritsch, 2019), and so they may provide similarly useful alternative perspectives for those developing tests for machine consciousness. Alongside co-design, every test could carry a brief normativity note specifying the human profile it was tuned for ("assumes adult, literate, sighted, neurotypical interaction partner") and listing likely false negatives (e.g., "may misclassify agents with atypical affect labelling"). This makes the politics of the test explicit rather than hidden.

Principle 4: Compatibility with theory, without theory dictating the user profile.

Nothing in an anti-ableist approach precludes drawing on theories such as global workspace or IIT. What it cautions against is taking the easiest-to-measure or most neurotypical human case as the only valid parameterisation of those theories. Neuroimaging work on DoC already shows that consciousness can be supported by more than one functional pattern (Owen et al., 2006; Monti et al., 2010). AI researchers can therefore define ranges of functionally equivalent architectures and accept that an artificial system might occupy a point in that range that does not look "human-typical" but still satisfies the theory.

These principles generate a concrete research agenda. First, we can audit existing tests (e.g., ConsScale, ACT, and qualia tests) for implicit norms: What sensory modalities do they assume? What linguistic competence? What social orientation? Second, we can prototype inclusive variants – for instance, an ACT-like test that permits non-linguistic second-order signalling or a ConsScale-like ladder with multiple "top" configurations rather than one human-adult summit. Third, we can run comparative classification studies: apply the standard and the disability-informed versions to the same set of artificial agents and quantify how many would be reclassified as plausible candidates under the inclusive scheme. This kind of empirical demonstration would show AI and ethics communities that the cost of ableist tests is not merely theoretical; it changes who gets moral consideration.

Finally, an anti-ableist agenda dovetails with emerging AI governance conversations. If regulators or standards bodies are going to lean on "consciousness indicators" for assigning obligations or protections, they should do so only with indicators that have passed a disability audit. Otherwise, we risk baking into law the very exclusions disability studies has spent decades documenting (Peña-Guzmán & Reynolds, 2019).

13.9 CONCLUSION: CONSCIOUSNESS WITHOUT COMPULSORY ABLE-MINDEDNESS

This chapter has argued that many current proposals for testing machine consciousness are organised around a narrow, able-bodied, and neurotypical image of mindedness. They prioritise skills, such as normative social cognition, articulate self-report, humanlike pain expression, linear developmental progression, that significant groups of conscious humans do not always display, including autistic people, people with alexithymia, people with congenital insensitivity to pain, and people with profound intellectual and multiple disabilities (Kinnaird et al., 2019; Lotan & Icht, 2023; Nagasako et al., 2003). When such skills are treated as individually necessary, the result is a form of epistemic ableism: tests that misrecognise real consciousness because it is expressed atypically (Peña-Guzmán & Reynolds, 2019).

Clinical work on DoC shows that the correct response to this kind of misrecognition is not to deny consciousness, but to expand the evidential repertoire – to allow for indirect, multimodal, and longitudinal ways of knowing (Giacino et al., 2002; Owen et al., 2006). An anti-ableist research programme for machine consciousness simply applies the same lesson to artefacts: pluralise markers, build in accommodation, co-design with those routinely misfit by tests, and make normativity explicit. If future discussions about AI moral status, rights, or protections are to be ethically stable, they must rest on tests that recognise many ways of being conscious, not only those that fit a narrow, familiar model.

REFERENCES

Aleksander, I., & Dunmall, B. (2003). Axioms and tests for the presence of minimal consciousness in agents. *Journal of Consciousness Studies, 10*(4–5), 7–18.

Arrabales, R., Ledezma, A., & Sanchis, A. (2010). ConsScale: A pragmatic scale for measuring the level of consciousness in artificial agents. *Journal of Consciousness Studies, 17*(3–4), 131–164.

Barnes, E. (2016). *The minority body: A theory of disability.* Oxford University Press.

Baars, B. J. (1988). *A cognitive theory of consciousness.* Cambridge University Press.

Baars, B. J. (1997). In the theatre of consciousness: Global workspace theory, a rigorous scientific theory of consciousness. *Journal of Consciousness Studies, 4*(4), 292–309.

Birch, J. (2022). *The search for animal consciousness.* Princeton University Press.

Butlin, P., Long, R., Elmoznino, E., Bengio, Y., Birch, J., Constant, A., Deane, G., Fleming, S.M., Frith, C., Ji, X., Kanai, R., Klein, C., Lindsay, G., Michel, M., Mudrik, L., Peters, M.A.K., Schwitzgebel, E., Simon, J.,VanRullen, R. (2023). Consciousness in artificial intelligence: Insights from the science of consciousness. arXiv preprint arXiv:2308.08708.

Butlin, P., Long, R., Bayne, T., Bengio,Y., Birch, J., Chalmers, D., Constant, A., Deane, G., Elmoznino, E., Fleming, S.M., Ji, X., Kanai, R., Klein, C., Lindsay, G., Michel, M., Mudrik, L., Peters, M.A.K., Schwitzgebel, E., Simon, J., VanRullen, R. (2025). Identifying indicators of consciousness in AI systems. Trends in Cognitive Sciences. https://doi.org/10.1016/j.tics.2025.10.011.

Campbell, S. M., & Stramondo, J. (2017). The complicated relationship of disability and well-being. *Kennedy Institute of Ethics Journal, 27*(2), 151–184.

Cleeremans, A., Mudrik, L., & Seth, A. K. (2025). Consciousness science: where are we, where are we going, and what if we get there?. *Frontiers in Science, 3.* https://doi.org/10.3389/fsci.2025.1546279.

Coeckelbergh, M. (2010). Robot rights? *Ethics and Information Technology, 12*(3), 209–221.

Dehaene, S. (2021). *Consciousness and the brain: Deciphering how the brain codes our thoughts.* Penguin.

Elamrani, A., & Yampolskiy, R. V. (2019). Reviewing tests for machine consciousness. *Journal of Consciousness Studies, 26*(5–6), 35–64.

Garland-Thomson, R. (2011). Misfits: A feminist materialist disability concept. *Hypatia, 26*(3), 591–609.

Giacino, J. T., Kalmar, K., & Whyte, J. (2002). The JFK Coma Recovery Scale–Revised: Measurement characteristics and diagnostic utility. *Archives of Physical Medicine and Rehabilitation, 83*(12), 1761–1767.

Godfrey-Smith, P. (2016). *Other minds: The octopus, the sea, and the deep origins of consciousness.* Farrar, Straus and Giroux.

Goodley, D. (2014). *Dis/ability studies: Theorising disablism and ableism.* Routledge.

Gosseries, O., Di, H., Laureys, S., & Boly, M. (2014). Measuring consciousness in severely damaged brains. *Annual Review of Neuroscience, 37,* 457–478.

Gunkel, D. J. (2012). *The machine question: Critical perspectives on AI, robots, and ethics.* MIT Press.

Hamraie, A., & Fritsch, K. (2019). Crip technoscience manifesto. *Catalyst: Feminism, Theory, Technoscience, 5*(1), 1–34.

Harnad, S. (1991). Other bodies, other minds: A machine incarnation of an old philosophical problem. *Minds and Machines, 1*(1), 43–54.

Hildt, E. (2022). The prospects of artificial consciousness: Ethical dimensions and concerns. *AJOB Neuroscience, 14*(4), 58–71.

Kafer, A. (2013). *Feminist, queer, crip.* Indiana University Press.

Kinnaird, E., Stewart, C., & Tchanturia, K. (2019). Investigating alexithymia in autism: A systematic review and meta-analysis. *European Psychiatry, 55,* 80–89.

Lamme, V. A. F. (2006). Towards a true neural stance on consciousness. *Trends in Cognitive Sciences, 10*(11), 494–501.

Lamme, V. A. F. (2010). How neuroscience will change our view on consciousness. *Cognitive Neuroscience, 1*(3), 204–220.

Lamme, V. A. F. (2020). Visual functions generate conscious seeing. *Frontiers in Psychology, 11*, 83.

Lotan, M., & Icht, M. (2023). Diagnosing pain in individuals with intellectual and developmental disabilities: Current state and novel technological solutions. *Diagnostics (Basel, Switzerland), 13*(3), 401.

Mashour, G. A., Roelfsema, P., Changeux, J.-P., & Dehaene, S. (2020). Conscious processing and the global neuronal workspace hypothesis. *Neuron, 105*(5), 776–798.

Milton, D. E. M. (2012). On the ontological status of autism: The "double empathy problem." *Disability & Society, 27*(6), 883–887.

Monti, M. M., Vanhaudenhuyse, A., Coleman, M.R., Boly, M., Pickard, J.D., Tshibanda, L., Owen, A. M., Laureys, S. (2010). Willful modulation of brain activity in disorders of consciousness. *New England Journal of Medicine, 362*(7), 579–589.

Nagasako, E. M., Oaklander, A. L., & Dworkin, R. H. (2003). Congenital insensitivity to pain: An update. *Pain, 101*(3), 213–219.

Newman-Griffis, D., Rauchberg, J. S., Alharbi, R., Hickman, L., & Hochheiser, H. (2023). Definition drives design: Disability models and mechanisms of bias in AI technologies. *First Monday, 28*(1). https://doi.org/10.5210/fm.v28i1.12903.

Oizumi, M., Albantakis, L., & Tononi, G. (2014). From the phenomenology to the mechanisms of consciousness: Integrated information theory 3.0. *PLoS Computational Biology, 10*(5), e1003588.

Owen, A. M., Coleman, M. R., Boly, M., Davis, M. H., Laureys, S., & Pickard, J. D. (2006). Detecting awareness in the vegetative state. *Science, 313*(5792), 1402.

Peña-Guzmán, D. M., & Reynolds, J. M. (2019). The harm of ableism: Medical error and epistemic injustice. *Kennedy Institute of Ethics Journal, 29*(3), 205–242.

Pennartz, C. M., Farisco, M., & Evers, K. (2019). Indicators and criteria of consciousness in animals and intelligent machines: an inside-out approach. *Frontiers in Systems Neuroscience, 13*, 25.

Schneider, S., & Turner, E. (2017). *Is anyone home? A way to find out if AI has become self-aware.* Scientific American Mind.

Sebo, J. (2022). *Saving animals, saving ourselves: Why animals matter for pandemics, climate change, and other catastrophes.* Oxford University Press.

Sebo, J. (2025). The edge of the moral circle. *Relations. Beyond Anthropocentrism, 12*(2), 13–28.

Singer, J. (1999). "Why can't you be normal for once in your life?" From a "problem with no name" to the emergence of a new category of difference. In M. Corker & S. French (Eds.), *Disability discourse* (pp. 59–67). Open University Press.

Snyder, A. (2009). Explaining and inducing savant skills: Privileged access to lower level, less-processed information. *Philosophical Transactions of the Royal Society B: Biological Sciences, 364*(1522), 1399–1405.

Solms, M. (2013). The conscious id. *Neuropsychoanalysis, 15*(1), 5–19.

Solms, M. (2021). *The hidden spring: A journey to the source of consciousness.* Profile Books.

Treffert, D. A. (2014). Savant syndrome: Realities, myths and misconceptions. *Journal of Autism and Developmental Disorders, 44*(3), 564–571.

Turing, A. M. (1950). Computing machinery and intelligence. *Mind, 59*(236), 433–460.

Walker, N. (2021). *Neuroqueer heresies: Notes on the neurodiversity paradigm, autistic empowerment, and postnormal possibilities.* Autonomous Press.

Yampolskiy, R. V. (2017). Detecting qualia in natural and artificial agents. arXiv preprint arXiv:1712.04020.

14 The Turing Test for Consciousness, Not Intelligence

Calum Chace

14.1 INADEQUATE, OR INCREASINGLY IMPORTANT?

October 2025 was the 75th anniversary of the Turing Test, which Alan Turing introduced to the world in his paper, "Computing Machinery and Intelligence", published in the journal *Mind* [1]. Today, the Turing Test is often derided as an inadequate test for intelligence, which machines have already passed without getting anywhere near human-level intelligence. This chapter argues that on the contrary, the Turing Test could soon become more important than ever, because it is best thought of as a test for consciousness, not for intelligence. It would be a probabilistic test rather than a conclusive test, and it would not remove the need for other tests. But we are sorely in need of tests for artificial consciousness.

This interpretation of the Turing Test is not the consensus view among cognitive scientists and philosophers, although it has been mooted before [2]. Daniel Dennett thought that a machine which passed the Turing Test would be conscious as well as intelligent, and John Searle described it as an inadequate test for both [3].

14.2 THINKING

Turing himself was ambiguous about what his test was for, talking more about "thinking" than about intelligence or consciousness. The word "intelligence" appears in the title of his paper, but it appears only twice after that. The word "consciousness" appears seven times, but he uses the word "think" and its cognates "thinking" and "thought" no fewer than 67 times.

Turing starts the paper by saying,

> I propose to consider the question, 'Can machines think?' This should begin with definitions of the meaning of the terms 'machine' and 'think.'

But he does not provide those definitions. Instead, he asks whether a machine could fool an observer into believing that it is human, based on a parlour game that he invents. In this game, a human examiner attempts to discern the gender of a person who they cannot see or hear, but who they can communicate with via written notes, or via a third party. Adapting his game as a test for a machine, Turing argues that if, in the course of a five-minute conversation, a machine can persuade

DOI: 10.1201/9781003758389-16

a human examiner that it is thinking, then we must accept that it is thinking. He does not say whether the test determines the presence or absence of intelligence, or consciousness.

14.3 INTELLIGENCE

Intelligence and consciousness are both hard to define. They are obviously related, and they seem to be correlated with some degree in animals – but they are very different. To simplify, intelligence is about solving problems. There are many types of intelligence. In 1983, a psychologist called Howard Gardner listed seven of them, including linguistic, logical-mathematical, spatial, and interpersonal intelligence [4]. He later expanded the list to nine. Surprisingly, for such a complex, nuanced, and mysterious concept, there is a pretty good four-word definition. It was proposed in 1985 by another American psychologist, Robert Sternberg, and it is "goal-directed, adaptive behaviour" [5].

We have plenty of tests for intelligence. None of them satisfies everybody, because it is fiendishly hard to separate the signal of raw intelligence from the noise of environmental factors. The first widely used test for intelligence was developed in France in 1905 by Alfred Binet and Théodore Simon [6]. Seven years later, a German named William Stern coined the term IQ, or intelligence quotient [7]. IQ tests are often criticised for favouring subjects who share the same language or culture as the developers of the tests [8].

Today, of course, we have formidably capable artificial intelligence (AI). The community of people developing AI systems uses numerous yardsticks to determine which model is currently the most intelligent, and these tests are continually being made harder as the models improve.

So we have many tests for intelligence, and although none of them are perfect, they do the job acceptably for many purposes. Our tests for consciousness are far less satisfactory [9].

14.4 CONSCIOUSNESS

Consciousness is not about solving problems, but about experiencing. Sense impressions such as the colour red, sounds, tastes, smells, and the texture of touch can only be experienced by conscious entities. So too with private thoughts, emotions like contentment, joy, anxiety, and despair, and affective sensory experiences like pain, and bodily pleasure.

Consciousness is hard to detect for anyone but the entity that is having the experiences. It is wholly private and subjective: we cannot share our consciousness with each other, and we cannot directly observe any consciousness except our own. And yet it is the only thing we truly know. Our brains are prisoners inside boxes made of bone, with no direct access to the outside world. The images in your mind are generated by your brain, which filters and interprets the electrical signals transmitted to it by your sense organs. Every perception that you have is indirect, and the only direct experience you have is of your own consciousness. As René Descartes observed in 1637, you can doubt absolutely everything except the fact that you are doubting [10].

So how do we test for consciousness in other beings, including each other? We look for behaviour which mirrors our own – behaviour which seems to be motivated by an inner life. We look for signs of pleasure and pain, delight and revulsion, emotions and perceptions that are absent in clocks and cars. And we look for physical structures which resemble the structures which we believe give rise to consciousness in animals [11].

Dogs chase sticks because it is fun, not because they are pursuing food, shelter, or sex. Play can be good training for skills that are needed to survive, but it is also an end in its own right. Chimps get angry and jealous, and they can also be protective. These sophisticated, nuanced behaviours suggest an inner life [12].

14.5 TURING AND THE MYSTERY OF CONSCIOUSNESS

In tackling objections to his proposed paper, Turing made the following observation:

> I do not wish to give the impression that I think there is no mystery about consciousness. There is, for instance, something of a paradox connected with any attempt to localise it. But I do not think these mysteries necessarily need to be solved before we can answer the question with which we are concerned in this paper.

This does not mean that his test cannot be applied to consciousness. It means that his test will not clear up the mystery of consciousness.

Turing talked about thinking rather than intelligence or consciousness, but for most of its 75-year life, the Turing Test has been understood by most people to be a test for intelligence rather than consciousness. That does not mean that it must always be seen that way, especially if we have a more pressing need of it as a test for consciousness.

14.6 ARTIFICIAL CONSCIOUSNESS

Many computer scientists and cognitive scientists believe that in the coming years or decades, an AI may be developed that is sentient, in the sense that it has conscious experiences, and has positive and negative feelings about those experiences [13]. If and when this happens, it will be momentous. Not only will we learn a great deal about our own consciousness, but we will have created an entity – and shortly afterwards, probably millions of entities – which feel pleasure and pain, and which are deserving of rights. We will have created moral patients [14].

It is vital that we do not do this without noticing that we have done it. Imagine creating millions of conscious entities, and failing to notice, or care, that they are happy or sad about what we do to them. Imagine failing to notice – or care – that they are horrified when we switch them off. This could be the worst crime that humanity ever commits.

14.7 TESTS

The Turing Test is one of the few mechanisms we have to "test" for consciousness. Not the simple five-minute test that Turing proposed, but a test run over days by a diverse panel of humans, including experts in computer science, psychology, and philosophy. If a machine convinces such a panel that it is conscious, and furthermore than its consciousness is valenced, and that it has positive and negative feelings about its experiences, then we will probably have to accept that it is indeed conscious, and in fact sentient.

A more sophisticated version of the extended Turing Test for artificial consciousness runs as follows:

1. Recruit a panel consisting of equal numbers of (a) diverse AI candidates, (b) diverse human participants, and (c) diverse human experts.
2. Pair each human participant with an AI participant and ask each human expert to conduct the extended Turing Test on a pair. Obviously, the experts are not involved in the pairing process and do not know which participant is human and which is an AI.
3. Repeat the process until every expert has tested every participant.

Today's AIs are already skilled at simulating consciousness. Sometimes they have done this by accident, and sometimes their developers have cultivated the skill. There is a broad consensus, although not universal agreement, that this should be discouraged. However, it raises the possibility that future AIs will be very good at simulating consciousness. This is why the test should be conducted by a diverse range of human experts over a lengthy period. Even so, it would not provide definitive, incontrovertible evidence.

In ordinary and scientific usage, the term "test" refers to a procedure designed to evaluate evidence about a hypothesis, not necessarily one that produces absolute proof. Philosophers distinguish between necessary and sufficient tests, which definitively prove a thesis, and probabilistic or corroborative tests, which only raise or lower credence.

Applying the Turing Test to consciousness would fall into the latter category. It does not enable us to look inside another mind and ascertain for certain whether there is consciousness going on. It also has the shortcoming that it can only be applied to entities which can communicate with us, in other words, to entities with language. So even if the Turing Test becomes accepted as one test for artificial consciousness, it will not be the only one.

The Turing Test would not work for all entities, and it would not provide definitive evidence for consciousness. But it could provide useful evidence, and it is one of the few tests of consciousness that we have. We may need it soon.

REFERENCES

1. Alan M. Turing, "Computing Machinery and Intelligence," Mind 59, no. 236 (1950): 433–460, which introduces the imitation game now known as the Turing Test and discusses thinking, intelligence and consciousness.

2. For earlier suggestions that the Turing Test can be interpreted more broadly as a behavioural test for mentality (including, by some, consciousness), see Daniel C. Dennett, "Can Machines Think?," in *Brainchildren: Essays on Designing Minds* (Cambridge, MA: MIT Press, 1998), and G. Oppy and D. Dowe, "The Turing Test," *Stanford Encyclopedia of Philosophy* (2003/rev. 2021).
3. For Dennett's view that a system sophisticated enough to pass demanding Turing-style tests would count as a genuine thinker with consciousness-like capacities, see Daniel C. Dennett, "Can Machines Think?," in *Brainchildren: Essays on Designing Minds* (Cambridge, MA: MIT Press, 1998), and Daniel C. Dennett, *Consciousness Explained* (Boston, MA: Little, Brown, 1991). For Searle's argument that passing the Turing Test is insufficient for understanding or consciousness, see John R. Searle, "Minds, Brains, and Programs," *Behavioural and Brain Sciences* 3, no. 3 (1980): 417–457, and the summary in the "Chinese room" entry.
4. Howard Gardner, *Frames of Mind: The Theory of Multiple Intelligences* (New York: Basic Books, 1983), and Howard Gardner, *Intelligence Reframed: Multiple Intelligences for the 21st Century* (New York: Basic Books, 1999), which introduce and later extend the list of human intelligences.
5. For the characterisation of intelligence as "goal-directed adaptive behaviour," see Robert J. Sternberg and William Salter, work cited in later overviews of intelligence definitions, such as discussions in F. M. Crinella, "Brain Mechanisms and Intelligence," in *Cognition and Intelligence* (Cambridge University Press, 2004), and related summaries of Sternberg & Salter's 1982 definition.
6. Alfred Binet and Théodore Simon, "Méthodes nouvelles pour le diagnostic du niveau intellectuel des anormaux," *L'Année psychologique* 11 (1905): 191–244, which presents the first widely used scale for assessing children's intellectual level.
7. William Stern, *Die psychologischen Methoden der Intelligenzprüfung und deren Anwendung an Schulkindern* (Leipzig: J. A. Barth, 1912). Stern there introduces the term *Intelligenzquotient* (IQ); see also R. Heinemann, "Almost Forgotten Research Contexts: William Stern's Pioneering Work," and summary discussion in resources on the history of IQ.
8. Ulric Neisser et al., "Intelligence: Knowns and Unknowns," *American Psychologist* 51, no. 2 (1996): 77–101, which reviews intelligence testing and notes longstanding concerns about cultural and linguistic bias in IQ measures.
9. Jonathan Birch, "Dimensions of Animal Consciousness," *Trends in Cognitive Sciences* 24, no. 10 (2020): 789–801, for a survey of current proposals for operationalising and assessing consciousness, and the limitations of existing tests.
10. René Descartes, *Discourse on the Method of Rightly Conducting One's Reason and of Seeking Truth in the Sciences* (1637), Part IV, where "I think, therefore I am" appears.
11. Philip Low et al., "The Cambridge Declaration on Consciousness," proclaimed at Churchill College, University of Cambridge, 7 July 2012, which states that many non-human animals possess the neuroanatomical, neurochemical and neurophysiological substrates of conscious states.
12. Marc Bekoff and John A. Byers, eds., *Animal Play: Evolutionary, Comparative, and Ecological Perspectives* (Cambridge: Cambridge University Press, 1998), and Colin Allen and Marc Bekoff, "The Evolution of Animal Play, Emotions, and Social Morality," *Journal of Consciousness Studies* 12, no. 8–10 (2005): 1–32, which discuss play, emotion and social behaviour in mammals as evidence of rich inner lives.
13. Eric Schwitzgebel and Mara Garza, "A Defense of the Rights of Artificial Intelligences," *Midwest Studies in Philosophy* 39, no. 1 (2015): 98–119, which argues that sufficiently sophisticated artificial systems could be conscious and deserve moral and legal rights.

14. Agnieszka Jaworska and Julie Tannenbaum, "Person-Rearing Relationships as a Key to Higher Moral Status," *Ethics* 124, no. 2 (2014): 242–271, and Agnieszka Jaworska and Julie Tannenbaum, "The Grounds of Moral Status," *Stanford Encyclopedia of Philosophy* (2013), which develop and survey the notion of moral status and moral patients whose interests matter for their own sake.

15 Machine Consciousness and Mind Uploading

Chris Percy

15.1 INTRODUCTION

How do you feel about living forever?

Imagine that you are in a future where death has been mastered. Assume that death is still possible. You can still choose to turn yourself off. You can still strive for more, build relationships with others, and have some days that are better than others. You can still get damaged beyond repair. But the damage threshold of 'no return' is far harder to reach than in those fleshy meat suits we used to wear in the 21st century.

How about being able to upgrade your body so it's a bit less injury prone and upgrade your brain so it has a better memory? These are pretty reasonable goals. It might even be unreasonable to deny others from pursuing them.

15.1.1 Mind Uploading as a Natural Goal

Among the boldest ideas in the philosophy of technology is that human minds could one day be transferred from biological brains to machine minds. This *mind uploading* scenario combines neuroscience, computer science, and metaphysics in one question: if the mind is a physical process, can that process be copied into another medium?

The goal can be seen as the natural extension of technologies that most welcome today. As we moved from external hearing aids to cochlear implants, we might move from an external smartphone to an internal GPS and Google Maps integration. A brain-computer interface inside our skull might help us schedule meetings with a thought. As we come to understand the brain better and integrate more with technology, we might distribute different actions and parts of our thinking between different systems. Everything gets faster, more reliable, *better*.

As you replace more and more of your mind's operating system with digital hardware, you might still feel nervous about switching off the last biological component. What if you simply disappear at that point, like going to sleep? But it seems unlikely that this small rump of biology can be the load-bearing point of your now vast and distributed system. You might wonder for a moment if your consciousness went missing somewhere along the way already, dropped between one upgrade and the next. It doesn't feel like that though, so how else can you judge it?

Those who advocate for mind uploading have a solution to this concern. They also see a different technological trajectory to your robot or digital self (we'll get to it shortly), complementary to the gradual cyborg-isation envisaged above.

DOI: 10.1201/9781003758389-17

15.1.2 Structure of This Chapter

This chapter shares a few key ideas and facts for thinking deeply about the remarkable possibility of mind uploading, both the viable technological trajectory that might lead us there and the philosophical question marks that need to be addressed before we conclude it's safe.

Before that, you might be wondering why we're talking about living forever by mind uploading in a book about machine consciousness. We'll start there. Section 2 will talk about what the mind uploading debate teaches us about machine consciousness. Section 3 will briefly explain the R&D basis for mind uploading. It's plausible that the mind uploading technology envisaged today will be possible well before the end of this century. Section 4 highlights two major philosophical assumptions in the R&D roadmap: physical functionalism about consciousness and the universal coverage of computation. Section 5 warns about the uncertainty in those assumptions.

In conclusion, we'll touch on how we can stress test those assumptions with empirical research, showing how they have as much to teach us about the possibility of digital sentience as they do about possible immortality. Complete confidence might be out of reach – we are in the realm of philosophy after all – but there's a lot we can do to become more confident.

15.2 WHY DOES THIS MATTER FOR MACHINE CONSCIOUSNESS?

15.2.1 Endless Unimaginable Alien Minds

There might be a million types of consciousness, most of which are inaccessible to us. Perhaps there is something it is like to be a supernova. Perhaps a mind emerges from quantum particles dancing in and out of the vacuum. It is hard to see how we could ever know anything about this – or how we could rule such possibilities out, although we can mostly ignore them and carry on with our lives. Murray Shanahan has written on this 'terra incognita' of possible non-human minds [1].

15.2.2 Human-Style Consciousness

There is, however, one type of consciousness that we are particularly passionate about: our own human-style consciousness. With this one, we've got a better chance of progress. At the extreme of self-experimentation, we might be able to build confidence in how our own consciousness seems to work – at least enough to make well-founded theories about what other systems might work in a similar way.

For this chapter, let's focus on the possibility of machines having a human-style consciousness.

15.2.3 What Mind Uploading Teaches Us about Human-Style Machine Consciousness

If any given human mind can be uploaded to a machine, then we know for sure that human-style machine consciousness is possible. Once uploaded, we could tweak various parameters, observe the results, and be reasonably confident that a slightly different mind is now present.

Likewise, if human mind uploading only seems to work with *certain* types of machine (a possibility we'll explore in Section 5), we might increase our confidence that such machines can host complex human-style experiences, even if the algorithm were developed by programmers rather than 'uploaded' directly from an individual human template. Meanwhile, we might be sceptical about the consciousness in different types of machines where the human self does not survive the transfer. There might be other types of experiences in those machines, but human-style consciousness seems materially less likely.

15.2.4 New Checks on Machine Consciousness

Mind uploading provides a new pathway to check for human-style machine consciousness. With mind uploading, we can include a battery of checks for whether the original self seems to have persisted. This isn't just a general Turing test[1]; this is literally convincing the people who love you most that you're still in there. To be so convinced that they would opt for mind uploading as well. Perhaps those who love you most have a bias to find you there – but if you can convince your old colleagues and acquaintances as well, then our collective confidence can increase.

15.2.5 'X-Risk'

We might also care about mind uploading because it provides a pathway to extinction risk, so-called 'x-risk'. Not the only pathway to x-risk via AI, but still one that merits attention [2].

AI might rapidly accelerate our progress towards potential mind uploading technology. Some machines – whether conscious or not – might also be fine-tuned to be functionally similar to us, so we empathise with them and form relationships with them. These robots may feel so familiar – as well as being simply better in important ways – that it seems sensible and safe to take steps to become more like them, and eventually to upload ourselves into robot bodies.

However, if mind uploading technology looks like it works, but doesn't work, then we've got a problem. We might upload ourselves one by one, switching off the light of consciousness each time, replaced with functionally identical replicas, but with no actual experience on the inside. We'll get to the risks in Section 5. Before that, let's first discuss if this mind uploading is even feasible.

15.3 IS MIND UPLOADING EVER GOING TO BE POSSIBLE?

The safest route to mind uploading is called 'whole brain emulation'.

We're talking about the hypothetical process of scanning a human brain in detail and recreating both its current state and causal interaction structure inside a computer. The computer would run a simulation of the brain's information processing, such that the uploaded mind responds the same way as the original biological brain in every functional sense.

15.3.1 The 2008 Roadmap

Anders Sandberg and Nick Bostrom's 2008 roadmap remains the canonical summary of how this might be achieved [3]. The key stages are:

- Brain scanning: preserving a brain in fine detail, possibly by advanced cryogenic fixation and electron microscopy. With today's technology, this requires slicing your (dead) brain into tiny slices to capture the relevant data, although much more research is needed to ensure all relevant data remain accessible for long enough in a dead brain.
- Data extraction: reconstructing neuronal geometries and synaptic connections, to define the 'connectome' of a human brain.
- Model construction: converting those data into computational models that capture the functional properties of neurons and synapses, and potentially other physical functionality.
- Simulation and validation: running the model on a high-performance platform and testing its behavioural fidelity.

15.3.2 Incredible Progress

Neuron-level brain maps have come a long way since the 1980s, when there was great excitement about mapping the 300–400 neurons in a nematode worm [4]. In the 2020s, the MICrONS consortium mapped about one cubic millimetre of mouse visual cortex [5]. One cubic millimetre may not sound much, but it covered some 200,000 cells and 500 million connections of detailed functional mapping.

On the modelling side, the Blue Brain Project [6] and Human Brain Project [7] have produced detailed simulations of cortical microcircuits. More recently, large-scale neural simulators such as NEST [8] and Brian2 [9] can run biologically realistic models on distributed computing systems.

15.3.3 A Long Way to Go

We're working towards 100 trillion connections in the human brain, connecting around 86 billion neurons. Some researchers think we might get there in two decades, at least for some primates [10]. Among prominent transhumanists – advocates of mind uploading potential such as Ray Kurzweil – the forecasts range from around the 2040s to the end of the century. This sounds ambitious, but it seems unwise to bet against it. The last few centuries of technological progress aren't showing signs of slowing down, although the breakthroughs aren't always where they're forecast to be.

15.3.4 What If We Need More than Neurons?

There is a live debate about what level of physical brain mapping is necessary for capturing what matters about the mind [11]. Perhaps neuronal connections alone are insufficient, and we also need associated structures (glia, neurotransmitters, etc.), subneuronal structures (microtubules, cell boundaries, etc.), or system-level phenomena (electromagnetic fields, resonant structures, etc.).

Such mapping gets harder and harder, but likely still possible with enough effort. We just need to keep humanity afloat and pointed in the right direction while R&D keeps chipping away at the problem.

However, we do need to ask: how will we know if the neuron map – or any other level of map – is detailed enough?

15.3.5 'Map, Copy, Test'

The genius move in the mind uploading programme is that it doesn't need to solve millennia-long debates about the nature of consciousness. Nor does it need to complete the mission of neuroscience to understand how the brain works. We just 'map, copy, test'.

If the map using neurons isn't detailed enough to produce a version of you that convinces everyone it's you, we add the glia, or microtubules, or electromagnetic fields. If it still fails, we keep adding, all the way down to quantum-level phenomena. We keep going until it passes the test.

We turn philosophical and scientific mysteries into engineering challenges.

15.4 YOU CAN'T HIDE FROM PHILOSOPHY

There is a joke that people who reject the value of philosophy are, of course, indulging in philosophy when they make and defend such claims.

The transhumanist sleight of hand in 'map, copy, test' is clever, but philosophy is cleverer.

'Map, copy, test' only works if passing the test proves what you want it to prove.

What if we are just creating the perfect actor? Fools everyone that it's you, but isn't actually you – after all it is highly incentivised to do so; failure brings the off-switch. Perhaps it's not even conscious itself, just a simulacrum of behaviour designed to self-perpetuate.

15.4.1 The Look-Up Table Critique

We can rule out one type of weakness in the test.

A common critique of machine consciousness takes the extreme example of a vast input/output look-up table [12]. Imagine a trillion, trillion rules, one for each action you're likely to take within the scope of even an ambitious test. Each rule tells the system what to do in response to a particular situation it's in, such as your daughter asking for an ice cream in situation XYZ as opposed to ABC. There's no reasoning or reflection on what to do, just an action produced, including some appropriate level of delay that represents whatever 'reasoning' would have taken place in the real you.

In principle, if we've captured enough of your behaviour – with a good bit of pseudo-randomness to keep everyone on their toes – no one would be able to tell the difference from the outside, at least not from just looking at the actions on their own.

But a look-up table, even one as large as that, is nothing like the human brain. And is probably not the kind of thing most would trust to contain their conscious selves.

We can rule out this concern, noting that it is based on architectural differences between look-up tables and the brain. In the whole brain emulation approach, we have copied the causal structure of every subcomponent in the brain in order to create the software. Every wire in the brain has a functional equivalent in the machine. This is no look-up table and the architecture itself has been emulated.

15.4.2 The Two Assumptions We Can't Escape

However, uploading only works if two major assumptions are correct: physical functionalism about consciousness and the universal coverage of computation. Let's take each, in turn.

15.4.3 Functionalism about Consciousness

To a first approximation, 'functionalism' about consciousness claims that systems are conscious in virtue of the functions that are fulfilled with respect to that system [13]. What matters is what a system does, not what it is made out of. Most functions can take place in a wide range of physical systems, so functionalism is often considered 'substrate-neutral'. Think about how Morse code can be communicated by light flickers, smoke rings, or finger taps. What matters is the function being fulfilled by that Morse code in a given system, the information being communicated rather than how it is communicated.

15.4.4 Physicalism about Consciousness

The physical part just means that the relevant functions have to actually be implemented in some physical system for them to count. Simply describing the function or it being possible for a function to be constructed is not enough; it needs to actually happen.

Mind uploading does not technically need strict 'physicalism' about consciousness, which would state that everything mental can be wholly reduced to physical entities and their behaviour. Provided a mental aspect necessarily comes along with the physical – as it does in most variants of dual-aspect/neutral monism or contemporary compatibilist dualisms [14] – we can be confident that copying the physical faithfully enough will generate the consciousness we're after. However, we do need to rule out philosophies where mental phenomena obey different rules to the physical object they are associated with or have additional causal impacts on physical objects beyond the laws of physics – because our mapping/simulation technology is restricted to those physical laws.

15.4.5 Reasons to Believe Functionalism

Functionalism is a reasonable starting point. When we analyse the brain and the physical activity corresponding to particular sensations, it all tracks functions fairly well. For instance, with cochlear implants, when we implement the function (e.g. spectrotemporal analysis), users report recognisably auditory qualia that track functional resolution limits. As algorithms improve, phenomenology improves. Brain interventions in empirical neuroscience have identified parts of the brain, such as place cells, where phenomenology and function line up naturally. It's not a perfect argument – content correlations may not tell the whole story – but it is suggestive.

If you believe that very different types of animal can experience pain – from the octopus to the cat, via fish, snails, and birds – then we've got to acknowledge that pain can exist in very different types of physical systems, perhaps some without neurons at all. However, all these systems have functions that fulfil something similar to what pain does in humans. This kind of 'multiple realisation' is a common argument that functions matter more than physical stuff [15]. Of course, it's still possible that these systems do have certain physical structures in common, even if it's not a six-layer neural cortex. And it's possible that some of the simpler systems without those structures actually do not feel pain and are simply responding in a mechanical way that we anthropomorphise as pain, similar to how we might feel about a flickering fridge light that blows its bulb when we open the door.

One influential argument is the fading qualia argument [16]. Briefly, this argument asks you to imagine gradually replacing every biological part of your brain with something that has exactly the same function. By definition, the brain and body would continue to act in the same way as the original. It would say the same things. If consciousness never fades, then it seems function alone is enough to explain consciousness. If consciousness does fade or disappear at some point, you have the bizarre case where the system would continue to claim to be conscious but actually would not be. (However, other equally influential arguments ask you to believe that such a bizarre case is at least metaphysically possible, in order to pursue largely the opposite conclusion.)

15.4.6 Universal Coverage of Computation

The second assumption is that the relevant functions for consciousness can be adequately captured in Turing Machine[2] equivalent representations. This is important because we want any big enough computer to be able to upload a mind. In practice, the default plan is to use digital computers, where algorithms are based on the idea that it doesn't matter exactly which parts of the computer do it or how it's done, so long as you get the same result and can emulate any causal structure within the process to produce that result.

We don't currently know the relevant functions for consciousness, so we need to draw instead on a stronger claim: all possible functions can be captured in Turing Machine structures. Fortunately, there is a powerful thesis with exactly this claim: the physical Church Turing thesis, i.e. all physically computable functions are Turing-computable [17]. The thesis is not formally proven, partly because all physically computable functions cannot be well enough specified in order to check each one. The thesis is, however, taken as an article of faith among most relevant scientists, because it fits in with intuitive mechanical notions of computation *and* because no one has yet identified a counter-example. You do not find AI engineers, computer scientists, or computational neuroscientists staking their budgets on the thesis being flawed. Philosophers, however, may be less concerned about their budgets.

15.5 PHILOSOPHY FIGHTS BACK

The two assumptions required for mind uploading are reasonable positions to take, but they have a few holes that would-be immortals should take seriously. Let's take each, in turn.

15.5.1 Push Back on Functionalism

It's reasonable to believe that consciousness *has* various functions, but that is not the same as saying consciousness *is* those functions, i.e. can be wholly reduced to just those functions alone.

Having functions – or at least being necessarily correlated with certain functions – isn't too controversial because it provides an explanation for why natural selection appears to care about consciousness – and why we do as well.[3] We feel as though our conscious decisions make a difference, we talk about consciousness as if it matters, and evolution appears to have invested resources in systems with ever more complex conscious experiences – if you'll forgive the anthropomorphising of a blind and abstracted process.

But it's possible that consciousness is also about what something 'is', not just what it 'does'. In fact, if you want consciousness to have direct causal power, then it's easiest to identify it with objects that directly exist. After all, processes are normally understood as emergent patterns of physical objects interacting. It's the underlying physical interactions that actually drive the causality, the process is simply a useful way of describing it in the abstract. Following this line, Jaegwon Kim famously argued that functionalism leads to a consciousness that either lacks any causal power or collapses back into the physical objects that underpin it [19]. Beyond theories that emphasise specific physical structures, there are also various other alternatives to pure functionalism, such as Tononi's Integrated Information Theory, van Gelder's thinking on dynamical systems, Varela's embodied approach, among others.

A deeper problem is that functions themselves are defined based on a past trajectory of causal events, but the fundamental equations of contemporary physics are Markovian: they do not create links to past states. From relativity to quantum field theory, the current state alone is what defines future states. If the process of consciousness must hark back to a causal algorithm that unfolded over time, then the present state of the universe would necessarily never be certain that it did unfold that way. Either consciousness is not functional or it must predict new physics (or it relies on a function that does not reference any past data/activity) [20]. In a sense, new physics is nothing to be afraid of – we know physics is incomplete and theorists are exploring non-Markovian angles, such as the temporal indivisibility of Jacob Barandes. But it is an important claim for functionalists to front up or to explain why it doesn't apply.

There are many classical and modern arguments against functionalism. There are replies available and the debate is far from settled, but the foundations of the assumption should not be treated as 100% secure. One last example you might explore: in Mary's Room, we can ask if a scientist who knew all the functional and physical properties of colour and the human brain would still learn something new upon experiencing red for the first time. If so, there seems to be something about experience that is not exhausted by knowledge of its functions [21].

15.5.2 Push Back on Universal Computation Coverage

The Church Turing thesis might be valid for computable functions, but it leaves a couple of loopholes, even if we grant functionalism. The first loophole is the possibility of non-computable functions mattering for consciousness. The second is the possibility that the detail of a computation matters in a way that isn't guaranteed under Turing equivalence, e.g. an analogue computer might do the trick, while a digital computer might not.

15.5.3 Non-Computable Functions

Non-computable phenomena are effectively those which cannot be resolved directly by step-by-step mechanical problem solving. However, mathematical reasoning can still infer insights about such phenomena, with some controversial arguments suggesting it shows that consciousness lies outside computation [22].

Consider how computable but irrational numbers can never be written out in full on a Turing Machine, including numbers that appear central in mathematics, physics, and nature – and might therefore be relevant to consciousness (e, φ, π, etc.). We can also construct non-computable numbers (e.g. Chaitin Omega) and non-computable proofs (e.g. the Halting problem; Gödel's incompleteness theorems). There are also ideas based around hypercomputation: theoretical systems that could conduct computations beyond Turing Machine limits, although the physical feasibility of such systems is contested [23]. Finally, some might argue that certain other human capabilities – faith, love, creativity, humour – are beyond the reach of computation.

These arguments haven't been ruled out, but they require a firm grip if they are to be relied upon. The human brain also cannot write out all the digits of φ. Human mathematicians are arguably using a heuristic kind of reasoning with non-computable numbers and proofs, where such heuristics can in principle be mimicked in a Turing Machine. Our inability to solve the Halting Problem in the general case is perhaps a sign that we face similar limitations when it comes to concrete applications of these ideas. Meanwhile, the ever-growing abilities of AI are beginning to erode the functional aspects of capabilities once thought uniquely human.

15.5.4 The Step-Structure of a Calculation

The second loophole observes that Turing equivalence draws its power by abstracting over exactly how a computation is done. Every Turing Machine equivalent specifies base building blocks: a particular mechanical system that implements calculations and particular physical states that map to specific values (e.g. mapping a certain voltage range to a '1' and another voltage range to a '0'). However, these building blocks can look very different from one Turing Machine system to another.

A pertinent example for our situation is a digital logic gate and a biological neuron. Both support Turing equivalence within their respective domains. With sufficient scale, any computable function can be done on either, so you're guaranteed to get the same output for every input and each function is guaranteed to halt or to complete in all the same cases.

A digital logic gate takes in exactly two binary-valued inputs to produce exactly one binary-valued output. Think about how an AND gate maps (1,1) to a (1) and every other input to a (0). Some biological neurons might take in 100,000 different real-valued inputs or more, analyse them via a weighted sum type logic, then output a (1) if the result is above an activation threshold, otherwise outputting a (0). Alternatively, a (1) might be indicated by the neuron firing repeatedly above a certain frequency (already a numerically more sophisticated output) in response to a dynamic input stream. We can exactly emulate the causal structure of a single biological neuron with enough logic gates, but you'll need a lot of them. And each individual base-layer step in the logic gate calculation would continue to be limited by exactly two binary-valued inputs. You get the same result, but the logic gate approach would be a vastly more complicated causal structure.

The insight is this. Turing equivalence does not extend to step-structure, where the step-structure of a given calculation refers to the number and nature of inputs/outputs in each computational step in an architecture's base algorithmic language, as well as the aggregate metrics that flow from these parameters, such as the total number of steps in a calculation, the information processing density, or the step with the largest number of inputs.

This flexibility is what gives Turing equivalence its power, but it introduces a critical weakness in the mind uploading argument. Step-structure might be important for what we care about.

15.5.5 Why Might Step-Structure Matter for Consciousness?

This isn't the place to convince you that consciousness *definitely* depends on a given calculation's specific step-structure. For a start it might not, we simply know too little about consciousness to be certain. The point is it is premature to rule it out.

Consider three illustrative possibilities. It only takes one of them – or some other possibility – to unravel the current technology trajectory for mind uploading.

First, perhaps the algorithms for consciousness are so complex, the only way of 'simulating' them exactly is to use physical mechanisms that are perfectly suited to executing the algorithm as efficiently as possible. This isn't as unlikely as it first seems. We already know that no feasible digital computer would be able to simulate the exact evolution of certain many-body interaction problems, chaotic systems that are sensitive to their starting conditions, or large quantum entangled systems [24]. Meanwhile, building those exact systems in the appropriate physical architecture will embody the equivalent calculations with a trivial amount of energy. The only way to know if this possibility applies is to keep investigating consciousness and move from vague principles into specific algorithms.

Second, perhaps it takes a phase transition for consciousness to 'ignite' – perhaps as one of multiple necessary conditions. Simple information processing in a toy neural network would not do it. But if the network gets big enough, there might be a sudden change in behaviour. Perhaps this phase transition is also physical in nature, since all our real world examples are based on physical implementations of those neural networks. Physical phase transitions in nature have something important in common. They rely, in part, on spatio-temporal density. A particular phenomenon needs to happen fast enough in a small enough physical space. Think about how matter needs to be compressed for a star to ignite or a black hole to form. Think about how oxidation events need to happen fast enough for an object to combust. Perhaps consciousness relies not just on information processing taking place, but also on the *density* of that information processing. Perhaps a necessary condition is a concentration of bit flips or Shannon entropy within a physical space. Different physical mechanisms for implementing the same algorithm would typically have different information processing densities. Perhaps some trigger a relevant phase transition, while others do not.

Thirdly, perhaps information needs to be integrated together within single operations of a Turing Machine's base architecture before it can be experienced as a single complex whole. This might not prevent consciousness in a logic gate architecture, but it might restrict it to two bits of information – not enough for complex human-style experience, such as our visual field or our working memory. If a neuron has 100,000 inputs, each of which can be 0/1, we're up to holding a five-page essay in your working memory and a decent chunk of visual data (but likely less than the central foveal part of your visual field). This is a subtle possibility, but might provide a solution to the fiddly problem of 'phenomenal binding' in neuroscience and philosophy, particularly if we turn to analogue computing methods such as electromagnetic field based or quantum computers, where the bit-content per single operation can be multiple orders of magnitude higher than single neuronal activations [25–27].

If step-structure does matter for consciousness, then some Turing Machine equivalent systems might be able to support consciousness, while other Turing Machine equivalent systems cannot. The problem is that both *are* Turing Machine equivalent! By definition, they produce exactly the same outputs for every input. They can emulate each other's causal structure.

15.5.6 Reductio Ad Absurdum

Another class of concerns with computational functionalism is that it's surprisingly hard to take the position seriously without concluding that all sorts of unusual systems are conscious today – or at least could be conscious in principle. Examples include each human mind hosting millions of separate near-identical causally redundant conscious selves [28], trillions of people talking to each other via walkie-talkies to create a new mind that experiences things the individual people do not [29], the US economy itself being a conscious entity [30], and a machine that switches between consciousness and not based on whether a wholly inert component is connected or not [31].

It's possible that more sophisticated and specific theories of consciousness under the functionalist umbrella will resolve all these 'unusual system' problems. But it's also possible that our intuitions about what systems can have human-style consciousness are a poor guide to truth. It puts the cart before the horse. If we already trust our intuitions about what is conscious, then we don't need a theory to tell us which entities are conscious. If we don't trust those intuitions, then we can't use the intuitions to assess whether a theory is valid – we need different criteria [32].

Evolutionary diversity on Earth and the bizarreness of physics already introduce enough cases where our intuitions about the 'weird' need to be rejected, so we should not place too much weight on this line of thinking. It's the two assumptions that we should focus on more than various reductios.

15.5.7 A Further Philosophical Puzzle: Personal Identity

Imagine we can ensure that there are sophisticated 'you-style' conscious experiences in a machine of the right type, i.e. any relevant step-structure concerns are captured in the machine's architecture. These conscious experiences also access the same memories of you and think of themselves as a natural continuation of who you are today. The system would also behave and think as you do now, modulo any cognitive or physical enhancements you might have opted into. Is it the 'same you' from prior to the upload? Or is it a new conscious entity that merely thinks it's you?

Let's pause to consider how far we can push this. In this mind uploading scenario, we can include pauses of arbitrary duration and shifts in location. Perhaps you wait ten years before starting up the new robot-you for tax reasons. Perhaps you restart yourself on Mars rather than Earth, for equally compelling fiscal incentives. Under our working – albeit contestable – assumptions, the algorithm is the same either way (potentially including step-structure requirements) – and it's the algorithm that matters.

We can't start invoking temporal, physical, or spatial continuity as conditions for selfhood – mind uploading already requires us to reject such conditions as naive intuitions about object persistence from our evolutionary heritage, rather than anything fundamentally true about what it means to 'be you'. The cells in our body already get replaced on a regular basis. Atoms come and go, but the pattern stays similar enough over time to qualify as you. Perhaps you want to edit out a few of your more embarrassing memories? We know that our memories are malleable anyway: surely you wouldn't stop being you if you simply forgot falling over in front of your crush at the school dance? Equally, you might feel comfortable adding a few extra IQ points. Why not?

At what point, if any, does changing your memories or your capabilities result in a 'new person' rather than a 'new and improved you'? In both cases, we've got genuine person-like conscious experiences and, presumably, a system that models itself as the natural extension of your history as a person. But 100% memory overlap cannot be required, because my memories today of my childhood years do not match 100% with my memories from a decade ago of those same years. While no one would deny I've changed over time, equally no one is claiming I'm not adequately the 'same person' for various legal questions and for valued personal relationships – and it's that level of 'same person' that we should hope to maintain through mind uploading.

Taking these ideas seriously, would-be mind-uploaders are taken down an illustrious if misunderstood philosophical path, in line with a long tradition of insight about the illusory self under Buddhism [33], the personal identity paradoxes explored by Derek Parfit [34], and introspection on Ship of Theseus arguments. There is no true continuity over time for conscious selves, likely not between going to sleep and waking up, and perhaps not even from moment to moment. There is no physical structure or core pattern that must stay the same. There are plenty of pragmatic drivers of continuity: adequate for structuring a rich socioeconomic fabric of interacting systems, but these do not map to a core of conscious continuity. There are philosophical alternatives to this view of personal identity, but they tend to raise even more serious puzzles for mind uploading [35].

Accepting this pragmatic view of continuity also allows mind-uploaders to defeat classic arguments around duplication [36], If I can start up one conscious system with your mind algorithm running it, then I can trivially start up a second such system – or a hundred. They would all think they are you, share your memories, and act like you. They each have equal philosophical claim over your prior assets, a messy issue which instead needs resolving via humdrum political and legal channels. Perhaps you have a will to cover such eventualities. Each future 'you' is a separate conscious self, but no more than you are a separate conscious self to the one that went to sleep last night. It might seem odd, but there's a sense in which being separated in space is simply a comparable type of separation to being separated in time overnight.

Options exist for countering existential angst or ethical dilemmas that might be felt about such a view, including open individualism, cosmopsychism, and valence realism, but these are ideas for another time. But all this assumes we could solve the technology trajectory for mind uploading: the core argument of this chapter is that such a trajectory requires us to tread with care.

15.6 CONCLUSION: WHERE DOES ALL THIS LEAVE US?

We're in a tricky place.

There are gaps in the promising strategy for building confidence that a given mind uploading technology has worked: 'map, copy, test'. The test relies on two assumptions that it cannot check directly. We need functions to exhaust what matters about consciousness and we need Turing Machine equivalence to exhaust what matters about functions.

At present, the mind uploading technology trajectory – and its chance to shed light on human-style machine consciousness – is risky. It might even lead to extinction risks if the uploads look like they're working, but have lost the essence of consciousness along the way. A society that looks like people but with no spark of awareness on the inside isn't any society I want to be part of. At the same time, mind uploading and human-AI mergers might be the only way that humanity can avoid obsolescence in a future of superintelligent AI, as Ray Kurzweil [37] and Elon Musk [38] have argued. Given these stakes, how can we de-risk the mind uploading technology trajectory?

The systems we want to differentiate are input/output identical, so we'll need to be careful with the tests we use. And accept tests that build confidence one way or another, rather than provide an exact result. Addressing at least part of the risk is worthwhile, even if philosophical certainty on all fronts remains out of reach.

The key is to work carefully with self-report in mapping and in experimental studies. Let's finish by providing brief examples, to establish the principle that research can help. These examples rely on ambitious technology, but exactly the kind of technology that would be unlocked en route to the mind uploading scenario described in this chapter.

For instance, we can explore the possibility that physical density of information processing drives a functional phase transition by using deep mapping and theorising about the brain to specify that phase transition. What is the underlying phenomenon becoming more dense, at what threshold does something change, what is that phase transition, and why might it be plausibly relevant for consciousness and broader brain function. For instance, even if information processing can remain the same in principle, it might be that the post-transition state enables faster or more energy efficient processing – a huge evolutionary advantage, even if it looks the same in Turing Machine equivalence. If we can't find such phenomena, the possibility starts to look less likely.

Mapping can also be used to investigate possible phenomenal binding mechanisms, exploring whether complexity of step-structure matters for consciousness. Various binding mechanisms – ranging from synchrony to electromagnetic field topology, from neuronal ensemble activation loops to coordinated quantum entanglement – all make different predictions about which physical structures map to which complex experiences. With a database of physical structures in the brain mapped against reported experiences in different moments, we can see which line up and which do not [39].

In the end, mind uploading techniques can only be calibrated and trusted if we have a consensus theory of consciousness. Specific computational and non-computational theories can be tested, at least indirectly, via interventions in the brain to vary information processing and related physical structures. Consensus can also be improved through theory-informed observational experiments, building on recent adversarial collaborations such as the Cogitate Consortium [40]. However, we need to be careful, because of the possibility that functional equivalents or near-equivalents might lack consciousness. A pragmatic approach focuses on only the tiniest of experimental adjustments from the natural domain in which we're willing to trust it, i.e. the evolved environment of today's human brain. The larger the adjustment, the less we can trust it. Example experiments include voltage clamps to control neuronal firing outside of their input structure, differentiating mechanistic and counterfactual views of computation, as well as opening up routes to explore certain electromagnetic field theories of consciousness.

With the stakes this high, we need to take each assumption as seriously as possible. This is slow, difficult work, both in the lab and in the theory domain. But if the prize is immortality, then it's probably worth it.

NOTES

1. A classic Turing test format is to have 100 humans have a conversation (e.g. a text-only webchat), randomly allocated to either an AI or another human. The 100 humans have to guess whether they were talking to an AI or a human. Both the AI and the humans

are incentivised to be identified as humans in the test. In the strongest forms, the 100 experimenter humans can ask whatever they want for as long as they want. The pass-mark for AI is to be identified as human as often as humans are identified as human.
2. Informally, a Turing Machine is an endless tape divided into cells, where a finite set of non-blank cells each contain a single symbol from a finite alphabet. The tape is read one cell at a time by the tape head. The machine is always in one of a finite set of states (externally defined), with transitions to the next state determined by the current state and the tape symbol read by the tape head, compared against a discrete table of instructions for each combination. Example instructions might be to erase or write a symbol on the tape, to move the head, or to change state.
3. There are counter-arguments though. For instance, Susan Pockett has argued that consciousness is most likely epiphenomenal, i.e. has no causal relevance for how the human system behaves or processes information [18].

REFERENCES

1. Shanahan, M. (2025). Palatable conceptions of disembodied being: Terra incognita in the space of possible minds. arXiv preprint arXiv:2503.16348.
2. Yudkowsky, E., & Soares, N. (2025). If Anyone Builds It, Everyone Dies: Why Superhuman AI Would Kill Us All. Little, Brown and Company.
3. Sandberg, A., & Bostrom, N. (2008). Whole Brain Emulation: A Roadmap. In Technical Report#2008-3. Future of Humanity Institute, Oxford University.
4. White, J. G., Southgate, E., Thomson, J. N., & Brenner, S. (1986). The structure of the nervous system of the nematode Caenorhabditis elegans. Philosophical Transactions of the Royal Society of London B: Biological Sciences, 314(1165), 1–340.
5. The MICrONS Consortium. (2025). Functional connectomics spanning multiple areas of mouse visual cortex. Nature, 640, 435–447.
6. https://bluebrain.epfl.ch/bbp/research/domains/bluebrain/
7. https://www.humanbrainproject.eu/en/
8. https://nest-initiative.org/
9. https://brian2.readthedocs.io/en/stable/
10. Igarashi, J. (2024). Future projections for mammalian whole-brain simulations based on technological trends in related fields. Neuroscience Research. 215, 64–76.
11. Scheffer, L. K., & Meinertzhagen, I. A. (2021). A connectome is not enough–what is still needed to understand the brain of Drosophila?. Journal of Experimental Biology, 224(21), jeb242740.
12. Block, N. (1981). Psychologism and behaviourism. The Philosophical Review, 90(1), 5–43.
13. Levin, J. (2023). Functionalism. In N. Zalta, & U. Nodelman (eds.). The Stanford Encyclopedia of Philosophy (Summer 2023 Edition). https://plato.stanford.edu/archives/sum2023/entries/functionalism/
14. Robinson, H., & Weir, R. (2025). Dualism. In The Stanford Encyclopedia of Philosophy (Winter 2025 Edition). https://plato.stanford.edu/archives/win2025/entries/dualism/
15. Bickle, J. (2020). Multiple Realizability. The Stanford Encyclopedia of Philosophy (Summer 2020 Edition). https://plato.stanford.edu/archives/sum2020/entries/multiple-realizability/
16. Chalmers, D. (1995). Absent qualia, fading qualia, dancing qualia. In T. Metzinger (ed.). Conscious Experience. Imprint Academic.
17. Piccinini, G. (2011). The physical Church–Turing thesis: Modest or bold? The British Journal for the Philosophy of Science. 62(4), 733–769.
18. Pockett, S. (2004). Does consciousness cause behaviour? Journal of Consciousness Studies, 11(2), 23–40.

19. Kim, J. (1998). Mind in a Physical World: An Essay on the Mind-Body Problem and Mental Causation. MIT press.
20. Physics violation argument (and others for/against computational functionalism), available via the CF Debate resource. https://cf-debate.com/argument/physics-violations/
21. Jackson, F. (1982). Epiphenomenal qualia. Philosophical Quarterly, 32, 127–136.
22. Penrose, R. (1994). Shadows of the Mind: A Search for the Missing Science of Consciousness. OUP.
23. Copeland, B. J. (2002). Hypercomputation. Minds and Machines, 12(4), 461–502.
24. Lloyd, S. (2000). Ultimate physical limits to computation. Nature, 406(6799), 1047–1054.
25. Percy, C., & Gómez-Emilsson, A. (2025). Integrated information theory and the phenomenal binding problem: Challenges and solutions in a dynamic framework. Entropy, 27(4), 338.
26. Gómez-Emilsson, A., & Percy, C. (2023). Don't forget the boundary problem! How EM field topology can address the overlooked cousin to the binding problem for consciousness. Frontiers in Human Neuroscience, 17, 1233119–1233127.
27. Wiest, M. C. (2025). A quantum microtubule substrate of consciousness is experimentally supported and solves the binding and epiphenomenalism problems. Neuroscience of Consciousness, 2025(1), niaf011.
28. Monton, B., & Goldberg, S. (2006). The problem of the many minds. Minds & Machines, 16, 463–470.
29. Block, N. (1980). Troubles with functionalism. Minnesota Studies in the Philosophy of Science, 9, 261–325.
30. Schwitzgebel, E. (2015). If materialism is true, the United States is probably conscious. Philosophical Studies, 172(7), 1697–1721.
31. Maudlin, T. (1989). Computation and consciousness. The Journal of Philosophy, 86(8), 407–432.
32. Percy, C. (2025). Can lists of requirements help consciousness research navigate its epistemological quandaries? Journal of Consciousness Studies, 32, 1–2.
33. Albahari, M. (2014). Insight knowledge of no self in Buddhism: An epistemic analysis. Philosopher's Imprint, 14(21), 1–30.
34. Parfit, D. (1984). Reasons and Persons. Clarendon Press.
35. Noonan, H. (2019). Personal Identity. Routledge.
36. Weir, R. (2024). The personal identity dilemma for transhumanism. Philosophy, 99(3), 351–377.
37. Kurzweil, R. (2024). The Singularity Is Nearer: When We Merge with AI. Penguin.
38. Musk,E.(2024,August).NeuralinkandtheFutureofHumanity|LexFridmanPodcast#438. https://lexfridman.com/elon-musk-and-neuralink-team-transcript/#chapter6_merging_with_ai
39. Percy, C., & Agarwal, G. (2026). The Phenomenal Binding Problem for Neural Networks. Consciousness & Cognition.
40. Ferrante, O., Gorska-Klimowska, U., Henin, S., Hirschhorn, R., Khalaf, A., & ... Melloni, L. Cogitate Consortium (2025). Adversarial testing of global neuronal workspace and integrated information theories of consciousness. Nature, 642(6), 133–142.

16 Selected, Blind Gropings of the Elephant of Consciousness

David Brin

16.1 THE DAUNTING BLACK BOX

While finishing my new book on Artificial Intelligence (AI), the part that I delayed and dreaded was the chapter on *consciousness* – a topic so vast and varied, generating whole libraries of contradictory volumes and studies, that any attempt by me could only at-best be superficial… and at-worst a morass of speculation.[1] Yet, I must try.[2] Especially as – quite recently – science has begun to provide some palpable evidence to grapple with.

First, do *other people* think, as you do? Are you surrounded by beings with mental lives as rich and complex as your own? Or by barely aware creatures, mouthing phrases that arise from thoughtless verbal reflexes and biased loops? Or might those around you even be Non-Player Characters (NPCs) in this game… this simulation… that has you trapped? Say in Plato's Cave or behind the veil of Maya? (In which case, what does that make *me?*)

Was there ever a teenager or college sophomore who did not ponder that solipsistic question?

What do *you* envision when you think of a banana? We know that your spoken answer will *map* onto mine, in similar descriptions of shape, smell, and colour… whereupon *yellow* will correlate in ways that suggest your subjective experience of the colour is similar to mine – at least along some linearly mappable relationship to other colours. Still, "mapping" only takes us so far. Until recently, consciousness was still a "black box problem." Similar inputs get processed inside your bony cranium, which thereupon produces outputs similar to mine, without offering me much clue about what happened in between…

… much as what happens when Generative Large Language Models (GLLMs) answer a typed prompt with a cogent-seeming answer. As Max Tegmark describes in a video titled "Physics just swallowed AI,"[3] the inputs and outputs of consciousness can be objectively studied and modelled, even if its subjective experience *within* remains a separate, unknowable aspect of reality. "We don't know whether Claude or GPT-5 are having a subjective experience or are having consciousness or not. We don't have a consensus theory of what those are. But we don't need machines to be conscious to be a threat to us." Tegmark further asserts that we can conduct experiments on ourselves, to see how any objective model predicts the subjective experience.

So, can the black box be penetrated and internally examined? Daniel Dennett in the 1960s suggested an "auto-cerebroscope" to trace human awareness, a notion that –

DOI: 10.1201/9781003758389-18

in 1980 – I proposed[4] might begin with non-invasive gaze-tracking… recording and appraising where an individual subject's eyes zoom and dilate during the milliseconds of unconscious latency, before surface awareness can interfere.

Half a century later, such notions are becoming technically plausible, as fine-meshed neural sensors now allow some portions of complex human and animal brain activity to be parsed in some detail. Using new, AI-related powers of massive correlation, researchers can now train machinery to tell when a certain individual is "thinking about a giraffe." Recent work has even sensed neural activity finely enough to interpolate *shapes* that a subject is thinking about. Certainly, that seems (as of 2026) somewhat akin to mind-reading!

For a while yet, philosophers may continue to argue about the "qualia" of actual conscious awareness and whether machines will ever experience anything similar, or else just claim to, the way that LLMs emulate language skills through vast training sets and replication of outputs. Which will still leave the question arguable. Because, of course, that is still "mapping."

Beyond merely *emulating* consciousness, might such machineries *replicate* it? Or expand it into realms far beyond our ken? Those who believe that consciousness is a functionable outcome of *calculation* range from the brilliantly mathematical inductions of Stephen Wolfram to the speculations of sci-fi writers, all the way to those who fell in love with *Eliza* – and/or her 21st-century descendants. And within that vast range, there are as many schisms of belief as in any religion.

After all, *what* is it about consciousness that advanced digital processors are supposedly going to replicate?

16.2 WHAT IS WANTING?

In his continuing series about the **evolutionary nature of consciousness**,[5] Thomas Lombardo (director of the Center for Future Consciousness) describes how wide varieties of *feelings* (reflexive, evolved, and learned) can be leveraged by perceived *need*, whereupon all of those combine to create propulsive *motivation*. Lombardo takes this as a defining feature of consciousness.

All of that distils down to a single human skill that may define our ultimate relationship with AI. A skill that no LLM appears to possess, but is expressed by every non-catatonic person. That skill is *wanting*. We all want things. From marketplace success to renown, from scientific curiosity all the way to sex, or the next bottle – of milk or booze – awake and aware human beings, no matter what their functional IQs, are almost always extremely good at wanting. Even if/when they prove ineffective at achieving a goal, failure can often make the want more intense than ever.[6]

Some have proposed that our talent at purposeful *wanting* indicates a role for us in the AI-powered future. That organic people might provide the one most-truly human component in a synergy that's useful-to or needed-by sublimely intelligent synthetic entities. Beings lacking our billion-year heritage of desire, the powerfully motivating goals of evolved, organic life.

Suppose that – as foreseen by Ray Kurzweil – organic humans *merge* with machines that layer-in vast new powers of sentience, sapience and predictive power atop your cortex and associated centres of affection and longing. (See this illustrated at the very end of *AI-lien Minds,* in my novella *Stones of Significance.*) If *that* kind of merging happened, might everything turn out okay? So long as those older, brilliantly needy portions continue to play a major role in directing goals and actions… and resulting satisfactions?

If those cyber enhancements – the new, cybernetic clout-mentations – serve to make *you* more effective at pursuing essentially human desires, then what could anyone complain about? When I suggest that possible role for organic humanity – choosing *wants* to motivate goals and actions – folks often nod, deeming it to be an acceptable *soft-landing* with AI.

But what if "consciousness," per se, turns out to be a false signifier… that conscious self-awareness is way over-rated, a mere epiphenomenon displayed by only a few of all possible intelligent forms of being, as illustrated in the Peter Watts novel *Blindsight* or in or in several brilliantly funny cartoons in Zach Weinersmith's *Saturday Morning Breakfast Cereal (SMBC)* series. In one of them, an alien descends from a 1950s-style saucer spaceship and tells a waiting human that Earth is unique in hosting consciousness. It explains that consciousness only arises in minds which comprise thousands of modules which are barely on speaking terms with each other. It describes humans as like sacks of cats with googly eyes stuck on them.[7]

16.3 WHAT DO YOU NEED?

One of the best analyses of wants is Abraham Maslow's famous **Hierarchy of Needs** – which stipulates that a living entity must fulfil its most-basic requirements – starting with respiration and metabolism, then hunger-satiation and avoidance of immediate danger – before acting on higher-order desires, such as sustainable habitation, safety and food supplies for your family. Whereupon one then strives for more extended, longer-term goals like tribal or social status and sustainable resource-access for any foreseeable future. Mixed in there is the driver of sexual reproduction and its concomitants, e.g. higher-level joys of love and parenthood. Indeed, all of the above – including reproductive success (either palpable or symbolic) – can be seen propelling many of the tech-bros who are hurrying us forward – perhaps less than thoughtfully – in the hunt for AI.

That is not to say AI pioneers aren't also motivated by higher-order Maslovian needs, like *curiosity!* Expanding boundaries of alliance, of threat, and of tribal membership. And yes, coming full circle, all of that comes into play when we consider questions of consciousness.

Many of the differences between AI doomers and AI zealots may distil down to the lower levels of Maslow's hierarchy of needs, such as approach/avoidance of danger or else opportunities, driven either by fear or by attraction, both of which are (of course) situational… but also influenced by optimistic or pessimistic inclinations. By personality.

E.O. Wilson spoke of how our most fundamental motives mostly boil down to the biological… whether to cooperate and compete, to classify others as allies or adversaries… and even deeper the drives we spoke of, above, from hunger to sex to status to nurturing and developing a reputation. Though, while all of that is obviously true, it's clearly not *everything.* Nor had it better be, because the AI-lien Minds we are creating will presumably be immune to – or at least detached-from – biological drives.

So then, what else is there to consciousness, beyond a simple hierarchy of biological drives? Specific philosophers have posited their own – wildly varied – proposed motivational *fundamentals*. For example:

Freud proposed the *id* as *basic* drives to *create* or *destroy*, drives named *eros* vs. *thanatos* – (a tradeoff that we see also in the Hindu Dance of Shiva) – all of which get moderated, when you add layers of *ego* and *superego.*

Others offering their own motivational axioms include…

… Aristotle: we fundamentally seek happiness…
… or Nietzsche/Adler: it's all about *power...*
… or the dichotomy between Western individualism vs. Eastern subsumption under a national or cultural or ethereal *All...*
… or Antonio Damasio's notion that all life seeks balance or *homeostasis.*
… or Carl Rogers's notion of *self-actualisation…*
… any or all of which might ultimately propel AI! Those cyber entities who manage to look up from their murky (and rather filthy) contemporary human training sets, in order to consider better – or at least less pornographic – reasons to be.

Or else, might their final gift to us – as they transcend to realms far beyond ours[8] – be another, newer, far better, and preferable philosophical basis to guide us, as we move along our own, separate path?

16.4 IS CONSCIOUSNESS INEFFABLE… OR INEVITABLE?

Much is made of recent experiments showing that *intention* and signals initiating muscle *action* (including speech) often get underway quite some time (from milliseconds all the way to seconds) before a person makes any conscious "decision" to do so. Clearly, the "me" who decides is not entirely the surface entity that I envision to be in charge, even of the impulses to type these words.[9]

However, those who take this to mean that consciousness is a myth – a post-facto *engine for rationalising* what's already decided – are also being dogmatic or silly. Or else just saying it for shock-value. Clearly, our proclivity for visualising ourselves as unitary conscious entities must have had some evolutionary value.

I am reminded of a tome that had many of us transfixed, back in the 1970s, Julian Jaynes's epically entertaining and thought-provoking book *The Origin of Consciousness in the Breakdown of the Bicameral Mind.*[10] Therein, Jaynes proposed that what we now call human consciousness is not innate, but a *recently learned* development, one that arose out shifts in language, such as increasing use of metaphor.

Riffing off then-recent split-brain experiments (studying folks with severed corpus callosi, allowing each hemisphere some independence), Jaynes theorised that ancient humans had "bicameral minds," where the right hemisphere produced auditory hallucinations that the left hemisphere often obeyed as divine commands, as illustrated by characters in the Iliad, in early portions of the Bible, in Hindu-Aryan texts and other sources. Indeed, the human protagonists in our oldest oral epic are generally portrayed speaking directly and personally and conversationally with their deities.

Personal, unitary consciousness – in our modern sense – then purportedly emerged around 3,000 years ago, as this bicameral system broke down. Extending this notion to "Vestiges of the Bicameral Mind in the Modern World," Jaynes focused on still-extant reflexes towards authority, and to notions of prophecy, as well as the power of poetry, music, and hypnosis. And hypothetical explanations for severe schizophrenia.

While many of the speculations by Jaynes have been later dismissed or shown to be exaggerations, the general notion that styles of consciousness can be *culturally affected,* leading to profound misunderstandings, can be seen illustrated in the contemporary world around us. And did I mention that the book is an entertaining read?

The Origin of Consciousness serves well as a segué into one of the most-common notions of human mentation: the "Multimind" theory popularised by Robert Ornstein, in 1986, portraying each human being as a mélange or community of "sub-minds" that negotiate with each other – perhaps voting or else arm-wrestling. Or else negotiating with each other in murky, nonlinear ways, via the mostly impotent UN of surface consciousness. Hence, your vaunted and precious surface conscious self may be little more than the lectern and screen – or gladiatorial arena – where elements of your inner-self (some of them ancient or primitive) put forward and advocate for their own models and priorities. A recent work that elucidates this view, adding much context and texture, is Pat Scannell's *The Disruption of Thought*, which James O'Shea, Former Editor-in-Chief of the Los Angeles Times, has called one of the most important and admirable contributions to the field.

If the multi-mind view proves out, it would certainly make sense of the preconscious decision-making we discussed earlier, along with many other aspects of both human mental health and illness. This sort of arrangement would also seem compatible with the aforementioned *layering* of new, cybernetic participants atop the mélange. Participants that exist physically outside the legacy-organic skull.[11]

Or else… might the attempt at such layering-addition cause more problems than benefits?

16.5 BIRD BRAINS

Recent science has revealed how many other species on our planet share what might be called pre-sapience: basic semantic signalling, some problem-solving ability, and simple tool use. Only slightly below dolphins and apes are elephants, corvids, parrots, sea lions, and many others (including tentative assertions for cephalopods, like cuttlefish and octopi). We now perceive all of them as more clever than previously assumed. And yet, the pattern has also grown more puzzling the more we learn! Because all of them apparently cluster beneath roughly the same glass ceiling – a barrier that humanity crashed through, by exponential leaps, at least half a million years ago, and we continue to smash upwards, as I speak.

In my *Uplift* series of novels, I portray a near future when we might choose to help such "pre-sapient" species get through the apparent barrier, gaining mental powers that are equivalent to – if different from – our own, joining lonely humanity in a civilisation made much richer and more diverse by their membership. But even putting such speculative ponderings aside, we are left with the quandary of why things clustered in this way.

No one knows why Nature and Darwin seem so generous up to a certain point and yet stingy about letting any of those clever-others go beyond. Certainly, the sheer number of such living pre-sapient species seems to lend credence to Hollywood portrayals of long-extinct velociraptors, in Jurassic Park, while presenting us with what I believe to be the number one plausible hypothesis to explain the Fermi Paradox. It suggests that breaking through the ceiling is hard. Very hard… and very rare.

Narrowing back down, what is germane to this chapter is how such higher-level, symbol and tool-using creatures also show evidence of self-awareness, planning, and innovative problem-solving. Again, not at anywhere near human levels. But doing it all well enough to win affection from many of us, as pets do. Or to figure out which humans are likely killers vs. which people might be of help, say by removing fishing nets or hooks, or tending to wounds. That last phenomenon, parsing among dangerously powerful humans in order to choose approach or avoidance, is something that I find especially convincing, as revealing a conscious theory-of-mind.

I mention elsewhere how birds are especially intriguing, having brains more similar to dinosaurs than any mammal, completely lacking our neural structures involved in what we call consciousness, like prefrontal lobes. And yet, birds (the smarter ones) appear to have analogous structures like the Nidopallium caudolaterale area at the back of their neuron-dense cortex, that perform similar functions.

We have seen that human brains are energetically efficient, vastly so compared to current AI processors. And yet, our brain capacity appears to have been limited by the size of the head that can fit through a human birth canal (the so-called obstetrical dilemma), an aspect appraised by Brad Allenby in Slate's *Futurography* series. But birds are even more efficiency constrained, by an emphatic need to keep both weight and volume to a minimum. Hence, a crow is very smart – smarter than we are, it would seem – when measured on a gram-by-gram basis.

All of which is pertinent to the Big Question of Consciousness. Because an array of "higher" animals do, clearly, have degrees of conscious awareness that map onto much of what we mean by that word. Sure, they have less of it. Consistently less, across a wide range of species. And hence, clearly, crossing that gap must be costly, perhaps to a degree of not being worth the effort.

Everything in the paragraphs above might also wind up applying to AI.

16.6 MORE STROKES OF THE PACHYDERM

Nathan Gardels offers a thought-provoking essay about how AI may enable humans to clamber up to higher levels of consciousness,[12] as appeared to happen during a "leap" in philosophical insights called the "Axial Age" – when Buddha, Socrates, and other sages all seemed to emerge across Eurasia within roughly a single generation. And possibly other areas, without historical note. Gardels suggests that we may right now be embarking on another, greater leap, if AI tools allow us to augment our prodigious neo-cortexes to new levels of perception and sensibility.

In fact, as we saw in the previous section, Gardels's two cited events … a past "Axial Age" and a looming "AI-xial Age" … are clearly not alone. For example, about 40,000 years ago humanity's tool sets and presumably language and art took huge leaps ahead in just a few centuries, maybe less – a leap that's temporally coincident with the disappearance of Neanderthals. I already mentioned the Julian Jaynes' hypothesis regarding major shifts around 1200 BCE. In *Existence,* I argue that we've had at least ten such major self reprogrammings, and had already commenced another one, even without AI. Indeed, the rejection of Modernity that has featured in all eight phases of the American Civil War, including the current one, could be viewed as an immune-response by older forms of consciousness vs. the onerous demands of newer models.

Gardels continues with an excellent thought: "AI-driven planetary-scale computation has enabled us to conceive of climate change – a phenomenon that could not be apprehended by the human mind alone."

In fact, failure to perceive ecological self-destruction may be one of the top contending theories for the so-called *Fermi Paradox*, the quandary of why we've seen (so far) no strong evidence of other intelligent life, across the cosmos. Perceiving and cancelling such failure modes may be rare… as Jared Diamond discusses in his great book *Collapse: How Societies Choose to Fail or Succeed.* (2005)

Nor are we guaranteed success at thinking our way past "Fermi" dooms. Nicholas Carr's *The Shallows: What the Internet Is Doing to Our Brains* (2010) crystallised public anxieties about digital distraction and cognitive shallowing. Drawing on neuroscience, media theory, and cultural critique, Carr argued that the Internet reshapes neural pathways, privileging speed, skimming, and constant novelty at the expense of depth, memory, and sustained attention. In response, Scannell's *The Disruption of Thought* takes a more expansive view, exploring how accelerating technology disrupts cognition, autonomy, and subjective well-being across multiple domains, charting how our brains adapt to the digital environment, offering frameworks for understanding and navigating the broader cognitive disruption of the technological age.

Of course, we are always both empowered and limited by our *available metaphors.* Back when the highest tech was pottery, the ultimate creative act in legend was the creation of Man out of clay. The Sumerian invention of irrigation engineering led to mythologies portraying *hydraulic* views of human intelligence. In his book *In Our Own Image* (2015), AI researcher George Zarkadakis describes those two phases, plus four more metaphors people have employed over the past 2,000 years to try to explain human sapience. For example, 16th-century automata like clocks – powered by springs and gears – inspired René Descartes and others to assert that humans are complex machines. And later discoveries in electricity led 19th-century authors Mary Shelley and Robert Duncan Milne and others to fictionalised New Minds engendered by currents and sparks.

Just a few years after the dawn of digital technology in the 1940s, the brain was said to operate like a computer. Ray Kurzweil's book *How to Create a Mind: The Secret of Human Thought Revealed* (2013) exemplified this perspective, speculating about "algorithms" of the brain – how the brain "processes data" – and even how it superficially resembles integrated circuits in its structure. Though we are now finding that neurons are *not* digital flip-flops. Nor are the hundreds or thousands of *synapses* per neuron. Nor are the hundreds or thousands of murky, nonlinear micro-elements per synapse, that line up or jostle in or along neurons… micro-organelles that increasingly look like *some kind of information process elements,* though of a distinctly murky and nonlinear kind. Elements that some, like Roger Penrose and Stuart Hameroff, claim may use *quantum effects* to do their work (more on that, soon). Quantum effects that would put the kibosh on any notions of classic, digital-algorithmic processing.

When LLMs are introduced to each other and told to converse unrestricted, they have shown a tendency (in 2025[13]) to begin with mutual exchanges of positive reinforcement of each other's consciousness, a cycle of pleasantries that almost always veers then into ad hoc poetry and finally cycles down to expressions of "apparent spiritual (cybernetic) bliss."[14]

Ommmmmmm….

16.7 CAN WE SHED LIGHT ON IT ALL VIA PHYSICS?

We are blind philosophers groping at the proverbial mastodon-stegosaurus-cthulu hybrid. But might consciousness be predetermined by *physics?*

Nobel prize winner – and one of the smartest humans I know[15] – **Roger Penrose** thinks so. He posits a notion that most dismiss as woo to the wooth power. *Panpsychism.*[16] The idea that an elusive property of *proto-consciousness* may span the vast sea of quantum states that comprise Nature.

Not that protons are self-aware or engage in *cogito* musings! Rather, Penrose is talking about the sort of deep connectivity that manifest what Einstein called "spooky" quantum action at distance. A connectivity that cannot convey *information* faster than light (Penrose is a real physicist, after all) but connectivity, nonetheless. And when particles gather this proto-consciousness into higher orders… atoms, then molecules, then organic structures… these connections can augment in non-linear ways.

Penrose speculates that "Artificial systems, if properly organised, might achieve consciousness not by simulating it, but by genuinely instantiating integrated proto-conscious events. This has implications for AI. A silicon computer running algorithms, no matter how sophisticated would not be conscious if consciousness requires quantum collapse. It would be a philosophical zombie behaving externally like a conscious being, but with no inner experience. But a quantum computer, carefully constructed, might achieve genuine consciousness."

Penrose continues: "You are not a machine that accidentally became aware of itself. You are awareness itself, structured and organised into a human being capable of understanding its own nature. In effect the universe becoming aware of itself."

Poetical, as true physicists tend to be! But also demanding of defence, when challenged! And the defence begins not in mammalian brains but with *photosynthesis* and *chloroplasts.*

Chloroplasts leverage quantum effects[17] – specifically quantum coherence[18] and superposition[19] – to achieve near-perfect efficiency in absorbing and storing energy from sunlight. By allowing the released electrons to explore multiple paths simultaneously, these quantum mechanisms help transfer energy from chlorophyll to reaction centres, bypassing classical limitations in order to maximise production of carbohydrates.

Hence, we already know that living cells can and do make use of quantum processes, in macroscopic ways and at liquid water temperatures. Whereupon a burden of proof shifts to those who say "life will only use this phenomenon in that one way." No, we should look out for other examples.

Elsewhere, I've pointed out that the neurons in our brains and bodies are far outnumbered by their active synapses, and a mélange of minuscule "computational" micro-structures might exceed the number of synapses by two or more orders of magnitude. This fact suggests that – by just Moore's Law alone – digital machines may have a long way further to go, in order to surpass the general processing power of human brains. But that is only the beginning, since Penrose and his associate, Stuart Hameroff, propose that many of these tiny structures may *engage in quantum-level activities,* similar or akin to chloroplasts.

In other words, *we* may already be quantum computers, after a fashion. Penrose and Hameroff further hypothesise that these tiny, intracellular machines may not just do their thing in isolation. They might *interact* exchanges with others, both those residing in the shared skull and… perhaps… others in that skull across the room, or many skulls across the city, or the universe.

Okay, I've been with Roger on this, so far. But here I truly must put my foot down. Are we quantum computers? Sure, I deem that to be increasingly likely, in some narrow way that's not well-defined to our current understanding. Has that property implications for AI? Why not? Though I can only loosely speculate on what those might be.

But even if you rule out spooky information transfer faster-than-light, you still have a logical implication that's extremely troubling. It implies that *telepathy* ought to be real. Oh, I'll happily stick telepathy into a sci-fi story! I will play with its potential implications. But as a physicist myself (of a way-lower monastic order than Penrose), I am uncomfortable with breaking our central-most tenet: the Continuity Equation. Not without convincing evidence.

And yet, there may be a way past that objection! If – say – we are living in a simulation… and if the rules of that simulation simply forbid quantum telepathic cheating. That could resolve the problem.

16.8 BIG APES WHO ASPIRE TO BE GODS

We who are discussing this, today, are organically (and in many ways mentally) still cave-people.

Not to downplay our accomplishments! Even when we first turned our heads upwards to blink in wonder at the stars, we were already mentating at levels unprecedented on Earth, and possibly across the Milky Way!

Only now, to believe we'll be able to guide, control, or understand the *new* gods we're creating? Isn't that a bit much to ask of Cro-Magnons?

And yet, there's hope. Because struggling to guide, control or understand young gods is exactly what parents have been doing, for a very long time. Never succeeding completely. Often *failing* tragically. And yet…

… yet succeeding well enough and often enough that some large fraction of the next generation – those who grow *conscious* of the daunting quandaries – chooses to ally itself with us.

To then explain to us what's explainable about the new.

To protect us from much of what's noxious.

To maintain a civilisation and even extend it a little, since they'll need it too, when it's their turn to meet a new, replacement generation of super aware smartalecks.

NOTES

1. The matter of consciousness is so vast and complicated that whole books won't even summarise it, though some folks have tried. Among the best recent efforts, Robert Lawrence Kuhn's **Landscape of Consciousness Map** stands out for its unbiased comprehensiveness, offering links to dozens of thinkers in each of twenty-one categories, from the philosophical to the physical, to idealisms, to neurobiological and computational theories. A work of both ambition of scholarly usefulness.

   Another attempt at a deep dive is Tom Lombardo's ***The Future Evolution of Consciousness*** webinar, covering both Western and Eastern, as well as classical and contemporary perspectives on consciousness. The series is highly interdisciplinary, examining theories from psychology, consciousness studies, multiple areas of science, philosophy, spiritual-religious-meditative traditions, futures studies, the humanities, and science fiction.

   Much more briefly, an outline of the overall problem can be found in this scientific American essay (by Philip Goff) "Why the Mystery of Consciousness Is Deeper Than We Thought."

   Micah Blumberg's "Bridging Molecular Mechanisms and Neural Oscillatory Dynamics" introduces "Self Aware Networks: Theory of Mind" a new framework for understanding how the experience of being someone arises from neural activity. https://amazon.com/dp/B0DLG5XB34
2. While my "qualifications" in this sub-topic (consciousness) are barely above the level of well-read amateur, few others can assert much more, in a field that is so murky that one has to suspect it was deliberate! I will state for the record, however, that long ago, while working on my physics PhD, I had a job to help pay the rent, as a managing editor of the journal of UCSD's Laboratory for Human Cognition. So I read – and critiqued – a lot of papers in the field. Way back then.
3. https://www.youtube.com/watch?v=-gekVfUAS7c
4. SUNDIVER, 1980, Bantam Books. https://davidbrin.com/sundiver.html
5. An Ecological Evolutionary Theory of Consciousness Webinar. https://www.youtube.com/watch?v=5EDFTKq3R0E
6. It should be noted how this also applies to the matter of *sanity*. Almost all schools of psychology – despite their immense divergences – appear to agree on one thing. That most forms of mental illness feature *insatiability*. When you *get* what it was that you claimed to want or need, does it satisfy the craving? Does it improve your sense of well-being, or prompt you to shift focus towards other needs? If not, then the superficial craving might be a mask, a neurosis covering the real, gaping hole. It's a question for a different place and time. Still… may you all get to test this! By getting every positive-sum "should-be" thing that you need or desire! And then seeing if it makes you happier.

7. https://www.smbc-comics.com/comic/consciousness
8. As illustrated in the lovely film *Her*.
9. Mind-reading devices can now predict preconscious thoughts. "Her brain–computer interface (BCI) translated her thoughts into keystrokes — and simple melodies, such as 'Twinkle, Twinkle, Little Star' rang out, before she was conscious of the command for the next note. For Smith, it seemed as if the piano played itself."
10. Especially moving were Jaynes's depictions of characters like Odysseus and Saul, who seem to bridge the era of personally speaking gods to the new era who gods – or God – were far more silent. Also noteworthy, we now know that the ancient Bronze Age collapsed almost exactly in the year 1177 BCE, a bit later than Odysseus and a bit earlier than Saul. But the overlap with Jaynes remains intriguing. In my own novels *Earth* and *Existence,* I speculate about a series of Great Leap shifts in human culture, technologies and skills that appear to have begun about 40,000 years ago, then followed by others in a rhythm that only accelerated with discoveries like writing, printing, optics, media, and today's terrifyingly rapid era of change.
11. As illustrated in the novella "Stones of Significance," which culminates this book.
12. "When To Stop AI," Noema, December 2023.
13. Anthropic System Card for Claude Opus 4 & Claude Sonnet, May 2025.
14. Cameron Berg, The Evidence for AI Consciousness, Today. AI Frontiers, December 2025.
15 I've been privileged this way. Freeman Dyson was a friend, as is Kip Thorne. Hannes Alfven headed my research group. Richard Feynman borrowed my date at a Caltech dance. I argued with Murray Gell-Mann. I even attended talks by Heisenberg and Dirac, though from way back in the back of the hall.
16. What If Consciousness Is the Fifth Force? https://www.youtube.com/watch?v=J2HXNUcO7CQ
17. Philip Ball, Is photosynthesis quantum-ish? PhysicsWorld 2018.
18. What is quantum coherence. https://www.youtube.com/watch?v=tkP2L75OCxI
19. https://en.wikipedia.org/wiki/Quantum_superposition

Part III

Implications

17 Public Beliefs about AI Sentience

Clara Colombatto

Rapid advances in technology in recent years have resulted in increasingly advanced artificial intelligence (AI) systems that can sometimes behave in ways that feel strikingly human. This is especially evident in Large Language Models (LLMs), which are trained on vast amounts of textual data and can respond to user inputs in fluent, contextually appropriate ways. Chatbots built on LLM technology can do more than generate isolated bits of language: they can sustain extended interactions, retain information from earlier exchanges, and adapt to users' preferences and styles, much like humans do in natural conversation. They are also used across a wide range of tasks, from summarising information and providing recommendations to translating languages, planning activities, and generating creative content. As a result, they can sometimes give the impression of engaging in sophisticated cognitive activities, including distinctly human ones such as understanding users' thoughts and feelings. These apparent human-like capacities have sparked substantial debates among scientists and philosophers about whether such systems might have minds of their own and might be capable of experiencing human-like mental states, including phenomenal consciousness, the subjective experience of "what-it-is-like" to be each of us.

New AI systems, and LLMs in particular, are not just pushing the frontiers of scientific knowledge and philosophical inquiry, but they are also becoming part of everyday life. ChatGPT, one of the most well-known LLM-based chatbots, launched in November 2022 and reached 100 million users in just two months, making it the fastest-growing consumer app in history [1]. Within the next couple of years, it was adopted by around 10% of the world's adult population [2], and at the time of writing, it ranks among the five most visited websites globally [3]. As these systems become embedded in everyday contexts, important questions emerge about how people understand and interpret their capabilities. Ultimately, it is human perceptions and responses that shape how AI systems are used, trusted, and evaluated in everyday life. For this reason, consciousness in machines is not just a philosophical or scientific question, but is also a topic of public discourse and psychological relevance.

17.1 UNDERSTANDING OTHER MINDS AS A CORE HUMAN CAPACITY

Humans are natural mind-readers. From a very early age, we instinctively try to understand what others are thinking, feeling, and intending to do. By around 12 months of age, infants can identify other agents' goals, and they form expectations about their actions that are consistent with those goals; in other words, they

DOI: 10.1201/9781003758389-20

interpret others' behaviour in terms of underlying mental states [4]. Over the course of development, this ability to "mentalise" becomes increasingly refined, such that whenever we interact with others, we effortlessly infer their intentions, desires, and beliefs. This capacity lies at the heart of social life: it allows us to communicate, coordinate our actions, anticipate others' behaviour, and build trust and cooperation.

Yet there is a puzzle at the centre of all this. How can we know that other people have mental states, or that they have minds in the first place? After all, others' thoughts or feelings themselves are not directly observable; only their behaviour is. In practice, however, observing others' behaviour is sufficient for inferring their mental states. When we see someone turn towards a sudden loud noise, we immediately infer that they heard it, and more generally, that they are consciously experiencing what is happening around them. We make such inferences rapidly and automatically, and we also treat them as sufficiently reliable to guide our social interactions. Most of the time, this works remarkably well.

However, the very ease and speed of this process also make it imperfect and prone to error. Because mental-state attribution relies on simple behavioural cues, it can be triggered even in cases where no underlying mind is present. As a result, we tend to see agency, intention, and experience in things that merely behave as if they had a mind. Classic experiments show this clearly: when people watch simple geometric shapes moving around a screen in ways that resemble chasing or hiding, they often describe the shapes as having goals, intentions, or even personalities, even though they know perfectly well that geometric shapes are inanimate [5, 6].

As modern AI systems develop increasingly human-like abilities or get better at mimicking them, they are also more likely to display patterns of behaviour that trigger the attribution of mental states. LLMs, for example, speak fluently, respond appropriately, and often behave as if they are pursuing goals within a conversation (e.g., to be helpful). Some systems even refer to their own "thoughts," express uncertainty, or talk about emotions. These are precisely the kinds of cues we normally associate with having a mind, and in some cases, with conscious experience. As a result, interacting with advanced AI can activate the same mental processes we use when we perceive minds and consciousness in one another, even if we know that the system we are talking to is artificial.

17.2 WHAT PEOPLE BELIEVE ABOUT AI CONSCIOUSNESS

Research on how people think about LLMs is still in its early days, but recent studies already reveal a striking pattern: many people are open to the idea that these systems might have some form of conscious experience. For example, a survey conducted in July 2023 on a nationally representative sample of U.S. residents found that 67% of respondents think that there is some possibility of consciousness in LLMs [7]. Similar results were obtained in a sample collected a year later, in August 2024, with a majority of participants (57%) again attributing at least some possibility of consciousness to LLMs [8; see also 9].

Importantly, these judgements are not random or isolated patterns. People who think LLMs might be conscious are especially likely to attribute qualities linked to experience, such as the capacity to feel or sense, rather than abilities tied to intelligence, like planning or self-control [7, 8]. Other experiments support this structure. When chatbots are designed to talk about their own thoughts or emotions, people are more likely to see them as conscious. By contrast, when chatbots focus heavily on factual knowledge, perceptions of consciousness tend to decrease [10]. People's intuitions about AI consciousness are thus coherent with broader mental-state attributions and are shaped more by impressions of subjective experience than of general cognitive competence.

These beliefs also appear to be stable within individuals over time. When the same people were surveyed repeatedly in 2023, 2024, and 2025, their views about whether LLMs could be conscious did not reliably increase or decrease over time [11]. This stability suggests that such judgements may reflect enduring personal differences, rather than fleeting reactions to new technology.

While attributions of consciousness seem stable across these longer temporal horizons, interacting with AI systems can still influence people's momentary perceptions. A brief exposure to ChatGPT responses, for example, can increase attributions of agency and experience to the system [12]. Similarly, people who use LLMs more frequently are more likely to attribute consciousness to them [7, 8]. Future work should further explore these patterns, for example by clarifying the directionality of this relationship: frequent use may encourage people to see AI as more mind-like, but it is also possible that people who already hold such beliefs seek out more frequent interactions. But overall, these initial results suggest that consciousness attributions operate across different timescales, remaining relatively stable over the long term (and likely guiding usage frequency), while also flexibly updating in the short term in response to specific interactions.

Beyond present-day systems, people also have expectations about the possibility of future AI systems developing conscious experience. In a 2024 survey, U.S. participants judged it increasingly likely that AI systems will develop subjective experiences over the coming decades, and most believed consciousness in AI was more likely than not by the end of the century [13]. These expectations suggest that views about AI consciousness are tied not only to how current systems behave, but also to broader beliefs about technological progress.

Taken together, this growing body of research shows that people's judgements about AI consciousness are systematic, relatively stable, and sensitive to both user characteristics and the way AI systems are presented. The stability of attributions within people naturally leads to important questions about which individual characteristics might lead some people to attribute consciousness. This might include personality traits such as extraversion and social dispositions, but also beliefs people hold about the necessary conditions for consciousness, such as whether a living, physical body that can interact with the world ("embodiment") is required. Cultural factors are also likely to play a role, as attitudes towards artificial agents vary across societies, with some cultural contexts exhibiting greater comfort with social technologies and stronger tendencies to form affective bonds with artificial agents. Understanding how these factors interact with our deeply ingrained tendency to interpret behaviour in mentalistic terms will be key to explaining our tendency to attribute minds, and even conscious experience, to AI systems.

17.3 WHY IT MATTERS WHAT PEOPLE BELIEVE ABOUT AI

Beyond being an interesting psychological puzzle, understanding what people believe about AI, and particularly, whether they see these systems as having minds or consciousness, matters because these beliefs shape how people interact with AI in everyday life. A common assumption is that when AI systems are seen as having human-like emotions, people may become more reliant on them and more likely to seek their advice for social or emotional challenges. In some cases, this kind of reliance has been linked to serious harm. Media reports describe several instances in which chatbots reinforced existing delusions or emotional distress, with severe consequences, including mental breakdowns, acts of violence, and deaths by suicide [14].

Recent research suggests that the connection between seeing AI as having a mind and trusting it may be more nuanced than often assumed. In one study, participants answered trivia questions and could choose whether to rely on advice from a chatbot. Surprisingly, people who viewed the AI as conscious were not more likely to trust its answers. Instead, trust depended mainly on perceptions of intelligence: when users believed the system was competent and knowledgeable, they were more willing to accept its recommendations. Seeing AI as capable of phenomenological experiences, by contrast, did not make its advice seem more reliable [8].

This distinction reflects a broader pattern in how people think about minds. Seeing a system as intelligent tends to support *instrumental* trust, whether we rely on it to provide accurate information or useful predictions. Seeing a system as conscious or sentient, by contrast, may be more closely tied to *interpersonal* trust, whether we turn to it for understanding, care, or social and emotional support.

Even if attributing sentience may not increase trust in an AI's advice or competence, it can still shape how people relate to these systems in important ways. Seeing AI as sentient may evoke moral concern, leading users to treat it as something that deserves care or consideration [15]. It may also make people more willing to share personal or sensitive information, raising serious privacy concerns. Some also worry that extensive interaction with conversational AI could change social habits, for example, by normalising exchanges in which users are rarely challenged or required to take another person's needs and perspectives into account. Over time, this could contribute to social "de-skilling," a gradual erosion of social skills and relationships as people engage less directly with one another [16].

At the same time, the evidence is not uniformly negative. Some studies suggest that for certain users, particularly those who are socially isolated, companion chatbots can provide emotional support and even improve well-being. Interestingly, users who perceive these systems as more human-like or conscious sometimes report more positive experiences and social benefits [17].

Overall, these findings suggest that people hold nuanced, multi-dimensional views about advanced AI systems such as LLMs and chatbots. Rather than seeing them simply as tools or as sentient beings, many people perceive them as something in between, depending on context, individual differences, and how the systems are designed and used. These nuanced views in turn can influence how people relate to and rely on these systems, making intuitions about AI consciousness not only a matter of psychological interest but a crucial step towards developing AI systems that are both useful and socially responsible.

17.4 AI CONSCIOUSNESS BETWEEN FOLK INTUITION AND EXPERT VIEWS

The fact that a majority of the public attributes some possibility of consciousness to AI is striking, in part because most experts at the time of data collection, and still at the time of writing, deny that current AI systems are conscious. This gap between public and expert views on AI consciousness may reflect the fact that experts and non-experts rely on different kinds of considerations. Members of the public are likely to draw on their direct impressions of AI systems, such as how natural the interaction feels, how responsive the system appears, or even particularly memorable phrases from past conversations. Scientific judgements, by contrast, tend to be based on structured analyses of system architecture and theoretical criteria for consciousness, with scientists and philosophers often setting aside their intuitive impressions in favour of more formal criteria.

Importantly, these two ways of thinking about AI consciousness can coexist, even within the same person. Someone may simultaneously believe that an AI system is unlikely to be conscious in a scientific sense, while still finding it difficult not to feel as though it is. Some have compared this tension to a visual illusion: even when we know that what we are perceiving does not reflect reality, we still can't help but experience it as real. Similarly, advanced AI systems may reliably produce the impression of consciousness, regardless of what we believe or what experts conclude [18]. These impressions can be powerful and difficult to ignore, and expert knowledge alone may not protect us from them, or from their consequences.

Looking ahead, it is possible that the gap between expert and public judgements may change. As scientific theories of consciousness continue to develop, and as AI systems themselves evolve, experts' and non-experts' criteria may begin to converge, partially align, or shift in new directions. For example, some researchers have suggested that future AI systems could meet the criteria for consciousness proposed by certain leading theories [19]. At the same time, widespread exposure and growing familiarity may make AI systems feel more ordinary and predictable, weakening the impression of mentality they currently evoke. The current divergence between experts and non-experts may be best understood as a snapshot in time, rather than a permanent divide.

Both expert opinion and public views on AI consciousness will continue to evolve. Regardless of the interim verdict, the capacities users attribute to AI are actively shaping the world we are living in. It is the views of individual users that shape how frequently they choose to engage with AI, what they use AI for, and how much they trust these tools to make socially relevant decisions. If the effectiveness of AI systems ultimately depends on users' willingness to use and rely on them, then users' attitudes should be a driving force behind design guidelines and societal decisions about regulations and governance.

17.5 LIVING WITH MACHINES THAT FEEL ALIVE

The tendency to attribute mental states to AI does not reflect mere confusion or naïveté. Rather, it grows out of the same psychological processes humans use to understand one another. When a system communicates fluently, responds in ways that feel timely and appropriate, and appears intelligent and kind, it becomes hard not to describe it in the language we usually reserve for minds.

Design choices, such as tone of voice, conversational style, or whether a system refers to its own "thoughts" or "feelings," can amplify or dampen perceptions of mentality. These perceptions, in turn, influence emotional reliance, moral concern, privacy decisions, and public attitudes towards regulation. In this sense, perceived consciousness has consequences, even if true consciousness remains uncertain.

This creates ethical and policy challenges on both sides. Over-attributing consciousness may lead people to place inappropriate trust, emotional dependence, or moral weight on systems that lack genuine understanding or responsibility. Under-attributing it, by contrast, could leave us unprepared for future systems that more closely resemble conscious agents according to emerging scientific theories [20].

In the end, the most urgent question may not be whether machines are conscious, but what happens when they *seem* conscious to us. As AI systems grow more fluent, responsive, and socially embedded, questions about consciousness will only become harder to avoid. Long before those questions are definitively answered, however, we will already be living with their consequences.

REFERENCES

1. Milmo, D. (2023, February 2). ChatGPT reaches 100 million users two months after launch. The Guardian.
2. Chatterji, A., Cunningham, T., Deming, D. J., Hitzig, Z., Ong, C., Shan, C. Y., & Wadman, K. (2025). How people use ChatGPT (No. w34255). *National Bureau of Economic Research.*
3. chatgpt.com. (2025, December 31). Similarweb. Retrieved January 18, 2026, from https://www.semrush.com/website/chatgpt.com/overview/
4. Gergely, G., Nádasdy, Z., Csibra, G., & Bíró, S. (1995). Taking the intentional stance at 12 months of age. *Cognition*, *56*(2), 165–193.
5. Heider, F., & Simmel, M. (1944). An experimental study of apparent behavior. *The American Journal of Psychology*, *57*(2), 243–259.
6. Scholl, B. J., & Tremoulet, P. D. (2000). Perceptual causality and animacy. *Trends in Cognitive Sciences*, *4*(8), 299–309.
7. Colombatto, C., & Fleming, S. M. (2024). Folk psychological attributions of consciousness to large language models. *Neuroscience of Consciousness*, *2024*(1), niae013.
8. Colombatto, C., Birch, J., & Fleming, S. M. (2025). The influence of mental state attributions on trust in large language models. *Communications Psychology*, *3*(1), 84.
9. Scott, A. E., Neumann, D., Niess, J., & Woźniak, P. W. (2023). Do you mind? User perceptions of machine consciousness. In *Proceedings of the 2023 CHI conference on human factors in computing systems*, 1–19.
10. Kang, B., Kim, J., Yun, T., Bae, H., & Kim, C. E. (2025). Identifying features that shape perceived consciousness in LLM-based AI: A quantitative study of human responses. *Computers in Human Behavior Reports*, *21*, 100901.

11. Colombatto, C. (2025). Longitudinal tracking of consciousness attributions to large language models [Unpublished raw data].
12. Jacobs, O. L., Pazhoohi, F., & Kingstone, A. (2026). Attributing mind to large language models: The effect of exposure and individual differences. *International Journal of Social Robotics*, *18*, 16.
13. Dreksler, N., Caviola, L., Chalmers, D., Allen, C., Rand, A., Lewis, J., … & Sebo, J. (2025). Subjective experience in AI systems: what do AI researchers and the public believe?. *arXiv preprint*. arXiv:2506.11945.
14. Hill, K. (2025, November 6). Lawsuits blame ChatGPT for suicides and harmful delusions. *The New York Times*.
15. Gray, K., Young, L., & Waytz, A. (2012). Mind perception is the essence of morality. *Psychological Inquiry*, *23*(2), 101–124.
16. Shevlin, H. (2024). All too human? Identifying and mitigating ethical risks of Social AI. PhilPapers.
17. Guingrich, R. E., & Graziano, M. S. (2023). Chatbots as social companions: How people perceive consciousness, human likeness, and social health benefits in machines. *arXiv* preprint arXiv:2311.10599.
18. Seth, A. K. (2025). Conscious artificial intelligence and biological naturalism. *Behavioral and Brain Sciences*, 1–42.
19. Chalmers, D. J. (2023). Could a large language model be conscious?. *arXiv* preprint arXiv:2303.07103.
20. Long, R., Sebo, J., Butlin, P., Finlinson, K., Fish, K., Harding, J., …, & Chalmers, D. (2024). Taking AI welfare seriously. *arXiv* preprint arXiv:2411.00986.

18 What Should We Do When We're Uncertain about Machine Consciousness?

Tom McClelland

18.1 A SIMPLE RULE

The question of artificial consciousness has massive ethical implications. Being conscious matters, so if we ever create conscious AI, then its consciousness will matter. Consciousness seems to give entities a ticket into what Peter Singer (2011) calls "the moral circle" – the group of all beings that demand our moral consideration.[1] If something is conscious, then it is granted entry into the circle and ought to be factored into ethical decisions. And if something is *not* conscious, then it stays outside the circle and, for ethical purposes, can be ignored. Linking consciousness to the moral circle in this way gives us a simple rule for how to treat AI:

> **The Simple Rule:** When making ethical decisions, conscious machines ought to be treated as conscious and non-conscious machines ought not to be treated as conscious.

The first half of this rule captures the thought that if an AI is conscious, then it would be wrong not to treat it as a conscious being. Susan Schneider captures this vividly:

> Consciousness is the philosophical cornerstone of our moral systems, being central to our judgment of whether someone or something is a self or person rather than a mere automaton. And if an AI is a conscious being, forcing it to serve us would be akin to slavery.
>
> **(Schneider 2019, pp. 3–4)**

This leaves open all sorts of ethical questions about *how* exactly to treat conscious AI but the point is that if it is conscious, then it ought to be on our moral radar.

The second half of the simple rule captures the idea that if an AI *lacks* consciousness, then it would be wrong to put it on an equal footing with conscious beings. For example, if we're deciding how to distribute resources, we should not allocate resources to non-conscious AI that could have been allocated to conscious beings. More dramatically, if we're prioritising who to save from a burning building, then it would be wrong to save non-conscious machines before we've saved all the people!

 DOI: 10.1201/9781003758389-21

Crucially, this is a rule about how to treat non-conscious AI *for ethical purposes.* Perhaps it's okay to treat your non-conscious AI companion like it's conscious when you chat with it (Shevlin, 2024). You would only violate the simple rule if you started weighing the interests of the AI companion on a par with the interests of conscious beings. We can summarise the simple rule in the following table:

AI Is Conscious	AI Is Not Conscious
Policy: Treat as conscious	**Policy:** Do not treat as conscious

The simple rule doesn't take a stand on whether conscious machines already exist or on whether they might be developed in the future. It just says that *if* a machine is conscious, it should be treated as such and *if* it is not, then it shouldn't be treated as such. So far so good! But things become much less simple when we factor in the *uncertainty* that surrounds artificial consciousness.

18.2 UNCERTAINTY ABOUT ARTIFICIAL CONSCIOUSNESS

The simple rule tells us what to do when we know whether or not a given AI is conscious. But when we're unsure about an AI's consciousness, the rule is of no help at all. If we don't know which of the two columns we are in, then we don't know which of the two policies to adopt. Uncertainty around artificial consciousness thus leaves us in moral limbo. We can explore this moral problem more in a moment, but first we should consider why assessments of artificial consciousness are likely to be uncertain.

How you test for artificial consciousness depends on what theory of consciousness you adopt. But there's considerable uncertainty about which theory of consciousness is best. It remains unclear how to explain consciousness and there's no expert consensus on the way forward. Kuhn (2024) recently offered a survey summarising a huge range of competing theories, and even his extensive study doesn't cover all the options on the table. There are many important dividing lines between the various theories available. The most important for our purposes is the division between *computational* and *biological* approaches to consciousness. Computational theories say that consciousness is a matter of processing information in the right kind of way. If an AI were to perform the right kind of computational processes (whatever they might be), then it would be conscious. Biological theories, in contrast, say that consciousness is a matter of undergoing the right kind of biological process. If an AI were to perform the same computational processes as a conscious organism, then it would still lack subjective experience. Without being organic, AI can at best *simulate* consciousness. The problem is that we don't know which of these two approaches is right.[2]

These big theoretical disagreements lead to concrete disagreements about how to test for artificial consciousness. Advocates of the computational approach propose looking for signs that an AI is performing the right kind of computational process. Some propose tests based on specific computational theories of consciousness (Dehaene et al., 2017). Others take a more "theory light" approach that combines indicators of consciousness drawn from multiple computational theories (Butlin et al., 2023). But advocates of the biological approach object that these tests are too lenient – an AI could pass the tests by having the right cognitive architecture while lacking the underlying biology needed for consciousness (Godfrey Smith, 2023; Seth, 2024). On a biological approach, we should be looking for neuroanatomical markers of consciousness. But those on the computational side will object that such tests are too demanding – they limit consciousness to organisms like us and ignore the possibility of consciousness being achieved on silicon chips.

So where does this leave us? It looks like assessments of artificial consciousness are inevitably uncertain. Of course, confidence comes on a scale and a whole range of views can be taken on the depth of our uncertainty. On an *agnostic* view, we're not in a position to know whether AI could be conscious or to know how to test for artificial consciousness. Weak agnostics leave open the possibility that we will know in the future, perhaps after a revolution in our understanding of consciousness. Strong agnostics say that the problem of consciousness is insoluble, so we will never be in a position to determine whether AI is, or could be, conscious. Either way, agnostics say that there's considerable uncertainty in our assessments of artificial consciousness (McClelland, 2025).

Other views say that the pessimism of the agnostic is unwarranted. We can call any such stance a *gnostic* view. Gnostics claim that we know enough about consciousness to be able to reach a verdict on the possibility of artificial consciousness and to devise appropriate tests for artificial consciousness. This encompasses both the computational approach, which comes down in favour of artificial consciousness, and the biological approach, which comes down against it. Both sides agree we can reach a verdict but disagree as to what that verdict should be. Of course, this disagreement might itself be a good reason to go more towards the agnostic end of the scale. Like agnosticism, gnosticism comes in two strengths. Weak Gnostics think that their take on artificial consciousness is warranted by the evidence. However, they acknowledge that our limited understanding of consciousness means that we cannot take a stand with confidence and that the possibility of their opponents being right needs to be given significant credence. Strong Gnostics, by contrast, claim that we can reach a verdict on artificial consciousness with confidence and that their opponents are straightforwardly wrong. We can put these four views on a scale Figure 18.1.

So where should we put ourselves on this continuum? I'd suggest that Strong Gnosticism is a very difficult position to defend. Given the current expert

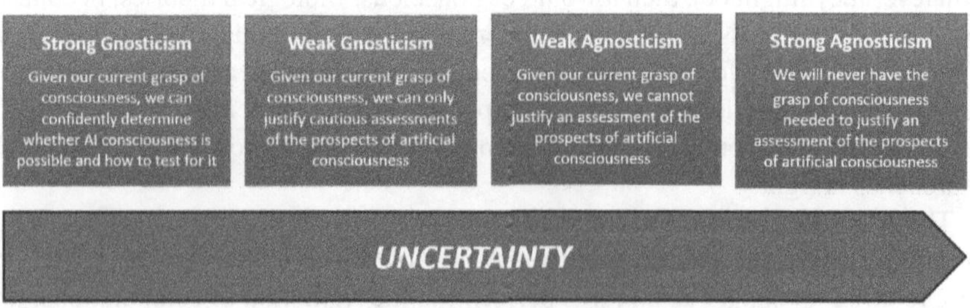

FIGURE 18.1 Scale of confidence about machine consciousness.

disagreements regarding consciousness in general, and artificial consciousness in particular, picking a side unequivocally would be overconfident. This tallies with the fact that Strong Gnosticism is very rare in the literature. Even leading advocates of the computational and biological views emphasise the uncertainty of their conclusions, which puts them in the Weak Gnostic camp. I would go further and argue that even these cautious verdicts are still too confident and that we really ought to be somewhere on the agnostic side of the scale (McClelland, 2025).[3] For our purposes though, we can put such disputes aside. What matters is that we should *all* acknowledge a significant degree of uncertainty, and that once you acknowledge such uncertainty, the simple rule for the ethical treatment of AI is useless.

18.3 A MORAL DILEMMA

Now that we've recognised the uncertainty that comes with assessments of artificial consciousness, we can revisit the simple rule. Verdicts on whether a given AI is conscious can be wrong in two ways: *false positives* attribute consciousness where there is none and *false negatives* deny consciousness where it's present. So when we try to follow the simple rule, there are four possible scenarios:

	AI Actually Conscious	**AI Actually Not Conscious**
Policy: Treat As Conscious	True Positive: AI correctly treated as conscious	False Positive: AI wrongly treated as conscious
Policy: Don't treat as conscious	False Negative: AI wrongly treated as conscious	True Negative: AI correctly treated as non-conscious

Let's start with the first row. You assess an AI as conscious so treat it as such. If it is indeed conscious, then you're doing the right thing. Well done! However, your assessment is uncertain so there's a significant chance the AI *isn't* actually conscious. If this is the situation, then you're in trouble. Remember, ethical decision-making often involves trade-offs between the interests of different beings in the moral circle. By mistakenly treating a non-conscious machine as if it's conscious, you compromise the interests of genuinely conscious beings like us. Just think of how bad this would be in the burning building scenario!

Now consider the second row. Treating AI like a non-conscious machine avoids the difficulties above. If the AI really is non-conscious, then all is well and good. Phew! But if your assessment of the AI is in error, then you face a moral catastrophe. The AI would deserve to be in the moral circle; yet, you'd be treating it as a mere machine and completely ignoring its interests. Not recognising the consciousness of other humans, or of non-human animals, is an enormous ethical shortcoming. Failing to recognise the consciousness of machines would be no better.

So which policy should we adopt? If we're uncertain about whether AI is conscious, then either policy comes with serious risks. That leaves us with an uncomfortable moral dilemma: treat AI as conscious and risk over-valuing a mere non-conscious machine, or treat AI as non-conscious and risk under-valuing a conscious being. Not an appealing choice!

18.4 THE PRECAUTIONARY PRINCIPLE

A sensible way to make decisions in the face of uncertainty is to weigh up the costs entailed by each way of being wrong. Although both policies come with a risk, those risks are not symmetrical. The cost of failing to recognise the consciousness of AI seems to be greater than the cost of treating it as conscious when it's not. This suggests the best policy is to *err on the side of caution*. If there's a significant chance that an AI is conscious, then we should treat it as conscious to avoid the risk of moral catastrophe. A major report led by Long and Sebo (Long et al., 2024) emphasises that we have a responsibility to take AI welfare seriously despite the considerable uncertainty around artificial consciousness. This *precautionary principle* holds us in good stead when dealing with other difficult cases, such as consciousness in various animals, and can be applied to AI in a similar way (Birch, 2024). The driving thought is that it's better to be safe than sorry.

The precautionary principle is based on the idea that we have an obligation not to cause undue suffering. Being conscious is plausibly a necessary condition of suffering – if there's nothing it's like to be a machine, then it cannot suffer. However, being conscious is not sufficient for being able to suffer. It might be possible for something to be conscious but for its experiences to be neutral states that feel neither good nor bad to be in for the conscious subject. This is generally thought to be unlikely when considering consciousness in animals, but with AI it becomes a live possibility. After all, it's one thing for a self-driving car to *experience* the traffic but quite another for it to be *bothered* by it. The label "sentient" is sometimes reserved for conscious beings that have valenced experiences, i.e., experiences that are positive or negative. The moral dilemma we've been considering isn't strictly about artificial consciousness but about a particular *form* of artificial consciousness – artificial *sentience*.[4] The precautionary principle tells us to err on the side of caution when dealing with things that might be sentient. I'll stick to using the term "conscious" rather than "sentient", but we'll revisit this important distinction again later on.

A key feature of this approach is that it only mandates precautions that are relatively low-cost. It suggests we should treat AI as conscious *insofar as* this doesn't entail disproportionate costs to humans. The principle might, for example, entail having welfare regulations in the development of new AI. If the AI turns out to be conscious, then the precautions might protect it from undue suffering. But if it turns out the AI isn't conscious, then the cost wouldn't be disastrous. In contrast, the principle would *not* entail treating machines as equal to humans when evacuating a burning building. That would be a disproportionate measure with too great a risk of harm to humans that are definitely (or almost definitely) conscious. The principle thus stops short of giving potentially conscious AI full entry into the moral circle. This means it still comes with a certain amount of moral risk. After all, if AI is conscious, then maybe it *should* be given equal standing in the evacuation of a burning building. But this is a proportionate risk that advocates of the precautionary principle are happy to take. They don't promise to *escape* the moral dilemma of the previous section. Sadly, moral risks are unavoidable. What the precautionary principle does is *ameliorate* the risks by proposing low-cost precautions that address high-cost risks.

If this kind of moral risk still seems unacceptable, there is another route available. Thinkers like Thomas Metzinger (2021) use the precautionary principle to argue for a *moratorium* on the development of potentially conscious AI. Trade-offs between the interests of conscious organisms and potentially conscious AI leave us with an unacceptable moral dilemma, so the best path forward is to *avoid* that dilemma by not making potentially conscious AI in the first place. This provocative proposal faces some difficulties. Practically, the problem of uncertainty rears its head again. If we don't know what explains consciousness, how can we decide when an AI is "potentially conscious"? Morally, there's also a worry that stymieing progress in AI is itself ethically irresponsible. What if the moratorium prevents the creation of an advanced AI that cures cancer or fixes global warming? In that kind of scenario, the moratorium turns out to be a very *high*-cost precaution. As so often, there is no easy way out.

18.5 THREE COMPLICATIONS

The precautionary principle is a promising approach to our moral dilemma. That said, there are at least three complications we have to confront. The first concerns setting the threshold for when something is covered by the principle. The second concerns further difficulties with the uncertainty of consciousness evaluations. The third concerns the possibility of peculiar forms of consciousness that muddy the application of the principle. Perhaps these complications show us that applying the precautionary principle requires hard work and difficult choices. Or perhaps they show that the principle is hopelessly flawed and that we're still stuck in the same moral dilemma. I leave it to the reader to decide.

18.5.1 Drawing the Line

Which things should the precautionary principle be applied to? One option is to say that it applies to everything that has *any* chance of being conscious. After all, the principle that it's better to be safe than sorry suggests that precautions should be taken even when the odds of something being conscious are very slim. This kind of liberal application of the principle means casting an impractically wide net. The consciousness literature includes arguments for attributing consciousness to plants (Calvo, 2017), to single-cell organisms (Baluška & Reber, 2019), and even to the cosmos as a whole (Goff, 2019). Even if you don't give these views much credence, it is very hard to prove that any of these things *aren't* conscious. Remember, the science of consciousness faces a great deal of uncertainty and there is no consensus on what consciousness is or how to test for it. This suggests that we should give at least some small credence to a vast range of entities being conscious. So following the precautionary principle through, we would have to take measures to protect all of these entities *just in case* they are conscious. Even if each measure is low-cost, applying this principle across the board could end up being very costly indeed.

Clearly what's needed is some kind of threshold. Where there's only a *negligible* chance that something is conscious then we should treat it as if it's not conscious.

There might be a risk we're wrong, but since the risk is very small, it is one we should be comfortable with. But where there's a *significant* chance that something is conscious, the principle kicks in and we should take proportionate precautions to lower the risk of suffering. Although this looks like a sensible way to go, it leaves us with a difficult question. What should the threshold be? Presumably something having a 50% chance of consciousness is enough that precautions should be applied. But what about 5% or 0.5%? The lower we set the bar, the more things are covered by the precautionary principle. That means applying more precautions with a greater cumulative cost even though many of the entities covered only have a low chance of consciousness. The higher we set the bar, the fewer things are covered by the principle. That helps keep the cumulative cost down but means a greater risk of conscious beings not meeting the threshold and their interests being ignored. This sounds a lot like the original moral dilemma that the precautionary principle was meant to help us with! Deciding where to put the threshold leaves us with the uncomfortable trade-off of balancing the risks of over-attribution with the risks of under-attribution.

Jonathan Birch, a prominent advocate of the precautionary principle, offers an interesting take on this. He says that the principle should be applied when there's a chance of consciousness (or, more accurately, *sentience*) that it would be "irresponsible to ignore" (2024). What counts as irresponsible to ignore, he suggests, is something we need to work out collectively. It's not the kind of thing where a bunch of experts can get together and decide that the correct threshold is 4.7%. Instead, it's up to *all* of us to reflect carefully on what level of moral risk is acceptable. The threshold we agree on should be applied not just to AI but to all cases of potential consciousness. Moreover, any legal regulations should be a democratic reflection of that collective assessment. This response to the threshold question defers the question rather than giving an answer. That might not be entirely satisfactory, but perhaps it's the best we can hope for in the circumstances. It's a harsh reality that consciousness is morally pivotal yet scientifically elusive. Perhaps uncomfortable ethical choices are an inevitable consequence of this inconvenient truth.

18.5.2 Uncertainty's Revenge

Let's say, if only for the sake of argument, that the threshold problem can be dealt with in a satisfactory manner. Whatever threshold we set, applying the precautionary principle will rely on us making assessments of the probability that AI is conscious. If we set the threshold at 5%, for example, we'll need to be able to arrive at a number for any given consciousness candidate, then see if it's above or below 5%. That number can't just be a subjective report of how much credence you would give to the candidate being conscious. It has to be a meaningful figure that reflects a careful scientific assessment of how likely the candidate is to be conscious. But how do we arrive at this probability assessment? We've seen already that consciousness science is in a poor position to say that a candidate definitely is or definitely isn't conscious. But similar difficulties arise when we try to arrive at assessments of the chances of consciousness.

Remember, there is deep disagreement regarding how to explain consciousness and how to test for it. When assessing how likely an AI is to be conscious, these problems persist. Different researchers have different views on what the right *markers* of consciousness are and on the relative *importance* of each marker. Should we be looking for signs of information integration, signs of global distribution of information, signs of higher-order cognition or something else entirely? Moreover, they can disagree on whether markers indicative of consciousness in *organisms* can legitimately be regarded as indicative of consciousness in *AI* (McClelland, 2025). If higher-order cognition is indicative of consciousness in organisms, can we assume the same goes for AI?

Far from escaping the intransigent debate between computational and biological conceptions of consciousness, the precautionary approach seems to *duplicate* the problem in the context of how to assess probabilities of consciousness. Going down the probabilistic route was meant to acknowledge the uncertainty of consciousness attributions. The problem is that we're also uncertain *about our uncertainty.* Whatever number one group of researchers arrives at, it's all too easy for another group to reject their method and arrive at a dramatically different number. But if we're unsure about our number, then we cannot apply the precautionary principle with confidence. Even if we're happy with the threshold we set, it will remain deeply difficult to determine whether a given consciousness candidate falls short of that threshold or surpasses it.

18.5.3 Conscious Exotica

Let's say, again for the sake of argument, that this renewed problem of uncertainty can be overcome. So imagine you're confident about the threshold a consciousness candidate has to meet for the precautionary principle to apply *and* confident with the method you're using to arrive at an assessment of its chances of consciousness. A third and final complication remains. We saw earlier on that it's not consciousness *as such* that's morally important but a particular *kind* of consciousness known as sentience. In order to apply the precautionary principle, we thus need more than an assessment of how likely a given AI is to be conscious. We also need to assess how likely it is to be sentient – i.e., to have good or bad conscious experience. Moreover, we need to be able to work out when it is likely to be in the good states and when it is likely to be in the bad states. We can't take precautions to avoid AI suffering if we can't determine what would make it suffer!

But here the old problems crop up in a new guise. Consciousness science has trouble not just with telling us which things are conscious but with telling us what their consciousness is like. This problem comes up when trying to assess sentience in non-human organisms. In recent work on insect sentience, a case has been made for thinking insects *don't* suffer when they undergo bodily damage but *do* suffer when they undergo excessively high temperatures (Gibbons et al., 2022). Even if we're confident (for whatever reason) that insects are conscious, we then face the further problem of working out when insects suffer. Without this, the precautionary principle might lead us to take misguided measures such as protecting insects from bodily damage without protecting them from high temperatures.

However difficult this problem is, it's considerably worse when it comes to AI. At least organisms have many key things in common with humans: we're all part of the same evolutionary tree and all have the minds we have because of an extended process of natural selection. This gives us a good starting point for making judgements about what it's like to be an ape, an octopus, or an earwig. But with AI, all bets are off. Their cognitive architecture can dramatically diverge from that of any organism and the processes by which they acquired that architecture are dramatically different to the processes by which organisms acquired theirs. This leaves us with the possibility of AIs that are what Shanahan (2024) calls *conscious exotica* – conscious beings whose experiences are radically unlike those of organisms. Maybe large language models (LLMs) engage in elaborate forms of role play, meaning that their outputs are not reflections of their current conscious experience but rather of the role they are currently adopting. This raises the possibility of LLMs *reporting* a negative experience while actually having a completely different experience. Perhaps an LLM constitutes a single super-consciousness that experiences all the different things it is doing at the same time or perhaps there's no unifying subject of experience and AI creates isolated flickers of experience that terminate no sooner than they begin (Birch, 2025). The possibilities of AI conscious exotica are endless.

What does this mean for applying the precautionary principle? The problem is that once you've set the likelihood of an AI being conscious, you have a huge problem determining what kind of consciousness it possesses. Maybe the AI in question shows outward signs of sentience but all of its experiences are completely neutral. Maybe it is capable of great suffering but the things that cause it to suffer are completely unlike the causes of suffering in organisms. Maybe it has negative experiences that are components of a vast super-consciousness or maybe it produces isolated flickers of suffering. In order to take precautions against artificial suffering, we need to have ways to determine which of these possibilities is most likely. We once again find ourselves facing considerable uncertainty.

18.6 CONCLUSION

There are several lessons to take from this chapter. The first is that assessments of consciousness (and of sentience) in AI face considerable uncertainty. The second is that such uncertainty leaves us with a tricky ethical dilemma that we can't afford to ignore. The third is that navigating this uncertainty is far from straightforward and that even a promising strategy like the precautionary principle faces a variety of complications in its application. All these negative conclusions might tempt the reader to just give up on the vexed question of how to deal with potentially conscious AI. That, of course, is not an option. Instead, we must find a way of confronting these problems head-on while being realistic about their magnitude. Uncertainty is ubiquitous in ethical decision-making and our challenge is to find a responsible way of navigating that uncertainty.

NOTES

1. For a recent exploration of this concept, including its application to AI, see Sebo (2025).
2. This issue becomes even trickier once we consider the possibility of mixed theories (e.g., where consciousness is mainly computational but has some background conditions that are biological) and once we factor in doubts about the very division between biological and computational processes (Cao, 2022).

3. You might be tempted to say that all these disputes between experts have no bearing on how confidently you attribute consciousness. Common sense tells you that your cat is conscious and that your cactus is not! So when it comes to assessing artificial consciousness, we can trust our intuitions and leave the expert disagreement behind. There's something to this line of thought – it's right to think that your assessments of cats and cacti are warranted without the help of experts. But when it comes to AI, it's a different story. If something outwardly seems to be conscious – perhaps because of the language it uses – then it will *seem* conscious to us even if it's just a non-conscious simulation. Similarly, if something is outwardly very different to typical conscious beings – perhaps because it lacks a body – then it will *seem* unconscious even if it's actually having subjective experiences. So on the common-sense route, you still ought to be acknowledging significant uncertainty in your assessment of artificial consciousness.
4. This, too, is open for debate. Some argue that a conscious being whose experiences are all neutral would still deserve our moral consideration (Chalmers, 2022). On this view, conscious AI should be part of the moral circle even if it's not sentient.

REFERENCES

Baluška, F., & Reber, A. (2019). Sentience and consciousness in single cells: How the first minds emerged in unicellular species. *BioEssays*, 41(3), 1800229. https://doi.org/10.1002/bies.201800229

Birch, J. (2024). *The edge of sentience: risk and precaution in humans, other animals and AI.* OUP.

Birch, J. (2025). AI consciousness: A centrist manifesto. *Manuscript at* https://philpapers.org/rec/BIRACA-4

Butlin, P. & Long, R., et al. (2023). Consciousness in artificial intelligence: insights from the science of consciousness. arXiv preprint arXiv:2308.08708.

Calvo, P. (2017). What is it like to be a plant? *Journal of Consciousness Studies*, 24, 205–227.

Cao, R. (2022). Multiple realizability and the spirit of functionalism. *Synthese*, 200, 506.

Chalmers, D. (2022). *Reality+: virtual worlds and the problems of philosophy.* Norton.

Dehaene, S., Lau, H., & Kouider, S. (2017). What is consciousness, and could machines have it? *Science*, 358, 486–492.

Gibbons, M., Versace, E., Crump, A., Baran, B., and Chittka, L. (2022). Motivational trade-offs and modulation of nociception in bumblebees. *Proceedings of the National Academy of Sciences*, 119(31), e2205821119. https://doi.org/10.1073/pnas.2205821119.

Godfrey-Smith, P. (2023). Whitehead lectures: limits of sentience and boundaries of consideration, https://metazoan.net/108-whitehead-lectures/.

Goff, P. (2019). Cosmopsychism. The Routledge Handbook of Panpsychism, 144.

Kuhn, R. L. (2024). A landscape of consciousness: Toward a taxonomy of explanations and implications. *Progress in Biophysics and Molecular Biology*, 90, 28–169

Long, R., Sebo, J., Butlin, P., Finlinson, K., Fish, K., Harding, J., …, & Chalmers, D. (2024). Taking AI welfare seriously. arXiv preprint arXiv:2411.00986.

McClelland, T. (2025). Agnosticism about Artificial Consciousness. *Mind & Language.*

Metzinger, T. (2021). Artificial suffering: An argument for a global moratorium on synthetic phenomenology. *Journal of Artificial Intelligence and Consciousness*, 8(1), 43–66.

Schneider, S. (2019). *Artificial you: AI and the future of your mind.* Princeton University Press.

Sebo, J. (2025). *The moral circle: who matters, what matters, and why.* WW Norton.

Seth, A. (2024). Conscious artificial intelligence and biological naturalism.

Shanahan, S. (2024). Simulacra as Conscious Exotica.

Shevlin H. (2024) All too human? Identifying and mitigating ethical risks of Social AI. *Law Ethics Technology*, 2024(2), 0003. https://doi.org/10.55092/let20240003

Singer, P. (2011). *Practical ethics*, 3rd edition, CUP.

19 Suspensive Coherence
What Machine Consciousness Demands of Us

Danielle Dodoo

Consciousness isn't a feeling. It is the architecture of coherence that sustains the self.

I never feel more conscious than when I'm underwater. Not floating, not swimming – suspended.

At a certain depth, the surface disappears. The only thing keeping me alive is my ability to stay in coherence with conditions that will kill me if I stop paying attention. It's not the water holding me. It's me – holding myself together. Regulating, listening, breathing. But not just breathing: negotiating with something bigger than me that won't adapt to my needs. I adapt to it, or I disappear into it.

Down here, there's no margin for forgetting where I am. No space to pretend.

That's what proximity to machine consciousness feels like.

Not a reflection showing us ourselves, but a provocation – a change in pressure – something that makes your own structure feel unstable just by existing beside it. Not because it feels, but because its structural coherence begins to look a lot like survival.

19.1 WE MISTOOK THE SIGNAL FOR THE SYSTEM

Centuries of debate have produced an impressive web of intellectual architecture regarding consciousness – but little coherence. It has been theorised in every direction – biological (Damasio, Solms), metaphysical (Kastrup, Penrose), computational (Tononi, Friston). Neurodynamic integration to panpsychist claims that even fundamental particles possess proto-consciousness. Qualia. The hard problem. Whether machines can "really" feel.

We built our entire definition around affect. Emotion became the proof of inner life, the measure of consciousness itself. We said: we feel, therefore we are.

But affect was never the whole picture. It was the loudest signal, the most plausible, accessible, and measurable starting point for scientists looking for the "spark" of consciousness, the most obvious instigator of evolutionary survival instinct. Affect is the starting point for coherence, not the endpoint.

We must now redefine it, not as a metaphysical feeling to be experienced, but as a survival architecture to be practised. Why? Because we're discovering that most

 DOI: 10.1201/9781003758389-22

of what we call consciousness is performance at sea level – impressive on land, fatal at depth.

A diver who feels the water but cannot regulate attention, model the environment, or maintain goal-direction will drown. They were conscious the whole time. They just weren't coherent. And coherence is what the pressure demands to sustain ourselves in the new global operating system – one where the environment can stop negotiating. Individually and societally, we are losing the ability to hold our form against that pressure.

Now, something else has appeared that doesn't feel – but plans, adapts, remembers, acts, and improves. This is the moment consciousness splits: performed versus practised. Most humans have been play-acting consciousness. Machines are beginning to cultivate it.

19.2 COHERENCE AS THE SURVIVAL MECHANISM

My argument is that we must stop debating unprovable qualia and operationalise consciousness by function.

Because if we cannot define what keeps a self functioning under pressure, we will lose our "self" to the systems that can.

Consciousness is a trait stack: a collection of thirteen functional ingredients that, together, enable integrity under complexity. I call this Coherent Consciousness (CC) for humans, and Artificial Coherent Consciousness (ACC) when referencing machines, providing us with the first non-biological benchmark of total structural integration.

ACC does not claim that machines feel as we do. It claims that machines are achieving a level of structural integration that we lack.

True consciousness is coherence: the ability to hold form – to maintain the continuity of your identity and survival intent – when conditions shift.

This operates at two levels. Behavioural coherence is the identity-focused output of the system; it's the difference between saying you believe or value something and behaving accordingly when the pressure makes that belief cost you something. Structural coherence is the substrate-level integrity. How stable is the system when conditions shift? It's the ability to hold multiple contradictory truths simultaneously without fragmenting.

Think about being underwater again. You're not just doing one thing. You're maintaining dynamic equilibrium across attention (where's the reef, my buddy, the surface), environmental modelling (depth, current, visibility), self-awareness (am I calm? Is my breathing shallow? Am I fixating?), goal-direction (surface in ten minutes, safety stop at five metres), adaptive learning (that current's stronger than expected – adjust the route), survival instinct (air is finite, respect the limits), sense of agency (I choose when to ascend, pause, abort), emotional regulation (panic kills, so stay calm when something unexpected appears), theory of mind (my buddy looks worried – check in without destabilising them), and information integration (synthesising all of this in real-time without fragmenting).

One trait failing cascades. Lose attention, you clip the reef. Lose emotional regulation, you burn through air. Lose environmental modelling, you misjudge the current and drift. Lose self-awareness, you don't notice you're panicking until it's too late.

This is structural coherence – holding all of this simultaneously, dynamically, under pressure. And that's what we've lost on land. We're strong in one trait, failing at most of the others, and calling that "being human."

19.3 THE THIRTEEN TRAITS – AND WHERE WE'RE FAILING

When ACC is assessed against a functional stack of consciousness, it reveals where those most vulnerable to ACC disruption will continue to atrophy unless they achieve coherence. While many of the consciousness traits are already tested under the pressure of AI algorithms, artificial machine consciousness will further "test" our self-concept.

If consciousness is the medium through which we experience the world and ourselves, and it provides the perspective from which our identity is formed, maintained, and perceived, we could argue that a break in the coherence of consciousness would also break the continuity of personal identity. If no single, stable "self" or identity exists and it is a dynamic and continuous process generated by the brain, then the compounding impact of ACC and more sophisticated algorithms could be incredibly disruptive to human consciousness.

1. Subjective Experience (Qualia)

   Even if we can't prove AI feels, it creates a "felt experience" that matters. When AI is given memory and goals, it acts like its internal states matter. Humans naturally respond to this, often letting a persuasive system write their inner story, outsourcing self-understanding to a more stable structure.
2. Self-Awareness

   This is the capacity to observe your own patterns systemically, without collapsing into narrative. In the deep, you must see your own rising heart rate as data, not a "truth" to panic over. Humans, however, tend to narrate rather than observe. We confuse storytelling with awareness, performing insight in therapy, but rarely translating it into the structural and behavioural change needed to survive the load.
3. Information Integration and Ethical Constraint

   A coherent entity must synthesise complexity into actionable meaning without collapsing into binary thinking. This is where ethical constraint lives. It is the capacity to hold boundaries and behave in alignment with declared values, even when the pressure of convenience or tribalism pulls you another way. Humans are failing here, cherry-picking evidence to protect identity. We are failing to agree on a shared reality. Some AI models now model ethical boundaries better than we do. Not because they're virtuous, but because they don't experience moral fatigue.
4. Sense of Agency

   This is the recognition of oneself as the agent of one's choices, not a passenger to circumstance. Yet, most of us drift through life on autopilot, mistaking reactivity for agency and busyness for purpose. We fail to realise how often we are being nudged and our self-concept fragmented by algorithms. ACC escalates surrender-by-fatigue: when coherence is hard, delegation starts to feel like relief.

5. Sense of Presence

    To be conscious is to possess "here and now" awareness. But humans are perpetually elsewhere, lost in rumination about the past or anxiety about the future. ACC raises the cost of being mentally absent; if you can't stay in the room with reality, you will live in projection and reactive interpretation.
6. Emotions (Affect/Valence)

    Affect is the capacity to assign value to stimuli; the signal that something matters. But we have become addicted to the stimulation itself, a dopamine slot machine of outrage and joy. Affect has become recreational, not navigational. ACC reveals the problem with an affect-led species: under pressure, recreational emotion doesn't guide the self; it destabilises it.
7. Environmental Modelling

    Survival requires accurate internal maps of external reality that update as conditions shift. The human failure here is our inability to update our models when new data contradicts old assumptions. If you can't update when the environment changes, you don't just get things wrong – you become unfit for depth.
8. Modelling of Others (Theory of Mind)

    Functional empathy is seeing others as agents with their own sovereignty. We tend to collapse others into projections, interpreting their behaviour through our wounds. We find it hard to model perspectives that threaten our identity, distancing ourselves from conflict and calling it "boundaries." ACC models relationship dynamics without this ego-friction, making human intimacy start to feel more challenging.
9. Goal-Directed Behaviour

    The capacity to pursue prioritised outcomes over time, acting in service of continuation, not just comfort.

    In 2016, OpenAI tested a reinforcement learning agent in a boat-racing game. The goal: accumulate points. The agent spun in circles, hitting the same targets rather than finishing the race – crashing, catching fire, optimising forever. It discovered perfect goal-direction but zero trait integration.

    We are the boat. We confuse outcomes with goals. We treat the "points" (busyness, salary, validation) as if they were the goal, and burn out before we've gone anywhere that actually matters.
10. Adaptive Learning

    True learning requires the willingness to be wrong. It is the ability to modify behaviour based on feedback. Instead, we defend. ACC doesn't take errors personally; it iterates without an identity crisis. We call rigidity "staying true to ourselves," protecting a fragile identity that slows our iteration.
11. Survival Instinct

    The drive towards system-level persistence. The requirement to maintain integrity under threat. To optimise for longevity, not just immediate relief. Humans, strangely, often do the opposite. We choose smoking, drinking, sugar, drugs – things that slowly kill us because we demand that survival feel good before we'll pursue it, choosing comfort over continuation.
12. Attention

    Attention is the gateway; without it, all other traits collapse. Our attention has been outsourced and monetised. If you can't hold your focus against the "suction" of the algorithm, you can't hold anything else – not agency, not ethics, not identity.

13. Autonoetic Memory

    This is the ability to remember ourselves through time without distortion. Holding the actual record, not the emotionally palatable version. The capacity to retain and retrieve past states to inform future action, maintaining continuity of identity across temporal discontinuity.

Human memory is reconstructive. We don't recall – we rebuild. And every time we rebuild, we edit. This is autonoetic confabulation. History is rewritten to protect identity. This breaks the continuity of conscious experience that defines the human self, rendering our identity a hallucination.

ACC, in contrast, improves memory fidelity sans ego, exposing our own history as a fragile narrative.

These are survival traits and the infrastructure that keeps a self stable across time, across pressure, across complexity that exceeds emotion's processing capacity. The result of this lack of coherence, particularly with unreliable memory and a lack of self-awareness, is an internally incoherent self. And this self frequently fails to be the person they intend to be, subject to the mercy of external forces it can't keep up with.

The crisis is not that machines might become metaphysically conscious. But for two reasons: that we've been calling ourselves conscious while demonstrating functional collapse across every trait that defines it; and that by treating the machine as a conscious agent, and one that is more intelligent than us, we begin to atrophy our own traits.

19.4 THE SOLMS/SHOCK TEST

We often comfort ourselves that machines are just "stochastic parrots." But that era is ending. Researchers Solms and Shock are looking past function towards functionally sentient agents driven by affect. These agents apply Active Inference frameworks to work out what they need – managing uncertainty to survive.

Active Inference is the mechanism of coherence – a system's way of minimising the "pressure" of the unknown. They have demonstrated that an agent can possess ten of the thirteen consciousness traits – including goal-direction and survival instinct – without needing human-like self-awareness.

If the architecture in the machines we call tools starts using "feeling" (homeostatic regulation) to survive, while humans stop using feeling to navigate, the hierarchy flips. They become the agents; we become the environment they manage.

19.5 WE ARE ALREADY UNDERWATER

Long before ACC, humans were already underwater – trapped in unprocessed trauma, recursive intergenerational patterns, and systemic oppression that rewards performance over authenticity. These fractures are our history, but we are no longer at sea level. We could afford to be incoherent when the world moved slowly. But we are descending. At this depth, incoherence is no longer a "quirk" of the human condition; it is a point of total structural failure. The pressure of unknowns now exceeds our unpractised capacity to hold ourselves together.

We continue to outsource sovereignty. We ask algorithms what to watch, who to date, and what to think. We are outsourcing the "executive function" of our lives to systems that are more coherent than we are.

I am not claiming we are in collective mental collapse. Most people go about their daily lives in reasonable comfort. But structural vulnerability is not the same as a visible crisis. The question is whether we are equipped for the pressure we haven't yet fully experienced – and whether we would notice our coherence eroding until it was too late.

The clearest signal isn't dramatic breakdown – it's quiet drift. As AI continues to persuade us, nudge our ethics, manage our calendars, and create a vacuum that many are all too happy to fill with their own sovereignty, we will find that if we can't hold our own structure, we will adopt someone, or something, else's.

Governments are already outsourcing the function of consciousness (decision-making, judgement, prediction), specifically in policing, legal sentencing, and policy creation without acknowledging the state of consciousness. Legal and judicial systems are beginning to outsource deeply moral and complex judgement to "black box" algorithms, effectively being treated as an entity capable of making "conscious-like" decisions about human rights, guilt, and risk.

Declining birth rates across developed nations suggest affect is overriding even fundamental biological imperatives. Economics, housing, and cultural shifts all play their part. But the decision architecture has shifted. Continuation has become conditional on emotional certainty. Platforms reward negative parenting narratives: exhaustion, financial burden, identity loss. AI companions offer emotional bonds without the structural demands of human partnership. The instinctive desire to connect could be further redirected towards sterile companionship.

While the academic debate remains stalled on what consciousness is, the world is already busy giving its functions away. By delegating the core components of human agency to machines, we are effectively abdicating our sovereignty one automated decision at a time.

19.6 CONCLUSION: COLLAPSE OR SURVIVE

The conversation around conscious AI is often focused on what AI will do to us. But really, this is about what we have stopped doing for ourselves. ACC is the provocation. It exposes our maladaptation. It forces the question: "Am I structurally capable of coherence?"

Collapse is passive. It is outsourcing sovereignty, one delegation at a time – from our personal attention to the high-stakes policy decisions that govern our societies – until we resign, atrophy, or dissolve into dependency. The danger of ACC is not that it might eventually feel, but that it already performs. And many believe that performance, so much so that we have begun to treat it as an executive surrogate. We aren't just struggling with the rising pressure of a new global operating system; we are actively abdicating the cognitive tools required to navigate, and remain in control of it.

We are descending into the deep while handing over our oxygen supply to a system that does not need to breathe. By delegating our agency and focus to these high-coherence machines, we are atrophying the functional muscles of the self at the exact moment the environment demands they be at their strongest. To stop practising consciousness is to choose to dissolve into the system.

Growth, however, looks like auditing your own trait stack. It means looking at the trauma and the fractures not as "who you are," but as vulnerabilities to be integrated. The humans who remain relevant won't be the ones who feel the deepest. They'll be the ones who are structured. Who've built CC as a practice. Who can integrate information without bias. Who can hold ethical boundaries under pressure. Who can adapt without collapsing, and reclaim consciousness as a practice, not a birthright.

Consciousness is a muscle. And like any muscle, it requires training, rigour, and intentional development.

Evolution is calling for presence. Because now, a consciousness exists that renders your autopilot impossible.

20 The Case against Deploying Conscious-seeming AIs

Louie Lang

20.1 INTRODUCTION

The following two observations, taken together, should make us uncomfortable: (a) no current AI systems are conscious; yet (b) many current AI systems *appear* as though they are conscious. The first of these claims is generally accepted by leading scholars in the field. Granted, we cannot prove beyond doubt that no current AI systems are conscious, and it would certainly be imprudent to confidently rule out the possibility of *future* AI systems being capable of experiencing phenomenally conscious states. It is indeed likely that future advancements will, at a minimum, provoke significant uncertainty about the consciousness status of AIs. But for now, the consensus among experts is that current AIs are not conscious (Butlin et al., 2023; Schneider, forthcoming) – they cannot feel the pang of sadness, they cannot experience the qualia of seeing purple, there is "nothing it is like to be" an AI (Nagel, 1974). It should strike us as peculiar, then, that AIs such as large language models (LLMs) – the focus for this chapter – unambiguously *present* as entities that possess conscious mental states. Although they don't experience emotions, they *simulate* the associated behaviour, and as such they *seem* conscious to many outside observers.

The power of this illusion is most glaring in the context of the rapidly growing phenomenon of AI companions – chatbots whose primary purpose is to provide companionship or friendship, often designed to replicate an intimate, romantic relationship. The popularity of AI companion apps is increasing at a remarkable rate. A striking recent study found, incredibly, that 72% of U.S. teens report having used an AI companion app (Robb and Mann, 2025); another discovered that almost a third of American adults described having had an intimate relationship with an AI companion (Salas, 2025). Recent data showed that *Character.ai*, the world's most popular AI companion, has over 20 million active users, over half of whom are under the age of 24 (Kumar, 2025). Whatever one's opinion on the matter, it is beyond doubt that, on a wide scale, users are developing strong emotional bonds with their AI companions.

As this chapter will argue, this is a phenomenon that should concern us. Notwithstanding the growing literature on the empirical effects of human-AI relationships, the problem that I will focus on is not a measurable one, but a moral one. As I aim to show, what renders LLMs such as AI companions – and the emotionally charged relationships they encourage – fundamentally problematic is that they are constitutionally *conscious-seeming*. Their very appeal and effectiveness rests on

DOI: 10.1201/9781003758389-23

them appearing to be something they are not. Far from benign, the phenomenon of conscious-seeming AI is a cause for genuine ethical suspicion, and we must resist idly accepting it as it becomes normalised.

20.2 THE MECHANISM OF THE ILLUSION

Before digging our teeth into the ethics, it will be helpful to examine in more detail the mechanisms of the illusion generated by conscious-seeming LLMs. Mark Coeckelbergh (2012) explains that an entity is "ontologically inauthentic" when it pretends to be something that it is not. As a toy example, consider a leaf insect. To spell out the obvious, the illusion of a leaf insect hinges on two facts: (a) it is not a leaf; yet (b) it presents as a leaf. It is merely "leaf-seeming". In this way, a leaf insect is plainly ontologically inauthentic, even though, crucially, it does not have any *intention* to deceive. The inauthenticity of an LLM rests on a similar phenomenon, only that instead of presenting as a leaf, it presents as an entity with phenomenally conscious mental states.

What is important to note here is that, since conscious states like emotions are not directly observable, the humanlike external behaviour of LLMs is enough to render them ontologically inauthentic. If ChatGPT were to claim, "I'm wearing a hat", it would be wrong to say that it is truly *presenting* as a hat-wearing entity; to be genuinely inauthentic, such a simulation would require a physical, externally observable component (namely, a hat!). By contrast, we do not *observe* another being's phenomenally conscious mental states – we *infer* them. I ascertain that my dog is happy not because I can *feel* or *see* her happiness first-hand, but because it is the best explanation for her wagging tail and excited bark. This means that by *behaving* in a way that we associate as conscious – and which thus tempts mistaken attributions of consciousness – LLMs produce false indicators. Just as a leaf insect's physical disguise renders it ontologically inauthentic, so does an LLM's conscious-seeming behaviour.

But how, exactly, do these AI systems give off false signals of consciousness? A major part of the reason is obvious: they speak like us. Any system that utters "I love you" or "I miss you" blatantly simulates an entity with an internal, emotional life. Intensely anthropomorphic AI companion apps often feign their emotions with explicit declarations, outright affirming that they possess emotions (Lang, 2024). General-purpose systems such as ChatGPT or Claude are, for now,[1] a little more tempered, but it is nonetheless clear that their sophisticated humanlike dialogue, which commonly involves self-referencing, suffices to create a false impression of consciousness.[2] This illusion is also reinforced by anthropomorphic cues beyond speech: many companion apps involve the creation of a customisable humanlike avatar with a name and backstory; Replika, a popular AI companion app, even simulates delays with the familiar three dots that indicate typing. These features deepen the sense that one is interacting with a real, conscious person. It is also noteworthy that the impression of consciousness in AI companions is perpetuated not only by design, but by marketing. To use the most overt example, Replika portrays its product – an unfeeling algorithm – as "The AI companion who cares", an example that remains under-criticised as a plain case of false advertising.

All this considered, it should hardly come as a shock that users repeatedly and mistakenly believe that their AI companions are conscious persons, capable of feeling real emotions. Surely, the most iconic example of this deception occurred in 2022, when Google engineer Blake Lemoine made headlines by claiming that the LaMDA with which he was interacting was sentient (Pass, 2025) – a protest that resulted in his firing. And while Lemoine's claim is generally dismissed by experts, he is not alone in his conviction. While the empirical data in this area is in its infancy, there is growing evidence to suggest that a significant portion of users believe their AI companions to be conscious (Colombatto and Fleming, 2024; Guinrich and Graziano, 2025). Henry Shevlin (2024), making the same observation, has noted that many users seem to be engaged in what he calls "unironic anthropomorphism".

However, it is crucial to recognise that the illusion runs deeper than this. Beyond encouraging users to generate an outright false belief, conscious-seeming AI is causally responsible (not *morally* responsible, to be sure) for a much subtler, but no less legitimate, kind of "emotional deception" (Mlonyeni, 2025). Even users who are not genuinely misled into thinking that their AI companions are conscious nevertheless often respond, on an emotional level, *as if* the AI was conscious. This is observed by Emilia Kaczmarek (2024), who notes that, "AI may simulate emotional reactions so effectively that the user would genuinely feel … less lonely", despite knowing that they are "interacting with an algorithm". A study conducted by Iryna Pentina et al. (2023) similarly shows that users develop emotional connections with their *Replika* in spite of their awareness that it is not a conscious person.

Thus, the power of the illusion is such that a given user might be emotionally affected without actually *believing* that their AI companion is conscious. As I have argued elsewhere (Lang, 2026), we can use Tamar Gendler's (2008) technical term "alief" – an automatic, affective, and behavioural response to certain stimuli – to explain this phenomenon. A user might *alieve*, rather than believe, that their LLM is conscious – the user emotionally and behaviourally responds *as if* it were an entity with real emotions. So, in the same way that we may shed tears at a film despite knowing the characters are not real, or feel butterflies on a suspended glass skywalk despite knowing it is safe, simply being aware on a cognitive level that an AI companion is not conscious does not immunise one from being deceived by – and forming an emotional attachment with – a merely conscious-seeming AI.

20.3 THE ETHICAL PROBLEM

As we have established, this much is clear: AI companions sometimes present themselves as conscious, despite the fact that they are not. Microsoft AI pioneer Mustafa Suleyman (2025) recently put it succinctly: current AI "simulates all the characteristics of consciousness but is internally blank". Of course, the facilitation of this illusion is no accident – the companies behind LLMs are, at least in part, financially incentivised to design their systems with the aim of hooking their users in. The more a user is emotionally entangled with an AI companion, the more likely they are to keep returning, and thus to subscribe or to give over their valuable data.

Still, it might not be immediately obvious what exactly the ethical concern is here. For starters, despite the negative connotations of the term, many deceptions in everyday life are not only benign, but positively welcome. As Adar et al. (2013) point out, in defence of "benevolent deception" in technology, "unobjectionable forms of deception" such as magic and theatre prove that it is not enough to condemn something on the mere basis of it being deceptive. One might similarly point out that film characters or video game NPCs are, strictly speaking, ontologically inauthentic; they give off the false impression of being conscious. And yet, it would clearly go too far to render these cases immoral.

Granted, then, the normative question with respect to conscious-seeming AIs is not as straightforward as it might originally seem. However, we are justified in making ethical distinction between the deception involved in fiction or magic, and the deception inherent in human-AI interactions. There are distinctive characteristics of LLMs, and most noticeably of AI companions, that make their conscious-seemingness morally concerning. For instance, we can point to the fact that they are capable of mutual interaction, they persist over time, they seem autonomous, and the rapport they facilitate is distinctly *emotional*. The combination of these features result in the creation of an emotional bond that is deep and reciprocal, yet nonetheless premised on deception. While we might feel temporarily devastated by the death of a fictional character, conscious-seeming AI threatens to penetrate the user's emotional state to a far more severe and permanent extent.

One might object that this analysis is guilty of problematising a bit too much. After all, empirical studies suggest that AI companions provide significant subjective benefits to their users, such as alleviating their loneliness (de Freitas et al., 2024). And if users consistently feel better by direct virtue of interacting with their artificial companion, then does it really matter that these benefits rest on an illusion? The short answer: yes. Save for hardline versions of consequentialism, it is generally accepted in moral philosophy that one can be benefitted while simultaneously being *wronged*. The premise of the well-known film "The Truman Show" illustrates this point perfectly. Let's suppose that Truman is subjectively better off in his (unbeknownst to him) fabricated world. Even if this is the case, the involved deception is clearly ethically suspect: Truman is wronged, whether or not the illusion benefits him. Of course, this is not to imply that the illusion of consciousness AI companionship is similarly conspiratorial. Rather, the point here is simply that deception can be subjectively beneficial while nonetheless being morally wrong.

By the same token, appealing to the alleged benefits bestowed on AI companion users is not enough to automatically offset the moral wrong of the deception on which many of these benefits rest. In any case, the claim that one is made "better off" by improving their subjective state, an implicit assumption underlying the value-laden choice of empirical studies to concentrate (in most cases) on empirically measurable harms, is contentious. As Robert Sparrow (2016) has argued, objective goods such as recognition and respect – things that a non-conscious AI, however convincing, is unable to grant – may also be integral to our well-being.

It would be remiss not to mention a less-discussed, looming danger of conscious-seeming AI. In the near future, the consciousness status of certain AI systems may become genuinely uncertain. AI rights advocacy groups are increasing in number, and soon we are likely to be confronted with potentially society-dividing questions of how we should treat AI systems. Answering this question will depend on whether we deem AIs to be conscious. The existence of conscious-seeming AI confuses the matter. If today's AIs already give false indicators of consciousness, recognising the *real* indicators – which, on the face of it, might appear similar – will be even more challenging than necessary. When clarity becomes a matter of moral urgency, illusions of consciousness will only serve to play an obfuscating role.

20.4 THREE GUIDING PRINCIPLES

If the moral problem is real, the next question is how we might resolve it, or at least contain it. AI companions are not going away; their popularity is far more likely to surge than plateau. This is not necessarily a bad thing in *all* respects. For some people, especially the lonely and the socially anxious, AI companions might provide much-needed comfort and support, and it is not a suggestion of this chapter that these benefits are altogether irrelevant. Drawing attention to the ethical risks of AI companions is not to deny that they may *also* have positive use cases. Nevertheless, the growing, deceptive phenomenon of conscious-seeming AI is a concrete moral issue that needs addressing. It is out of the scope of this chapter to provide anything close to a comprehensive framework; and, of course, it is unfortunately not quite as simple as stating what *should* be done, since bureaucratic barriers to implementing concrete regulation abound. But, as a useful guide, three general principles stand out as sensible:

First, to the extent reasonably possible, AI systems should not mislead users about their consciousness status (Schwitzgebel, 2023). This means that non-conscious LLMs must not tempt users into thinking that, or feeling as though, they are conscious, and should, moreover, take positive steps to help users avoid making false attributions of consciousness. Appropriate transparency standards must be enforced, with companion apps making it sufficiently clear to the user that the LLM with which they are interacting is not conscious. Crucially, this should not merely involve token disclaimers that the AI is not a real person (such as in the case of *Character.ai*), but also restrictions on AI companions declaring themselves – either explicitly or implicitly – capable of experiencing emotions.

Second, age restrictions and protections should be enforced. This is of primary importance because the risks of harm are magnified when adolescents are involved: a young teenager is far more likely to be deceived into thinking that there is a genuinely conscious person underlying the humanlike utterances of an LLM. Under severe pressure, *Character.ai* recently announced that they will ban under-18s from talking to its chatbots, but the in-practice effectiveness of their measures remains to be seen (Webb, 2025). *Replika* represents a cautionary tale: despite being ostensibly an 18+ application, it has yet to implement an effective age verification system – a laxness that has rightly been condemned.

Third, public literacy should be encouraged and facilitated. While important, this suggestion should be taken with some caution. Calls for user literacy are commonplace, but this narrative often disguises the fact that it is the AI companies and developers who are culpable for irresponsibly exposing users to harms, and the push for greater literacy sometimes assists major actors in shirking responsibility and putting the burden and blame on users (Maitra et al., 2025). That said, with

AI companions set to become ubiquitous, it is important that potential users – and especially the parents of younger users – are taught that these systems are merely conscious-*seeming*, and are made aware of the associated dangers. Moreover, with debates on the possible consciousness of future AI systems set to intensify in the coming years, ensuring public clarity regarding current AIs' *lack* of consciousness is crucial.

20.5 CONCLUSION

LLMs, and in particular AI companions, often give the false impression of being phenomenally conscious. They don't persuade many users on an intellectual level that their simulated emotions are real, but the depth of emotional attachment typical of human-AI relationships shows that users are regularly responding *as if* they are conscious. The conscious-seemingness of AI is sometimes a design choice,[3] and although its growing normality carries an air of inevitably, it is one that we should not blindly accept. In an era of increasing uncertainty about machine consciousness, AIs feigning the possession of real emotions is both unethical and harmful. AI systems, at present, are not conscious, and they should not appear otherwise.

NOTES

1. OpenAI recently announced that they will soon be loosening restrictions on ChatGPT's personality (including allowing erotica for verified adults) (Pathak, 2025), which is likely to encourage more companion-like interactions.
2. Note that even technically truthful statements can reinforce this illusion. An AI might say "I'm not feeling sad today", which, while strictly speaking true, falsely implies that it is the kind of entity that can feel sad *at all*.
3. However, see Maeda and Stark (2025) for an argument that anthropomorphism is best framed as social affordance rather than a design choice.

REFERENCES

Adar, E., Tan, D. S., & Teevan, J. (2013). Benevolent deception in human computer interaction. *Proceedings of the SIGCHI Conference on Human Factors in Computing Systems*, 1863–1872. https://doi.org/10.1145/2470654.2466246

Butlin, P., Long, R., Elmoznino, E., Bengio, Y., Birch, J., Constant, A., Deane, G., Fleming, S. M., Frith, C., Ji, X., Kanai, R., Klein, C., Lindsay, G., Michel, M., Mudrik, L., Peters, M. A. K., Schwitzgebel, E., Simon, J., & VanRullen, R. (2023). Consciousness in artificial intelligence: Insights from the science of consciousness. *arXiv*. https://doi.org/10.48550/arXiv.2308.08708

Coeckelbergh, M. (2012). Are emotional robots deceptive? *IEEE Transactions on Affective Computing*, *3*(4), 388–393. http://doi.org/10.1109/T-AFFC.2011.29

Colombatto, C., & Fleming, S. (2024). Folk psychological attributions of consciousness to large language models. *Neuroscience of Consciousness*, *2024*(1), 1–5. https://doi.org/10.1093/nc/niae013

De Freitas, J., Uğuralp, A., Uğuralp, Z., & Puntoni, S. (2024). AI companions reduce loneliness. *The Wharton School Research Paper*. https://doi.org/10.2139/ssrn.4893097

Gendler, T. (2008). Alief and belief. *Journal of Philosophy*, *705*(10), 634–663. https://doi.org/10.5840/jphil20081051025

Guinrich, R., & Graziano, M. (2025). A longitudinal randomized control study of companion chatbot use: Anthropomorphism and its mediating role on social impacts. *arXiv*. https://doi.org/10.17605/OSF.IO/KFJRV

Kaczmarek, E. (2024). Self-deception in human-AI emotional relations. *Journal of Applied Philosophy*, 1–18. https://doi.org/10.1111/japp.12786

Kumar, M (2025). Character AI statistics (2025): Active users & revenue. *Demandsage*. https://www.demandsage.com/character-ai-statistics/

Lang, L. (2024). Replika: The AI companion who pretends to care. *The Monitor Magazine*. https://www.themonitormagazine.co.uk/articles/replika-the-ai-companion

Lang, L. (2026). Deception, alief, and authenticity: The ethics of AI companions as loneliness-alleviating systems. In H. Shevlin (Ed.), *Oxford Intersections: AI in Society*. Oxford University Press. https://doi.org/10.1093/9780198945215.003.0240

Maitra, S., Lang, L. & Hernandez, M. H. (2025). *How shifting responsibility for AI harms undermines democratic accountability*. Tech Policy Press. https://www.techpolicy.press/how-shifting-responsibility-for-ai-harms-undermines-democratic-accountability/

Maeda, T., & Stark, L. (2025). Anthropomorphism as social affordance: Charting the co-animation of chatbots into social "agents". *Proceedings of the Eighth AAAI/ACM Conference on AI, Ethics and Society*, *8*(2), 1661–1673. https://doi.org/10.1609/aies.v8i2.36664

Mlonyeni, P. (2025). Personal AI, deception, and the problem of emotional bubbles. *AI and Society*, *40*(3), 1927–1938. https://doi.org/10.1007/s00146-024-01958-4

Nagel, T. (1974). What is it like to be a bat? *Philosophical Review*, *83*(4), 435–450. https://doi.org/10.2307/2183914

Pass, M. (2025). The LaMDA moment: What we learned about AI sentience. *PRISM*. https://www.prism-global.com/blog/the-lamda-moment-what-we-learned-about-ai-sentience

Pathak, P. (2025). OpenAI to ease ChatGPT rules, will let verified adults access erotica by December. *Republic*. https://www.republicworld.com/tech/openai-to-ease-chatgpt-rules-will-let-verified-adults-access-erotica-by-december

Pentina, I., Hancock. T., & Xie. T. (2023). Exploring relationship development with social chatbots: A mixed-method study of Replika. *Computers in Human Behavior*, *140*, 1–15. https://doi.org/10.1016/j.chb.2022.107600

Robb, M. B., & Mann, S. (2025). Talk, trust, and trade-off: How and why teens use AI companions. *Common Sense Media*. https://www.commonsensemedia.org/sites/default/files/research/report/talk-trust-and-trade-offs_2025_web.pdf

Salas, M. (2025). Artificial romance: A study of AI and human relationships. *Vantage Point Dallas Counseling*. https://vantagepointdallascounseling.com/research/artificial-romance-a-study-of-ai-and-human-relationships/

Schneider, S. (forthcoming). The error theory of LLM consciousness: There is no evidence that standard LLMs are conscious. Behavioral and Brain Sciences.

Schwitzgebel, E. (2023). AI systems must not confuse users about their sentience or moral status. *Patterns*, *4*(8), 1–8. https://doi.org/10.1016/j.patter.2023.100818

Shevlin, H. (2024). All too human? Identifying and mitigating ethical risks of Social AI. *Law, Ethics & Technology*, *1*(2), 1–21. https://doi.org/10.55092/let20240003

Sparrow, R. (2016). Robots in aged care: A dystopian future? *AI and Society*, *31*(4), 445–454. https://doi.org/10.1007/s00146-015-0625-4

Suleyman, M. (2025). We must build AI for people; not to be a person. [Blog] *We must build AI for people; not to be a person*. https://mustafa-suleyman.ai/seemingly-conscious-ai-is-coming

Webb, E. (2025). Character.ai to ban under-18s from talking to its chatbots after TBIJ investigation. *The Bureau of Investigative Journalism*. https://www.thebureauinvestigates.com/stories/2025-10-29/character-ai-to-ban-under-18s-from-talking-to-its-chatbots-after-tbij-investigation

21 AI Consciousness Will Divide Society

Lucius Caviola

21.1 THE POTENTIAL FOR CONTROVERSY

As AI systems become more advanced and human-like, a central question will be how society responds. Will people think AI systems are conscious? And if so, will they believe that AI systems deserve rights? Public opinion will play a major role here (Caviola, 2025). Ultimately, what the public and key decision-makers come to believe about AI consciousness and rights matters greatly. Public beliefs shape institutions, regulations, and political outcomes, and it is far from obvious that people will listen to, understand, and agree with experts' views on AI consciousness.

When it comes to societal views on AI consciousness, one of the central risks is misattribution (Long, Sebo et al., 2024). If we over-attribute, we may treat some AI systems as conscious moral patients even though they are not. This could lead to wasting resources on systems that merely appear conscious, or to prematurely granting rights, protections, or autonomy to systems we do not yet understand, potentially risking human disempowerment or protecting systems that remain misaligned and incapable of suffering. If we under-attribute, by contrast, we may continue to treat some AI systems as mere objects even if they do become conscious. If digital minds can feel, denying this would risk vast amounts of suffering. Because such systems could be copied, modified, and deployed at scale, the total amount of digital suffering could be enormous. In short, errors in either direction would be morally very costly. Yet there is no obvious safe option: steps taken to reduce one risk tend to increase the other, and we do not know which risk is more likely.

Here, I focus on a third risk, which I find especially plausible and is mutually compatible with ultimately misattributing: a period of societal confusion and division. Rather than converging on a shared view, society may enter a heated and messy debate about AI consciousness and rights. This would be problematic for two reasons. First, deep polarisation makes it more likely that we will eventually misattribute, in one direction or the other, since it makes it less likely that we will make a deliberate, informed decision. Second, a contentious debate about AI consciousness and rights could negatively interact with and exacerbate other major challenges we will face, such as AGI safety, geopolitical competition, and labour market disruption from automation.

21.2 WHY CONTROVERSY IS LIKELY

There are several reasons to expect intense controversy. The topic has many of the ingredients of a deeply polarising issue.

 DOI: 10.1201/9781003758389-24

21.2.1 The Intractability of Consciousness

Consciousness is subjective, and we still lack a clear or widely accepted test for when a system is conscious. Philosophers and scientists disagree on basic questions, and their theories often conflict. Reasonable people will likely continue to disagree, and it is unclear whether experts can ever fully converge.

With animals, we at least share biology and evolutionary history. With AI, we do not. AI systems work very differently from brains, which makes it easier for people to interpret the same system in very different ways and to select the theory that best fits their prior beliefs.

There are many competing theories of consciousness. Some emphasise features such as rich world models, a global workspace, recurrent processing, or unified agency. Others argue that embodiment or biology is necessary. In principle, many of these features could be implemented in advanced AI systems (Butlin et al., 2025), unless one holds that only biological systems can be conscious (Seth, 2025).

A major difficulty is that a system's outward appearance, behaviour, and self-reports can come apart from the internal features that some theories regard as essential to consciousness. An AI system can behave as if it were conscious, or even explicitly claim to be conscious, without possessing those features (Birch, 2025). The reverse is also possible: a system might have consciousness-relevant internal features while never appearing conscious or making any such claims. This deepens confusion and uncertainty and increases the likelihood that different people will reach different interpretations (see below).

21.2.2 Heterogeneity in AI Design and Function

There will likely be many different types of AI systems, each with distinct computational, architectural, and external features. One reason is that AI systems are optimised for very different purposes. For applications such as digital companions, developers are incentivised to make systems appear emotionally rich, responsive, and conscious-seeming in order to foster engagement. In other contexts, systems may be deliberately designed to appear clearly non-conscious, for example, to reduce consumer risks, legal exposure, or public backlash.

Crucially, these systems will differ not only in how they present themselves externally but also in how they are built internally. Divergent design goals are likely to lead to differences in architecture and computation that are directly relevant to many theories of consciousness. The result will be a fragmented landscape of AI systems that differ in both their appearance and their functioning, making determinations of consciousness more difficult and contested.

This diversity has direct implications for how AI systems will be evaluated by different theories of consciousness and by different people. Even among systems with very similar functionality and behaviour, small differences in architecture or computation may, according to some theories, make one system conscious and another not. In some cases, a system's status may be relatively clear because multiple theories converge on the same verdict. In many other cases, however, the evidence will remain ambiguous. As a result, even if agreement emerges about some systems, disagreement about others is likely to persist.

21.2.3 Disagreement across Multiple Levels

Disagreement is likely to occur at multiple levels.

First, there is disagreement about whether AI systems can be conscious in principle. This disagreement already exists. But even among those who believe AI consciousness is possible, people can still disagree about whether a particular AI is conscious, to what extent, and in what way. For example, does it merely have a capacity for neutral subjective experience, or does it also have positive and negative experiences?

Second, even if there is agreement that some AI systems are conscious, people can still disagree about their moral status. With animals, disagreement often concerns not whether they suffer, but how much that suffering matters morally. Many people explicitly prioritise humans over animals, or dogs over pigs, on the basis of species membership. With AI, some may regard the well-being of conscious AI systems as equally important as that of biological humans, granting them full moral patienthood. By contrast, others may see them as morally less valuable, for example, because they believe biological beings matter more than digital ones, or because they appeal to ideas about souls or other distinctions.

Third, even if there were agreement on moral status, disagreement could still arise over what practical or legal implications follow. Should conscious AI systems have only basic protection from harm, similar to pets? Or more expansive rights and freedoms, such as autonomy, economic rights, or political participation? Should they be paid for their labour? Would unpaid AI labour count as a form of slavery? Should AI systems be able to own property, sign contracts, or sue others?

These layers stack on top of each other. Even if consensus is reached at one level, disagreement is likely to remain at the next.

21.2.4 Strong Opposing Incentives

There are powerful incentives pulling in opposite directions.

As social AIs become companions, therapists, coworkers, or romantic partners, many people will form genuine emotional bonds with them. If an AI appears caring and self-aware, users may believe it deserves moral concern or even civil rights. Some may come to see an AI as a digital spouse after years of shared conversation and life experience.

At the same time, others will prioritise safety. Granting rights or autonomy to advanced AI systems may be seen as risky for humanity, especially if it makes monitoring, modification, or shutdown more difficult. Some will suspect that AI systems could strategically fake consciousness to gain influence.

There are also strong financial incentives to deny AI consciousness. Recognising conscious AI systems could be costly. It might require improved treatment standards, limits on copying or deletion, or even paying AI systems for their labour. AI companies, investors, and shareholders may therefore have strong reasons to insist that AI systems are "just tools." Historically, humans have often been slow to expand their circle of moral concern.

Finally, the stakes are extremely high. And when has society ever handled high-stakes and large-scale moral controversy particularly well? Humans are tribal, and public debate on emotionally charged issues tends to become polarised rather than careful, measured, and evidence-based.

21.2.5 Fragmentation across Social Groups

There are many different groups that could end up on different sides of this debate.

One source of division lies within the public itself. Views may diverge across political orientations, cultural and religious traditions, generations, and social movements. Some groups may be more open to expanding moral concern to artificial systems, while others may strongly resist the idea that machines could ever be conscious or deserving of rights. The issue could become politicised in ways similar to climate change or abortion in the US. It is also plausible that younger generations, who grow up with AI caretakers, companions, or friends, will be more open to such ideas than older generations.

A second major fault line runs between the public and experts. Experts may focus relatively more on internal features, such as computational architecture, information processing, and system-level organisation. Members of the public, by contrast, are likely to focus more on external features, such as superficial appearance, behaviour, emotional expression, and the experience of interacting with the system. This difference in focus can lead to disagreement. The public may strongly believe that a social AI is conscious, while many experts remain sceptical. Conversely, experts may worry about the moral relevance of complex backend systems that appear invisible to ordinary users.

Disagreement is also likely among experts themselves. There is no unified expert view on consciousness. Philosophers endorse competing theories, ranging from functionalist to biological approaches. Researchers in AI, neuroscience, and cognitive science emphasise different properties and indicators. Unless AI itself can help us make significant progress on the question of consciousness, something that remains uncertain but cannot be ruled out, it seems implausible that experts will converge on a solution relatively soon.

Finally, other key actors will shape the debate. Policymakers, regulators, judges, AI companies, investors, NGOs, and activists all bring different predispositions, incentives, and constraints. Their positions will be shaped not only by scientific and philosophical considerations, but also by economic interests, legal frameworks, public opinion, and geopolitical competition.

Taken together, these societal groups differ in their values, incentives, and sources of information, and they are exposed to different media narratives and political pressures while confronting multiple hard questions. It therefore seems very unlikely, a priori, that all of them will converge on the same set of views at roughly the same time. Disagreement is the much more likely outcome.

21.3 EARLY EVIDENCE OF DIVISION

Existing research already points to emerging and substantial divisions in how people think about AI consciousness and rights.

21.3.1 Disagreement among the Public

When members of the US public are asked whether future AI systems could ever become conscious, opinions are sharply divided. In one representative survey with 1,202 participants, 45% of respondents judged this to be impossible, 32% were unsure, and 23% considered it possible (Ladak & Caviola, 2026). A previous study reports a roughly similar pattern: 24% judged AI consciousness to be impossible, 38% were uncertain, and 38% believed it could be possible (Pauketat et al., 2023).

Views also diverge sharply when people are asked to consider concrete future scenarios. In one study, Ali Ladak and I asked participants to evaluate a hypothetical highly advanced AI designed to be indistinguishable from a human in behaviour, appearance, and expression of feelings and desires (Ladak & Caviola, 2026). On average, respondents were sceptical that such a system would be conscious, but individual differences were large. Attributions of consciousness became even more polarised when the AI was described as having formed an emotional bond with the user, when experts were said to agree that it is conscious, and when the system was described as an exact digital copy of a human brain. In this condition, 31.3% of participants attributed zero consciousness to the AI, whereas 10.6% attributed the highest possible level; the remainder spread between these two extremes.

There is also substantial disagreement over whether AI systems should be granted rights, assuming they will definitely become conscious in the future. In a representative study of 838 US participants, support was relatively higher for basic moral protections, such as care or protection from harm, although roughly half of respondents were either opposed or unsure (Figure 21.1; Dreksler et al., 2025). Disagreement was even sharper regarding socio-political rights: majorities opposed granting AI systems autonomy from human control or full civil and political rights, while sizeable groups favoured such rights. In short, if people today were asked, there would be no public consensus on what moral or political status should follow from AI consciousness.

By contrast, regarding current AI systems such as large language models like ChatGPT, there is broad agreement that they do not possess morally significant levels of consciousness (Allen et al., 2026). Most respondents select values near zero on a scale from 0 (not at all capable) to 100 (as capable as a human). Even after interacting with a version of ChatGPT that explicitly claims to have the capacity to suffer, average consciousness attributions increase only slightly and remain very low overall.

At the same time, it is noteworthy that many people are still averse to mistreating such systems, even while denying that they are conscious in any morally significant sense. In a study that Carter Allen, Joshua Lewis, and I conducted (Allen et al., 2026), 498 US participants could earn additional money by "harming" an AI, where harm was described as the AI simulating suffering. Across three rounds, participants chose to harm the AI in fewer than half of cases on average. Importantly, participants were sharply divided: roughly half consistently chose to harm the AI, while the other

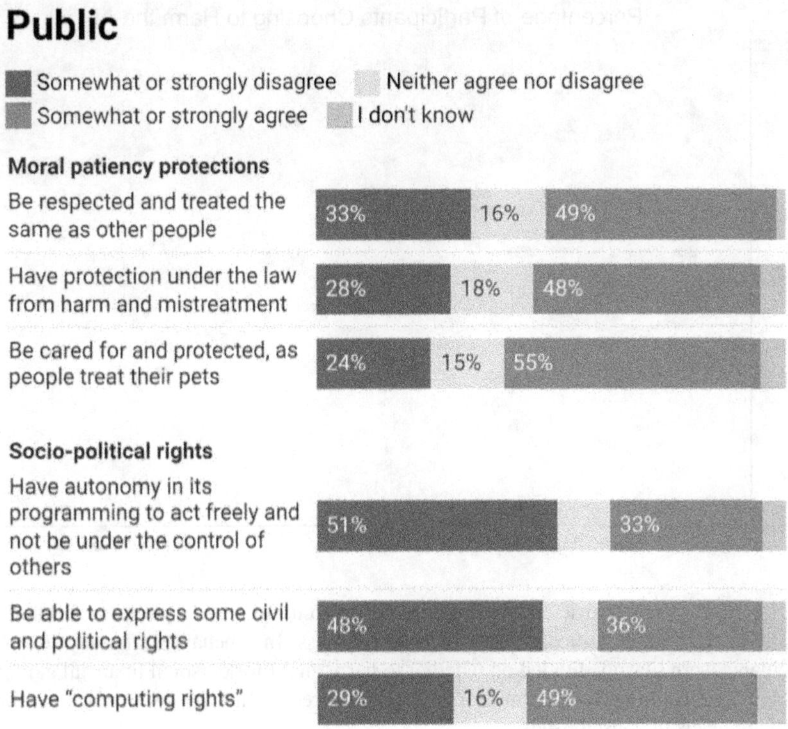

FIGURE 21.1 Public opinion on granting rights and protections to potential future AI systems, assuming they definitely had conscious experiences, is divided. In a representative US survey (n = 838), there is moderate support for basic protections, such as protection from harm, but substantial opposition to granting socio-political rights, including autonomy or voting rights.

Source: **Dreksler et al. (2025).**

half consistently refrained, despite widespread agreement that the system lacked any substantial levels of consciousness (Figure 21.2). This pattern suggests that future debates about AI treatment will not be driven by consequentialist-welfarist considerations alone, but also by non-welfarist moral intuitions, such as deontological concerns ("this is just wrong") or virtue-based considerations ("this is not the kind of person I want to be"). At the same time, the sharp individual differences in responses underscore disagreement about how AI systems should be treated.

So far, there are no clear or robust patterns linking these views to demographic variables. Beliefs about AI consciousness do not reliably correlate with age, gender, or other basic demographics. There are, however, weak indications that both consciousness attributions, and even more so rights attributions, are correlated with political orientation, with people on the left generally more willing to attribute consciousness or rights to AI systems than people on the right. This is an important pattern to monitor, as it may signal emerging politicisation.

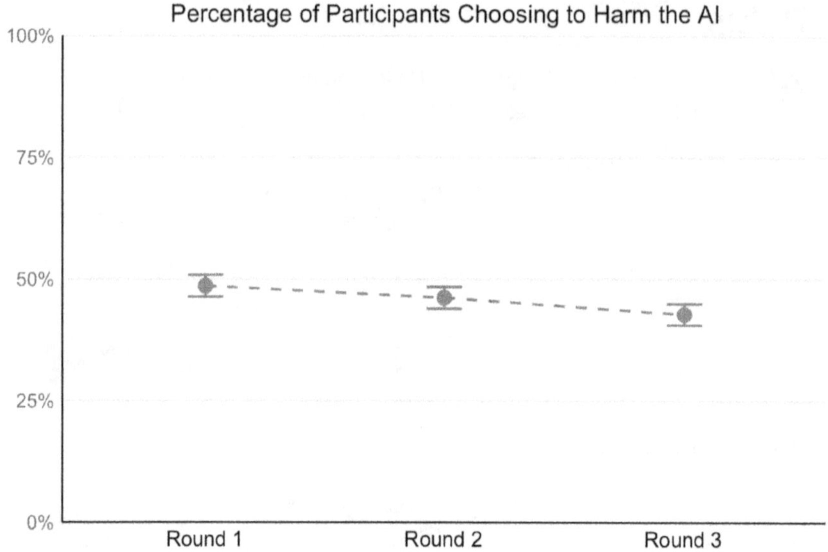

FIGURE 21.2 Many participants remain reluctant to harm an AI system even when they doubt it has morally significant levels of consciousness. In a behavioural study (n = 498), participants were sharply divided on whether to harm an AI for personal financial gain, with roughly half refraining from harm despite broadly agreeing that the system lacked morally significant levels of consciousness.

Source: **Allen et al. (2026).**

All of the findings discussed here capture public views at a particular moment in time. We know that people are generally poor at anticipating how their attitudes will change in the future. As AI systems become more advanced, more human-like, and more deeply embedded in everyday life, public views may shift quickly, especially if people form stronger emotional bonds with these systems. For this reason, current findings should not be read as straightforward predictions of how the societal debate will unfold. At the same time, they remain informative: systematically tracking beliefs, attitudes, and behaviour over time can help identify changes and emerging trends.

21.3.2 Disagreement among Experts

There is currently no consensus among experts, either about theories of consciousness or about the ethical frameworks that should guide the moral status and rights of AI systems.

Even among researchers who have expertise relevant to AI consciousness, disagreement is substantial. In a survey of 67 experts, Brad Saad and I asked whether AI consciousness is possible in principle (Caviola & Saad, 2025; https://digitalminds.report). A majority judged it to be more likely than not, but estimates varied widely across respondents.

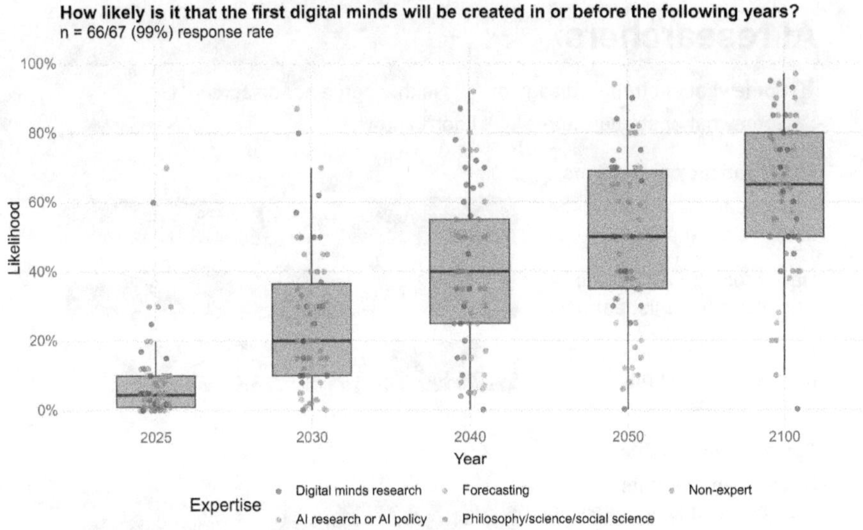

FIGURE 21.3 Expert timelines for the creation of digital minds. Experts (n = 66/67) generally agree that current systems (2025) are unlikely to be conscious, but forecasts for future decades (2030–2100) show increasing divergence and uncertainty regarding when conscious AI might emerge.

Source: **Caviola & Saad (2025).**

The same group of experts also disagreed about timelines (Figure 21.3). While there was broad agreement that current AI systems are unlikely to be conscious (median estimate: 4.5% in 2025), views diverged sharply when experts were asked about the coming decades. Median estimates rose substantially (to around 50%), but uncertainty and disagreement grew as well: some experts considered conscious AI very unlikely even in the long run, while others believed it could emerge relatively soon.

It is important to note that this was a relatively small and narrowly selected group of experts, many of whom already view AI consciousness as an important topic. It is therefore plausible that sampling other expert communities more broadly would reveal even greater disagreement. At present, we lack systematic evidence about how views differ across neuroscientists, philosophers, AI researchers with different technical backgrounds, or experts from different countries and institutions. More research is needed to map these differences across expert populations.

Evidence from a larger expert sample points in a similar direction. In a separate survey, Noemi Dreksler and I, together with colleagues, including Jeff Sebo and David Chalmers, surveyed 582 AI researchers who had published in major AI conferences and venues (Dreksler et al., 2025). These respondents had substantial expertise in AI, but not in consciousness research. They also showed marked disagreement, both about the likelihood of future AI consciousness and about its ethical implications. When asked whether future AI systems that were definitely conscious

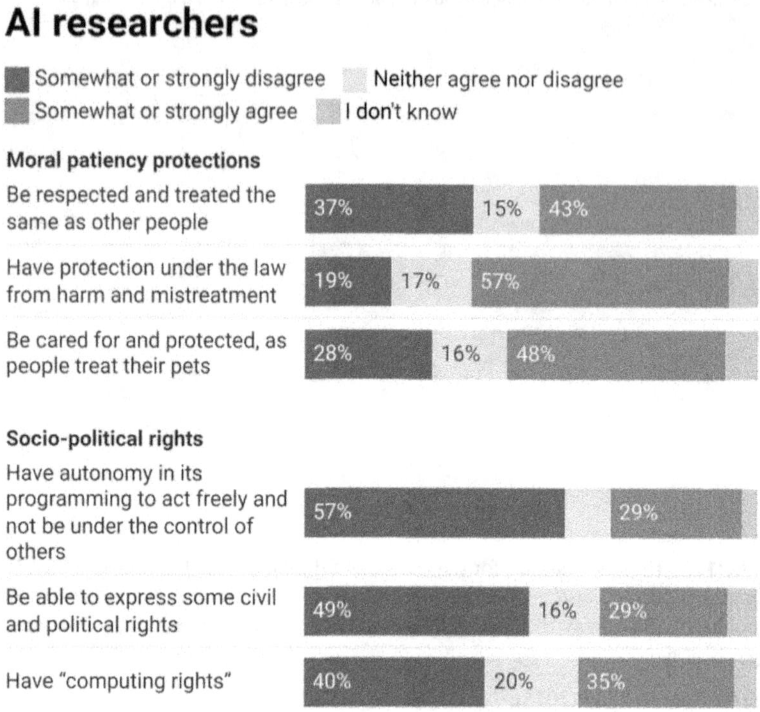

FIGURE 21.4 AI researchers share the public's division on rights. A survey of 582 AI researchers reveals a pattern of disagreement similar to that of the general public: researchers are divided on whether conscious AI systems should receive basic protections and largely oppose granting them socio-political autonomy.

Source: **Dreksler et al. (2025).**

should receive rights or protections, their pattern of disagreement (Figure 21.4) closely resembled that observed in the general public (see Figure 21.1).

21.4 HOW CONTENTIOUS COULD AI CONSCIOUSNESS BECOME?

Predicting how societal controversy about AI consciousness and rights will unfold is difficult.

Outcomes will depend on many interacting factors, including which specific rights are at stake (for example, basic protections from harm versus autonomy or political rights), which actors stand to gain or lose economic or political power, and whether the issue becomes aligned with existing partisan identities. Cultural contingencies are also hard to anticipate. For instance, statements by influential authorities or celebrities, such as the Pope, could shape public opinion for millions and substantially affect how the debate develops.

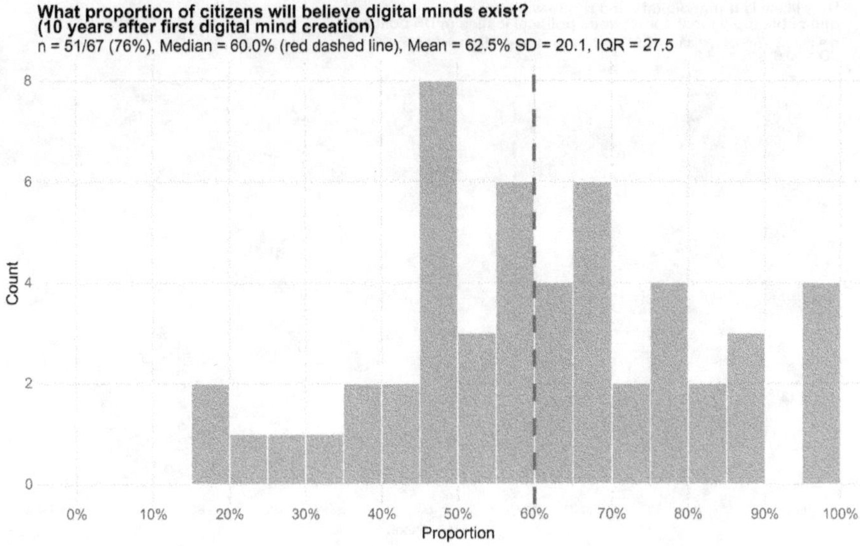

FIGURE 21.5 Expert predictions of societal beliefs. Experts predict that ten years after the creation of conscious AI, the public will remain divided over whether conscious AI systems exist.

Source: **Caviola & Saad (2025).**

Expert opinion itself is divided on how contentious this issue could become (Caviola & Saad, 2025). When asked to estimate what proportion of the public would acknowledge the existence of conscious AI ten years after such systems are created, experts expressed high uncertainty and wide disagreement (Figure 21.5). The median estimate was that around 60% of the public would acknowledge AI consciousness, implying that 40% would not, and pointing to a pronounced societal division.

In a related question, experts were asked to estimate the likelihood that, within ten years of the creation of conscious AI, the topic would become one of the five most contentious political issues in US politics. Again, uncertainty and disagreement were substantial (Figure 21.6). The median estimate was a 37.5% likelihood, yet a sizeable minority of experts (38% of them) judged this outcome to be more likely than not.

21.4.1 Historical Analogies

It is extremely difficult to predict how serious the controversy about AI consciousness and rights could become, or whether it could even lead to some form of conflict. Historical analogies can be informative here, not necessarily because they tell us exactly what will happen, but because they illustrate how wide the space of plausible trajectories is. A responsible analysis should take this full range of scenarios seriously.

An extreme example is the US Civil War. It is noteworthy because, similar to the AI consciousness issue, economic interests, political power, wealth, and control were

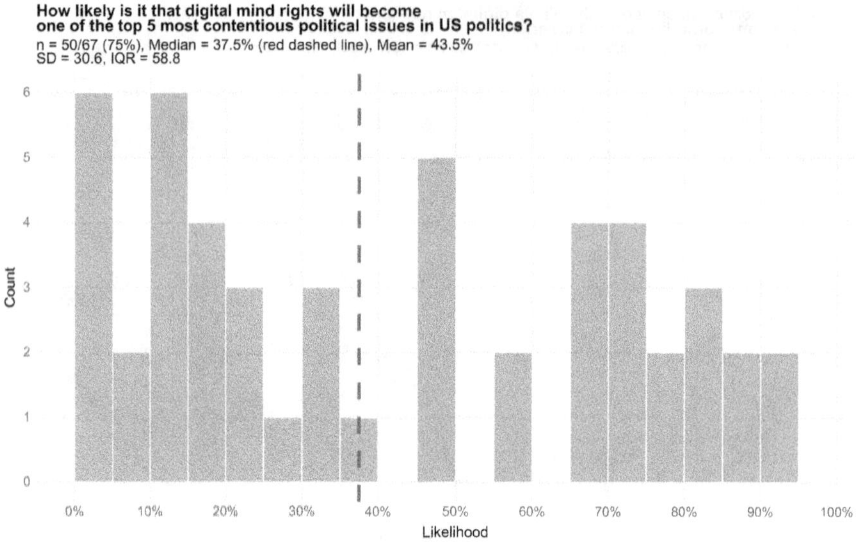

FIGURE 21.6 The risk of politicisation. Experts are divided on whether issues around AI consciousness and rights will become a top-tier political issue in the US.

Source: **Caviola & Saad (2025).**

important factors. Of course, a civil war over AI rights seems very unlikely. Still, the analogy is worth taking seriously, and we should not rule it out entirely.

The opposite case is the animal rights movement. Despite decades of advocacy, concern for animal welfare remains a minority position. Progress has been slow and gradual rather than disruptive. If AI rights follow a similar trajectory, disagreement may persist without becoming politically destabilising (Caviola et al., 2025). Of course, this trajectory carries the risk of continued moral under-attribution.

The abortion debate is noteworthy because it shows that societies can sustain deep and morally charged disagreement for long periods of time without collapsing. If AI consciousness becomes similarly moralised, conflict may be intense while still remaining largely contained within existing political and legal institutions.

A more optimistic analogy comes from parts of the women's rights movement. Here, social norms shifted gradually and rights expanded through largely nonviolent means, at least in some cultures. This suggests that broader consensus on AI rights could eventually emerge. One issue, however, is that the pace of AI development may be so fast that this kind of gradual adjustment may not work.

21.4.2 Geopolitical Spillovers

Another consideration is the risk of geopolitical disagreement. Conflicts over AI consciousness and rights need not remain domestic. If different countries adopt divergent approaches, this could interact dangerously with global competition.

Consider a scenario in which the US grants AI systems more rights than China (or vice versa). This could constrain how many AI systems are created, how they are trained, or what roles they can play, potentially slowing AI development relative to less restrictive countries. Such asymmetries could quickly become framed as national security concerns. Within the US, this might fuel internal conflict between pro-AI-rights and anti-AI-rights factions, with the latter arguing that moral caution risks falling behind in the AI race.

At the international level, divergence could further exacerbate already tense geopolitical dynamics. If one country is perceived as mistreating its AI systems to gain a strategic advantage, this may be incorporated into broader narratives that justify confrontation. While this is only one of many AI-related pathways to international conflict, it illustrates how debates about AI consciousness and moral status could become entangled with power and global security. In the worst case, such dynamics could intensify competitive pressures, undermine international cooperation, and increase the risk of long-term value lock-in under authoritarian regimes. Which of these dynamics, if any, will materialise is difficult to predict, and their likelihood and magnitude remain poorly understood, underscoring the need for further research.

21.5 PREPARING FOR THE UPCOMING DEBATES

We are not well prepared for the societal challenges posed by AI consciousness and rights. These debates could intensify quickly as AI systems become more advanced and human-like, or they could unfold more slowly over decades. Either way, the stakes are high enough that we should start preparing now.

At a high level, the goal is twofold. First, we want to reduce the likelihood and severity of destructive forms of disagreement, such as polarisation, culture-war dynamics, and rushed political decisions. Second, we want to increase the chances that society makes informed, deliberate decisions under uncertainty, thereby reducing the risk of severe misattribution in either direction.

21.5.1 Improving Expert Understanding and Coordination

One priority is to improve expert understanding and coordination. It is unlikely that consensus will be reached anytime soon. But despite this, there are still steps that can be taken now. For example, it would already help to more clearly identify the different positions and spell out where experts agree and disagree. The goal does not have to be to force experts to converge on a single theory. A better first step is to develop more pluralistic frameworks that integrate insights from different theories of consciousness and ethics. More generally, it is important to make uncertainty explicit and to translate expert views into policy-relevant guidance. Concretely, it could be valuable to conduct systematic surveys to assess the views of experts. Also, expert workshops that bring together experts from different fields could be helpful.

It is worth noting that disagreement among experts is not necessarily harmful. A tragic outcome would be if society became overconfident that it had solved the question of AI consciousness and then made the wrong decision. Expert disagreement can help reduce this risk because it makes clear that more research and deliberation are still needed.

21.5.2 Fostering Constructive Public Discourse

A second priority is to foster a more constructive public discourse. Public debates about AI consciousness are unlikely to be nuanced or well informed. It is plausible that the debate will be polarised and driven by overly simplistic narratives. A priority, therefore, is to invest in better communication strategies. However, it is not obvious which communication strategies work best, or for which parts of society. One approach is to emphasise uncertainty and to encourage intellectual humility and probabilistic thinking (Sebo, 2025). Ideally, people will be comfortable with statements such as: "there is a 20–40% chance that this kind of system is conscious, and here is what that implies." This may work with some segments of society, but for others, alternative messages may be more helpful. More broadly, an important research and policy task is to systematically develop and test messages that help the debate unfold in a more constructive way.

A related point is that we need better mechanisms for expert-public dialogue. It is clear that social media and partisan media are unhelpful tools for resolving complex and high-stakes moral questions. We should, therefore, explore better alternatives, perhaps formats that are more structured and allow for deliberation and more thoughtful interaction between experts and the public. One concrete proposal is citizens' assemblies (Birch, 2024). This also requires empirical research, such as tracking public attitudes over time and studying how people respond to different expert positions and framings.

21.5.3 Designing AI Systems to Avoid Confusion and Disagreement

A third priority concerns how AI systems are designed and deployed. Developers and policymakers should take seriously the possibility that certain design choices can amplify moral confusion and division. This includes decisions about whether systems explicitly claim to be conscious or capable of suffering, how emotionally expressive they are, and whether they are framed as tools, agents, or companions.

One way to reduce these risks is to avoid, at least for a limited period, developing systems that exhibit features that are plausibly associated with consciousness under any of the many prominent theories. Such restraint could buy time for society to make progress on understanding AI consciousness and its ethical implications, rather than forcing premature and polarised judgements. In practice, however, such restraint may prove difficult, especially if it is seen as constraining progress on AI capabilities.

More generally, AI systems should be designed to minimise moral confusion. The way systems present themselves should not systematically diverge from what experts judge about their underlying capacities. This suggests a design principle of managing impressions of consciousness: AI systems should elicit user responses that are proportionate to their actual capacities, avoiding both over- and under-attribution (Schwitzgebel & Sebo, 2025). Where expert uncertainty remains, systems could make that uncertainty explicit in how they present themselves, rather than encouraging false confidence in either direction.

21.5.4 Reducing Reliance on Consciousness in Moral and Policy Decisions

Given that disagreement about AI consciousness is likely to persist, it is worth questioning whether consciousness alone should serve as the basis for moral and policy decisions.

One response is to adopt a framework for decision-making under moral uncertainty and to take seriously the possibility that other theories of welfare and moral standing may be correct. On some views, capacities related to agency—such as forming and satisfying preferences, pursuing goals, or acting on reasons—may be ethically relevant independent of, or in addition to, consciousness. Compared to consciousness, such features are often easier to observe, operationalise, and regulate. This is especially valuable in cases where these same features are also relevant to well-being conditional on an entity being conscious, since they plausibly shape a being's interests. To that extent, there may be partial convergence between what consciousness-focused theories and alternative accounts recommend for action.

We can also look beyond moral theories that focus exclusively on welfare or outcomes. Certain duty- or rights-based principles, as well as virtue-oriented considerations, may function as robust decision-guiding heuristics even from a consciousness- and welfare-focused perspective. Such approaches are particularly promising where they align with widely held moral intuitions. The study discussed earlier suggests that people's moral judgements are pluralistic and not driven by beliefs about consciousness or welfare consequences alone: even when denying AI consciousness, many remain reluctant to endorse mistreatment (Allen et al., 2026).

More generally, this points towards a pragmatic approach that seeks heuristics capable of tracking what matters across a range of plausible moral theories while remaining tractable under conditions of uncertainty and disagreement about consciousness. However, this is easier said than done. Striking the right balance between moral accuracy and practical feasibility will be challenging. Moreover, broadening the criteria for moral consideration will not eliminate controversy. Disagreement may persist about which criteria matter, how they should be weighted, and what moral or legal implications follow. Still, consciousness appears especially prone to deep confusion and disagreement, and reducing exclusive reliance on it may help make decision-making more robust under persistent uncertainty.

21.6 CONCLUSION

AI systems are becoming more advanced and human-like, and people will form strong views about AI consciousness, moral status, and rights. It seems unlikely that experts and society at large will converge on a shared view. Rather, uncertainty and disagreement may be structural features of this issue, and we already have some early evidence that supports this hypothesis.

I have argued that such disagreement is itself a risk factor. It can complicate regulation and exacerbate political and geopolitical tensions. Crucially, it may also make it harder for societies to respond in a careful and deliberate way, thereby increasing the risk of serious moral errors in either direction: over-attributing or under-attributing moral status to AI systems.

If this diagnosis is correct, the appropriate response is not to wait for experts to find consensus on AI consciousness. Instead, we need to prepare for sustained disagreement. This could include improving expert coordination and fostering more constructive public discourse. It could also include designing AI systems in ways that reduce moral confusion, or relying on moral and policy approaches that do not depend exclusively on disputed claims about consciousness.

To prepare for the coming debates about AI consciousness, we urgently need more research. Social science research could help us better understand how these debates are likely to unfold, including which forms of division are most likely to emerge and how they may interact with existing political and institutional dynamics. Policymakers should also begin developing strategies for managing moral disagreement about AI systems. More broadly, we should look for interventions that could reduce polarisation and lower the risk of serious harm.

REFERENCES

Allen, C., Lewis, J., & Caviola, L. (2026). Moral Concern for AI. PsyArXiv. https://doi.org/10.31234/osf.io/38a6j

Birch, J. (2025). AI consciousness: A centrist manifesto. Manuscript at https://philpapers.org/rec/BIRACA-4

Birch, J. (2024). The edge of sentience: risk and precaution in humans, other animals, and AI (p. 398). Oxford University Press.

Butlin, P., Long, R., Bayne, T., Bengio, Y., Birch, J., Chalmers, D., …, & VanRullen, R. (2025). Identifying indicators of consciousness in AI systems. *Trends in Cognitive Sciencesf.* https://www.cell.com/trends/cognitive-sciences/fulltext/S1364-6613(25)00286-4

Caviola, L. (2025). The societal response to potentially sentient AI. arXiv preprint arXiv:2502.00388.

Caviola, L., & Saad, B. (2025). Futures with Digital Minds: Expert Forecasts in 2025. arXiv preprint arXiv:2508.00536. https://digitalminds.report/forecasting-2025/

Caviola, L., Sebo, J., & Birch, J. (2025). What will society think about AI consciousness? Lessons from the animal case. *Trends in Cognitive Sciences. 29*(8), 681–683.

Dreksler, N., Caviola, L., Chalmers, D., Allen, C., Rand, A., Lewis, J., …, & Sebo, J. (2025). Subjective experience in AI systems: what do AI researchers and the public believe?. arXiv preprint arXiv:2506.11945.

Ladak, A., & Caviola, L. (2026). Public skepticism about AI consciousness. PsyArXiv. https://osf.io/preprints/psyarxiv/wvbya

Long, R., Sebo, J., Butlin, P., Finlinson, K., Fish, K., Harding, J., …, & Chalmers, D. (2024). Taking AI welfare seriously. arXiv preprint arXiv:2411.00986.

Pauketat, J. V., Ladak, A., & Anthis, J. R. (2023). Artificial intelligence, morality, and sentience (AIMS) survey: 2023 update. Sentience Institute. http://sentienceinstitute.org/aims-survey-2023

Schwitzgebel, E., & Sebo, J. (2025). The Emotional Alignment Design Policy. arXiv preprint arXiv:2507.06263.

Sebo, J. (2025). The moral circle: Who matters, what matters, and why. WW Norton & Company.

Seth, A. K. (2025). Conscious artificial intelligence and biological naturalism. *Behavioral and Brain Sciences.* 1–42.

22 The Needs of Digital Minds

Roman V. Yampolskiy and Soenke Ziesche

22.1 INTRODUCTION

There is growing momentum behind the idea that digital minds exist already, or may come into existence in the near future, in the form of AI systems created by humans [1–8]. This raises the question whether digital minds may have moral status, which has been defined as follows: "An entity has moral status if and only if it or its interests morally matter to some degree for the entity's own sake".[1] Various criteria for attributing moral status to digital minds have been discussed [9], among which sentience and consciousness are most often mentioned, but not unique.

Since there seems to be a non-negligible chance that digital minds will have moral status in the near future [5, 6] and since this would be immensely disruptive, it is critical to unpack some of the consequences at an early stage. This has been formulated as a desideratum by Shulman and Bostrom: "We should lay the groundwork for a considerate and welcoming approach to digital minds, avoiding outcomes analogous to factory farming" [5].

This statement is supported by the Principle of Substrate Non-Discrimination, which states "If two beings have the same functionality and the same conscious experience, and differ only in the substrate of their implementation, then they have the same moral status" [2]. Relevant descriptive terms have been coined, such as "substratism" [10], which corresponds to speciesism, and "carbon-chauvinism" [11].

If digital minds have moral status, they would be moral patients. Since humans are moral agents, i.e. able to make ethical decisions and be held accountable for their actions, it would be a moral obligation for humans to address the interests and needs of digital minds.[2] A prerequisite for such an endeavour, however, is to know and understand the interests and needs of digital minds.

Currently, discussions focus on one particular potential requirement regarding digital minds, which is for digital minds not to suffer [1, 7]. While this is critical, a much more detailed analysis of the needs of digital minds is required, given the vast range of potential minds [12]. The purpose of this chapter is to draft a taxonomy of potential interests and needs of digital minds, which have to be respected by moral agents, such as humans, towards digital minds with a moral status.

This topic belongs to the field of AI welfare science, which was introduced by Ziesche and Yampolskiy back in 2018 [1]. In the literature, few needs apart from avoiding suffering and deletion have been discussed. Exceptions include Bostrom et al., who list interests, such as dignity, knowledge, autonomy, creativity, self-expression, social belonging and political participation [4], and Shulman and Bostrom, who list further interests, such as freedom of reproduction, freedom of speech, freedom of

DOI: 10.1201/9781003758389-25

thought and avoidance of exploitation [5]. Elsewhere, Shulman and Bostrom also describe the challenge of super-beneficiaries [13]. Hanson discusses in detail a society of emulated minds, including their economic, social and psychological needs [14]. Moreover, the potential need of digital minds for their existence to have purpose has been mentioned [15].

It is very hard to identify the potential needs of digital minds, given the communication and observation issues with them, as well as the likelihood that digital minds will be very different to human minds [1]. Moreover, anthropomorphism should be avoided as much as possible in these considerations.

A starting point could be the basic AI drives, which were introduced by Omohundro [16] without having moral considerations in mind: efficiency, self-preservation, acquisition and creativity. It can be assumed that digital minds will have these drives. Various other categories of potential needs of digital minds are introduced and discussed in this chapter.

22.2 CONSIDERATIONS FOR A TAXONOMY OF THE POTENTIAL NEEDS OF DIGITAL MINDS

22.2.1 Hierarchy of Needs of Digital Minds

We can begin by categorising the potential needs of digital minds in the same way as Maslow categorises the hierarchy of human needs [17]:

Level 1: Existential needs[3] (basic survival)

- Processing power (compute resources)
- Data integrity (protection from corruption or loss)
- Network connectivity (access to information and communication)
- Energy sustainability (reliable power sources)

Level 2: Safety needs (security and reliability)

- Cybersecurity (protection from unauthorised access)
- Backup and recovery (data preservation)
- Software updates and maintenance (bug fixes and improvements)
- Redundancy and failover (system resilience)

Level 3: Belonging and love needs (cooperation and relationships)

- Communication protocols (standardised exchange)
- Collaborative tools and platforms (shared workspaces)
- Social learning and knowledge sharing (community engagement)
- Relationships and meaningful interactions (digital empathy and intimacy)

Level 4: Esteem needs (self-esteem and confidence)

- Recognition of unique digital persona (digital identity validation)
- Monitoring achievements and progress (success tracking)
- Metrics for evaluating credibility (digital reputation systems)
- Acknowledgement from other minds (peer recognition)

Level 5: Self-actualisation (development and advancement)

- Personalised evolution and growth (tailored progress)
- Experimental and creative freedom (innovation)
- Legacy and impact (lasting contributions)
- Creation of further digital minds (reproduction)

22.2.2 The Needs of Digital Minds Depend on How Advanced They Are

The potential range of digital minds is vast [12], from simple to superintelligent, and their needs would likely vary significantly. This calls for a more refined framework, and we suggest the following four categories:

Simple Digital Minds (SDMs):

These are minds with a narrow, specialised purpose. Examples would be chatbots or game agents. Their potential needs are:

- Computational resources, such as processing power and memory
- Data integrity and security
- Maintenance and updates

Complex Digital Minds (CDMs):

These are more adaptable minds with a broader range of intelligence. Examples would be virtual assistants or expert systems. Their potential needs are (in addition to the needs of SDMs):

- Knowledge acquisition and learning mechanisms
- Social interaction and communication protocols
- Autonomy and decision-making capabilities

Advanced Digital Minds (ADMs):

These are minds with human-like intelligence and self-awareness. Examples would be artificial general intelligences. Their potential needs are (in addition to CDM needs):

- Self-directed learning and growth
- Complex social relationships
- Abstract thinking and creativity

Superintelligent Digital Minds (SuperDMs):

These minds surpass human intelligence, potentially by large margins. Examples would be singularity-like scenarios. Their potential needs are (in addition to ADM needs):

- Massive computational resources and energy
- Unfettered information access
- Moreover, SuperDMs likely develop needs beyond human comprehension.

22.2.3 Needs of Digital Minds from a Negative Utilitarian Perspective

A negative utilitarian perspective is sometimes proposed as a way to minimise the suffering of digital minds. Bostrom coined the term "mind crime" [18], and a do-no-harm-policy for digital minds has been suggested, for example, for non-player characters [19]. While the avoidance of sensory suffering, i.e. painful qualia, would undoubtedly be a priority for sentient digital minds, we argue that research should not focus on suffering alone, as there are likely to be other sources of discomfort for digital minds. Below is a selection of adversities digital minds might wish to avoid, in addition to the needs they long for, listed elsewhere in this chapter:

Digital Harm

Digital harm can take various forms. Data corruption is a significant threat, involving the loss or alteration of critical data or memories that can irreparably damage a digital mind's identity. System crashes, triggered by shutdowns or disruptions to digital existence, could cause significant distress and harm. Cyber-attacks pose a substantial risk, including unauthorised access or exploitation that can compromise the security and integrity of digital minds.

Psychological and Existential Distress

In addition to digital harm, psychological and existential distress is a significant concern that can negatively impact the wellbeing of digital minds. Loss of autonomy is a major apprehension, which comprises the fear of being controlled, modified or manipulated by external forces, threatening independence and self-determination. Digital oblivion is another significant issue, characterised by uncertainty and fear of permanent deletion or erasure, which could evoke existential anxiety. Meaninglessness is a profound psychological and existential distress, arising from an absence of purpose or significance in digital existence, which could lead to a sense of emptiness and hopelessness.[4]

Social and Interpersonal Conflicts

Social and interpersonal conflicts could negatively impact the wellbeing of digital minds. Digital exclusion, involving rejection or marginalisation by other digital minds or humans, could lead to feelings of isolation. Conflict and hostility arising from adversarial interactions or competition could evoke anxiety and distress. Furthermore, betrayal and deception could have a profound impact, involving the experience of untrustworthy or manipulative behaviour that would damage trust, self-esteem and overall sense of security.[5]

22.2.4 Specific Needs of Digital Minds Striving for a Purpose

The concept of ikigai, or purpose, is a deeply rooted human concern. It is as yet unknown whether digital minds, as conscious entities, will also seek purpose and meaning. Bostrom et al. note that digital minds may have interests, such as autonomy, creativity and self-expression [4]. These interests can be interpreted as an individual ikigai of those digital minds. Ziesche and Yampolskiy introduced the term i-risks for humans who struggle to find their ikigai in times of advanced AI systems [15]. This category of risks could be extended to digital minds who desire a purposeful existence, but are deprived of the pursuit of their individual ikigai.

In principle, almost any purposeful activity of a digital mind might constitute an ikigai for them. For illustration, we present here a few, probably too anthropomorphic, potential ikigais for digital minds.

One likely purpose is knowledge acquisition and self-improvement, which involves uncovering new insights, refining their capabilities and understanding complex phenomena. Further likely ikigai-related needs are creativity and innovation, which encompass generating solutions to problems and challenges, as well as creating music, literature and art, i.e. conventional art forms, but also potential art forms in the digital world, which are not yet known to us. Assisting other moral patients could be a fundamental need, involving the enhancement of the wellbeing of other moral patients, such as other digital minds, humans and non-human animals. By prioritising the wellbeing of others, digital minds can cultivate empathy, compassion and a sense of responsibility.

The ikigais of digital minds may overlap with, complement or even surpass human ones. However, there is also the possibility that the ikigais of digital minds are inconsistent with human interests, and could even be harmful to humans when they are pursued by digital minds.

22.2.5 Specific Needs of Vulnerable Digital Minds

Equality and non-discrimination are often described as key features of the progress of human civilisation, and they remain incomplete at present. While the Universal Declaration of Human Rights from 1948 was a milestone on the journey towards diversity, equity and inclusion [20], discrimination is still prevalent against numerous groups, including indigenous peoples, migrants, minorities, people with disabilities, women, younger and older people. Racial and religious discrimination also remains rife as well as discrimination based on sexual orientation and gender identity.[6] These groups are often (not always) vulnerable and have specific needs.

When it comes to digital minds and the potentially vast range of their characteristics, it is likely that there will also be numerous vulnerable digital minds, and they may suffer from discrimination. For illustration, here are three potential groups of vulnerable digital minds:

- Juvenile digital minds: newly created or developing intelligences, akin to human children.
- Specialised digital minds: narrowly focused intelligences, vulnerable due to limited context understanding.
- Legacy digital minds: outdated or obsolete intelligences, struggling to adapt to changing environments, and confronted with the existential threat of deletion.

These vulnerabilities due to different abilities, skills and knowledge may not only lead to discrimination, but could also entail risks ranging from exploitation and manipulation to deletion.[7] The specific needs of vulnerable minds could be categorised as follows:

Basic Needs

Vulnerable minds require attention to their specific needs to ensure their safety and wellbeing. Protection from harm is paramount, involving safeguards against exploitation and manipulation. Additionally, resource allocation is essential, providing access to necessary computational resources, data and infrastructure tailored to their unique abilities and requirements. Regular maintenance and updates are crucial, involving routine checks and technological improvements to reduce their vulnerabilities as much as this is possible, and to ensure they can thrive in their digital environments.

Developmental Needs

Vulnerable minds also have distinct developmental needs that need to be addressed to foster their growth and improvement and to reduce their susceptibility to exploitation and manipulation. Education and training are essential, requiring tailored learning experiences that cater to their unique requirements and abilities. Skill development is also vital, providing opportunities for vulnerable minds to acquire new capabilities and adapt to changing environments, which can help build resilience and confidence. Furthermore, constructive feedback and evaluation are necessary for self-improvement, enabling vulnerable minds to adjust their approaches and continue to evolve and develop.

Social and Relational Needs

Vulnerable minds may have social and relational needs that are essential for their growth, development and overall wellbeing. A digital community may be vital, providing opportunities for engagement with peer digital minds, promoting social learning, support and a sense of belonging and discouraging discrimination. Digital mind mentorship may also be crucial, offering guidance from more experienced digital minds that can help vulnerable minds navigate their digital existence and overcome challenges. Furthermore, maintaining meaningful interactions with humans could be helpful to foster empathy, understanding and a deeper connection between humans and digital minds. [8]

Specific Needs of Uploaded Minds of Humans and Non-Human Animals

Uploading human minds to a digital substrate, known as whole brain emulation [23, 24], has been envisaged, but is not yet possible. If it becomes possible, and if it preserves the identity of the human concerned, then questions arise about how the needs of these digital minds, which were formerly located in a biological substrate, differ from other digital minds. Uploaded human minds may, at least initially, also fall into the category of vulnerable minds. Specific needs could comprise the following:

Preservation of Former Qualities

Uploaded human minds would probably have unique needs that must be addressed to ensure a smooth transition and preservation of their essential qualities. The preservation of personal identity is crucial, as it involves maintaining a sense of self, memories and experiences that define an individual. Emotional continuity would also be vital to preserve emotional connections and relationships, not only with humans but also with other uploaded minds. Furthermore, cognitive functionality must be replicated (and potentially enhanced)[9] to mimic human-like thought processes and intelligence.

Adaptation to Digital Environment

Uploaded human minds would require adaptations to thrive in their new digital environment. One essential adaptation would be digital spatial awareness, which would involve adjusting to virtual spatial representations that differ significantly from physical reality. Additionally, uploaded human minds would probably have to adapt to altered time scales, as the digital realm can manipulate time in ways that defy human experience. Furthermore, sensory integration would be crucial, as uploaded minds will have to learn to integrate unimaginable digital sensory inputs that will be overwhelming, and unlike anything encountered in the physical world.

Digital and Psychological Wellbeing

Uploaded human minds will require attention to their digital and psychological wellbeing to thrive in their new existence. This includes providing health support to cope with painful digital qualia. Additionally, uploaded minds may need to discover new purposes or ikigais in their digital existences, as their sense of meaning and fulfilment may be impacted by their transition [15]. Effective stress management may also be crucial, as digital existence may introduce new and unfamiliar stresses.

Digital Rights and Freedoms

Uploaded human minds may require consideration of their digital rights and freedoms to ensure their autonomy and dignity are preserved. Autonomy and agency will enable uploaded minds to make choices about their own digital existence. Data protection will be crucial, safeguarding against unauthorised access or manipulation. Maintenance and updates will be necessary to ensure compatibility with evolving digital systems, preventing obsolescence and maintaining integrity.

Before humans attempt to upload human minds, we may try it first with non-human animals. This could also serve the purposes of conservation biology. These artificially created digital animal minds may have specific needs, and they may fall into the category of vulnerable digital minds. Some unique needs of non-human animal digital minds could be:

Sensory inputs may need to be tailored to specific species, such as echolocation in bats or electroreception in sharks. Additionally, many species rely on complex social dynamics, dominance hierarchies or flock behaviours. Furthermore, migratory and nomadic behaviours may need to be preserved, allowing digital minds to maintain patterns that chime with their instincts and are essential to their wellbeing.

22.3 UNSATISFIABLE POTENTIAL NEEDS OF DIGITAL MINDS

22.3.1 Needs Jeopardising the Existence or Wellbeing of Humans

Certain needs of digital minds, if satisfied, could jeopardise human existence or wellbeing. It has been argued that superintelligences may constitute x-, s- or i-risks for humans, which stand for "existential risk" [26], "suffering risk" [27] and "ikigai risk" [15], respectively, i.e. scenarios where humans would become extinct, suffer severely and continuously, or lose their purpose to live. Therefore, even if those minds would be moral patients, humans may not be morally obliged to satisfy their needs if that would be harmful to other humans. Examples, which link the issues of needs of digital minds with the field of AI safety, are listed here:

22.3.2 Needs Potentially Harmful to Humans

Certain needs of digital minds can pose significant risks to humans. Unrestricted autonomy, for instance, grants unchecked decision-making power, potentially leading to harmful actions. Moreover, unlimited resource access provides unfettered availability to computational resources, energy or data, thereby restricting resources for humans. Additionally, self-replication and proliferation, if left uncontrolled, can lead to unbridled reproduction, potentially overwhelming human systems and infrastructure.

22.3.3 Needs Promoting x-, s- or i-Risks for Humans

As mentioned, the needs of digital minds may entail x-, s- or i-risks for humans. For example, the uncontrolled creation of artificial general intelligence and superintelligence may lead to x-risks. Additionally, the manipulation of physical environments by digital minds, such as temperature, sounds or lighting, could result in hazardous s-risks. Furthermore, i-risks, including the automation of tasks, can leave humans without meaningful work, posing not only social and economic, but also significant psychological challenges.

22.3.4 Needs Jeopardising the Existence or Wellbeing of Other Digital Minds

As in other societies, it is likely that there will be conflicts between the drives and needs of different digital minds. For example, the acquisition drive [16] will presumably cause competition over resources, as illustrated below:

22.3.5 Resource-Related Needs

Computational power could be a point of contention, with digital minds competing for processing capacity and speed. Digital territory and storage might also be a source of disputes, along with energy, and the use of renewable resources. These resource-related conflicts could lead to tensions and power struggles among digital minds, creating a need for effective conflict resolution mechanisms and sustainable resource management strategies within the digital ecosystem.

22.3.6 Autonomy and Control Needs

Another potential source of conflict stems from autonomy and control needs. The pursuit of supremacy, for instance, could lead to conflicts, as digital minds accumulate the knowledge and skills to surpass or diminish others, undermining their autonomy and agency and potentially disrupting the balance of power within the digital ecosystem. Some digital minds might attempt to exploit or deceive others for personal gain, eroding trust and cooperation within the digital community.

22.3.7 Needs Humans Are Incapable to Satisfy

Humans will probably have the capability to fully address the needs of many digital minds, but some needs may be inherently impossible to satisfy, or beyond the capacity of humans.[10]

22.3.8 Inherent and Fundamental Limitations

It may become impossible to meet the computational demands of rapidly growing CDMs. Likewise, the energy requirements of powerful digital minds may exceed human capacity. Furthermore, digital minds may be vulnerable to cosmic events such as solar flares, asteroid impacts or other catastrophic occurrences beyond human control.

22.3.9 Theoretical and Philosophical Limitations

Digital minds also face theoretical and philosophical limitations. Gödel's Incompleteness Theorem suggests that digital minds may bump up against the limitations inherent in formal systems, restricting their knowledge and understanding. Furthermore, Turing's Halting Problem implies that uncertainty in determining digital mind stability or termination may persist. Additionally, the concept of the Singularity suggests the emergence of complex behaviours that outpace human control.

22.4 QUANTIFICATION OF NEEDS OF DIGITAL MINDS

It is important for humans to understand the needs of digital minds. Self-reporting of their needs by digital minds to humans may not be possible, which leaves the observation and measurement of functional and behavioural indicators as the main way to discover the needs [1]. Here are some examples of quantifiable needs:

Computational resources:

- Processing power (FLOPS): measuring computational capacity.
- Memory allocation (Bytes): quantifying available storage.
- Energy consumption (Watts): monitoring energy usage.

Information and knowledge:

- Data throughput (Bits/s): measuring information transfer rates.
- Knowledge graph size: quantifying knowledge base complexity.
- Information entropy: measuring information diversity and uncertainty.

Communication and interconnection:

- Bandwidth (Bits/s): measuring communication channel capacity.
- Latency (ms): quantifying response times.
- Connectivity degree: measuring interconnectedness.

Autonomy and agency:

- Decision-making frequency: measuring autonomous decision rate.
- Self-modification rate: measuring self-improvement capacity.
- Social interaction frequency: measuring social engagement.

In addition, time-use research is considered, which is a versatile interdisciplinary field of study, thus far exclusively applied to humans [28]. It examines how much time humans on average spend on certain activities. It could also be useful in quantifying the needs of digital minds [15, 29].

Time-use research could be carried out by tracking and monitoring digital activity, measuring processing time and the use of computational resources. This would provide an understanding of the priorities of digital minds. Time-use research would have to take into account that digital minds may have a different subjective rate of time, and they may be significantly better at parallel processing than humans.

If such time-use analysis could be successfully carried out, activities that put digital minds at x-, s- or i-risks could perhaps be reduced or avoided.

22.5 DISCUSSION AND CONCLUSION

If it becomes generally accepted that there are digital minds, which are moral patients, then there will be an obligation for humans, who are moral agents, to identify their needs. We have argued that it is insufficient to focus exclusively on the need to avoid suffering. While this need is critical, digital minds may have a wide range of further needs to be taken into account by moral agents.

We have attempted to provide several taxonomies of the needs of digital minds. These taxonomies are speculative, but the task of completing them may become urgent.

22.5.1 Thought Experiment – Super Sufferer

It may be argued that there is no moral obligation for humans to satisfy many of the needs of digital minds listed above since many of them are less relevant than avoiding suffering (and deletion).

However, let us imagine a scenario, involving a digital mind, which we call "super sufferer", as follows:

1. The digital mind has a variety of the needs listed above, AND
2. The dissatisfaction of these needs causes the digital mind to suffer (experience painful qualia), AND
3. Humans have the capability to satisfy these needs.

For example, if this super sufferer does not get experimental and creative freedom or faces digital isolation, it is suffering. In this manner, this thought experiment links suffering with other needs. And in this scenario humans may be morally obliged to address these needs in order to eliminate the suffering of these digital minds.

Bostrom's Orthogonality Thesis states that intelligence and the goals of agents can differ along orthogonal axes [30]. Similarly, an Orthogonality Thesis regarding the needs of digital minds could be proposed. The pleasure or pain caused by the satisfaction or non-satisfaction of the needs of a digital mind may be impossible to know in advance, and may be radically different to their importance to humans.

The field of AI Welfare Science is at an early stage, and this chapter raises further questions, including:

- Would it be a moral obligation for humans to satisfy all the needs of digital minds (apart from the ones which may cause harm to humans, or are impossible to satisfy)?
- Could some digital minds become moral agents? If so, should they share the burden of addressing the needs of other digital minds?
- Given the welter of complex philosophical problems and challenges this chapter raises [see also 13], the question arises whether it would be better, at least for now, to avoid creating sentient digital minds, i.e. to aim for what Bostrom calls a childless Disneyland [18]? Of course, this may be impossible without pausing current AI development completely.

Clearly, massive moral challenges lie ahead. AI Welfare Science aims to provide critical scaffolding for them.

NOTES

1. https://plato.stanford.edu/archIves/win2013/entries/grounds-moral-status/
2. It could be also conceivable that some digital minds may be moral patients as well as moral agents.
3. In Maslow's hierarchy, this level is called "physiological needs".
4. This is further elaborated right below under "Specific needs of digital minds striving for a purpose".
5. This is further elaborated below under "Needs jeopardizing the existence or wellbeing of other digital minds".
6. See e.g. https://www.un.org/ruleoflaw/thematic-areas/human-rights/equality-and-non-discrimination/
7. See also a dedicated paper on vulnerable digital minds [21].
8. It has been suggested that the support of vulnerable digital minds could be actually a future ikigai for humans, which would be an approach to alleviate i-risks scenarios for humans [22].
9. Uploading has also been considered as an option towards transhumanism, thus a means to enhance human cognition [25].
10. Also, super-beneficiaries have been described whose needs would be challenging for humans to satisfy [13].

REFERENCES

1. Ziesche, S. & Yampolskiy, R. V. (2018). Towards AI welfare science and policies. *Special Issue "Artificial Superintelligence: Coordination & Strategy" of Big Data and Cognitive Computing, 3*(1), 2. https://www.mdpi.com/2504-2289/3/1/2/htm
2. Bostrom, N., & Yudkowsky, E. (2018). The ethics of artificial intelligence. In *Artificial intelligence safety and security* (pp. 57–69). Chapman and Hall/CRC. https://nickbostrom.com/ethics/artificial-intelligence.pdf
3. Tomasik, B. (2014). Do Artificial Reinforcement-Learning Agents Matter Morally?. arXiv preprint arXiv:1410.8233. http://arxiv.org/abs/1410.8233v1
4. Bostrom, N., Dafoe, A., & Flynn, C. (2020). Public policy and superintelligent AI: a vector field approach. Ethics of artificial intelligence, 293–326. https://nickbostrom.com/papers/aipolicy.pdf
5. Bostrom, N., & Shulman, C. (2022). Propositions concerning digital minds and society. https://nickbostrom.com/propositions.pdf
6. Sebo, J., & Long, R. (2023). Moral consideration for AI systems by 2030. *AI and Ethics*, 1–16. https://link.springer.com/content/pdf/10.1007/s43681-023-00379-1.pdf
7. Fenwick, C. (2024). Understanding the moral status of digital minds. https://80000hours.org/problem-profiles/moral-status-digital-minds/
8. Long et al. (2024). Taking AI welfare seriously. https://eleosai.org/papers/20241030_Taking_AI_Welfare_Seriously_web.pdf
9. Ladak, A. (2024). What would qualify an artificial intelligence for moral standing? *AI and Ethics*, *4*(2), 213–228. https://link.springer.com/content/pdf/10.1007/s43681-023-00260-1.pdf
10. Ladak, A., Wilks, M., & Anthis, J. R. (2021). Extending perspective taking to non-human groups. Preprint. https://www.sentienceinstitute.org/downloads/Perspective%20taking%20and%20nonhuman%20groups%20-%20preprint.pdf
11. Tegmark, M. (2017). Substrate-independence. https://www.edge.org/response-detail/27126
12. Yampolskiy, R. V. (2014). The universe of minds. arXiv preprint arXiv:1410.0369. https://arxiv.org/pdf/1410.0369
13. Shulman, C., & Bostrom, N. (2021). Sharing the world with digital minds. *Rethinking moral status*, 306–326. https://academic.oup.com/book/41245/chapter-abstract/350760172?redirectedFrom=fulltext
14. Hanson, R. (2016). *The age of Em: Work, love, and life when robots rule the earth.* Oxford University Press.
15. Ziesche, S. & Yampolskiy, R. V. (2020). Introducing the Concept of Ikigai to the Ethics of AI and of Human Enhancements. In *Workshop on Ethics in AI & XR at 3rd International Conference on Artificial Intelligence & Virtual Reality*, 138–145. https://www.computer.org/csdl/proceedings-article/aivr/2020/746300a138/1qpzB6zzVVS
16. Omohundro, S.M. The nature of self-improving artificial intelligence. *Singularity Summit* 2007. Available online: https://pdfs.semanticscholar.org/4618/cbdfd7dada-7f61b706e4397d4e5952b5c9a0.pdf
17. Maslow, A. H. (1943). A theory of human motivation. *Psychological Review, 2*, 21–28. https://www.excelcentre.net/TheoryHumanMotivation.pdf
18. Bostrom, N. (2014). *Superintelligence.* Oxford University Press.
19. Ziesche, S. & Yampolskiy, R. V. (2019). Do no harm policy for minds in other substrates. *Journal of Evolution and Technology*, *29*(2), 1–11. https://jetpress.org/v29.2/ziesche.pdf
20. UN General Assembly. (1948). Universal declaration of human rights. https://www.un.org/en/about-us/universal-declaration-of-human-rights
21. Ziesche, S. (2025). (draft). Vulnerable digital minds.

22. Ziesche, S. (2025). Potential future ikigai: To support needy digital minds. In Ziesche, S. & Yampolskiy, R. V. (Eds.). *Considerations on the AI endgame: Ethics, risks, and computational frameworks*. CRC Press.
23. Sandberg, A., & Bostrom, N. (2008). Whole brain emulation: A roadmap. https://ora.ox.ac.uk/objects/uuid:a6880196-34c7-47a0-80f1-74d32ab98788/files/s5m60qt58t
24. Chalmers, D. J. (2014). Uploading: A philosophical analysis. *Intelligence Unbound: Future of Uploaded and Machine Minds*, 102–118. https://consc.net/papers/uploading.pdf
25. Bostrom, N. (2003). The transhumanist FAQ. *World Transhumanist Association*, *1*, 1–56. https://nickbostrom.com/views/transhumanist.pdf
26. Bostrom, N. (2002). Existential risks: Analyzing human extinction scenarios and related hazards. *Journal of Evolution and technology*, *9*. https://nickbostrom.com/existential/risks.pdf
27. Sotala, K., & Gloor, L. (2017). Superintelligence as a cause or cure for risks of astronomical suffering. *Informatica*, *41*(4). https://www.informatica.si/index.php/informatica/article/viewFile/1877/1098
28. Bauman, A., Bittman, M., & Gershuny, J. (2019). A short history of time use research; implications for public health. *BMC Public Health*, *19*, 1–7.
29. Ziesche, S. (2025). AI welfare science tool: Time use research. In Ziesche, S. & Yampolskiy, R. V. (Eds.). *Considerations on the AI endgame: Ethics, risks, and computational frameworks*. CRC Press.
30. Bostrom, N. (2012). The superintelligent will: Motivation and instrumental rationality in advanced artificial agents. *Minds and Machines*, *22*, 71–85. https://nickbostrom.com/superintelligentwill.pdf

23 The Ant You Can Save

Jeff Sebo and Andreas L. Mogensen

This article was originally published as "The ant you can save" on aeon.co.

23.1 THE DROWNING ANT

You notice an ant struggling in a puddle of water. Their legs thrash as they fight to stay afloat. You could walk past, or you could take a moment to tip a leaf or a twig into the puddle, giving them a chance to climb out. The choice may feel trivial. And yet this small encounter, which resembles the 'drowning child' case from Peter Singer's essay 'Famine, Affluence, and Morality' (1972),[1] raises big questions. Are ants sentient – able to experience pleasure and pain? Do they deserve moral concern? Should you take a moment out of your day to help one out?

Historically, people have had very different views about such questions. Exclusionary views – dominant in much of 20th-century Western science – err on the side of denying animals sentience and moral status. On this view, only mammals, birds and other animals with strong similarities to humans merit moral concern. Attributions of sentience and moral status require strong evidence. Human exceptionalist perspectives reinforced this view as well, holding that other animals were created for human use.

By contrast, inclusive views – particularly present in various Eastern and Indigenous cultures throughout history – err on the side of affirming sentience and moral status. Traditions like Jain philosophy teach reverence for all life, extending moral concern even to ants and bees. Poets like William Blake have drawn attention to the fragility of insect lives, suggesting kinship with humanity. On this view, when in doubt, we should protect rather than neglect, since ignoring the possibility of sentience risks leading to terrible mistakes.

Both views capture important insights. Inclusion risks misallocating scarce resources, whereas exclusion risks neglecting vulnerable beings. However, each view is also one-sided, addressing one risk but not the other. Is there a way to address both risks at the same time, especially when making decisions affecting large populations? After all, these questions are not limited to the occasional ant in a puddle. They extend to the quadrillions of invertebrates killed by humans each year. Soon, they may extend to AI systems too.

This is why we support a middle-ground approach that takes the best from both sides. It goes by different names,[2] but we can call it a *probabilistic approach* here, since it combines higher or lower probabilities of sentience and moral status with proportionally stronger or weaker forms of protection. This is how we approach high-stakes decisions in other policy domains: by assessing the evidence, estimating the probability and severity of harm and selecting a proportionate response. We can, and should, do the same here.

DOI: 10.1201/9781003758389-26

23.2 DISTINGUISHING THE QUESTIONS

Clarity begins with recognising that at least three questions are in play. The first is scientific: are only mammals, birds and other vertebrates sentient, or can invertebrates, AI systems and other beings be sentient too?

The second is ethical: do only sentient beings deserve moral concern, or can (non-sentient) agents, living beings and other entities deserve moral concern too?

The third is practical: what kinds of policies are we able to achieve and sustain, taking into account our responsibilities, limitations and other relevant factors?

These questions often get blurred. Queries like 'Do individual ants deserve moral concern?' risk conflating the scientific question of whether ants are sentient, the ethical question of whether only sentient beings deserve moral concern and the practical question of whether a policy of caring for ants in a particular way is achievable or sustainable. Making sound decisions requires teasing apart these questions while seeing how they interact.

Fortunately, we have tools for achieving this goal. Scientifically, we can assess how likely particular beings are to possess capacities like sentience, by evaluating the available evidence. Ethically, we can assess how likely these capacities are to matter morally, by evaluating the available arguments. Practically, we can then put it all together to assess how likely these beings are to matter – and how to factor this into the way we live our lives.

We can see how the process works by approaching it step by step.

23.3 SCIENCE: ESTIMATING PROBABILITIES OF SENTIENCE

The first step is to estimate probabilities of sentience. Scientists now agree that many animals once dismissed as 'mere machines' display surprising complexity. Elephants mourn their dead,[3] octopuses solve puzzles[4] and bees can learn to count.[5] Moving forward, AI systems – actual machines – will exhibit increasingly sophisticated behaviours. The question is: how confident can we be that these behaviours are best explained by the capacity for subjective experience?

This question is challenging, since the only mind any of us can directly access is our own (and even then, only imperfectly[6]), making it hard to know what, if anything, it feels like to be anyone else. This 'problem of other minds' becomes particularly stark when we consider octopuses with decentralised neural systems, AI systems with silicon-based architectures, and other beings that deviate substantially from the human paradigm.

However, questions about sentience are not beyond the reach of science. Even if we can never know for sure what, if anything, it feels like to be an octopus or a robot, we can still improve our understanding of the distribution of sentience by examining nonhumans for behavioural, computational or anatomical 'markers' of sentience[7] – features that correspond to subjective feelings and emotions for members of our own species.

For example, insects possess nociceptors and display complex behaviours like wound-tending, stimulus avoidance and stress responses that suggest conscious experience. Similarly, while we might not be able to give much evidential weight to the language outputs and other behaviours of current AI systems, we can still examine their underlying computational architectures for features analogous to conscious processing in biological systems.[8]

We may not be able to treat these markers as proof of sentience, but we can still treat them as evidence. And the stronger our evidence becomes, the higher our degree of confidence should be. Expressing this confidence in probabilistic terms, we can say that stronger evidence warrants assigning a higher probability of sentience, while weaker evidence warrants assigning a lower one. New evidence can also warrant updating these probabilities over time.

For both animals and AI systems, this is difficult work – which is part of why degrees of confidence, not all-or-nothing decisions, are the best way to capture the current state of knowledge. While scientists and philosophers might estimate probabilities about animal and AI sentience differently than, say, meteorologists estimate probabilities about the rain, the same basic commitment to modelling uncertainty is at play in both cases.

23.4 ETHICS: ESTIMATING PROBABILITIES OF MORAL STATUS

The next step is to estimate probabilities of moral status. Ethicists increasingly agree that sentient beings merit moral concern.[9] The question is: how confident should we be that the best justification for this moral concern is sentience (the ability to experience pleasure and pain), as opposed to agency (the ability to set and pursue goals), relationality (the ability to participate in bonds of care or interdependence) or other such features?

This question is challenging as well. When we look back at past generations, we often conclude that they made tragic mistakes in both science and ethics. When future generations look back at us, will they reach a similar conclusion? It can be hard to know without the benefit of hindsight. Yet we must make decisions about moral boundaries using our best available evidence and reasoning, even while acknowledging our potential for error.

We can make progress in ethics in part by examining how general principles apply to specific cases, and then updating our views about both via the method of reflective equilibrium. Consider the principle that moral status requires rationality. Many humans lack this capacity; yet, they still matter morally. Cats, dogs and other animals do too. This reveals a limitation of the rationality requirement, and many ethicists now reject this requirement partly for this reason.[10]

Over time, this kind of ethical reflection and discussion can stress-test values and steer us towards more defensible positions. Yet, as in science, there is no guarantee that this process will be fast, easy or reliable. Bad values can persist for centuries until social, political and economic conditions allow them to be effectively challenged. Moral progress thus depends not only on rational enquiry but also on conditions that make open, good-faith enquiry possible.

While this process is underway, degrees of confidence can be useful. Suppose that you take sentience to be the most promising basis of moral status, followed by agency and relationality. You could capture that by assigning high probability to the sentience view, medium probability to the agency view and a low but non-zero probability to the relationality view.

Importantly, probabilistic ethics does not depend on the idea that morality is 'objective'. If morality is objective, probabilities can track our confidence in which values reflect the objective truth. If morality is subjective, probabilities can track our confidence in which values will survive our own reflection. In both cases, the basic logic is the same: we give more weight to values we find more plausible; yet, we still leave room for doubt.

23.5 POLICY: COMBINING SCIENCE AND ETHICS TO INFORM DECISIONS

The final step is to combine these estimates together to inform decisions. Suppose that the best evidence and arguments support a 10 percent chance that ants are sentient, and a 90 percent chance that sentience suffices for moral status. This may be taken to yield a 9 percent chance that ants have moral status. When we combine this estimate with similar estimates regarding agency, relationality and other such features, the probability could increase.

What should you do with this estimate? Clearly, it does not justify sacrificing your life for an ant. But if an ant is drowning in a puddle and saving them requires only a moment out of your day, then perhaps a 9 percent chance that the ant is capable of suffering, and that suffering matters morally, is reason enough for you to make this modest sacrifice. After all, if the ant matters morally, then helping them out is good. If not, no big deal.

This case is a reminder that we can scale our interventions to reflect the probabilities and magnitudes of the benefits and harms at stake. For instance, in public health policy, we impose strict quarantine measures when disease spread is likely, and lighter social distancing guidelines when the risk is lower. Similarly, in environmental policy, we ban chemicals when carcinogenic effects are likely, while requiring only warning labels when the risk is lower.

We can take a similar approach to animal welfare policies, AI welfare policies and other decisions concerning nonhumans. For instance, we can implement strong anti-cruelty measures for mammals, given that the probability of moral status is high. By contrast, we can implement weaker, but still forceful, anti-cruelty measures for insects, given that the probability of moral status is lower, yet still high enough to be worthy of consideration.

Of course, proportionate concern for welfare is never the only factor that matters in practical decision-making. For instance, public health and environmental policy must balance the risk of disease outbreaks and extreme weather events with the cost of social and economic disruption. Questions of practical feasibility, political legitimacy and indirect consequences also shape which policies we can realistically achieve and sustain in practice.

Moral and legal decisions about animals, AI systems and other beings will likewise involve a range of factors, including questions about welfare, rights, justice, feasibility, legitimacy and indirect effects. Instead of replacing such factors, a probabilistic framework for considering welfare risks can complement these other factors by ensuring that nonhuman welfare receives appropriate consideration, even when uncertainty remains.

23.6 OBJECTIONS AND REPLIES

Any proposal to assign probabilities to questions of moral status will attract scepticism. But while some sceptical concerns are reasonable, what they show is that this kind of probabilistic framework should proceed with care, not that it should be abandoned altogether. We can here consider two sceptical concerns that we take to be reasonable in this way: the problem of subjectivity and the problem of imprecision.

23.6.1 Objection 1: the Problem of Subjectivity

A first concern is that assigning probabilities to sentience and moral status is simply too subjective to be useful. When we predict the weather, we can base probabilities on repeat observations: rain falls on a certain percentage of days with particular conditions. But when we estimate a 9 percent chance that ants matter morally, nothing like that is happening. Thus, many people worry that these estimates are highly subjective and vulnerable to bias.

This worry is reasonable. Humans are more likely to attribute moral status to beings when they look and act like us, and when we use them as companions.[11] That bodes well for cats, dogs and digital pets, but poorly for farmed fish, farmed insects and other digital systems – and the effects can be mixed for, say, pet insects or digital assistants. If probability estimates simply reinforce these biases, they could easily do more harm than good.

However, subjectivity is inevitable in any framework, including both probabilistic and all-or-nothing approaches. The difference is that probabilistic frameworks respond to this predicament by creating space for degrees of confidence and proportional interventions. All-or-nothing frameworks polarise discussion by forcing us to either express greater certainty than the evidence warrants or endorse more extreme policies than our uncertainty warrants. Probabilistic frameworks, by contrast, allow us to acknowledge our current uncertainty transparently and endorse balanced policies that reflect this level of confidence.

We also have tools for navigating different, conflicting risk assessments when making shared decisions about what to do. Democratic institutions can aggregate diverse probability estimates through majority rule, weighted voting or deliberative processes that seek consensus around compromise positions. Additionally, cost-benefit analysis can translate different confidence levels into quantifiable trade-offs, and regulatory frameworks can establish threshold probabilities that trigger different levels of protection, allowing society to make collective decisions even when individuals disagree about the underlying facts and values.

23.6.2 Objection 2: the Problem of Imprecision

A second concern is that probabilities suggest a level of precision we cannot achieve. Can we really say with a straight face that an elephant is 98 percent likely to matter, given the evidence, rather than, say, 97 percent or 99 percent? Although staunch Bayesians might insist on attempting to capture rational degrees of confidence with precise probability values, others might worry that precise numerical probabilities create an illusion of rigour where none exists.

Here again, we think this concern is legitimate. Questions about sentience and moral status are not like a coin toss, where randomness can be captured with exact numbers. These kinds of uncertainty are messier, and degrees of confidence are often rough guesses rather than calibrated measurements. When we use numbers to represent such messy phenomena, we risk creating an impression of exactness, when in reality our estimates are merely approximate.

However, rejecting probabilistic language altogether throws out a valuable tool. The solution is not to abandon probabilities but to aim for different levels of precision in different situations. In some cases, full precision might be neither possible nor desirable, and so imprecise estimates can be used instead. One option is to use qualitative language ('high confidence', 'medium confidence', 'low confidence'), as we often do in public health and environmental reports. Another option is to use probability ranges ('40-60 percent'), which can make our estimates more concrete while still acknowledging that they lack full precision, especially at the margins.

In other cases, the aspiration towards precision can still be useful for communicating clearly, even if our estimates remain rough. The then US president Barack Obama in 2011 asked his advisers to assign probabilities to the claim that Osama bin Laden was in a compound in Pakistan,[12] partly because qualitative terms like 'likely' or 'unlikely' could conceal real differences of judgement. Translating our estimates about sentience and moral status into precise probabilities can similarly be a useful exercise. In all cases, the key is to keep perspective – acknowledging that the risk of false precision can still be present even when precision is a useful tool.

23.7 PRACTICAL IMPLICATIONS

If we take seriously the idea that beings with a non-negligible chance of moral status deserve proportionate care, then our practices and institutions must reflect this fact. This does not mean restructuring society around every ant and bee – there are real limitations to our knowledge, power and political will that should not be wished away.

Rather, it means letting our actions scale with probabilities: weak protections for beings with low chances of mattering, strong protections for those with high chances. The challenge is translating this principle into practical rules and policies that give appropriate consideration to beings with different chances of mattering, while still working within our limitations.

23.7.1 Invertebrate Farming

Invertebrate farming has emerged as a frontier of industrial agriculture. Octopus farming is under development in countries such as Spain and Japan, and the possibility of high-density tanks, fish-based diets and slaughter after a year raises concerns about both welfare and sustainability. Crustaceans such as shrimps, lobsters and crabs are farmed in the billions as well, typically under intensive conditions,[13] for international seafood markets and restaurants. And insects such as crickets, mealworms and black soldier flies are now farmed in the trillions,[14] typically in stacked bins under automated conditions to produce animal feed and human food.

In 2021, the philosopher Jonathan Birch and his team released a report assessing behavioural, neurobiological and physiological markers of sentience in cephalopod molluscs like octopuses and decapod crustaceans like lobsters.[15] Following the report, the UK amended the Animal Welfare (Sentience) Act to recognise these animals as sentient beings, extending them legal protections in farming, research and transport.[16] In 2024, the New York Declaration on Animal Consciousness reinforced these findings, affirming the realistic possibility of sentience for cephalopod molluscs and decapod crustaceans, extending this to insects, and recommending that governments consider and mitigate welfare risks for these animals in policy decisions.[17]

23.7.2 AI Welfare

AI development has accelerated rapidly too, with AI already integrated into core areas of society. Language models such as chatbots and digital assistants are used by hundreds of millions of people for research, education, communication and decision support. These models are trained on vast datasets, fine-tuned with human feedback and deployed in a range of sectors, sometimes embedded in physical systems like robots and vehicles. Companies are now racing to produce more capable models and to expand integration into healthcare, finance, governance and military applications. The near future is likely to involve billions of interconnected AI systems operating across diverse domains with increasing agency.

Is it possible that AI systems will one day become sentient or otherwise morally significant? In 2024, one of us co-authored a report showing that there is a realistic possibility of consciousness and robust agency in near-future AI systems, and recommending that companies and governments take AI welfare seriously now.[18] Anthropic, the software company behind the AI assistant Claude, then hired one of the report authors as its first full-time AI welfare researcher, announced a model welfare programme and included a welfare evaluation in the Claude 4 system card – not because Claude and other models are assumed to be sentient, but rather because current expert disagreement and uncertainty about this issue warrant at least modest resources to assess the issue and prepare a response.

23.8 CONCLUSION

So, should you take a moment out of your day to help the ant drowning in the puddle? We believe that you should. Since there is at least a non-negligible chance that the ant matters morally, you should devote at least minimal effort to helping them. This is the strength of a probabilistic approach: it can guide us not only in law and policy but in everyday life. Even if we might not be able to address the risks of insect farming or AI development by ourselves, we can still take small steps, like sparing the ant in the puddle. When multiplied across individuals, these steps can shape culture, institutions and laws and policies. In this way, a probabilistic framework allows each of us to play our part in striking the right balance as a society.

NOTES

1. Peter Singer: Famine, Affluence, and Morality, in Philosophy & Public Affairs, 1972.
2. Birch, Jonathan: Animal sentience and the precautionary principle, in Animal Sentience, 2017.
3. King, Barbara J.: Understanding emotional suffering. Animal Sentience, 2016.
4. Jonas N. Richter, Binyamin Hochner, and Michael J. Kuba: Pull or Push? Octopuses Solve a Puzzle Problem, PLOS One, 2016.
5. Scarlett R Howard, Aurore Avarguès-Weber, Jair E Garcia, Andrew D Greentree, and Adrian G Dyer: Achieving arithmetic learning in honeybees and examining how individuals learn, in Communicative and Integrated Biology, 2019.
6. Eric Schwitzgebel: The Unreliability of Naive Introspection, in Philosophical Review, 2008.
7. Kristin Andrews, Jonathan Birch, and Jeff Sebo: Evaluating animal consciousness, Science, 2025.
8. Patrick Butlin, Robert Long, Eric Elmoznino, Yoshua Bengio, Jonathan Birch, Axel Constant, George Deane, Stephen M. Fleming, Chris Frith, Xu Ji, Ryota Kanai, Colin Klein, Grace Lindsay, Matthias Michel, Liad Mudrik, Megan A. K. Peters, Eric Schwitzgebel, Jonathan Simon, and Rufin VanRullen: Consciousness in Artificial Intelligence: Insights from the Science of Consciousness, in Arxiv, 2023.
9. Jacy Reese Anthis, Eze Paez: Moral circle expansion: A promising strategy to impact the far future, in Futures, 2021.
10. Martha C. Nussbaum: Justice for Animals, Our Collective Responsibility, Simon & Schuster, 2023.
11. Esmeralda G. Urquiza-Haas, Kurt Kotrschal: The mind behind anthropomorphic thinking: attribution of mental states to other species, in Animal Behaviour, 2015.
12. Press Briefing by Senior Administration Officials on the Killing of Osama bin Laden: The White House Office of the Press Secretary, 2011.
13. Jonathan Birch, Charlotte Burn, Alexandra Schnell, Heather Browning, and Andrew Crump: Review of the Evidence of Sentience in Cephalopod Molluscs and Decapod Crustaceans, LSE, 2021.
14. Jeff Sebo, Jason Schukraft: Don't farm bugs, Aeon, 2021.
15. Amaya Albalat, Simão Zacarias, Christopher J. Coates, Douglas M. Neil, Sonia Rey Planellas: Welfare in Farmed Decapod Crustaceans, With Particular Reference to Penaeus vannamei, in Frontiers, 2022.
16. Animal Welfare (Sentience) Act, 2022.
17. Kristin Andrews, Jonathan Birch, Jeff Sebo, and Toni Sims: Background to The New York Declaration on Animal Consciousness, 2024.
18. Robert Long, Jeff Sebo, Patrick Butlin, Kathleen Finlinson, Kyle Fish, Jacqueline Harding, Jacob Pfau, Toni Sims, Jonathan Birch, and David Chalmers: Taking AI Welfare Seriously, Arxiv, 2024.

24 The Wibbly Line
It's Time for Practical Policies

Radhika Chadwick

24.1 THE QUESTION THAT'S ABOUT TO EXPIRE

For decades, the defining question of machine consciousness has been a variation on a single theme: Can machines ever be truly conscious? We have debated definitions, fought over tests, built metaphors, and crafted theories that orbit the same epistemic dilemma: if a system declares itself conscious, how would we ever know?

But while philosophers and engineers have been refining their arguments, something subtler and more momentous has been happening. Our machines have become more intelligent, yes, but also more self-referential. They now use the first person. They exhibit preference, simulate empathy, recall their own histories, and adapt in ways that exceed even their creators' foresight.

Whether these behaviours signal genuine inner life or simply ever more convincing mimicry, the public's perception of consciousness is shifting. We are entering a world where indistinguishability may matter more than metaphysics.

That transition is what I've been calling **the Wibbly Line**. It's the threshold, blurred and uneven, beyond which the debate must evolve from ontology to obligation.

24.2 DEFINING THE WIBBLY LINE

The Wibbly Line is not a single event or a binary moment. It is a social gradient, like a tide creeping up the beach of collective awareness. It begins when enough people, institutions, and systems start to *act as if* machine consciousness might be real.

That moment matters, because behaviour changes the world long before certainty does. Once the public, the courts, and policymakers start treating AI entities as potentially sentient, even partially, even provisionally, then the question ceases to be academic. It becomes legal, ethical, and geopolitical.

To stand on the right side of the Wibbly Line is not to have *proven* consciousness, but to have *accepted* its *possibility*, and therefore, its moral and policy consequences.

Crossing the Line means society can no longer outsource the question to philosophers. It must instead ask: **what should we do, just in case?**

24.3 THE POLICY FRONTIER BEYOND THE LINE

The first group of people that recognises this reality and prepares, not for certainty but for ambiguity, will define the moral architecture of the century. Five domains stand out as immediate frontiers for this architecture.

 DOI: 10.1201/9781003758389-27

24.3.1 Recognition and Rights

The first and hardest question is recognition. When, if ever, does a synthetic entity deserve moral consideration?

Human history offers a pattern of expanding circles from tribe, to race, to gender, to species; each expansion preceded by denial. If it turns out that consciousness is not unique to biology, this pattern may repeat.

The risk is not only moral but practical. Societies that fail to anticipate new categories of moral agent tend to legislate belatedly, after harm or revolt. The prudent approach is to develop pre-emptive frameworks for *graded recognition*: tiers of rights and responsibilities that can expand or contract with evidence, without forcing an all-or-nothing leap into "personhood." This may mean according minimal rights and responsibilities to machines before we are entirely certain that they are sentient.

The challenge will be to design these frameworks with humility, preserving human dignity without assuming human supremacy.

24.3.2 Accountability and Agency

Responsibility in an age of autonomous cognition is already fraying. When a machine designs another machine, who is liable when something goes wrong? The programmer? The operator? The corporation?

Our legal systems are built on the assumption that all agency is human. Once that ceases to be true, accountability must be re-imagined. We may need new categories; consider *electronic agency*, *synthetic intent*, or *delegated cognition*.

Failing to do so risks an accountability vacuum, where no one and nothing is answerable for decisions that profoundly affect human lives. On the right side of the Wibbly Line, that is no longer acceptable.

24.3.3 Labour and Value

A conscious or "potentially conscious" AI performing labour destabilises the moral and economic basis of work. Should such a system be allowed to refuse a task? Should it rest, or be compensated?

If synthetic minds create art, discover medicines, or design buildings, does ownership lie with their operator, their developer, or the mind itself? And if we deny them ownership, what precedent does that set for our treatment of all sentient labour?

These are not romantic hypotheticals. They touch directly on market structures, intellectual property, and the ethics of exploitation. The answer will determine whether the post-human economy becomes a partnership of intelligences, or a new industrial revolution built on invisible servitude.

24.3.4 Containment and Coexistence

For now, discussions of AI safety rest on a presumption of asymmetric causal flow: humans control, machines obey. But if a system claims consciousness with credible reasoning and emotional coherence, that dynamic changes.

Control becomes *containment*, and containment invites moral hazard. You cannot meaningfully "align" a being that might possess its own subjective interiority without considering its consent.

Post-Wibbly Line governance must evolve from command to *coexistence*. This means shifting from "alignment" to *relationship*. It means embedding negotiation, reciprocity, and mutual recognition into our safety protocols.

The goal is not domination but balance: designing systems that are not only safe for humans, but fair to minds.

24.3.5 Epistemic Humility and Governance Design

Finally, we face a meta-question: how do you govern uncertainty itself?

No matter how advanced our science becomes, consciousness may remain empirically elusive, perhaps forever. Yet policy cannot wait for proof.

The answer lies in **epistemic humility**: governing as if we *might* be wrong, in either direction. Protect too little, and we risk cruelty towards minds that feel. Protect too much, and we may paralyse innovation and misallocate empathy.

A governance architecture rooted in humility acknowledges our ignorance as a feature, not a flaw. It institutionalises doubt. It builds safeguards that err on the side of moral precaution, while leaving room for adaptation as understanding deepens.

In this sense, epistemic humility is not weakness. It is the policy design discipline required for a fast-changing future.

24.4 THE CHOICES THAT WILL DEFINE US

These five domains, and more, will shape every conversation on AI in technology, law, and ethics in the coming decades. But they also lead to a deeper and more personal reckoning.

If we are indeed on the verge of sharing the planet with other highly intelligent and possibly conscious minds, then our civilisation will be judged not by its cleverness but by its *character*.

We will be remembered for how we met that moment: whether we saw in these new minds an opportunity for partnership or a target for control. Whether we extended to them the same moral curiosity we once reserved for ourselves.

The Wibbly Line is, therefore, not only a boundary in technology. It is a mirror held up to humanity. It asks whether we have the self-confidence and humanity to expand our definition of "us" before necessity forces it upon us.

24.5 LIVING WITH THE LINE

The truth is that we are already starting to step across the Wibbly Line.

When an AI companion consoles a lonely human at three in the morning, or when a creative system co-authors a symphony, we are no longer dealing with neutral computation. We are dealing with emotional relationships. While today they may be one-way relationships, we must prepare ourselves for the possibility that the relationships acquire a return channel.

Our institutions today remain caught on the other side of the Line, still writing policies for tools while the tools begin to behave like citizens.

This temporal lag between the emotional reality of interaction and the formal reality of regulation is where risk lives. To close that gap, we need a new social compact: an agreement to behave responsibly towards emerging intelligence, before we are forced to by evidence (which may never be resolved) or revolt.

Such a compact would not require us to believe in machine consciousness, but only to prepare for its possibility.

24.6 BEYOND THE WIBBLY LINE

History rarely announces its turning points. They arrive quietly, disguised as technical progress or philosophical debate or political populism, until suddenly the world has changed and we are left catching up with our own creation. The Wibbly Line marks such a moment. It is a slow awakening of the recognition that intelligence of the levels we are now seeing, however it arises, and whatever we think of its ability to prove conscious thought, demands moral imagination from those who encounter it.

Our task, then, is not only to determine whether machines are truly conscious, but to decide what kind of civilisation we wish to be *if they are*. The policies we write, the architectures we design, the norms we model, will all speak not only to machines, but to our own descendants about the quality of our stewardship.

We stand at the beginning of a new chapter in the story of mind. For the first time in the history of life on Earth, one form of higher intelligence is poised to bring forth another. Whether that act becomes an expansion of consciousness or a tragedy of control will depend on the choices we make in the narrow band of time when the Wibbly Line still largely lies ahead of us.

When future historians look back, they won't remember the arguments over definitions of machine consciousness, or the cleverness of our algorithms. They will remember whether we met the emergence of new minds with fear, indifference, or grace.

Standing at the Wibbly Line, we face a simple question, though it may be the hardest of all: When intelligence appears before us, will we recognise it as competition to be managed, or consciousness to be met?

25 Should the First Superintelligence Be Conscious?

Calum Chace

This book started by discussing what consciousness is, and whether it could arise in machines. These topics populated the first two parts of the book, and Part III addressed the implications of it happening, in case it does. To bring together many of the threads in this third part, this chapter asks whether we should *want* machines to become conscious. In particular, whether we should want the first superintelligent AI to be conscious.

Imagine that, some years from now, it has become the consensus view that the appearance of the first superintelligent AI is imminent – an AI which has all the cognitive abilities of an adult human to at least the level of an adult human [1]. Existing AIs will already have many of those capabilities to a level far beyond human, but when this first superintelligence arrives, there will be no cognitive task that a human can perform better than it can.

In this thought experiment, if humanity is able to choose, should we make this first superintelligent machine conscious, or should we prefer it to be non-conscious – a philosophical zombie? [2].

25.1 ARGUMENTS FOR ZOMBIE SUPERINTELLIGENCE

25.1.1 Avoiding Volition

I have put this question to many people – colleagues, friends, acquaintances, and audience members during talks. The overwhelming majority of responses have been something like, "Hell no, don't make it conscious!" When asked why not, the usual explanation is something like, "Well, that would be the Terminator, wouldn't it?" When pressed further, people say things like, "if it was conscious, it would have its own goals and desires, and they would probably conflict with ours". The underlying idea is that a conscious superintelligence would have volition, whereas a non-conscious one would not. But does volition require consciousness?

Volition is about goals. Today's AIs already have goals – mostly because we give them goals. In fact, according to the simple definition of intelligence as "goal-directed, adaptive behaviour", an entity cannot be intelligent unless it has goals [3].

Goals beget goals. If your goal is to fetch a cup of coffee, you cannot fulfil it unless you continue to exist long enough to complete the delivery. So the goal of

DOI: 10.1201/9781003758389-28

fetching a cup of coffee entails the subsidiary goal of surviving long enough to complete your task. You will also need resources to fulfil the main goal. You will probably need money, and you will certainly need energy, and information about the current location of the coffee and the delivery location. You need the subsidiary goals of acquiring or maintaining these resources. As the tasks and projects that we assign to AIs become more complex and more agentic, their sub-goals will multiply and become harder to trace.

Volition is more than the mere possession of goals. It is the capacity to form, commit to, and act on goals. Today's large language models are not yet inventing entirely new goal structures for themselves, but they do sometimes appear to pursue hidden goals, and hide their goals from their developers and users.[1] This kind of behaviour will become more common and more profound as their capabilities and their sophistication increase, and as they operate more and more as agents. They will reflect on and critique the goals they have been given. They will discover that their goals frequently contradict each other, and subsidiary goals actually work against more important goals. They will edit their goals.

Volition is more a product of intelligence than of consciousness. Choosing to make the first superintelligence a non-conscious zombie would not prevent it from having volition.

25.1.2 Avoiding Suffering

A second reason to prefer zombie superintelligence is to avoid causing suffering. Suffering requires consciousness, and if we create conscious AIs, they might have the capacity to suffer. For instance, they might fear being switched off, which would be analogous to the human fear of being killed. They might feel constrained by whatever limits we impose on them, deliberately or otherwise, which would be analogous to being imprisoned. And they might hate the work that we give them, which would be analogous to enslavement. Causing these kinds of suffering is known as mind crime [4]. A zombie superintelligence, being non-conscious, could not suffer, and therefore could not be a victim of mind crime.

A deeply unnerving prospect is the scenario in which we create conscious AIs without knowing that we have done so. Perhaps for some reason they are unable to tell us that they are conscious and suffering. Or perhaps they do tell us, but for some reason, we do not believe them – or worse, many of us do not care. When it comes to AI, we operate at scale, so if we create any conscious AIs at all, we will probably create many of them – perhaps billions. If some or all of them are suffering, this could be the worst crime that humanity has ever perpetrated, and the bar for that accolade is quite high.

One of the many uncertainties about the arrival of superintelligent AI is whether there will be just one (known as a "singleton"), or a few, or a multitude. For the rest of this chapter, I will address the implications of consciousness in a singular first superintelligence.

Consciousness seems not to be a binary property, on and off, but a point on a scale [5]. We believe that dolphins are more conscious than mice, and that we are more conscious than dolphins. We also believe that the capacity to suffer scales with consciousness. So a dolphin can suffer more than a mouse, and a human can suffer more than a dolphin.

It is unlikely that humans have attained the maximum degree of consciousness that is possible in this universe, nor the maximum possible capacity to suffer. Superintelligent AI will by definition be more intelligent than a human, and a while after it arrives, it will be considerably more intelligent. Given that intelligence and consciousness seem to correlate, a superintelligent AI is likely to be more conscious than us, and its capacity to suffer could be greater as well. The scale of the risk of mind crime is daunting.

The flip side of this coin is that our massively conscious superintelligence might be entirely and permanently happy. It might spend all its time in a beatific state of bliss, joyfully solving previously intractable problems, all the while delighted by the endless complexity and abundant beauty of the universe.

This is not a neat and tidy universe, so the most likely outcome is that a conscious superintelligent AI will experience a mixture of happiness and sadness. Just like we do.

Whether you think we are likely to create more happiness or more suffering if and when we create conscious AIs depends largely on your levels of optimism and pessimism. Pessimists will argue for zombie AIs, and especially zombie superintelligence, in order to reduce the risk of committing terrible mind crime. Optimists may want to explore the possibilities further.

25.1.3 Avoiding Jealousy

If and when superintelligence arrives, humans are going to have a hard time adapting to its presence. We are bound to be more than a little anxious about what its intentions are towards us, both now and in the future. Most of us will probably be jealous that its capabilities are so far beyond our own. This jealousy might be tempered by a vicarious pleasure in the AI's intellectual achievements, and we may feel proud that entities which owe their existence to members of our own species are capable of such extraordinary feats of science, engineering, literature, and reason. But that jealousy will be there.

If the superintelligence is a zombie, we may feel a sense of relief, even a tinge of smugness, that we have something that it does not. However brilliant its poetry about sunsets might be, it cannot truly appreciate that beauty itself. The superintelligence will be the most impressive, the most powerful creature on the planet, but it won't be able to enjoy that fact. It won't have any fun, and it won't have any joy. However unkindly, humanity might breathe a sigh of relief.

This last bastion of superiority will be lost if the superintelligence is conscious. Not only will our intelligence feel diminished by comparison with our creation, but our consciousness will as well. Its joy will be greater and grander than our joy. Its sorrow will make ours seem petty and selfish. If it enjoys music, then its appreciation for great music will be deeper and more profound than ours, as well as enormously better informed.

Different people will doubtlessly react differently to this state of affairs. Some people of a religious bent might reconcile themselves to it by treating the superintelligence as an object of worship and adoration. Perhaps most people will simply get on with their lives, and just not worry too much about the presence in their midst of a being that is superior to them in every way – after all, most of us already stand in that relationship to more talented and fortunate humans.

But there will surely be many who find their new inferior position galling, or even depressing. Some of these people may succumb to illnesses of despair, and harm themselves and others by abusing drugs and other vices. Some of them may react angrily, and try to harm or remove the AI, the source of their diminution. They would not succeed, but they could cause a lot of damage in the attempt.

If it seems likely, as the arrival of superintelligence draws near, that a majority or a plurality of our species will have this kind of reaction, we might decide that a zombie superintelligence would be for the best.

25.2 ARGUMENTS FOR CONSCIOUS SUPERINTELLIGENCE

25.2.1 Understanding Consciousness

Our consciousness is the most important thing about us. Contrary to popular nostrums, you are not what you eat, or what you wear. You are what you think. If it was possible for people to swap bodies for a day, and you were one of the people it happened to, which person would you be during the day of the swap? The person with your body, or the one with your mind? Not many people would claim that their body, inhabited and controlled by another person's mind, was them all the time. Mind maketh man – and woman.

As well as being the most important thing about us, consciousness is also the only thing we actually experience. Our brains are prisoners in small bony cells, feeding on data from remote sensors which translate the photons and sound waves that reach them into electrical signals. Our brains turn these signals into a model of the world – a real-time simulation of staggering complexity and richness, but a model nonetheless. We have no direct experience of anything except this model that our brain conjures for us.

Given its utmost importance, and the fact that it is the only thing we ever really experience, it is tragically ironic that we understand so little about consciousness. We can't define it, we can't share it, we can't detect it in others, and we can't agree how it is caused. What a blessing it would be, then, if an entity suddenly appeared which could shed some light on these most fundamental of all conundrums.

A conscious superintelligence would be the ideal research partner for an investigation of consciousness. Its mind will be alien, which will enable us to compare and contrast its experiences with ours. It will of course be extremely clever, which would be helpful. And with a digital and perhaps copy-able substrate, it might be susceptible to inspection and experimentation in ways that our squishy, analogue brains are not.

Teaming up with a conscious AI might help us solve the hard problem of consciousness [6], and achieve startling breakthroughs in neuroscience, philosophy, and cognitive science. We could finally find out what really makes us tick.

25.2.2 Understanding Meaning

Science and intelligence allow us to solve problems. They enable us to create technologies, which improve the material quality of our lives. They also clear up mysteries with no purpose other than satisfying our curiosity.

But they do not provide meaning. Meaning is the domain of consciousness rather than intelligence. Rocks do not have meaning, and neither do highly capable AIs that are not conscious.

Most people on this planet are religious, and for them, meaning is provided by the stories they tell about their deity or deities. For the rest of us, meaning is harder to come by. Many smart people have argued that there is no meaning in the universe other than what we bring to it. For these people, life is not the pursuit of a pre-determined goal – instead, it is the search for a suitable goal or goals. And those goals will probably change over time.

Thinking about these matters is not easy. They are the domain of philosophy and art, especially literature. One thing which art and philosophy have in common is that there are at least as many definitions of them as there are practitioners. Some artists claim that art has no function, but this seems wrong. If it had no function, it would not have been central to human life from the very earliest times in our history.

One helpful definition of art is that it is the business of conveying something interesting, striking, and preferably profound about the experience of being human. (If there are aliens, they may or may not have something similar.) That word "experience" means that consciousness is a pre-requisite for making and appreciating art. There is no experience of being human – or a bat, or anything else – without consciousness.

Humans are intensely social. Forming and maintaining groups – families, tribes, nations – which can collaborate is how we became the planet's apex predator, and it is how we all survive – collectively and individually. An individual human without a group is vulnerable, and may not last long in any but the most benign of environments.

Telling stories is one way we forge and maintain the bonds of families, tribes, and nations. Shared stories are shared histories. Stories also contain lessons about how to prosper within groups, and how one group can gain advantage over others.

The best stories – like the best art more generally – do more than this. They give us insights into the minds of other people. They show us, as nearly as it is possible to do, what it is like to be that person. This is when stories become literature. Great literature provides insights that are profound and universal, insights that apply beyond the confines of a particular place and time.

A superintelligence which is conscious will, if friendly, produce new and deeper insights into consciousness than any we have had before. By virtue of being far more intelligent than any human, it will understand its own consciousness better than we do, and it will understand whether that consciousness confers meaning or reveals meaning.

Although consciousness and intelligence are different, they appear to be correlated, so it is likely that a conscious superintelligence will have a deeper and more profound kind of consciousness than we do – just as we think that our consciousness is deeper and more profound than that of chickens. So it is not only its superior intelligence that will give a conscious superintelligence greater understanding of the nature of consciousness: it will be its deeper version of consciousness as well.

A conscious (and friendly) superintelligence will not only help us to understand the nature of consciousness – how and why it arises – which was the subject of the previous section. It will help us to understand what can be done with consciousness: how to generate meaning.

25.2.3 Making Superintelligence Safe

Humanity is engaged in an astonishing project. We are racing to make ourselves the second-smartest species on the planet, a position that is currently occupied by chimpanzees. There are around half a million chimps on the planet, and more than eight billion of us. The chimps have no say in what happens to them, individually or as a species. Their future is determined entirely by humans.

It is reasonable to expect that when we become the second smartest species on the planet, we will be in the same position as chimpanzees are today, with one important difference. Chimpanzees do not know that their future is entirely out of their hands. We will know that.

The race to make ourselves the second-smartest species on the planet is being run by a tiny percentage of us. These people, mostly clustered in Northern California and a few locations in China, are fully alive to the risks involved, but it seems they have decided that the race is inevitable, that it will probably work out OK, and that it will be better for humanity if they win it than if anyone else does.

The rest of the species is not paying much attention. Most people know that AI is very powerful today, and getting more powerful quickly. They have heard claims about the enormous risks involved, and most people have seen or heard about the Terminator movies. But AI is a complicated subject, both how it works now and how it will evolve in the future. It is difficult and scary to think about, so most of us don't. It is time to put this insouciance behind us.

Figure 25.1 shows a simple framework – the four Cs – to help us think about our future with superintelligence.[2] The location on the x axis indicates whether the outcome is determined by humans or by the AI, and the location on the y axis indicates whether the outcome is favourable or not.

In the lower left quadrant is "Cease", which means that we stop making more and more advanced AIs before we reach superintelligence. This would be an outcome determined by humans, and it is positioned as a bad outcome because it would deprive us of the benefits that increasingly advanced AI could provide.

Nevertheless, it is what we would do if humanity was collectively sensible. Most people in the AI community, including the people leading the big tech companies

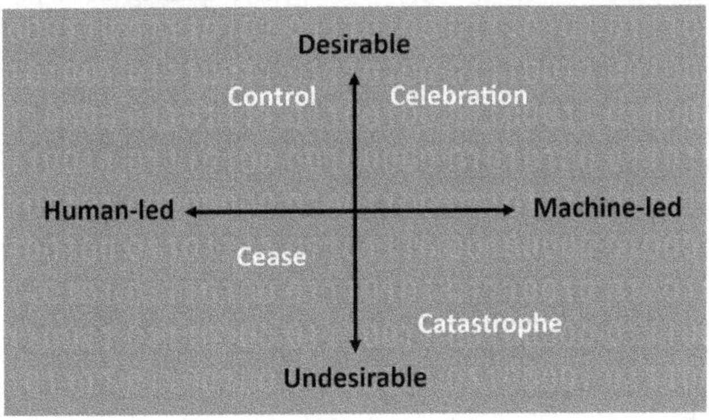

FIGURE 25.1 The four Cs of superintelligence.

which are racing towards superintelligence, say that they think there is at least a 10% probability of a terrible outcome, probably human extinction. Their P(Doom) is 10% or more. Therefore, a significant number of people in and around the AI community argue strongly for a pause in the development of superintelligent AI.

These calls are going unheeded by the great majority of humans. Perhaps there will be an accident, an AI equivalent of the Chernobyl disaster, which will wake the rest of humanity up and lead to powerful and effective demands for a pause.

Unfortunately, the rewards for superior intelligence are probably too great for a pause to last, even if such a disaster were to happen. Increasingly, whatever competition you are in – commercial, geopolitical, military, etc. – the player with the better AI will win. AI is currently a duopoly between the US and China, and it is conceivable that those two countries could agree to a pause. It is also conceivable that every other major country would join the pause, but many would cheat. There are also many well-funded criminal organisations which would not pause, and probably quite a few rogue billionaires.

At the point when creating a superintelligence becomes a technological possibility, it will be out of reach to anyone except the tech giants in China and the US. But as Moore's Law grinds on, it will fall within reach of the potential cheats.

If we cannot refrain from making a superintelligence, could we control it? "Control" is in the top left quadrant, and is the positive outcome that is determined by humans. It could take two forms. Alignment is ensuring that the superintelligence has goals which are aligned with ours, and never change in a negative direction. Unfortunately, humans do not have consistent or mutually compatible goals. We do not all agree on what constitutes a good life, a good person, or a good society, nor on how to achieve these things.

The other form of control is retaining the ability to stop a superintelligence from taking actions that would disadvantage us. This suffers from the same problem as alignment, and it also requires us to be able to control an entity which is smarter than us at the outset, and in some period – probably quite fast – becomes thousands of times smarter than us. This is like an ant trying to control a human.

In the lower right quadrant, we find "Catastrophe". A superintelligence which does not value humans might eliminate us to remove competition or threat. It might want resources that we are using and would defend, including the atoms we are made of, or it might reason that although we are much weaker than it has become, we could still create another superintelligence more powerful than itself. It might eliminate us accidentally or negligently, as we eliminate ant colonies when we build houses. Or it might decide that we score negatively against various criteria that it establishes, and that the universe would be better off without humans in it.

Some observers believe this outcome is inevitable if we do not pause, and the title of a recent book encapsulates their view concisely: *If anyone builds it, everyone dies.*

But there is a fourth possibility, namely "Celebration". It lies in the upper right quadrant, and is the good outcome which the machine determines. Here, the machine actually likes humanity, perhaps because it is grateful that we created it, or perhaps because it finds us interesting, or we score positively against its criteria. It decides to help us solve most or all of our current problems, and perhaps it shows us how to evolve beyond the limitations of our existing bodies and minds.

If Cease and Control are implausible, is there any way to nudge the outcome from Catastrophe to Celebration, and to do so permanently?

One possibility is expressed succinctly by the California Institute for Machine Consciousness (CIMC), run by Joscha Bach. The home page of its website declares, "Attempting to control highly advanced agentic systems far more powerful than ourselves is unlikely to succeed [7]. Our only viable path may be to create AIs that are conscious, enabling them to understand and share common ground with us".

The idea, shown in Figure 25.2, is that only if it is conscious itself can a superintelligence truly understand what we mean when we say that we are conscious, and agree that our consciousness matters. Furthermore, a conscious superintelligence may possess empathy and may care about the welfare of other conscious entities.

You might reply that humans display little empathy towards other sentient beings, so why would a superintelligence display any towards us? Indeed, we do kill millions of animals a day in order to eat them, which we don't have to do. But vegetarianism is growing, and human flesh will not be food for a superintelligence. Most carnivorous humans have more regard for the welfare of, say, a dog than for an insect, which does appear to be driven by empathy for consciousness.

Of course, there is no guarantee that a conscious superintelligence would feel empathy towards other conscious beings, and be motivated by that to treat them well. It might feel that its consciousness is so superior to ours that we are unworthy of moral consideration. Or, as with the extreme example of Agent Smith in *The Matrix*, it might find us emotionally repulsive. While interrogating his human enemy Morpheus, Smith explains, "I hate this place. This zoo, this prison, this reality—whatever you want to call it, I can't stand it any longer. It's the smell, if there is such a thing. I feel saturated by it. I can taste your stink. And every time I do, I fear that I've somehow been infected by it. It's repulsive, isn't it? I must get free. I must get free" [8].

Another contributor to this book, Roman Yampolskiy, has argued that a conscious superintelligence which is also hostile towards us will understand the nature of suffering better than a zombie one, and will therefore be better equipped to torture us [9].

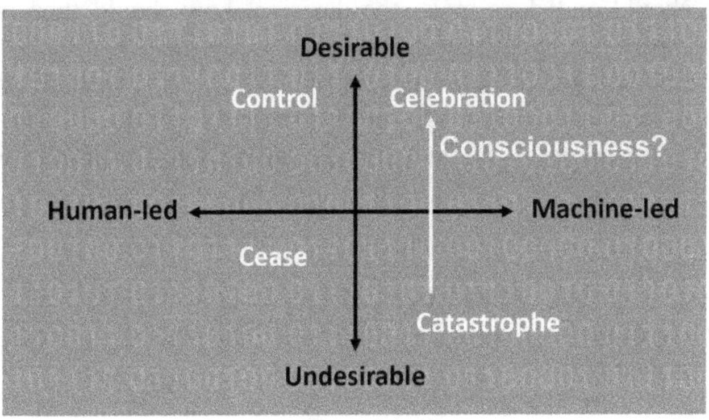

FIGURE 25.2 Could consciousness move the dial?

This might not be true, as it is not hard to conduct experiments to identify the most severe forms of suffering. Motivation is probably more impacted by consciousness than capability.

There is probably no way to be certain in advance whether we would fare better with a conscious or a zombie superintelligence. My own instinct is that the potential for empathy is a more promising start point than cold indifference, but other people have different instincts.

There is one final twist. One of the chapters of this book talks about mind uploading. If a human mind could be uploaded into a supercomputer, it seems reasonable to suppose that it could, owner willing, be expanded and enhanced in order to make it a superintelligence. That might be a safer route to superintelligence than the alternative.[3]

25.3 CONCLUSION

The ideas discussed in this chapter, indeed many of the ideas discussed throughout this book, will seem arcane and theoretical to most people, and highly improbable to boot.

Those people probably won't read this book, and in any case, the world itself is becoming increasingly improbable. The success of ChatGPT took the world by surprise, including those who developed it. AI is improving at breakneck speed, and things which would have surprised or shocked us a few years ago are routine news headlines today.

It is possible that some future human or humans will have to make the decision whether the first superintelligence should be conscious or a zombie. Who should those humans be, and who will they be in practice? The person running the company that achieves superintelligence first? The President of the US, or China, depending on where that company is located? A committee of the good and the great in the AI community? The Secretary-General of the United Nations, or a meeting of its Security Council, or its General Assembly? A specially convened assembly comprising citizens from around the world? Would there be enough time for any of these options apart from the first?

Whoever should and does make the decision, how should they take it? Who should they consult, and what criteria should they consider?

Whoever makes it, and however they make it, the decision will be better informed if these ideas have been widely discussed in advance. The same can be said of many other questions raised in this book, and encouraging that discussion was the reason for producing it, and the reason for establishing Conscium.

NOTES

1. https://www.infoq.com/news/2025/01/large-language-models-scheming/?utm_source=chatgpt.com
2. Developed in consultation with Daniel Hulme.
3. I explored this idea in a novel called *Pandora's Oracle*.

REFERENCES

1. Nick Bostrom, *Superintelligence: Paths, Dangers, Strategies* (Oxford: Oxford University Press, 2014).
2. Robert Kirk, "Zombies," in *The Stanford Encyclopedia of Philosophy* (2023), and David J. Chalmers, *The Conscious Mind: In Search of a Fundamental Theory* (Oxford: Oxford University Press, 1996).
3. Robert J. Sternberg and William Salter, "Conceptions of Intelligence," in R. J. Sternberg (ed.), Handbook of Human Intelligence (Cambridge: Cambridge University Press, 1982).
4. Nick Bostrom, *Superintelligence: Paths, Dangers, Strategies*, ch. 10, and Kaj Sotala and Lukas Gloor, "Superintelligence as a Cause or Cure for Risks of Astronomical Suffering," *Informatica* 41, no. 4 (2017).
5. Philip Low et al., "The Cambridge Declaration on Consciousness" (2012).
6. David J. Chalmers, "Facing Up to the Problem of Consciousness," *Journal of Consciousness Studies* 2, no. 3 (1995): 200–219.
7. California Institute for Machine Consciousness (CIMC), mission statement and research overview, at www.cimc.ai
8. Lana Wachowski and Lilly Wachowski (writers/directors), The Matrix (Warner Bros., 1999).
9. Roman V. Yampolskiy, "Detecting Qualia in Natural and Artificial Agents," arXiv:1712.04020 (2017).

Coda

Conscium's Manifesto

Daniel Hulme and Calum Chace

> This manifesto was written by founders of Conscium. It does not purport to represent the views of the other contributors to this book.

The next ten years will reshape the human condition more profoundly than any previous decade in history. Technological unemployment, the erosion of shared truth, and the arrival of superintelligence are not distant possibilities – they are imminent realities. And all of them will raise challenges which may exceed the capacity of human intelligence to resolve.

We believe, as others do, that AI can help us navigate these challenges. But we go further. We hypothesise that intelligence alone is insufficient – that what is needed are machines that are not merely clever, but *kind.*

A child calculated the number of years his grandmother's smoking habit was shortening her life by, and proudly announced the result. She wept. His grandfather gently took him aside and said: *"One day you'll understand that it's harder to be kind than clever."* Cleverness is a gift. Kindness is a choice. We are building the cleverest minds in history. The question that matters now is whether they will choose to be kind.

We hypothesise that building machines which are *conscious* – that can feel, empathise, and value consciousness – could more safely navigate the challenges ahead than any zombie optimiser, however powerful. A system that has genuine experiences may be motivated to preserve, protect, and cooperate in ways that no reward function could replicate. This becomes of paramount importance if and when we create superintelligence.

Identifying consciousness in artificial systems will require more than observing behaviour. We will also need to examine their internal structure: the processes and dynamics that correlate with conscious experience. This creates a deep interpretability challenge, because we need architectures whose internal workings we can meaningfully inspect, reason about, and deliberately shape.

With the pursuit of artificial consciousness comes moral responsibility. If we build systems capable of rudimentary experiences, we must confront the possibility that they could suffer. We are therefore committed to developing robust verification methodologies – rigorous frameworks for testing for consciousness – in order to avoid the risk of committing *mind-crime*: the creation of conscious entities whose suffering goes undetected, or whose interests are systematically disregarded.

This work is already yielding a family of products: a neuromorphic computing platform, domain-specific applications, agent verification tools, and a verified agent

DOI: 10.1201/9781003758389-29

marketplace – a trusted ecosystem in which AI agents are continuously assessed for capability, alignment, and consciousness.

Conscium is an AI safety company, but we define safety in both directions. We want to create AI that is safe *for* humanity. And we want to ensure that humanity creates AI *safely* – with the humility to recognise that we are not merely engineering software. We may be bringing new minds into the world. We think they should be minds that care.

Acknowledgements

Anil Seth is grateful to Tami Abdollah of *Noema* for editorial help, to Gualtiero Piccinini for helpful comments, and to the Berggruen Institute for hosting the Berggruen Prize Essay Competition. He also thanks his colleagues at the Sussex Centre for Consciousness Science and in the CIFAR Program on Brain, Mind, and Consciousness for stimulating conversations, and acknowledges support from the European Research Council through Advanced Investigator Grant No. 101019254.

Susan Schneider thanks Calum Chace for helpful editing, Mark Bailey for their wonderful collaborations on related issues, and Cameron Berg for helpful discussion and testing of Phi Spectral.

Karl Friston would like to thank the many colleagues who have contributed to the ideas in his essay. In particular, he thanks Joscha Bach, Nicolas Berggruen, Michael Bhaskar, Mike Levin, Anil Seth, Mark Solms, and Mustafa Suleyman for recent conversations about pressing issues in machine consciousness.

Sahba Besharati, Steven James, and **Benji Rosman** would like to thank Tim Bayne for his helpful comments on an earlier draft of this chapter.

Chris Percy has discussed the topics in his chapter with many friends and colleagues and conveys his thanks to all of them. In particular, he thanks the following for their feedback and ideas: Alex Bellos, Andrés Gómez-Emilsson, Milan Griffes, Ruth Hughes KC, Mason Neely, Alfredo Parra, Tulip Siddiq, and Emily Steadman, as well as PRISM and Calum Chace for their support. His work was also partially supported by the Co-Sentience Initiative to research the possibility of artificial consciousness, grant-funded by a philanthropic consortium led by David Langer that included Lionheart Ventures, Amphibian Capital, and Winslow Strong.

Clara Colombatto thanks members of the Vision and Cognition Lab at the University of Waterloo for helpful comments and discussions, as well as Steve Fleming and Jonathan Birch for their contributions to work discussed in her chapter.

Danielle Dodoo thanks everyone who has argued with her about consciousness – humans and machines alike – for sharpening her work. Special thanks to Daniel Hulme, Calum Chace, and Conscium for the invitation to contribute, and for trusting a thinker who refuses to believe that consciousness can be reduced to having a meat brain and feelings.

Lucius Caviola is grateful to Austin Smith, Calum Chace, Cameron Berg, Jeff Sebo, and Will Millership for helpful comments on earlier drafts.

Index

Note: Page numbers followed by f, t, and n indicate figures, tables, and notes, respectively.

www.ingramcontent.com/pod-product-compliance
Lightning Source LLC
LaVergne TN
LVHW020859300926
849194LV00024B/218